MĀRGA

WAYS OF LIBERATION, EMPOWERMENT, AND SOCIAL CHANGE IN MAHARASHTRA

MĀRGA

Ways of Liberation, Empowerment, and Social Change in Maharashtra

Edited by

M. NAITO
I. SHIMA
H. KOTANI

MANOHAR
2008

First published 2008

ISBN 81-7304-762-6

Published by

Ajay Kumar Jain for
Manohar Publishers & Distributors
4753/23 Ansari Road, Daryaganj
New Delhi 110 002

Typeset at

Digigrafics
New Delhi 110 049

Printed at

Lordson Publishers Pvt. Ltd.
Delhi 110 007

Contents

PART IV: PILGRIMAGE AND FOLK RELIGIOUS PRACTICES

Preface

The present volume is a selection of papers read at the Eleventh International Conference on Maharashtra: Culture and Society held in Tokyo from 22 to 24 August 2005 (Convener: Prof. Masao Naito of the Senshu University. Venue: Kanda Campus of the Senshu University. See the Appendix written by Dr. Meera Kosambi for a short history of the International Conference on Maharashtra: Culture and Society). Three papers in this volume (Zelliot, Ferrié and Feldhaus), however, were not read at the Conference but contributed afterwards. The conference theme was *mārg(a)*. The term can accommodate a very wide range of interpretation or understanding. For example, there are such *mārgas* to spiritual liberation as *jñāna mārga, karma mārga* and, most relevant to the Conference, *bhakti mārga.* Another interpretation is the *mārg(a)* traversed by pilgrims to sacred places. *Mārg(a)* can also be understood in cultural, social and political contexts. *Satyāgraha,* as an example, can be interpreted as a *mārg(a)* to political liberation and at the same time the process of cultural self-realization. Thus the participants interpreted the Conference theme *mārg(a)* according to their own understanding or liking, based on their respective disciplines or academic interests.

The volume consits of twenty-two papers which are divided into four sections. The first section includes five papers, of which three (Lele, Shima and Koiso) deal with the *Jñāneśvarī* (in popular Marathi, *Dnyaneshwari*), the Marathi reinterpretation of the *Bhagavadgītā,* written by Jñāneśvara or Jñānadeva (in popular Marathi, Dnyaneshwar, *c.* 1275-96) in the last decade of the thirteenth century in Maharashtra. Jñāneśvara, the very first of a series of medieval Maratha *sants,* was born in a Brahman family living in the vicinity of Pune. In his teens he explained the *Bhagavadgītā* to the public using the Marathi language understood by people at the time but soon after writing it he died. His *samādhi* in Alandi near Pune is still a great pilgrimage place in Maharashtra. One paper in this section (Bhagwat) takes up another Maratha *sant*, Eknāth (*c.* 1533-99) who prepared the edition of *Jñāneśvarī*. Eknāth was born in a Brahman family in Paithan on the Godavari River and learned Sanskrit but grew up to be a great Maratha *sant* situated chronologically between Jñāneśvara and Tukārām (1608-49). The theme of the last paper in this section (Zelliot) is the thinking of B.R. Ambedkar (1891-1956) on Buddhism which might appear to have no relevance to the *sant* tradition of Maharashtra discussed in these four papers. Sympathy with the lives of the ordinary people including the depressed and those longing for uplift, however, is shared, though often implicitly, by Maratha *sants* and Ambedkar who, inspite of his hatred towards Hinduism, was fond of the Maratha *sant* tradition, especially Tukārām.

The first three papers of the second section dwell on social-cum-cultural problems involving language, especially problems pertaining to the relationship between elite-hegemonic and popular-regional languages. The role of the elite-hegemonic languages such as Sanskrit (Kotani), Persian (Guha) and lastly English (Adachi) in regulating the way of life of a populace who did not understand them is one of the most problematic aspects of the history of Maharashtra. The other three papers of the section in their own ways deal with the problems of evil social practice, social injustice and social reform. From the view point of gender the heated controversy in the last decades of the nineteeth century over whether political liberation had priority over social liberation or vice versa is criticized (Kosambi). In the same period there was another major controversy in Bombay over social reform or religious reform involving a Brahmo leader (Tikekar). In Dalit literature not only the discrimination against them (social injustice) but also the evil social practices of Dalit themselves are described (Ishida).

The papers grouped in the third section have more or less a similar orientation in dealing with the problems of politics in socio-cultural contexts. In many cases, politics has been deeply intermingled with the socio-cultural uplift or self-realization of the people concerned. The *satyāgrahas* analyzed in two papers

(Masselos and Vora) clearly exemplify the point. Peasant movements in contemporary Maharashtra also drew on *satyāgraha* as a means of realizing their goals (Pendse). The conversion to Buddhism of Ambedkar and his followers also demonstrates it (Guru). Politics and culture often have a more direct relationship when, as an example, popular culture like *lok nāṭak* is utilized to inspire and mobilize the masses (Naregal). The relationship between politics and religion is one of the most difficult problems in India nowadays. The problem is observed not only on the national level but also, more routinely, on the regional or rural level such as in local sacred places in the Maharashtrian countryside (Palshikar and Deshpande).

The fourth section consists of five papers for which the focal point is religious practice, especially pilgrimage to sacred places in both the all-India and regional scale. Such sacred places as Varanasi and Prayaga on the Ganges River and Gaya in the Ganges plain, though geographically far away from Maharashtra, have been places to be visited for the people of Maharashtra by whatever means available (Glushkova). The *sant* tradition of Maharashtra has Pandharpur as its great pilgrimage center where even now a huge number of pilgrims (*vārkarī*) swarm to every year (Manjul). The religious practice of *vārkarī kīrtan* performed, in its ideal manner, on the way to Pandharpur is discussed in comparison with *nāradiya*, the other type of *kīrtan* (Ferrié). There are many more pilgrimage-type religious practices in present day Maharashtra which involve carrying holy objects from one place to another (Feldhaus). Folk religious practice in Maharashtra includes as its essential part the worship of goddesses such as Mariai (Tachikawa).

Thus the conference theme *mārg(a)* has been discussed in a variety of ways in this volume, so that it will provide the readers with a spectrum of images or ideas concerning Maharashtrian culture and society in history and at present.

Here, however, some explanation will be needed of the stylistic discrepancies in this volume. The most conspicuous is those authors mostly dealing with themes pertaining to precolonial periods have used diacritical marks to romanize Indian terms but authors mainly dealing with themes pertaining to modern and contemporary periods have not, while others have used a different romanizing style such as *mee* (*mī*) and *raat* (*rāt*). These discrepancies might have been adjusted beforehand but the editors have decided to leave these discrepancies as they are, since the editors wish to publish this volume as the accumulated efforts of all the contributors who have their own policy regarding writing style, not as the exclusive editorial work of the editors.

Finally we are pleased to thank the Japan Foundation for the financial aid granted to us without which it would have been difficult to organize the Conference. We are also thankful to all the contributors who have readily cooperated with us in the many tasks required for the publication of this volume and especially Kyosuke Adachi, one of the contributors, who has helped us in rearranging the draft papers in various formats into a unified format.

30 April 2007 EDITORS

Contributors

Jayant Lele: Professor Emeritus of Political Studies, Sociology and Development Studies, Queen's University, Kingston, Ontario, Canada.

Iwao Shima: The late Professor, Kanazawa University, Japan: Indology.

Chihiro Koiso: Part-time Lecturer, Hyogo Iryol University, Japan: Hinduism.

Vidyut Bhagwat: Professor KSPWSC, University of Pune, India: Researcher in the field of Social History.

Eleanor Zelliot: Laird Bell Professor of History emerita, Carleton College, Northfield, Minnesota, USA: Social history, especially the Ambedkar Movement; Cokhamela and Eknath of the Medieval Bhakti Movement.

Hiroyuki Kotani: Member of the Science Council of Japan: Professor Emeritus, Tokyo Metropolitan University: Medieval and Modern History.

Sumit Guha: Professor, Department of History, Rutgers: The State University of New Jersey, USA: Medieval and Modern History.

Kyosuke Adachi: Ph.D. candidate, Graduate School of Area and Culture Studies, Tokyo University of Foreign Studies, Japan: Modern History.

Meera Kosambi: Ex-Director, Research Centre for Women's Studies, SNDT Women's University, Mumbai, India: Sociology with a special interest in Urban Studies and Women's Studies.

Aroon Tikekar: Adjunct Professor, Dept. of Journalism, University of Pune, India; Editor Director, *Sakal*; former Editor of *Loksatta*; historian of the University of Mumbai, special interest in 19th-century Bombay Presidency.

Hideaki Ishida: Associate Professor, Daito Bunka University, Japan: Modern Hindi and Marathi Literature.

Jim Masselos: Honorary Reader, School of Philosophical and Historical Inquiry, the University of Sydney, Australia: Modern South Asian History.

Rajendra Vora: The former Lokmanya Tilak Professor of Politics and Public Administration, University of Pune, India: Indian politics, and Indian political thought.

Aruna Pendse: Reader in Politics, Department of Civics and Politics, University of Mumbai.

Gopal Guru: Professor, Jawaharlal Nehru University, India: History of Idea/Indian politics.

Veena Naregal: Institute of Economic Growth, Delhi, India.

Suhas Palshikar: Professor, Department of Politics and Public Administration, University of Pune, India.

Rajeshwari Deshpande: Reader, Department of Politics and Public Administration, University of Pune, India.

Irina Glushkova: Leading (a post) research scholar, Center for Indian Studies, Institute of Oriental Studies of Russian Academy of Sciences, Moscow, Russia: Hinduism and Indian Philology.

V.L. Manjul: Ex-Librarian, Bhandarkar Oriental Research Institute, Pune, India.

Eric Ferrié: Department of Anthropology, University of Paris X, Nanterre, France.

Anne Feldhaus: Foundation Professor, Arizona State University, USA: Religious Studies.

Musashi Tachikawa: Professor, Aichi Gakuin University, Japan: Indian and Buddhist Studies.

PART I

HERITAGE OF *SANT* TRADITION

1

Ganesh at the Crossroads: Reflections on Dnyaneshwar's Theory of Dialogue[1]

JAYANT LELE

Taise Prayag hota samarasyace
Vari vosan tarat satvikace
Te samvad catuspathice
Ganesh jale

With streams of meanings confluent
With satvik distilled floating on the surface
They became Ganesh
At the crossroads of dialogue

INTRODUCTION

No. 108 is by far the most intriguing *ovi* in the tenth chapter of *Dnyaneshwari* (hereafter *DN*). Many commentators have simply ignored the nuances associated with the use of the metaphors involved. Those few who have tried to explore them (Dhere and Kavade, for example) have remained caught within the orthodox, spiritual-transcendental (*paramarthika*), understanding of the message of *DN*. In this paper I propose to explore those nuances in view of my earlier suggestion (Lele 1981) that *DN* could be fruitfully understood as a discourse on communicative action (i.e. action oriented to, as well as arising from the intention of, "making sense together").

It will not be possible to sketch all the elements of what I have called the discourse on communicative action in such a short paper. Of the many references to dialogue (or communication) in *DN*, 10: 108 seems to encapsulate some of the basic principles of a theory of dialogue that I am discovering in his work. The word *catuspatha* (the crossroads) occurs prominently in this *ovi*. It captures what I see as one of the key concepts of this theory. In view of the theme of the conference, I shall try to show how it helps us make the message of *DN* relevant and meaningful for our times. The bringing together of the terms *samvad, catuspatha, samarasya* and *sattvika,* in this *ovi,* as well as the names Prayag and Ganesh, presents an unusual challenge for his interpreters. The use of *samvad, catuspatha* and Ganesh in the last two lines of the stanza is a perplexing juxtaposition of three very potent images. Each one of them carries with it an enormous weight of distinct substantive historical contexts. Dnyaneshwar uses the unique context of Krishna–Arjun dialogue as a multi-polar device for exploring the various dimensions of human relations (including the divine dimension) as dialogic encounters.[2]

Ovi 10: 108 speaks of the moment of arriving (in dialectical sense) at an understanding, by the participants in a dialogue, or as a moment of their making sense, new sense, together. This is the meaning of the term *samarasya,* as employed here by Dnyaneshwar. This idea of *samarasya* as the moment of arrival at a shared understanding, as a moment of transcendence, is of course amenable to both critical as well as orthodox brahmanic interpretations.

CONVENTIONAL INTERPRETATIONS

Over the years a large number of interpretations of Dnyaneshwar's work, especially of *DN,* have been written in Marathi. By bringing together powerful concepts such as *samvad, catuspatha, samarasya* and *sattvika* and a reference to Ganesh in one single stanza (10: 108), *DN* invites us to explore the depths of their multiple contexts and thus the possibility of arriving at an enriched meaning that is likely to result. And yet, most of the orthodox interpreters have not made any effort to explore the possibilities created by it. Most have offered little in the way of comprehensive explanation beyond a literal translation.[3] Dandekar edition, for example, provides the following gloss for this *ovi* (see Kavade 2003):

Just as Ganga and Yamuna form a confluence at Prayag, in the same way, meaning when *bhaktas* meet *bhaktas*, there forms a confluence of a distillation of their oneness (*aikyarasa*). And on the flood of that distillation floats the rubbish of the eight *sattvik bhavas*. Those *bhaktas* become Ganapati on the crossroads (*cavhata*).

Pandit, in his *Gudharth Dipika* gives a similar meaning for the *ovi* but offers a useful additional note, in the form of an explanation of the terms *samvad, catuspatha* and Ganesh (see Kavade 2003).

Samvad: a unified treatment of contradictory theses from a variety of different (*nirniralya*) *sastras*.
Catuspatha: the place where four roads arriving from opposite directions come together.[4]
Ganesh: the deity that understands the intended (*vivakshit*) meaning of the word and enlightens the intellect (*buddhi*) of the other with that same meaning.

Khandarkar also follows the Dandekar meaning but adds an explanation claiming that (see Kavade 2003):

in old times, according to the science of town planning, there was the common practice of building a Ganesh temple or an open Ganesh platform (*par*) at the crossroads of the town. Even today one finds this to be the case in old towns. The purpose behind it was that any citizen out on an auspicious occasion should attain *darsan* of the alleviator of danger or when an outsider enters the town should be able to have *darsan* of the initiator of auspicious events.

He goes on to add that:

like this Ganesh at the crossroads, *bhakta sants* can also be seen, at all times, engaged in a discussion (*carca*) on subjects such as *jiva, jagat, bramha, maya,* with fellow *sants* or eager (*jidnyasu*) disciples.

Kavade, in his review of these writers, finds that the *ovis* that occur before and after 10: 108 (in his account it is 10: 124[5]), support the idea, on which all interpreters seem to agree, of a confluence of equally mighty streams (and hence the reference to Prayag). He finds, however, that none of them explains the noticeable dramatic shift to Ganesh in the second half; nor do they discus how or how well it fits within the semantic flow of the surrounding *ovis*. Their translation of the term *vosan* as debris, sticks or rubbish is also totally incompatible with the idea of *sattvika*. None of them suggests an alternative, a meaning that is more appropriate to the spirit of the *ovi*. Kavade offers the following alternate meaning:

When two waves or streams, having confronted each other meet and riding on each other, crashing into each other, become one and rise to a peak and then begin to recede, their receding, undulating parts are *osan*.[6]

For *samvad*, he offers the following clarification:

As a result of mutual merging into each other (*ekrupata*), on attaining total identity (*tadatmya*) the rapturous, thoroughly united (*ekwat*), undifferentiated (*abhinna*) state of love (*premabhava*) that springs forth and the unadulterated (*nirbhel*) transcendent joy (*brahmananda*) that one gains from it is *samvad*.[7]

Despite his pioneering and insightful analysis of 10:108 and a number of highly suggestive possibilities emerging from it and his thorough knowledge and a lifetime dedication to the message of *DN*, he settles in the end, unfortunately for us (as this gloss on *samvad* shows), for a solution that remains completely bounded by an artificially abridged domain of the spiritual.[8]

I have been arguing, over the years, (see, for example, Lele 1981, 1987a, 1987b, 1989, 1994 and 1995), that the distinguishing feature of *Varkari bhakti* in Maharashtra has been its unstinting commitment to the unity of our material existence, our everyday life of joy and sorrows (*vyavahara*) with our spiritual selves seeking transcendence (*paramartha*) and with our sense of community (*lokahita*) with our fellow human beings as unique beings (who demonstrate, as species being, the unity of body and mind, matter and spirit, nature and culture and individual and society). All *Varkari sants*, Dnyaneshwar in particular, show how our quest for the transcendent, for divinity, is intimately linked to finding the cause of sorrow and consists in making efforts to find ways to overcome it in this life so as to create a joyful and mutually caring community (as a community of *sants*) on this earth. The artificial bisection of that unity, the unity of the real and the transcendent, by declaring one as ephemeral and illusory while glorifying only the other as eternal and unendingly joyful, violates that commitment and distorts the real, unique message of Dnyaneshwar.[9]

The consequences of such a violation through an abridged dualism that valorizes an intuitively attained and hence inexplicably individualized divine experience, attained through bodily discipline (such as *yoga*) is that the socially anchored and community-based practices of *Varkaris* are ignored or treated as mere ancillaries to the seeking of the divine experience as an egoistic self-experience in isolation from the community.[10] Professor Kavade's attempt to equate *catuspatha* with Bharata's eight *sattvika bhavas* (through an interesting arithmetic of reducing eight to four) and to equate Ganesh with the meta-joy (*mahasukha*) of *samvad*[11] is not convincing. A more detailed examination of the treatment of this *ovi* by him or in the conventional literature on *bhakti* is beyond the scope of this paper. However, in the following brief account of what I have called Dnyaneshwar's theory of communicative action, some of my reservations about the dualism on which these treatments have come to rest will, I hope, become clearer.

ON THE APPROPRIATION OF TRADITION

My idea, that there is a coherent theory of (or at least a framework for) communicative action in Dnyaneshwar's writings, is at an early stage of its development. I cannot present all its elements and the evidence to support it in this short paper. What I hope to demonstrate, however, is the possible method for excavating the foundations on which such a theory can come to rest. The review of the conventional meanings attached to 10: 108 gave us a glimpse of one of the ways in which tradition is interpreted and appropriated in order to sustain the legitimacy of Brahmanism. It showed us how distortions of meanings become systematically imposed on and entrenched in once critical insights from Indian traditions. The standard shadow-boxing within the conventional metaphysical debates on *dvaita-advaita* cannot, however, help us break through the crusts of such ideological distortions. What is needed, perhaps, is some "conceptual archeology" to excavate the layers of accretion with which these critical insights have been appropriated by brahmanic orthodoxy.[12] Take, for example, the word *bhakti.* In the conventional literature it is routinely translated as "devotion". Jaiswal traced the origins of the idea of *bhakti* to prevedic, communal, tribal life. In such relatively egalitarian social orders "*bhagavata* originally denoted primitive tribal group which owned all tribal wealth, *bhakti* meant a share thereof and *bhakta* an individual, who had received such a share" (Jaiswal 1981: 8). This possible original intention of *bhakti* has certain affinity with the idea of partnership in dialogue.[13] The notion of devotion, ultimately, perpetuates subservience while that of partnership questions it.[14] Understood in this way *samvad* in 10: 108 is still a dialogue with the divine but where the divine, as *bhagawan,* symbolizes the community and becomes a co-sharer of knowledge and action with all the *bhaktas.*[15]

I locate my own work on *bhakti* in the framework that stands in contrast and is best described as critical appropriation of tradition. The primary concern of this framework is the place of tradition, of our beliefs about the self and the world shaped by it, in the contemporary world dominated by the ideas of natural science and reason. The most rewarding insights on this issue are to be found in the now well-known Gadamer-Habermas debate and the intervention by Paul Ricoeur.[16] For me the major insight arising from the debate is an understanding of tradition that I have called the modernity of tradition (see Lele 1981). I have argued that tradition is constituted by moments of critique and hegemonic appropriation arising from an ongoing state of transition mediated by reflection that tests all our prior understanding of self and of the world against the changing material context of our everyday life.[17] My attempt to "excavate" a theory of communicative action in Dnyaneshwar's texts has emerged from within that framework.

While I place all of my study of *DN* in the larger context of the modernity of tradition, in this paper my focus is on the question of discovery of meaning through dialogue as reflection. I am concerned with the idea of 'arriving at a meaning', a meaning that departs from the previous understandings (prejudices in

Gadamer's terms) of the interlocutors but emerges as a transcendence of these for both (all) interlocutors. Such transcendence, however, can only be momentary because it must remain open to further reflection and thus to further disputation and dialogue. All traditions display this dynamic quality whereas perspectives and interpretations (as different paths) meet and clash. The idea that transcendence of the shared meaning is always "momentary" in nature distinguishes this dynamic approach to tradition, the one that recognizes its modernity in a dialectical sense, from the conventional understanding of tradition as that which is handed down without change, as *sanatan* in the case of Indian orthodoxy.

This paper deals with *DN* as a text. When we approach a text, our preconceptions can, to use Gadamer's expression, be "pulled up short" if the text were to reveal an entirely new sense, as a result of our reflection on our context. This can only happen, however, if we are open to it. What may prevent such openness is the hegemony of dominant ideas that hold sway as a result of institutional mechanisms of "pedagogic violence" (Lele 1996). This is true of tradition as embodied in a text or of tradition itself as a text. A text as a product of human reflection invariably houses within itself the dominant discourse and a potential subaltern, critical discourse. Hence reading a text in the critical hermeneutic framework involves treading a sensitive but delicate path that mediates between the two by, what discourse theory calls, reading against the grain of the apparent sense that a text presents to the reader at the outset.

I also deal with *DN* as a text that is structured as a dialogue.[18] It is about a dialogue and is presented as a dialogue. In other words it emphasizes, by its very nature, the prime intention of a dialogue: that of arriving at shared sense.[19] The text is understood as "standing alone" in terms of its trans-temporality, its ability to make sense in diverse temporal contexts. As such an understanding of its meaning cannot be reduced to dissection of its parts or of its literary merit. The context of the author includes, among other things, the sources of his/her motivation, the available forms of expression and the choice made. The third element of the analysis is the context of the interpreter. Critical hermeneutic inquiry requires that none of these three elements be ignored and that all of them must be examined in relation to each other and not in isolation from each other. In this short paper I can only attempt to present a glimpse of such analysis of *DN*. I have chosen 10: 108 because it encapsulates the essentials of its theory of communicative action. The three dimensions of a critical hermeneutic framework of analysis are presented in the following diagram.[20]

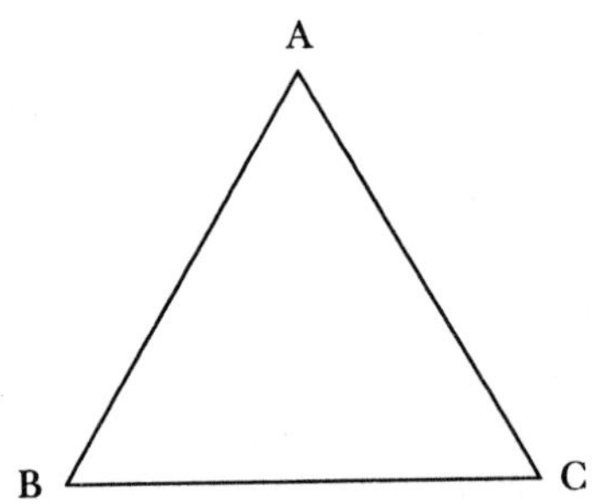

CRITICAL HERMENEUTIC TRIANGLES

A : The Text
B : Author in Context
C : Interpreter in Context

	Δ1	Δ2	Δ3
A :	*Dnyaneshwari* (*DN*)	*Bhagavadgita* (*BG*)	*BG* & *DN*
B :	Dnyaneshwar & his Times	*BG* in Context of Origin	Their Times (The times of crises of Brahmanism)
C :	'We' (the Interpreters in Our Times)	Dnyaneshwar as Interpreter	We and Our Context

DNYANESHWAR'S THEORY OF COMMUNICATIVE ACTION

Given the insistence on indivisible but differentiated unity of everyday life and the quest of divinity in Dnyaneshwar's tradition[21] the message emerging from his works speaks to the dream of a new moral-ethical order which will overcome the artificial trifurcation of our life into specialized cognitive, expressive and normative domains. Such fragmentation helps perpetuate the status quo beyond its material viability.[22] The brahmanic insistence on the separation of the two worlds of *vyavahar* and *paramartha*, I suggest, has the same effect, that of perpetuating injustice in society.[23]

Let us return to 10: 108 and to the distinction I made between *samvad* or dialogue as a process and the coming to a shared understanding as its intended culminating moment. Most *ovis* just before and after 10: 108 celebrate that moment. In 10: 108 also Dnyaneshwar speaks of it as "Prayag (confluence) of *samarasya*". In this case *samarasya* can only mean total sharing, in all its dimensions (cognitive, expressive and intersubjective), of meaning (or truth) which is grasped as a result of *samvad* or the dialogue. The aesthetic power with which Dnyaneshwar expresses the unique and unprecedented nature of that moment, as intended but still unanticipated (and therefore transcendent), speaks also to the tension, uncertainty and risk that surround the process of dialogue. The convergence at the crossroads is obviously that of roads, ways or paths (*marg*, *vat* or *patha* in Marathi). On this even the conventional interpretations seem to agree.

These roads are the various approaches to the discovery of meaning or truth and to gaining knowledge of which *BG* is itself a sort of compendium. *DN* is an original and insightful re-interpretation of the message of *BG*. It puts an entirely new light on the paths that *BG* has dealt with. Dnyaneshwar begins with the recognition that there are different ways of arriving at truth and that they often conflict with each other unless they can be transcended and contained within a new understanding that overcomes their contradictions. The task of a true *sant*, we know not only from the writings of Dnyaneshwar but also from those of other *Varkari sants*, is to attain that transcendence and to discover a meaning of the truth that goes beyond the truth claims of all the *margas* dealt with in *BG*. The power to make an ongoing transcendence possible, transcendence that keeps discovering truth that is always contemporary for the changing times, says Dnyaneshwar, is the essence of *Gita* (*gitatattva*), and for that reason alone it can express itself forever in new ways. It is thus unknowable as it is eternally new (*nityanutan*).[24] Conventional interpretations treat the state of *samarasya,* what is in fact the moment of revelation of a newly shared, contemporary meaning, as its opposite. For them it amounts to a *bhakta's* isolated, egoistic experience of becoming one with the divine in some mystical ways. Brahmanism wants to ensure that this will not result in a call for transformative action from the community of *sants.*

The idiom used by Dnyaneshwar in describing this discovery of new meaning is that of a *bhakta's* discovery of and merger with the divine ("with me, the lord" as *BG* puts it). This usage is no doubt consistent with that of *BG* and with the understanding of the role of knowledge in his times. The brahmanic orthodoxy sees it as adequate for our times as well. It is thus able to continue its attempts to feed the quietistic abridgement of *Varkari* tradition, which it has systematically controlled since its appropriation in the seventeenth century.[25] The discovery of a shared meaning is not something that can be taken for granted or assumed as an assured outcome of a dialogue. When it does happen, and that takes a whole range of prerequisites for it to become possible, it is indeed a moment when words cease. It is to that moment that the description from the *Naradiya Sukta* (67, 68) so eminently applies. The distillation of the churning of the various *margas* produces a state of body-mind that is *sattvika.*[26] Bharata, in his *Natyasastra,* graphically describes the eightfold bodily sensation as the manifestation of the *sattvika bhava.*[27]

Given the unity of theory and practice as the basic tenet of the *Varkari* way, the new sense that overcomes the crisis of understanding must translate into transformative action in order to overcome the crisis at the everyday *vyavaharika* level. For indications of a model of such action one must turn to *Varkari* practice. An important component of that practice is treatment of God as the mother, a teacher, a playmate, a lover or, in some cases, someone who chips in to finish the "impure" menial tasks of *bhaktas.* A careful study of the *guru* tradition in the *Varkari* way will also point in the same direction.[28]

While the entire text of *DN* is replete with insights that add up to a rich theory of communicative action,[29] 10: 108 encapsulates its most significant elements. At the risk of sounding mechanistic let me attempt to present what I see as the four elements revealed by 10: 108.

1. the presence of diverse and often contradictory perspectives or paths that interlocutors or participants in communicative action hold prior to their commitment to engage in a dialogue (*patha*).
2. the presence of an arena, a space, a sphere (real or virtual) that makes it possible for these diverse perspectives to arrive at and meet with the intention of creating a shared understanding, a common meaning, an agreed upon truth, that takes them (and us) beyond their points of departure by transcending the contradictions that inhere in their positions and by containing their perspectives (and not by submerging, substituting, subordinating or eliminating them) (*catuspatha*).
3. the process itself through which the participants attempt to overcome the contradictions in their positions (*samvad*).
4. the moment of arrival, of reaching an understanding, a consensus, of discovering "truth" as the confluence of meanings (*samarasya*).

DIALOGUE AT THE CROSSROADS

All the four elements of the theory of dialogue that I have outlined above will have to be explored and developed in greater detail. For example, with respect to (1), the interests represented by the diverse perspectives, the power relations they may represent, their internal contradictions and the challenges that confront them in the dialogue will have to be specified. In case of (2), the nature and conditions for the existence of such a space and for the emergence of an intention of creating a shared understanding that make dialogue possible will have to be clearly specified. As to (3), the dialogue itself, the preconditions for the possibility of its successful completion will have to be clearly specified. This calls for a detailed discussion of the impact of inequality of interlocutors on the process, largely missing in current theories that claim the status of theories of communicative action such as those of Gadamer, Habermas and Ricoeur that I have drawn on. Similar explorations are necessary with respect to (4) where the structure, quality, durability and consequences of the emergent "truth" will have to be specified.

In view of the theme of the conference I will explore only the issues that are related to the crossroads, understood as an arena in which diverse perspectives meet with the intention of arriving at a way of making shared sense and to come to an agreed upon understanding that goes beyond the initial perspectives that the participants bring to the encounter.[30] The question remains, however, as to why the proponents of these perspectives, of these trusted and long practiced ways of making sense, become motivated to bring them up for disputation and resolution of the kind implied in 10: 108.

What conditions must exist for those who have their ways of making sense to become interested in a dialogue that brings them under the searchlight of critical reflection? The obvious answer is that this becomes necessary because of a crisis precipitated by the changes in the phenomena that have previously been amenable to the existing ways of making sense.[31] Such crises seem inevitable when the reality that they claim to comprehend (and indeed, expect to manage, manipulate or alter) changes, despite their efforts to maintain the status quo.[32] I have argued elsewhere (Lele 2000) that our three dimensional human existence: of living as individuals in the two worlds of nature and society at the same time, of being and confronting nature and culture, body and mind as well as objects and symbols, while remaining united within our selves, implies a creative tension that propels the exercise of our reflexive capabilities.[33] This necessary reflexive activity in our everyday life initiates and facilitates change, in many miniscule ways, in the way we do things and think about them (unless, of course, systematically prevented from doing so). These small quantitative changes have a tendency to accumulate and acquire a qualitative dimension that makes the established and sanctioned ways of thinking and doing problematic.[34] As they start to become fetters on the ongoing exercise of reflection, but are still sustained and enforced by those with vested interests, they may provoke concerted questioning and challenges that could precipitate a crisis. A crisis of this order would force the upholders of the established perspectives onto an arena of disputation with those who are contesting their ways and may have found access to other, more relevant ways of making sense.[35]

In English (and in French) the idea of the crossroads is associated with the possibility of a dramatic shift in the existing conditions as a result of some momentous decisions. It therefore implies a feeling of fear and uncertainty, a sense of risk, on the part of those at the crossroads, about the likely, as yet unpredictable, outcome of the contemplated action. It also presupposes certain dissatisfaction about the way things are and has, as a result prompted the need for a decision and action. It also suggests a certain kind of immobility on the part of the agent who is engulfed by a sense of indecision and foreboding. To be at the crossroads is to be in a state of crisis. Societies experience such moments of crisis when the micro-moments of reflection and innovation accumulate and pose major qualitative questions. Habermas (1975: 1-8) refers to the use of the idea of crisis in the fields of medicine and literature to show the link between crisis and critique at the societal level. A critique is the reflection, rethinking and churning that goes on under conditions of crisis. All previously held convictions are brought into question. New meanings and new guidance for remedial or transformative action are sought. When an effective solution is found, a decision is made and appropriate action follows, a crisis is resolved. If not so resolved, it holds the prospect of demise for the one in that state.

Dnyaneshwar's use of *catuspatha* in 10: 108 corresponds to this usage. Many of the conventional interpreters of the *ovi* seem to agree that it refers to the coming together and clashing of contradictory perspectives that in the end produces an understanding (*samarasya*) that takes us beyond the contradictions.[36] The context in which such coming together becomes possible is the context of crisis. The future of all those who seek resolution (the leaders and their subjects/followers as well) is at stake. A recognition that the old is no longer viable but the new has yet to arrive permeates the atmosphere. Only a crisis of this order can bring the dominant interpretations that govern the existing social order into question. It forces the orthodoxy and its critics onto a forum for deliberation and propels the desire for a satisfactory solution, for *samarasya.* Fear of risk, uncertainty and foreboding are the sentiments that dominate the deliberations. This is the period of Gramsci's interregnum (1971:

276). Not surprisingly, resolution produces an unprecedented sense of liberation and bliss. The crossroads, *catuspatha* is the arena where this dramatic transition can occur. The feeling of awe and fear about *catuspatha* is not alien to the Indian tradition.[37]

DN is an attempt by Dnyaneshwar to critique a text so as to make its message relevant to his own times. The choice of *BG* in this case also could not have been accidental. As I have argued (Lele 1990), *BG* was a product of an era of crisis. Its response to the crisis of Brahmanism was to forestall transformative challenges through the strategy of adaptation. It did prove to be successful but that was as much because of the political-economic context as it was, as Kosambi would have it, because some "remarkably keen" minds "capable of deep and sympathetic study" took the essentials from each prior doctrine and arranged them and fitted them together "with consummate skill and literary ability, and cemented (them) by *bhakti* without developing their contradictions" (Kosambi 1962: 29). It seems the times of Dnyaneshwar were also the times of a crisis of Brahmanism (Lele 1987).[38] However, *DN* is fundamentally different from *BG* in a number of ways. It offers, as I have shown elsewhere, a highly nuanced critique of Brahmanism. Echoes of some of the issues raised in it, about critical appropriation of tradition, are to be found in contemporary critical hermeneutics (see Lele 1987).[39]

There is one more aspect of the idea of crossroads that is crucial for our purposes. Kavade refers to *DN* 18: 1607 (1588 in Rajwade/Godbole version) where Dnayneshwar refers to Sanjay (who has been narrating *BG*, as part of the narrative of Mahabharata, to Dhrtarastra) as becoming the *cohota* of *samvad sukha* or the bliss of dialogue. The word *cohota* has a meaning similar to *catuspatha.* Two other words in Marathi, *cauk* and *cavata,* also carry similar meanings. Unlike *catuspatha* and *cauk,* however, the other two refer to a platform in front of a house where friends and family tend to meet. It is an open space in which neighbors and passers-by may also join in as participants in conversation. It is this latter sense of incidental participation in dialogue that the term *cohota* is used in reference to Sanjay.[40] *Catuspatha* and *cauk* mean only the meeting of four roads.[41] What is common to all the four words and is crucial for our purposes is the sense of openness or publicness of the implicated space.[42] It is this denial of claims of privacy and hidden agendas of private interests (which both the state and the privileged classes seek to keep concealed from the purview of dialogue and discussion), implied in the use of the term *catuspatha*, which lends it a special significance for Dnyaneshwar's theory of communicative action. *Catuspatha*, in other words, is the equivalent of what Habermas and his associates who promote deliberative democracy would call "the public sphere".[43]

This brings us to the second question about *catuspatha* as the public sphere. What are the preconditions for the possibility of a successful completion of the process of deliberation? This successful outcome is what *DN* celebrates as *samvad sukha*. What are the prerequisites for the agents engaged in dialogue to see beyond their existing ways by taking the arguments of the other agents seriously, on their own terms, and be willing to be guided by a "common will" and towards the "common good"? Questions of this nature have been raised in the context of formal democracies in the West.[44] The contemporary social science literature on *bhakti* often raises doubts about the claims of a transformative intent, the intent to promote social justice and equality made on behalf of the *Varkari* tradition. I have argued elsewhere (see Lele 1987a and 1991, for example) that before raising such questions one must place the *Varkari* critique in its historical context and treat that historical context in a non-linear, dynamic and dialectical framework.[45] Rather than repeating those arguments, let me come to that point with a different question: how does Dnyaneshwar deal with the fact that all social interactions, including those aimed to arriving at a new understanding, must confront the fact that dialogue in such situations is always a dialogue between unequals?

For a brief sketchy answer let us return to the point I made in the first section about the commitment to the unity of our material and spiritual existence in *Varkari* theory and practice. In my reading, the *Varkari* answer to the question of inequality is encapsulated in the two main attributes of the movement: its conception of the community of *sants* (as "potential community") and the way it treats the relationship between God and the *bhakta* and between the *bhakta* and his/her *guru*. *DN* makes it very clear that there is no distinction to be made between these relationships. God and *guru* are practically on par. Both are, above all, dialogic relationships. The second unique feature of those relationships is that even when seen as involving the process of arriving at a new sense, of coming to know, it is not viewed in terms of some artificially isolated cognitive domain. The essential unity of the three dimensions of our human existence on earth, cognitive, communicative and self-expressive[46] are all equally active in the dialogue. This tri-dimensional relationship between God, *guru* and the *bhakta* is expressed both in the ideal of the community of *sants* as "potential community" (on this see Lele 1981: 105-6) and in the way that community conducts *guru-sisya samvad.*

The most potent example of how the *guru* and God are seen as one and the same is of course that of the dialogue between Krishna and Arjuna. But Dnyaneshwar's references in *DN* to his own *guru*, Nivruttinath, are on par with those to the first pair.[47] Consistent with the entire *Varkari* tradition[48] this relationship of initial inequality is modeled after the mother-child relationship of inequality which looks towards equality as its outcome. The greatest joy for a mother or a *guru* (and hence for God) is to see their pupils become autonomous and independent full-fledged human beings on par with their teacher-care givers. That is what *samvad sukha* is all about. A successful culmination of *guru-sisya samvad* has, therefore, an unmistakable divine quality to it. To become one with God is to become God and that essentially means recognizing that every other living being is God. This promise permeates Dnyaneshwar's discourse on dialogue. That is why his *bhaktas*, as those who have successfully arrived at a shared understanding, celebrate that moment of transcendence in which all doubt has ceased and all questions have been answered. This is how such a pedagogic encounter between God or *guru* and *bhakta* unfolds for Dnyaneshwar:

Pudha sneha pazare
maga calàti akshare
shabdu maghara avatare
krpa adhi.

Loving kindness springs forth first
Then follows the march of letters
Words arrive later
Compassion first.

WHY GANESH?

Finally, in calling those who share that divine understanding Ganesh, Dnyaneshwar invites us to explore the goldmine of possible meanings emerging from the complex history of the multiple origin myths and diverse trajectories of evolution of this most fascinating of all the non-Vedic deities.[49] Dnyaneshwar summons Ganesh in many places in *DN* to take advantage of his multiple origin myths and his diverse attributes.[50] In a fascinating display of an aesthetically appropriated essence of the diverse metaphysical schools of Indian traditions, the very first twenty *ovis* of *DN* list for us all the *paths* that are in contention and require transcendence as the attributes of Ganesh. Here *samvad* is his tooth and its perfect whiteness (*subhravarnu*) is *samata* (at least one of its meanings being equality). For Dnyaneshwar, his *guru's* blessing is also Ganesh (10: 6), because it allows his "childish efforts" to pass through the gates of high literature (*saraswat*).

The words Ganesh or Ganapati also mean the leader of a community, of *gana*.[51] His past as a *yaksha* and a *vighnakarta* also puts him in a class of gods to be dreaded and propitiated, like the *matrakas* who had to be propitiated at the crossroads and with whom he has been associated.[52] As noted earlier, in many ancient traditions crossroads are associated with a dark, mysterious and uncertain future and with the deities who either contribute to or help alleviate such mystery and uncertainty. Ganesh as the initiator (*vighnakarta*) and alleviator of crises (*vighnaharta*) is often seen as the god of the crossroads. He is also a *yaksha* who eventually gets brahmanized as a god (see Dhavalikar 1991: 57-60). Dialogue is an encounter at the crossroads, with an uncertain future for those engaged in it. It is full of promise as well as possible disappointment. Ganesh is the deity who understands the intended (*vivakshit*) meaning of the word and has the capability to enlighten the intellect of others with that same meaning (see Kavade 2003: 86). Who but the god who represents both possibilities as well as the possible transcendence should have the privilege of presiding over such divine encounters?

The idea of this paper emerged from my total puzzlement with 10: 108. My sense of mystery about the Ganesh reference arose also from the knowledge of the dialectic of his position as both the creator and destroyer of obstacles. In this paper I have tried to solve that puzzle with the use of what I understand as the method of critical hermeneutics. The anticipated result of this exercise was to demonstrate the significance of reading *DN* as the source for contemporary reflection. I have attempted to show in a brief sketch, how this form of critique can throw new light on the role of tradition in contemporary life and in addressing some of the basic issues of the possibilities for dialogue under conditions of unceasing material inequality.

NOTES

1. I am grateful to Amod Lele, Nissim Mannathukaren and Rajendra Singh for their critical comments. I am alone responsible for the various inadequacies that still remain.
2. There are four different dialogic encounters occurring simultaneously in *DN*, three of them dyadic, the central one being that between Krishna and Arjuna. There is also the Sanjay-Dhrtarastra dialogue, inherited from *Bhagvadgita* (hereafter *BG*) and the one between the author and his *guru*. In addition the narrative as a whole is structured as a dialogue between the narrator Dnyaneshwar and his audience.
3. For this section I have drawn heavily on an excellent, uniquely sensitive attempt (Kavade 2003) at exploring the nuances of the puzzle posed by 10: 108. I am grateful to Professor Kavade for doing this and to P.K. Lele for bringing this to my attention.
4. Kavade (2003: 86) argues that the meanings to *samvad* and *catuspatha*, given by Pandit, speak to the same oppositional/contradictory nature of meanings that converge, making the use of *catuspatha* somewhat redundant. In fact Pandit seems to distinguish between *catuspatha* and *samvad* as I do. Thus his note takes us a step closer to our intended meaning (see pp. 29-30).
5. Those familiar with *DN* will recognize that my reference is to the Rajwade version. The citations to which Kavade refers all use the traditional brahmanic version of *DN*, found in Kunte and Dandekar editions. I hope to deal with the controversy surrounding the two

versions, in a subsequent paper. For some indication of this see Prabha Rao's statement in the revised government sponsored version of 1977 (Government of Maharashtra 1977) and Dhere (1967: 146). For this paper I have mostly used the Godbole edition of the Rajwade version (Godbole 1977).

6. I see in this definition a welcome attempt to capture the dynamics of dialogue (*samvad*) (more on this later).
7. Under this interpretation of *samvad*, however, there is no need for *samvad* as dialogue since the unity/uniformity of meaning is prior to this coming together. This is contrary to the strong avowal of differentiated unity in much of the text of *DN*. For me it violates the spirit of the *Varkari* understanding of divinity, the central place accorded to *DN* in it and the associated practice in which the *sants* approached and spoke about the divine in terms of their daily life practice as tailors, barbers and holders of other village service occupations or housewives and servants.
8. This is not surprising and not something that I take issue with. For those who work within that widely shared and almost universally accepted dualistic view of the world, his contribution represents an unquestionably enriching advance over prior interpretations. For us it opens a remarkably potent possibility to illustrate the uniquely undualistic way in which Dnyaneshwar and the *Varkari sant* tradition treat dialogue.
9. Even those who assert the *advaita* claim systematically downplay the material-social dimension of that unity.
10. Apart from the orthodox interpretations of Dnyaneshwar there are also equally asocial readings of Dnyaneshwar by scholars of literature who expound on its "literary merit" in isolation from his trans-temporal appeal to people of all classes and castes, both genders and various levels of literacy.
11. The main problem, as I hope it will become clear, is that while Kavade treats *samvad* as an end point I, following Dnyaneshwar, treat it as a process that culminates in a shared understanding which is intended but not always necessarily attained. Dnyaneshwar's term for that moment of arrival is *samarasya.*
12. We find the beginnings of this method in D.D. Kosambi's *Myth and Reality*. "Anyone with aesthetic sense can enjoy the beauty of the lily (of Indian philosophy)", but, he says, "it takes considerable scientific effort to discover the physiological process whereby the lily grew out of the mud and filth (of the swamp of popular superstition)" (1962: 1).
13. The idea of *bhagawan* as the designated leader and distributor of the shares in surplus, to be trusted to uphold the principle of justice (as equality), may invoke a sense of gratefulness. It may thus seem to

account for the evolution of the idea of *bhakti* as devotion. It then becomes available for ideological exploitation for legitimizing the deviations from the ideal of community, once the leadership has transformed itself into rulership (I owe this point to Rajendra Singh).

14. Tracing the affinity of *bhakti* to partnership brings its meaning closer to the needs of our times and can thus become relevant for possible communicative action aimed at the pursuit of greater participation of communities in the governance of their everyday life, thus enlarging the prospects for justice and equality (I owe this clarification to Amod Lele).
15. This identity of community (with an emphasis on equality of members) with divinity was the driving force for the rapid increase in the popularity of various *bhagavata* sects and is reflected still in the various practices (now hidden under a brahmanic ritualistic crust) of the followers of *Varkari panth*.
16. For a brief introduction to the debate and intervention see McCarthy 1982.
17. Unless structurally (and ideologically) prevented from doing so by institutions, from religious to educational and by various other mechanisms of manufacturing consent (see Lele 1996; Herman and Chomsky 1988).
18. As pointed out earlier there are four different dialogues at work here.
19. Here I am drawing on the point argued in detail by Habermas (1970) that a dialogue implies a commitment to arriving at shared sense or to reach an understanding that is mutual. Apart from this commitment, he also discusses, as "dialogue constitutive universals", three types of validity standards (about the implicit truth claims) and three types of expressions, all grounded in the three-dimensional human existence as (a) in and as nature, (b) as subject or "the other" of nature and (c) as an "intersubject" or a social being.
20. While I cannot deal with it in full detail in this short paper, I should clarify that in my usage a critical-hermeneutic inquiry of this kind entails critical examination of the following: (a) the text itself (b) the material and ideological context of its author and of the creation of the text and (c) the context in which the text (still) makes sense, meaning the context of the interpreter of the text. In the kind of study I attempt here we are dealing with a complex of relationships involving all three aspects of *DN* as well as a second triad of *BG* as the text, its context of creation and the context in which *DN* was offered as its interpretation. The basic critical hermeneutic question for me is this: what makes the text (in our case *DN* in particular but also *BG*) relevant to our times? Having pointed out that brahmanic orthodoxy understands its meaningfulness in a particular way, I have criticized its consequences

for the basic human values of truth, justice and freedom (their foundational nature is a matter of debate but to be taken up elsewhere). I then go on to suggest that perhaps a careful look at Dnyaneshwar's own context of interpretation as well as a reading of the text of *DN*, on its own terms (this may perhaps involve a discussion of some standard criteria of literary criticism but that too cannot be taken up here, but also its equally important relationship to its own context, which is hinted at here) will reveal a meaning nexus that upholds rather than violates those basic human values.

21. Dnyaneshwar expresses this unity in a variety of ways and in several places in the text. Take the following two, for example:
pari srutismrtice arth/je apana houni moort/
anushthane jaga det/vadil je ga (17: 85)
The true meanings of the scriptures can be comprehended
by the world only when they express themselves
through the actions of those who claim their authority
and
aang vari carci/janate vanci
to jaan adnyanaci/khani yeth (13: 659)
One who holds hollow discourses on knowledge
and thus practices deception on his people
is a veritable mine of ignorance
Also see Sardar (1970: 13-17).
22. This is, as Max Weber pointed out, the basic feature of Western modernity. On its role in the perpetuation of an unjust social order see Jurgen Habermas' work, especially his idea of the unfinished project of modernity. For critical discussions on these ideas see Honneth et al. 1992.
23. For my discussion on the relationship between Indian traditions and modernity see Lele 1995: 51-80.
24. Hence:
teth haru mhane jevi nenije/devi jaise ka swarup tuze/ he nityanutan dekhije/ gitatattva (*DN.* 1: 71).
Said Hara, not unlike your own unfathomable beautiful disposition my beloved, the meaning of *Gita* is eternally new.
This gives Dnyaneshwar an excuse, a reason, the freedom to offer his own new meanings of *gitatattva.*
25. See Lele 1991.
26. "Such incomparable *bhaktas*, in a state of horripilation (*romanch uthlele*) and with tearful eyes conversing with each other, purify their own clans and the universe" (my English translation of Kavade's Marathi rendering of 68). See Kavade 2003. Even Narada does not ignore the social, universal dimension of this *sattvika* stage!

27. It includes immobility, perspiration, horripilation, inarticulate speech, trembling, color change, tears, and deep mental absorption. I intend to take up the liberating aesthetic dimension of this transcendence in another paper.
28. The choice of *BG* by Dnyaneshwar as the backdrop for his original treatise on dialogic discovery of truth seems also to be guided by the fact that in this case God and *guru* are the same. I hope to explore this theme of God, *guru* and *bhakta* relation in *DN* in a subsequent paper.
29. Communicative action is an action oriented to, as well as arising from, an attempt to make sense together and leads to an action to implement that new sense.
30. All the traditional interpreters of this *ovi*, reviewed by Kavade, seem to accept that this was the intended use of the word by Dnyaneshwar.
31. This is demonstrated most clearly in the domain of natural sciences since the pioneering work of Thomas Kuhn on paradigm shifts.
32. It should be made clear that here we are talking about those who have entrusted themselves with the task of maintaining a given social order and with the creation and upholding of ideological-explanatory frameworks that legitimize and thus sustain it.
33. To sum it up in the words of Habermas (1975: 15): "not learning but not-learning is the phenomenon that requires explanation at the socio-cultural stage of development".
34. The most obvious illustration of this can be found in technological change. See Anderson 1978 (182-96) on medieval Europe.
35. Attempts to contain challenges by adjusting legitimating ideologies to the changing conditions without letting the demands for total transformation turn into a battle cry are very common. The entire history of Brahmanism can be traced in these terms as has been shown by several critical historians starting with D.D. Kosambi. His critique of *BG* points at its role in adaptation of the old. Also see Jaiswal (1981) on *BG*.
36. The conventional thought, not surprisingly, limits this process to the world of ideas and perspectives and has nothing to say about its origins in and impact on the real, material social world.
37. Kosambi (1962: 82-109) provides us with a fascinating survey of the historical context that has made the texts and legends of Buddhist and brahmanic traditions treat crossroads as dangerous places full of risk and uncertainty and thus places of worship of deities that may spell danger as well as security.
38. There is sufficient evidence to suggest that the Yadava regime under which *DN* was written was a period of rapid decline of the preceding years of prosperity. With the arrival of Khilji's campaign against the regime in 1296, the state of disarray at the political level became

obvious. The socio-cultural crisis of the times was at the same time reflected in the massive proliferation of rituals of the *vrata* and *udyapana* variety, indicating the crisis of Brahmanism (see Gadgil 1979; Sardar 1970).

39. In the article cited above I take issue with Kosambi (1962: 12-41) for his dismissal of both texts for legitimizing Brahmanism. Here Kosambi seems to have succumbed to his own orthodoxy in not being able to capture the nuance in *DN* that distinguishes it from *BG* in fundamental ways. Unlike *BG* I believe it qualifies as a voice, no matter how muted, of the subaltern classes and rightfully belongs, as the tradition claims, beside the works of Tukaram, Bahinabai and other *Varkari sant* poets.
40. This is clearly noticeable in the different endings of Kavade's *DN* 1607 and Rajwade/Godbole's 18: 1588, where *samvadsukhaca cohota* (the crossroads of dialogue) becomes *bhavabhavanica cohota* (the platform in front of the house of *bhavas*)!
41. In Hindi, Singh reminds me, *chaupal* (and *chavadi* in Marathi) is where the village *panchayat* meets, as do less formal meetings in the village.
42. Openness implies (a) the absence of restrictions on the availability of information and (b) the denial of secrecy (see Ku 1997).
43. Great importance is attached to the openness of deliberations on a society's future, whether under normal conditions or those of crisis, in contemporary democratic theory. Its taken for grantedness in "traditional" communities is often remarked on by Westerners who encounter it for the first time (more on this in a future paper).
44. Promoters of deliberative democracy insist that upon entering the public domain citizens (must/should/do) treat each other as equals. The presence of institutions that promote such bracketed equality are considered to be adequate for the purpose by some. Others take recourse to the ideas of "civic culture" or "culture of democracy" or the rule of law, under which the citizens of "mature" Western democracies are brought up, as satisfactory mechanisms for ensuring formal equality. Those who are willing to look critically at the pathologies of formal democracies as they are practiced in the West and elsewhere challenge these claims.
45. Nissim Mannathukaren (personal communication) has raised the question of non-comparability of the notions of deliberative democracy with its prerequisites that presume the existence of an autonomous self as coming to deliberate with similar individual selves and the idea of dialogue in Dnyaneshwar. The associated concepts of citizenship and individual rights were also conspicuously absent in Dnyaneshwar's times. While recognizing that the material basis for dialogue has dramatically changed with the advent of capitalism and the institutions that have emerged since, the specific point I am making here is that

the persistent pathologies of these institutions reflect the fundamental absence of material equality among the participants of the so-called deliberative democracy and that inequality as the basis of social organization is what grounds both discourses of dialogue and makes them the source of tension between potentiality and actuality (on the tension between potential and actual community, see Lele 1981).

46. As captured by Dnyaneshwar in his treatment of *satcitanada* in *Amratanubhav* 5-10 and 12. See Lele 1981: 108.
47. See, for example, 10: 1-15.
48. In looking at contemporary *Varkari* practice we must again look at the current explanations critically and attempt to excavate the traces of the original associations that have become encrusted in layers of brahmanical interpretations.
49. For a sample of reflections on the multiple contexts and contents of these myths and functions see the papers in Brown 1991.
50. Kavade and Dhere (1967: 6-7) point to another important historical detail as one possible source of inspiration for Dnyaneshwar's reference to Ganesh in 10: 108: a contemporary inscription of a Yadava general on a Ganesh temple at the crossroads, describing those long distance travelers arriving from all four directions resting happily at all times in that temple.
51. On the various uses of *gana*, including an important link to the non-monarchical states of Ancient India, see Narain 1991: 21.
52. See Kosambi 1962: 82-109 as well as Brown 1991: 7-8. The association of Ganesh with the *matrakas* in the ancient texts and with the trade routes and crossroads in the alien lands through which the migrating mendicants of Buddhism, Jainism and Brahmanism traveled south of the Vindhyas, will be explored further in relation to Dnyaneshwar's multiple and complex references to Ganesh in a later paper.

REFERENCES

Anderson, Perry, 1978: *Passages from Antiquity to Feudalism.* London: Verso.

Brown, Robert L. (ed.), 1991: *Ganesh: Studies of an Asian God.* Albany: State University of New York Press.

Dhavalikar, M.K., 1991: "Ganesa: Myth and Reality", in Brown (ed.): *Ganesh: Studies of an Asian God.* Albany: State University of New York Press.

Dhere, R.C., 1967: *Vividha.* Pune: Neelakantha Prakashan.

Gadgil, S.R., 1979: *Vaidic Yadnya, Madhyayugin Tantrasadhana ani Dnyaneshwar Pranit Bhaktiyog.* Pune: Dastane Ramchandra ani Company.

Godbole, M.S. (ed.), 1977: *Sartha Shri Dnyaneshwari.* Pune: Shri Vidya Prakashan.

Gramsci, Antonio, 1971: *Selections from the Prison Notebooks.* London: Lawrence and Wishart.

Habermas, Jurgen, 1970: "Toward a Theory of Communicative Competence", in H.P. Dreitzel, *Recent Sociology*: No. 2. New York: Macmillan.

Habermas, 1975: *Legitimation Crisis.* Boston: Beacon Press.

Herman, Edward S. and N. Chomsky, 1988: *Manufacturing Consent: A Propaganda Model.* New York: Pantheon Books.

Honneth, Axel, Thomas McCarthy, Claus Offe and Albrecht Wellmer (eds.), 1992: *Philosophical Interventions in the Unfinished Project of Enlightenment.* Cambridge: The MIT Press.

Jaiswal, Suvira, 1981: *The Origins and Development of Vaishnavism.* Delhi: Munshiram Manoharlal.

Kavade, S.S., 2003: "Te Samvad Catuspathice Ganesh Jale", in *Baparukhamadevivaru.* Pune, 8 November 2003.

Kosambi, D.D., 1962: *Myth and Reality.* Bombay: Popular Prakashan.

Ku, Agnes S., 1997: "Boundary Politics in the Public Sphere: Openness, Secrecy, and Leak", *Sociological Theory* 16 (2) July.

Lele, Jayant, 1981: "Community, Discourse and Critique in Jnyaneshwar", in Jayant Lele (ed.), *Tradition and Modernity in Bhakti Movements.* Leiden: E.J. Brill.

——, 1987a: "Jnanesvar and Tukaram: An Exercise in Critical Hermenutics", in N.K. Wagle and M. Israel (eds.), *Religion and Society in Maharashtra.* Toronto: University of Toronto, Centre for South Asian Studies.

——, 1987b: "Language and Litereture of Dalits and Sants: Some Missed Opportunities", in I. Narain and L. Lutze (eds.), *Literature, Social Consciousness and Polity.* New Delhi: Manohar.

——, 1989: "Tradition and Intellectuals in a Third World Society", in J.K. Lele and R. Singh, *Language and Society: Steps towards an Integrated Theory.* Leiden: E.J. Brill.

——, 1990: "On Regaining the Meaning of the Bhagavad Gita". *Journal of South Asian Literature* 23(2).

——, 1991: "*Varkari* Sampradayatil Krantikarak Ashay", in *Samaj Prabodhan Patrika,* October-November.

——, 1994: "*Varkari* Sampradaya as a Critique of State Power", in V. Subramaniam (ed.), *Political Theorizing in Asia.* Delhi: Ajanta Publications.

——, 1995: "The Political Appropriation of Bhakti: Hegemony and Dominance in Medieval Maharashtra", in Lele, *Hindutva: The Emergence of the Right.* Madras: Earthworm Books.

——, 1996: "Hindutva as Pedagogic Violence", in Nigel Cook (ed.), *Transmission of Knowledge in South Asia.* Bombay: Oxford University Press.

——, 2000: "By Faith Alone: History as a Weapon in the Politics of Hindutva", in H. Kotani and F. Oshikawa (eds.), *Fussing Modernity: Appropriation of*

History and Political Mobilization in South Asia. Osaka: The Japan Center for Area Studies (JCAS), National Museum of Ethnology.

Maharashtra Rajya Shikshan Vibhag, 1977: *Shri Dnyaneshwari.*

McCarthy, Thomas, 1982: "Rationality and Relativism: Habermas's 'Overcoming' of Hermeneutics", in John B. Thompson and D. Held (eds.), *Habermas: Critical Debates.* Cambridge: The MIT Press.

Narain, A.K., 1991: "Ganesa: A Protohistory of the Idea and the Icon", in Robert L. Brown (ed.), *Ganensh: Studies of an Asian God.* Albany: State University of New York Press.

Sardar, G.B., 1970: *Sant Vangmayaci Samajik Phalasruti.* Pune: Maharashtra Sahitya Parishad.

2

A Way to Liberation: *Kuṇḍalinīyoga* in the *Jñāneśvarī*

IWAO SHIMA

INTRODUCTION

Bhakti and Tantrism are the two main religous streams that characterize medieval Hinduism. The *bhakti* movement, which originated from the *Bhagavadgītā*, appears to have developed in medieval India in the following manner.

With the rise of the *bhakti* movement in Tamil (seventh-ninth centuries), *bhakti* began to occupy a central position in the three ways to salvation (*karman*, *jñāna* and *bhakti*). Thereafter, this *bhakti* was absorbed into the Brahmanical tradition and spread all over India. Three stages can be distinguished in the development of the *bhakti* movement. During the first stage, the *bhakti* movement, which originated in a non-Aryan environment (Tamil), was absorbed into the orthodox Brahmanical tradition and was reconciled with this tradition of knowledge (*jñāna*) and meditation (*upāsanā*). Rāmānuja and Madhva are representatives of this stage. They attempted to reconcile *bhakti* with the Upaniṣadic tradition of *jñāna* and *upāsanā* and identified *bhakti* with knowledge (*vedanā*) and meditation (*upāsanā*). However, as a result of the reconciliation with the Upaniṣadic tradition of knowledge and meditation, their *bhakti* came to lose its original emotional character to a certain extent.

With the spread of the *bhakti* movement to west and north

India and among the lower castes, *bhakti* gradually became free from the Upaniṣadic tradition of *jñāna* and *upāsanā* and recovered its original emotional character. This is the second stage in the development of the *bhakti* movement. This stage has two aspects. One is that *bhakti* spread all over India through the Sanskrit language, which supported the Brahmanical tradition as the sacred language of the Brahmins; thus, emotional *bhakti* came to permeate the Brahmanical tradition itself. Vallabha, Nimbarka and others are representatives of this aspect. The other aspect is that *bhakti* spread even among the lower castes through the local languages with the help of local sages from various parts of India. Jñānadeva is one of the representatives of this aspect.[1]

The thought of Jñānadeva has been discussed by scholars from the following three points of view.

1. Some scholars have pointed out the influence of Śaṅkara or Advaitavedānta on Jñānadeva's thought.[2]
2. Others have discussed the *bhakti* elements in the thought of Jñānadeva in relation to the *bhakti* movement that developed through the Marathi language in Maharashtra.[3]
3. Still others have found influences of the Nātha sect in Jñānadeva's thought.[4]

It is true that we find these three aspects in the *Jñāneśvarī* composed by Jñānadeva, but how are these aspects interconnected and unified in one and the same work? It appears to me that a study on the *Jñāneśvarī* itself would be insufficient to clarify this point because the *Jñāneśvarī* is a commentary on the *Bhagavadgītā* and its framework follows that of the *Bhagavadgītā*. Therefore, in this paper, I will first discuss the interconnection and unification of the three above-mentioned aspects in the *Jñāneśvarī* (chapters 1-6) within the framework of the interpretation of the *Bhagavadgītā* in comparison with three previous commentaries on the *Bhagavadgītā*, i.e. the *Śāṅkarabhāṣya*, *Rāmānujabhāṣya* and *Madhvabhāṣya*.[5]

Let us first examine the kinds of religious traditions that Jñānadeva succeeded to in the *Jñāneśvarī*.

RELIGIOUS TRADITIONS SUCCEEDED BY JÑĀNADEVA IN THE *JÑĀNEŚVARĪ*

FROM THE INTRODUCTION OF THE *JÑĀNEŚVARĪ*

In the introduction of the *Jñāneśvarī*, Jñānadeva pays homage to Gaṇapati and describes the different parts of Gaṇapati as corresponding to different religious traditions, as shown in Table 1.

TABLE 1: PARTS OF GAṆAPATI AND THEIR CORRESPONDENCE TO RELIGIOUS TRADITIONS (*JÑĀNEŚVARĪ* 1.3-14)

Parts of Gaṇapati	*Religious traditions*
beautiful form	Śabdabrahma (Veda)
limbs	Smṛti
ornaments	eighteen Purāṇas
multi-colored garment	Sāhitya
jingling bells	Kāvyaṇāṭakā
waist-cloth and its tassled end	wisdom of Vyāsa, etc.
six arms	six schools of Indian philosophy

In the introduction, Jñānadeva clarifies that his work continues the orthodox Brahmanical religious traditions, such as the Veda, the Smṛti, the eighteen Purāṇas, the *Mahābhārata* and the six schools of Indian philosophy.

However, Jñānadeva did not consider the six schools of Indian philosophy as opposing each other, although these schools clashed with each other within the orthodox Brahmanical religious traditions.

Among the six schools of Indian philosophy, the Vedānta, which continued the Upaniṣadic tradition, particularly Dvaitavedānta and Advaitavedānta, appears to have special importance for Jñānadeva, as shown in Table 2.

After having paid homage to the orthodox Brahmanical religious traditions, Jñānadeva ends by paying homage to Goddess Śāradā (1.21) and the Nātha *yogin* Nivṛtti (1.22-7). Then, he discusses the excellence of the *Mahābhārata* and the *Bhagavadgītā* and makes references to *sants* (saints) and *bhaktas* (1.53-4) in Maharashtra.

TABLE 2: UPPER PARTS OF GAṆAPATI AND THEIR CORRESPONDENCE TO RELIGIOUS TRADITIONS (*JÑĀNEŚVARĪ* 1.16-18)

Parts of Gaṇapati	*Religious traditions*
two ears	two Mīmāṃsās
temple	Dvaita and Advaita unified
fragrant flowers adorning the crown of the head	ten Upaniṣads

From this introductory portion of the *Jñāneśvarī*, we can infer the following three points. The *Jñāneśvarī* is:

1. based on the ten Upaniṣads on the scriptural level;
2. influenced by Dvaitavedānta and Advaitavedānta on the philosophical level;
3. influenced by faith in Goddess Śaradā, the Nātha sect and the *bhakti* of *sants* at the local, religious, traditional levels.[6]

PHILOSOPHICAL LEVEL: INFLUENCE OF ADVAITAVEDĀNTA?

Among the six schools of Indian philosophy, it appears that the influence of Advaitavedānta is prevalent, particularly in the first six chapters of the *Jñāneśvarī*.

Thus, although we find many ideas of Advaitavedānta in the first six chapters of the *Jñāneśvarī* at present, it cannot be said that these six chapters are influenced by Advaitavedānta. This is so because even Rāmānuja, who opposed Śaṅkara, interprets these six chapters as preaching the realization (*sākṣātkāra*) of *ātman*, although his interpretation of the relationship between action (*karman*) and knowledge (*jñāna*) is rather different from that of Śaṅkara. In order to understand this point, we should first grasp the basic framework of the interpretation of the *Bhagavadgītā* by Jñānadeva in the historical development of the interpretations of the *Bhagavadgītā*. Let us first examine the basic framework of the interpretation of the *Bhagavadgītā* in the previous three Sanskrit commentaries.[7]

BASIC FRAMEWORK OF THE INTERPRETATION OF THE *BHAGAVADGĪTĀ* (CHAPTERS 1-6)

ŚAṄKARA'S INTERPRETATION OF THE *BHAGAVADGĪTĀ*

Śaṅkara interprets the *Bhagavadgītā* based on the following two *dharmas*: (1) the *dharma* characterized by non-action (= *jñānayoga*), which directly leads to liberation, and (2) the *dharma* characterized by action (= *karmayoga*), which indirectly leads to liberation through the purification of the mind, the attainment of knowledge and the renunciation (*sannyāsa*) of all actions, when it is practiced in a spirit of complete devotion to the Lord without expecting any result. Further these two types of *dharmas* are the two fundamental schemes of Śaṅkara's interpretation of the entire *Bhagavadgītā*.

Although Śaṅkara considers the first of these two fundamental schemes to be more essential, when he follows the second fundamental scheme, he argues at various instances that *karmayoga* leads to *jñānayoga* through the purification of the mind and finally leads to liberation through *jñānayoga* (*Śāṅkarabhāṣya* III.3, etc.). This process of liberation consists of the following four stages: (1) *karmayoga* dedicated to the Lord and practiced without expecting any result, (2) the purification of the mind, (3) the attainment of the knowledge of *ātman* and (4) the renunciation of all actions followed by liberation (*Śāṅkarabhāṣya* V.12; V.27).

Thus, in short, Saṅkara interprets the entire *Bhagavadgītā* within the framework of *karman* and *jñāna*. In other words, he interprets the entire *Bhagavadgītā* within the double framework of the Vedic tradition of rituals and the Upaniṣadic tradition of knowledge.[8]

RĀMĀNUJA'S INTERPRETATION OF THE *BHAGAVADGĪTĀ*

In contrast to the dichotomic framework of Śaṅkara's interpretation, Rāmānuja, following Yāmuna's interpretation, uses a triadic framework of interpretation, namely, *karman*, *jñāna* and *bhakti*. According to Rāmānuja, the purpose of the *Bhagavadgītā* is *bhaktiyoga* that is fostered by *jñānayoga* and *karmayoga*. Based upon this relationship of the three means to salvation and following

Yāmuna's idea (*Gītārthasaṃgraha* 2-4), Rāmānuja divides the chapters of the *Bhagavadgītā* into the following three groups according to their subject: *karmayoga* and *jñānayoga* (chapters 1-6), *bhaktiyoga* (chapters 7-12) and other miscellaneous topics (chapters 13-18). Let us now consider the first of these three groups.

After discussing *sāṃkhyabuddhi* (the consciousness of the difference between the body and *ātman*) and the *yogabuddhi* (the application of *sāṃkhyabuddhi* to the daily performance of acts, presupposing the knowledge of *ātman*) in the second chapter, Rāmānuja briefly summarizes the stages to salvation in the introductory portion of the third chapter as follows: the knowledge of *ātman* combined with *karmayoga* (= *yogabuddhi*) leads to *jñānayoga*. This *jñānayoga* (the constant consciousness of the knowledge of *ātman*) leads to the contemplation of *ātman*, which culminates in the realization (*sākṣātkāra*) of *ātman*; this realization again leads to *bhaktiyoga*, and this *bhaktiyoga* alone leads to the attainment of God or salvation. Rāmānuja then discusses the relationship between *karmayoga* and *jñānayoga* in the remainder of chapter 3 and *karmayoga* in the fourth and fifth chapters.

In sum, Rāmānuja appears to distinguish the following stages to salvation: (1) the knowledge of *ātman* (discussed in chapter 2), (2) *karmayoga* or *jñānayoga* (discussed in chapters 3-5), (3) the contemplation of *ātman* culminating in the realization of *ātman*, (4) *bhaktiyoga*, and (5) the attainment of God or salvation. Accordingly, in the sixth chapter, he explains the contemplation of *ātman*, which presupposes *karmayoga* and/or *jñānayoga*, and in chapters 7-12 he proceeds to explain *bhaktiyoga*, which presupposes the realization of *ātman*. Thus, Rāmānuja interprets the *Bhagavadgītā* (chapters 1-12) according to the stages of salvation and places *bhakti* as the final stage after the realization of *ātman*, which is the goal of Advaitavedānta.[9]

MADHVA'S INTERPRETATION OF THE *BHAGAVADGĪTĀ*

Like Rāmānuja, Madhva also follows a triadic framework of interpretation, namely, *karman*, *jñāna* and *bhakti*, and divides the chapters of the *Bhagavadgītā* into three groups, i.e. *karmayoga* and *jñānayoga* (chapters 1-6), *bhaktiyoga* (chapters 7-12) and other miscellaneous topics (chapters 13-18).

According to Madhva, the second chapter deals with the knowlege of *ātman* and the means of the knowledge of *ātman*, and the third chapter deals with the criticism of non-action and the performance of action (= *karmayoga*).

The topics of the fourth chapter are *jñāna* and *karman*, and the topic of the fifth chapter is *karmayoga*, which was discussed in relation to the renunciation of action (*karmasannyāsa*) in the previous two chapters.

The topic of the sixth chapter is contemplation, and this contemplation finally culminates in the direct vision (*aparokṣa-jñāna*) of the Highest God, as shown at the beginning of the seventh chapter. Thus, according to Madhva, *karmayoga* and *jñānayoga*, discussed in the first five chapters of the *Bhagavadgītā*, culminate in contemplation discussed in the sixth chapter, which leads to *aparokṣajñāna*. Next, *bhakti* to the Highest God, which presupposes this *aparokṣajñāna*, is discussed in the following six chapters (chapters 7-12).[10]

Jñānadeva's Interpretation of the *Bhagavadgītā*

Like Rāmānuja and Madhva, Jñānadeva also follows a triadic framework of interpretation, namely, *karma*, *jñāna* and *bhakti* and divides the chapters of the *Bhagavadgītā* into three groups, i.e. *karmayoga* and *jñānayoga* (chapters 1-6), *bhaktiyoga* (chapters 7-12) and other miscellaneous topics (chapters 13-18).

In the second chapter, Jñānadeva states that the *yoga* of pure intelligence (*buddhiyoga* = *jñānayoga*) presupposes *karmayoga*, and thus emphasizes the necessity of *karmayoga*, which, in many ways, appears to be inferior to *buddhiyoga*.

In the third chapter, Jñānadeva describes two paths to final liberation, i.e. *jñānayoga* and *karmayoga*. Through *jñānayoga*, philosophers instantly become one with the Self and attain final liberation (*mokṣa*), which appears to be the final goal of Advaitavedānta. Through *karmayoga*, on the other hand, practitioners or *yogins* attain final liberation (*nirvāṇa* or perfection) in course of time. However, these two paths ultimately become one. Thus, even here Jñānadeva emphasizes the necessity of *karmayoga*.

In the fourth chapter, *jñānayoga* is considered to be the discrimination between *ātman* and non-*ātman*, which is the subject of Advaitavedānta.

Just as in the third chapter, in the fifth chapter as well, Jñānadeva again emphasizes the oneness of *karmasannyāsa* (= *jñānayoga*) and *karmayoga*, and thus once again points out the importance of *karmayoga* in the way to final liberation. What, then, is this *karmayoga*, which is easier to practice but takes more time in leading to final liberation as compared to *jñānayoga*? After a brief explanation of *kuṇḍalinīyoga* by Lord Kṛṣṇa, Arjuna addresses Him as follows:

> Similarly, the path of *yoga* is easier than the path of knowledge for people as weak as we are. Though this *yoga* is attainable after a long time, we will be patient (5.165).

Here, the path of yoga (*karmayoga*), which is mentioned as being easier than that of knowledge (*sāṃkhyayoga jñānayoga*), is related to the *kuṇḍalinīyoga* of the Nātha sect, which Jñānadeva's teacher, Nivṛtti, followed.

The sixth chapter deals with the essence of the meaning of the *Bhagavadgītā*, the other shore of the ocean of discrimination, the treasure of the riches of *yoga* and the resting place of primordial matter. Further, this topic cannot be expressed by the Vedas, which means that it does not belong to the Vedic tradition. Jñānadeva talks about this topic in the local language (Marāṭhī). This is indeed the *kuṇḍalinīyoga* of the Nātha sect, which will be discussed in detail in 6.152-330.

In sum, according to Jñānadeva:

1. The topics of the first six chapters of the *Bhagavadgītā* are *jñānayoga* and *karmayoga*;
2. *Jñānayoga* is a quick but difficult way to final liberation and corresponds to the Advaitavedāntic way to final liberation;
3. *Karmayoga*, which is recommended to *sants*, is an easy but slow way to final liberation and is identical with the *kuṇḍalinīyoga* of the Nātha sect.

In this manner, Jñānadeva interprets the first six chapters of the *Bhagavadgītā* as culminating in the *kuṇḍalinīyoga* of the Nātha sect in the sixth chapter.[11] This appears to be a remarkable feature of the *Jñāneśvarī* in comparison with three other commentaries on the *Bhagavadgītā*.

A WAY TO LIBERATION: *KUṆḌALINĪYOGA* IN THE *JÑĀNEŚVARĪ*

In the fifth chapter (5.149-57), a way of meditation to attain Brahmanhood without abandoning one's body is described as follows:

> A *yogin* casts out all objects of desire by means of dispassion, and concentrates his mind within the body (5.150). Then, he fixes his gaze turned inwards on the knot (*granthi*) between the eyebrows where the three *nāḍīs* (*iḍā, piṅgalā* and *suṣumṇā*) meet (5.151). Then, he stops his breath through his right and left nostrils and equates his outgoing and ingoing breath (*prāṇa* and *apāna*), and causes his mind to go up to the crown center (*vyoma* = *brahmarandhra*) on the top of the head (5.152). When, by means of restraint of his breath, the mind is absorbed into the crown center, the various desires also disappear (5.154). Thus, when the mind has disappeared, where is there any place for egoism or other passions? Therefore, a *yogin* who has realized [the Self] becomes Brahman even when still in the body (5.156).

This is undoubtedly a description of a *kuṇḍalinīyoga*. Further, this *kuṇḍalinīyoga* is explained again in the sixth chapter as follows:

> There [i.e. on the royal road of *yoga* = *kuṇḍalinīyoga*] can be seen the abundant fruits of the cessation of action (*nivṛtti*) lying at the foot of the tree of action (*pravṛtti*). Even Mahesh is still a pilgrim on this road (6.153). Multitudes of *yogins* have set out quickly to the crown center (*ākāśa*) on the top of the head through the vertical path [i.e. *suṣumṇā*], and the footprints of their experience have made an easy path (6.154).

Futher, this *kuṇḍalinīyoga* consists of the following stages.

PLACE FOR MEDITATION

First, a *yogin* should find a suitable place for meditation, which is described as follows (6.164-80):

> It should be a place where one can sit comfortably, not feel the desire to rise and such that when one sees it, one's intention towards dispassion

increases (6.164). It should be very beautiful so that one wishes to practise *yoga* there and the heart experiences self-realization (6.166). It should be frequented by seekers of *yoga* and not disturbed by the footsteps of passers-by (6.172). It should be surrounded by a grove of shady trees that have roots as sweet as nectar and that are always bearing fruits (6.173). The air should not be hot but cool, and gentle breezes should blow softly over it (6.175). There should be a secluded hermitage near the spot or a temple of Siva (6.179).

This is just a general description of a suitable place for meditation.

Seat for Meditation

The *yogin* should then create a seat for meditation; the procedure for this is described as follows (6.181-5):

One should place a pure deer skin on the top, a folded cloth in the middle and unbroken blades of *kuśa* grass on the ground (6.182). The tender *kuśa* grass should be placed with care so that it remains well bound and even (6.183). If the seat is too high, the body might sway; if too low, it will be affected by contact with the earth (6.184). It should be neither too high nor too low (6.185).

This also is a general description of the seat for meditation and does not include anything specific.

Preparation for Meditation—Concentration of Mind and Control over the Senses and Mind

Then, the *yogin* should concentrate his mind and control his senses and mind. This is the preparation for *kuṇḍalinīyoga* and the first step of meditation (6.186-91).

With concentration of the mind, the *yogin* should remember his *guru* (6.186). While remembering his *guru*, a sense of purity pervades inside his body and the hardness of egoism is melted away (6.187). Then, the sense of objects is forgotten, the restlessness of the senses stops and the mind becomes quietened within the heart (6.188). While sitting on the seat, the outgoing activities of the mind are withdrawn and a sense of repose is felt within. Now, all the preparations for meditation (*abhyāsa*) are complete (6.191).

YOGIC POSTURE OF *KUṆḌALINĪYOGA*: *MŪLABANDHA* AT THE *ĀDHĀRACAKRA*

Then, a description of *kuṇḍalinīyoga* is provided. First, a yogic posture (*mudrā*) named *mūlabandha,* which is also referred to as *vajrāsana,* is described as follows (6.192-206):

Lifting the calves of the legs up on to the thighs seated on the ground (6.192), the soles of the feet should be placed firmly at the root of the tree called *ādhāracakra* (6.193).[12] Let the right foot press against the middle of the seam-like line between the anus and the penis, so that the left foot rests on it easily (6.194). The ankles should be held in such a way that the lower part of the body is raised so slightly that one is not aware of it (6.197). Oh Pārtha, now, the whole body comes to be resting completely on the top of one heel (6.198). Oh Arjuna, know that this is what is called the *mūlabandha* posture, otherwise known as *vajrāsana* (6.199).

When this posture is established at the *ādhāracakra,* the lower passages of the body are closed and the downward life-breath (*apāna*) cannot find a way to go down.

Thus, once this posture is established at the *ādhāracakra,* the lower passages of the body are closed and the downward life-breath begins to withdraw within the body (6.200).

STRUGGLE OF *APĀNA* AGAINST *MAṆIPŪRACAKRA*

Then, this downward life-breath begins to rise in the body and struggle against the *maṇipūracakra* and destroys the body of the *yogin* (6.214-20).

The downward life-breath (*apāna*), being confined by the *mūlabandha* posture, turns back and, becoming compressed, begins to go up (6.214). More and more, it is agitated and in the freer space above, it rumbles and struggles against the *maṇipūracakra* (6.215). Then, this strong storm (*apāna*) disturbs the house (i.e. the body of the *yogin*) and drives all the impurities from childhood out of the body (6.216). It looses the ocean of the humours of the body, reduces the fat and even draws out the marrow from the bones (6.218). It clears the *nāḍīs* and destroys the body [of the *yogin*] (6.219).

AWAKENING OF *KUṆḌALINĪ*

Kuṇḍalinī, on the other hand, is awakened by the heat caused by the *mūlabandha* posture, and begins to eat the flesh inside the body of the *yogin*. It is described as follows (6.221-41):

On the other hand, Oh Wielder of the bow, the heat induced by the practice of this posture (*mūlabandha*) awakens a *Śakti* called *Kuṇḍalinī* (6.221). This *Kuṇḍalinī* was sleeping, very small and curled in three and a half circles, like a female serpent with her head turned downwards (6.223), and was firmly confined in a small space; but being compressed by *vajrāsana* (= *mūlabandha*), she is awakened (6.225). For long years, she has hungered for this awakening, and being irritated, she extends her mouth upwards with great eagerness (6.228). The fire arising from her spreads upwards and downwards and begins to consume the flesh of the *yogin* (6.230).

Then, after devouring all the flesh, blood, bones and two elements (earth and water) of the body, *Kuṇḍalinī* is fully satistfied and being pacified, remains close to the *suṣumṇā* (6.231-40). Then, she begins to emit poison from her mouth, by which the body of the *yogin* regains the vitality that she had previously taken away to satisfy her hunger (6.241-2).

Then, the curtains of the six *cakras*[12] open out, and *Kuṇḍalinī* enters into the *suṣumṇā*. This is described as follows (6.243-6):

The *iḍā* and *piṅgalā* merge into one, the knot of the three [*nāḍīs*] is loosened, and the curtains of the six *cakras* open out (6.244). The energy of mental activity dies down and the sense of smell that remains in the knot enters into the *suṣumṇā* with *Kuṇḍalinī* (6.246).

KUṆḌALINĪ DRINKS MOON NECTAR

At this moment, moon nectar pours itself into the mouth of *Kuṇḍalinī* and this nectar fills the entire body of the *yogin*. It is described as follows (6.247-8):

Slowly, from above, the reservoir of moon nectar situated at the *ājñācakra* turns downwards on one side and the moon nectar pours itself into the mouth of *Kuṇḍalinī* (6.247). This nectar circulates the *nāḍīs* with the life-breath and fills the entire body and is absorbed in every part of the body (6.248).

Then, the body of the *yogin* changes into supernatural form (6.249-68).

The dried surface of the skin flakes off as husks are shed from grain (6.252). The beauty of the limbs seems like natural marble or the sprouting of seed-jewels (6.253). So appears the body [of the *yogin*] when *Kuṇḍalinī* has drunk the nectar, and even the god of death is afraid to look at it (6.259).

Further, the *yogin* aquires various supernatural powers (6.268-70).

Listen, though the body has the appearance of gold, yet it has the lightness of air, for no earthly or watery elements remain in it (6.268). The *yogin* can then see beyond all oceans, hear the thoughts of the heavens and read the mind of the ant (6.269). He rides on the horses of the winds, walks on the surface of the water, though his feet do not touch it, and in such ways, he acquires many supernatural powers (6.270).

Kuṇḍalinī Enters the Heart (*Anāhatacakra*)

Then, *Kuṇḍalinī,* ascending the steps of the *suṣumṇā,* enters the heart (i.e. the *anāhatacakra*).

Please listen to this. Grasping the life-breath (*prāṇa*) by the hand, ascending the stairway of ether, *Kuṇḍalinī* enters the heart by the steps of the *suṣumṇā* (6.271).

When *Kuṇḍalinī* enters the heart, the *anāhata* sound[13] is heard and the windows of the crown center (*brahmarandhra*) open (6.274-9).

When *Kuṇḍalinī* enters inside the heart, the *anāhata* sound is heard (6.274). When the etheric space reverberates with the thunder of this *anāhata* sound, the windows of the crown center suddenly burst open (6.279).

In the great space of the crown center, there is the pure consciousness (*caitanya*) to whom *Kuṇḍalinī* offers her own lustre, and she becomes the life-breath (*prāṇa*). It is described as follows (6.280-8):

Listen; here (in the *brahmarandhra*), exists still another great space in the form of a lotus bud, where the pure consciousness stays half satisfied (6.280). In the innermost cavity of the heart, *Kuṇḍalinī* offers the feast of her own lustre to the pure consciousness (6.281). Her brilliance then vanishes and is transformed into the life-breath (6.283ab). She appears as a necklet of gold as far as the lotus-like heart center (*anāhatacakra*), or a stream of brilliant light flowing into [the lotus-like heart center] (6.286). Then, [*Kuṇḍalinī*] is absorbed in the earth of the hollow of the heart. Thus, a form of *Śakti* [*Kuṇḍalinī*] is merged into *Śakti* (6.287).

Disappearance of the Body

When *Kuṇḍalinī* loses her lustre, the body of the *yogin* becomes invisible and the three grosser elements (earth, water and fire) that constitute the body are merged into etheric space. It is described as follows (6.293-301):

Listen! When *Kuṇḍalinī* loses her lustre, the body of the *yogin* disappears and it is no longer visible to physical sight (6.293). When such is the condition of the body, the *yogin* is called *khecara* (one who moves in the air). When this happens, his body causes various miracles (6.296). But we are not concerned with these; Oh Arjuna, bear in mind that the three grosser elements of the body have disappeared with the body itself (6.289). The water dissolves the earth, the fire absorbs the water and in the heart center, the air consumes the fire (6.299). The air alone is left, but it continues in the form of the body and after a time, it is even merged into etheric space (6.300).

Kuṇḍalinī Arrives at the *Brahmarandhra*

Then, *Kuṇḍalinī* ascends further in the *suṣumṇā* and finally arrives at the *brahmarandhra* on the top of the head, where she unites with the Supreme Self (*paramātman*). This is described as follows (6.302-28ab):

Now, she leaves the heart center (*anāhatacakra*), breaks through the end of the *suṣumṇā* and enters the space (*brahmarandhra*) at the top of the head (6.302). After settling in the *brahmarandhra*, she reaches out with the arms of her consciousness of unity with the self and embraces the *liṅga* of the Supreme Self (6.305). At that moment, the veil of the five elements is rent asunder and *Kuṇḍalinī* and the Supreme Self are united; then, all, including the etheric space [of the *brahmarandhra*], is absorbed in that union (6.306).

This is the final goal of the *kuṇḍalinīyoga* in the *Jñāneśvarī,* and this union is futher described as follows:

As water from the ocean is drawn up into the clouds and pours down again into itself as rain (6.307), so *Kuṇḍalinī,* having lived in bodily form, enters into the Supreme Self. Oh Pāṇḍava, such is this union (6.308).

In this final stage, the *yogin* attains the following state:

As it happens that the space [of the *brahmarandhra*] merges into the space of the pure consciousness, so is this state of union realized by experience and the *yogin* remains in it (6.310). He becomes the lustre, which manifested itself in the form of the four-armed (Kṛṣṇa), seeing that the godless have persecuted the multitudes of my devotees (6.324). He enjoys the indescribable bliss of being one with the reality (Brahman) (6.325). He, who follows the method prescribed by me (Kṛṣṇa) within the body, reaches a state comparable to mine (6.326). It seems as though the liquid of the Supreme Brahman had been poured into the mould of his body (6.327).

At this point, I focus on the following descriptions:

1. *Kuṇḍalinī* embraces the *liṅga* of the Supreme Self (*paramātmaliṅga*) (6.305), and *Kuṇḍalinī* and the Supreme Self are united (6.306).
2. *Kuṇḍalinī,* having lived in bodily form, enters into the Supreme Self (6.308).
3. The *yogin* becomes the lustre, which has manifested itself in the form of the four-armed (Kṛṣṇa) (6.308).
4. The *yogin* enjoys the indescribable bliss of being one with reality (Brahman) (6.325).
5. He, who follows the method prescribed by me (Kṛṣṇa) within the body, reaches a state comparable to mine (6.326).
6. It seems as though the liquid of the Supreme Brahman had been poured into the mould of his body (6.327).

In these descriptions, we find the following three elements of different religious traditions mixed together.

1. The union of *Kuṇḍalinī* (*Śakti*) and the Supreme Self (*paramātman*), which is the goal of the Tantric practice (*kuṇḍalinīyoga*) of the *Jñāneśvarī*. Further the word *paramātmaliṅga* indicates the union of Śiva (*liṅga*) and *Śakti*, which is the goal of Tantrism.
2. The identity of the individual self and the Supreme Self or Brahman, which is originally the goal of Advaitavedānta.
3. The union of the *yogin* and Kṛṣṇa, which is the goal of *bhakti*.

At this point, by means of *kuṇḍalinīyoga*, a *yogin* finally attains the union of *Kuṇḍalinī* and the Supreme Self (*paramātman*); however, this union is considered to be the identity of one's *ātman* with *paramātman* or Brahman, which is generally the goal of Advaitavedānta. Then, in chapters 7-12, Jñānadeva proceeds to explain *bhaktiyoga*, which presupposes the realization of the identity of *ātman* with *paramātman* or Brahman mentioned above in the sixth chapter.

CONCLUSION

I have discussed the features of the *Jñāneśvarī* (chapters 1-6) in comparison with the previous three commentaries on the *Bhagavadgītā*, i.e. the *Śāṅkarabhāṣya*, *Rāmānujabhāṣya* and *Madhvabhāṣya*.

Here, as a concluding remark, I point out two outstanding features of the *Jñāneśvarī*.

1. In the *Jñāneśvarī*, Tantric practice (*kuṇḍalinīyoga*) is considered to be the means to attain the identity of one's *ātman* with *paramātman* or Brahman, which is generally the goal of Advaitavedānta.
2. *Bhakti* and Tantrism are generally considered to be the two main different religous streams in medieval Hinduism, but in the *Jñāneśvarī*, these two streams meet.

Then, how can these two features be understood? Is this a form of the combination of Tantrism and *bhakti* or Tantrism and Advaitavedānta? At present, this point is difficult to answer. It will be necessary for me to proceed to read the *Jñāneśvarī* (chapters 7-12), where *bhakti* is disscussed. Another point to be disscussed in the future will be the similarity and difference in the *kuṇḍalinīyoga* between the general Nātha sect and the *Jñāneśvarī*.

NOTES

1. Cf. Shima 1992b: 2.
2. Cf. Bahirat 1984; Ranade 1982.
3. Cf. Deleury 1960; Kiehnle 1997b; Mokashi 1987; Sardar 1969; Vaudeville 1969; Vaudeville 1996; Tulpule 1984; Zelliot & Berntsen 1988.
4. Cf. Kiehnle 1997a.
5. Cf. Shima 2004: 669-70.
6. Cf. Shima 2004: 670-1.
7. Cf. Shima 2004: 673.
8. Cf. Shima 1992a.
9. Cf. Shima 1992b: 6-8.
10. Cf. Shima 2004: 675-6.
11. Cf. Shima 2004: 677-80.
12. There are six *cakras* in the body.
    1. *Mulādhāracakra*, between the anus and the penis, which is the starting point of the *suṣumṇā*.
    2. *Svādhiṣṭhānacakra*, at the root of the penis.
    3. *Maṇipūrakacakra*, at the center of the navel.
    4. *Anāhatacakra*, at the heart.
    5. *Viśuddhacakra*, at the throat.
    6. *Ājñācakra*, between the eyebrows.

    After awakening, *Kuṇḍalinī* ascends in the *suṣumṇā*, breaking through these six *cakras* and arrives at the *brahmarandhra* on the top of the head.
13. The *anāhata* sound belongs to *madhyamā*, which is the second stage of the evolution of the word. This sound is not perceptible by ordinary human beings. The *hata* sound, on the other hand, is perceptible by ordinary human beings, because it belongs to the third stage of the evolution of the word, i.e. *vaikharī*.

REFERENCES

TEXTS AND TRANSLATIONS

The Bhagavadgītā with Eleven Commentaries, ed. S.G.S. Sadhale, Bombay: Gujarati Printing Press, 1933.

Sri Jñāneśvarī, ed. V.K. Rajavade, Bombay: Government Central Press, 1963.

Dandekar, S.V. (ed. & tr.), *Sārtha Jñāneśvarī*, Pune: Svanand Prakasan, 1986.

Mangrulakar, A. & V.M. Kelkar (eds. & trs.), *Jñāneśvarī* (3 vols), Bombay: University of Bombay, 1994.

Pradhan, V. G. (tr.), *Jñāneśvarī: A Song-Sermon on the Bhagavadgītā* (2 vols), London: George Allen & Unwin Publication, 1969.

Shima, I. (tr.), "A Japanese Translation of the *Jñāneśvarī* (Chapter 1)", *Mahārāṣṭra* 5, 1999, pp. 43-72.

—— (tr.), "A Japanese Translation of the *Jñāneśvarī* (Chapter 2)", *Mahārāṣṭra* 6, 2000, pp. 27-70.

—— (tr.), "A Japanese Translation of the *Jñāneśvarī* (Chapter 3)", *Mahārāṣṭra* 7, 2001, pp. 101-28.

—— (tr.), "A Japanese Translation of the *Jñāneśvarī* (Chapter 4)", *Mahārāṣṭra* 8, 2003, pp. 93-117.

—— (tr.), "A Japanese Translation of the *Jñāneśvarī* (Chapter 5)", *Mahārāṣṭra* 9, 2004, pp. 105-24.

—— (tr.), "A Japanese Translation of the *Jñāneśvarī* (Chapter 6 1-191)", *Mahārāṣṭra* 10, 2005.12, pp. 61-79.

Yardi, M.R. (tr.), *Surasa Jñāneśvarī*, Pune: Bharatiya Vidya Bhavan, 1991.

SECONDARY WORKS

Bahirat, B.P., 1984: *The Philosophy of Jñānadeva*. Delhi: Motilal Banarsidass.

Deleury, G.A., 1960: *The Cult of Viṭhobā*. Poona: Deccan College.

Kiehnle, C., 1997a: *Song on Yoga: Texts and Teachings of the Mahārāṣṭrian Nāthas*. Alt- und Neu-Indishe Studien herausgegeben vom Institute für Kulture und Geschichte Indiens und Tibets an der Universität Hamburg 48.1. Stuttgart: Franz Steiner Verlag.

——, 1997b: *The Conservative Vaiṣṇava: Anonymous Songs of the Jñāndev Gāthā*, Alt- und Neu-Indishe Studien herausgegeben vom Institute für Kulture und Geschichte Indiens und Tibets an der Universität Hamburg 48.2. Stuttgart: Franz Steiner Verlag.

Mokashi, D.B., 1987: *Palkhi*, tr. by Philip Engblom. Albany: State University of New York Press.

Ranade, R.D., 1982: *Mysticism in Maharashtra*. Delhi: Motilal Banarsidass.

Sardar, G.B., 1969: *The Saint-Poets of Mahārāshtra*, tr. by K. A. Mehta. Bombay: Orient Longmans.

Shima, I., 1990: "Śaṅkara's Interpretation of the *Bhagavadgītā*", *Journal of Indian and Buddhist Studies* 39-1, pp. 501-4.

——, 1992a: "Śaṅkara's Interpretation of the *Bhagavadgītā*: *Jñāna*, *Karman* and *Bhakti*" (in Japanese), *Journal of Naritasan Institute for Buddhist Studies* 15 (II), pp. 187-205.

——, 1992b: "Historical Development of Salvation Theories Found in Commentaries on the *Bhagavadgītā*: From Śaṅkara to Rāmānuja", *Journal of the Japanese Association for South Asian Studies* 4, pp. 1-14.

——, 1996: "Jñāneśvara's Interpretation of the *Bhagavadgītā* V-VI" (in Japanese), *Indian Thoughts and Buddhist Culture: Essays in Honour of Professor Junkichi Imanishi on His Sixtieth Birthday*. Tokyo: Shunjusha, pp. 29-42.

——, 2004: "The *Jñāneśvarī* as a Commentary on the *Bhagavadgītā* (Chapters 1-6)", in S. Hino & T. Wada, eds., *Three Mountains and Seven Rivers: Prof. Musashi Tachikawa's Felicitation Volume*. Delhi: Motilal Banarsidass, pp. 669-83.

Tulpule, S.G., 1984: *Mysticism in Medieval India*. Wiesbaden: Otto Harrassowitz.

Vaudeville, C., 1969: *L'Invocation, Le Haripāṭh de Dnyāndev*, Publications de l'Ecole Francaise sd'Extreme-Orient, vol. LXXIII. Paris: Adrien-Maisonneuve.

——, 1996: *Myths, Saints and Legends in Medieval India*. Delhi: Oxford University Press.

Zelliot, E. & M. Berntsen, eds., 1988: *The Experience of Hinduism: Essays on Religion in Maharashtra*. Albany: State University of New York Press.

3

Bhakti Mārga of Jñāneśvara: Social Aspect of his *Advaita-Bhakti*

CHIHIRO KOISO

INTRODUCTION

Jñāneśvara's approach to *bhakti* is unique in the history of *bhakti* tradition. His contribution to *Bhāgavata dharma* in Maharashtra is especially great. As Bahinābāī describes in her *abhaṅga, Jñānadeve racilā pāyā* (Jñānadeva laid the foundation), if we consider *Bhāgavata dharma* as a temple, Jñāneśvara laid its foundation. And this foundation is firm and profound. Jñāneśvara adds a philosophical basis to *Bhāgavata dharma*. His contribution lies not only in his philosophical concept of *bhakti* which is advaitic, but also in making *Bhāgavata dharma* a movement, or a living force controlling the lives of the devotees. Zelliot (1976: 143) credits "*bhakti* movement with securing the final triumph of Hinduism over Buddhism and Jainism, with bringing the vernaculars into being as literary languages, spreading the concepts of the great tradition of brahmanical Hinduism to the common man."

Jñāneśvara says, "All human beings are naturally inclined to worship my divine being" (J. 4-67). He is pointing out that *bhakti* is a natural instinct of the human being, therefore, *bhakti* must be as old as the human being. In this paper I want to try to examine the significance of *bhakti* in Jñāneśvara's philosophy. Here the notion of *advaita-bhakti* which is also called *jñāna-bhakti, sādhya-bhakti,* and *parā-bhakti* is propounded and discussed with reference to the original texts, *Jñāneśvarī* and *Amṛtānubhava*. Jñāneśvara propounds that *bhakti* has an intrinsic or absolute value. According to him, *bhakti* is not an external mode of approach to God, but it forms the very essence of Reality as it is self-experienced (*svasaṃvedya*) and self-illuminated (*svasaṃvitti*). On the basis of these discussions, the social content of *bhakti* is considered. The social aspect of *bhakti* is examined and the application of *advaita-bhakti* to day-to-day life. Discussing *advaita-bhakti* is easy but practicing it in daily life is very difficult. The concrete example of a true *bhakta* and description of his way of life is shown. Here the central notion is to conceive God in all beings. So, serving God is equivalent to serving all beings. What is important is the way to serve. The attitude required is *niṣkāmatā*. According to Jñāneśvara, all our activities should be done with *tyāga* (renouncement) of *phala* (fruit of result). We should do our duties as *yajña* (sacrifice) and *pūjā* (worship).

BRIEF OUTLINE OF JÑĀNEŚVARA'S PHILOSOPHY

Jñāneśvara's philosophical approach can be traced to his various works, *Jñāneśvarī*, *Amṛtānubhava*, *Cāṅgādeva pāsaṣṭi*, *Haripāṭha* and the *Abhaṅgas*. It is clear from all of these works that his approach is advaitic and aupanisadic. The essence of his advaitic philosophy is summed up in the 65 verses of *Cāṅgādeva pāsaṣṭi*. Here he expresses the necessity or the essential unity of *ātman* and *brahman*. As this unity is a matter of direct experience and beyond word (indescribable = *aniruvācanīya*), it is of mystical character. Ranade (1982: 50) says that Jñāneśvara's interpretation of the *Gītā* in his *Jñāneśvarī* is "absolutely mystical and in a way super Vedantic". And he praises Jñāneśvara's interpretation as a "unique combination of philosophy, poetry and mysticism". (Ranade 1982: 50) Jñāneśvara's contribution to Indian culture in general and Maharashtrian culture in particular is immense. N. Macnicol (1968: 120) says, "Jñāneśvara is more of a thinker, and that in India almost necessarily means more of a pantheistic thinker than others of this brotherhood of saints". Jñāneśvara used Marathi language as a medium to express his philosophy. Therefore his philosophy could reach the masses.

His spiritual life is a combination of *yoga* of the *Nātha-pantha* and *bhakti* of the *Bhāgavata-sampradāya* or *Vārkarī-sampradāya*. Both *yoga* and *bhakti* are synthesized in his philosophical writings. Jñāneśvara says, "By way of *jñāna* one obtains the unmanifested form of God, by *bhakti* one obtains manifested form of God" (J. 12-23). According to Farquhar (1984: 235), "Jñāneśvara's approach is that of an enthusiastic *bhakta*". Jñāneśvara holds *bhakti* as the main means to pursue the Ultimate Reality. He seems to suggest that *bhakti* is equivalent to *jñāna*.

Many scholars discuss where to place Jñāneśvara's philosophy in the Indian philosophical tradition. Some scholars point out the influence of Śaṅkarācārya on his philosophy. The positive aspect of his *advaita* philosophy forms the sound foundation for his conception of *bhakti-yoga* and, through it, his philosophy of life which we call *Bhāgavat dharma*. His philosophical standpoint is very unique, in the sense that he sees the world absolutely positively.[1]

The terms *cidvilāsa* (where *vilāsa* is more than just "expression"; and *cid* is cosmic consciousness), and *pūrṇādvaita* (perfect monism) may be said to be the key words to understand Jñāneśvara's philosophy. We shall consider *cidvilāsa* first.

According to Jñāneśvara this world is nothing but the expression of *ātman*. *Cidvilāsa* can be said to be a positive theory of the world. According to Jñāneśvara, the whole world is the manifestation of divinity, which is of the nature of pure consciousness. Manifestation of Being of the nature of *ānanda* (bliss) is called *vilāsa*. This term *vilāsa* cannot be translated exactly, but it may be roughly translated as " splendid, beautiful movements". He states that "the manifestation of the world is not due to *avidyā* (illusory knowledge) but is the very expression of pure *jñāna*, and the triad of *jñāna* (knowledge), *jñeya* (object of knowledge), and *jñātā* (knower) does not spring from *ajñāna* (ignorance), but is enlightened by the Universe" (Bahirat 1984: 72). It is necessary to consider his conception of *ātman* and "*ajñāna-khaṇḍana* (refutation of *ajñāna*)" carefully to understand the notion of *cidvilāsa*. First, *ajñāna* should be considered properly. There are two main meanings of *ajñāna*: (1) *jñānābhāva* (non-existence of knowledge), and (2) *mithyā* or *viparīta jñāna* (false knowledge) or, *adhyāsa* (super-imposition); he gives the example of *rajjū sarpa* (snake like rope). Jñāneśvara refutes *ajñāna* in the former sense, i.e. *jñānābhāva*. According to Jñāneśvara, "*ātman* is beyond both *jñāna* and *ajñāna*, and is of the nature of pure and absolute *jñāna*" (A. 3-23). It is known as *cinmātra*. He continues, "Knowledge that shines by destroying Ignorance, is itself swallowed up by Absolute Knowledge, which leaves no distinction between Knowledge and Ignorance, as the Sun that fills the whole universe and leaves no room for any distinction between light and darkness" (A. 4-11, 12, 14). In the seventh chapter of the *Amṛtānubhava*, Jñāneśvara refutes *ajñāna*. He declares that "Knowledge and Ignorance are like twins that resemble each other, and that knowledge is, therefore, itself a kind of Ignorance" (A. 7-6). "But for knowledge, the very name of Ignorance would never have been heard. For Ignorance is as illusory as the horses in a picture, which cannot be used for war" (A. 7-1, 4). He gives many metaphors to explain the non-existence of Ignorance: "It is as vain to search for it in real Knowledge, as to seek for the waves of a mirage in moonlight" (A. 7-5). In Indian philosophy, the relation of *jīva* (man), *jagat* (world), and *Īśvara* (God) is important. One should note Jñāneśvara's views about the nature of the world. According to him, the world is *citsvarūpa*, *sadvastu*, and its *vilāsa*. He clearly states, "*jaga asakī* | *vastu prabhā* ||" (the whole world is an illumination of the Absolute) (A. 7-289). He declares that "to regard the world, which is really a form of the *ātman* who is absolute knowledge, as but a flood of ignorance, is as foolish as to call the light of the Sun darkness" (A. 7-95, 100).

"The world, which, as the sport of the *ātman*, proceeds from the *ātman*, who is all knowledge, cannot be anything but knowledge. If one were to call such a world Ignorance, he knows not of what nature knowledge would be; for whatever exists is the *ātman*" (A. 7-101). Jñāneśvara concludes that "it is therefore unjust to call the *ātman* Ignorance, when all the universe is the vibration of knowledge" (A. 7-277). Here *caitanya*, *saṃvitti*, *vastu*, *cit*, and *cidrūpa*, are used as synonym of *ātman*. All stand for self-illumination and pure consciousness.

Jñāneśvara shows us that our particular awareness is a hindrance to grasping the reality. Four constituents of particular awareness, according to him, are *śabda* (language), *avidyā*, *ajñāna* and *jñāna*, which condition human consciousness. It is true that language distinguishes man from the other animals. Because of language man became more cultured. According to Jñāneśvara, *śabda* is useful as a reminder. But by itself, *śabda* is useless in the pursuit of realization of *ātman*, "because the self-conceived *ātman*, that is all-knowledge, stands in no need of any obligation of being reminded by means of word" (A. 6-13). Secondly, "it is not right to suppose that the word can show *ātman* to himself by destroying Ignorance, which by its very nature has no existence whatsoever" (A. 6-20). He says that *avidyā* is a fact but is *anirvācanīya* (indescribable in words), is like saying that non-existence is capable of negating itself. Word is like a mirror, he says, which shows us our figure through reflection. It reflects the formless by giving it as a form (A. 6-2). According to Jñāneśvara, *avidyā* is made up of a word-based belief, a mere ideation, which has no existence in the world of reality. "Now the knowledge and ignorance whose very life pitiably depends upon the word, are as real as the forest in a picture" (A. 6-102). "Now *avidyā*, being non-existent, there is no destruction of it, and when *ātman* is self-evident what is there to be proved by any means?" (A. 6-97).

Jñāneśvara's philosophical stand-point is rooted in the Upaniṣads. We can easily trace Upaniṣadic influence on his philosophy. Jñāneśvara's main *siddhānta* (theory) of *cidvilāsa*, "*jaga asakī* | *vastu prabhā* ||" is nothing else but the notion of *sarvam khalvidam brahmā* in the *Chāndogya Upaniṣad* (3-14-1), and *Īśāvāsyamidam sarvam* in the *Īśa Upaniṣad*[1] and so on. They state the positive view of life, which is stated philosophically. They are said to be the *anvayī* (positive) aspect of *advaita*. On the contrary, *neti, neti* (not this, not this) in *Āraṇyaka Upaniṣad* (2-3-6) is said to be the *vyatirekī* (negative) aspect of *advaita*. Jñāneśvara expounds both the *anvayī* and the *vyatirekī* aspects of *advaita*. In his philosophical discourse, he gives the examples of *anvayī* as *suvarṇa* and *alaṅkāra* (gold and ornaments), *kalloḷa-udaka* (wave and sea water), and so on, to explain the Reality. For example, "*sone sonepanā uṇe* | *na yetanci žale leṇe* | *tevī na vecatā jage hoṇe* | *aṅge jayā* || (the gold without destroying its properties takes various shapes in ornaments. Similarly, he becomes the world being least affected)" (C. 4).[2] Another example is, "*kalloḷakancuka* | *na pheḍita ughaḍe udaka* | *tevī jagesī samyaka* | *svarūpa jo* || (the water is water though it is covered with the ripples and waves. Similarly, what we see is the factual expansion of the *paramātman*)" (C. 5). The world is filled with one Reality. We have seen many different forms of one Reality. Though names and forms are different, they imply only the Reality.

Advaita is propounded in *vyatirekī* ways by means of terms such as *māyā, māyānadī* (illusion-river), *avidyā, rajjū-sarpa* (rope-snake), *mṛgajala* (mirage), *svapna* (dream), *vandhyāputra* (son of a barren woman), and so on. For example, "*modoni māyā kunjaru* | *mukta motiyācā vogaru* | *jevavita sadguru* | *Nivṛtti vandu* || (I bow to the spiritual teacher Nivṛtti, who by killing the elephant in the form of *māyā,* offers him the dish of the pearls taken from its temple)" (A. 2-3).[3]

To describe Jñāneśvara's approach, S.V. Dandekar uses the term *pūrṇādvaita.* According to him, the philosophical approach of Jñāneśvara is not much different from Śaṅkarācārya's. Śaṅkarācārya uses only its *vyatirekī* aspect to expound *advaita,* while Jñāneśvara considers both *anvayī* and *vyatirekī* aspects, that is why it may be called *pūrṇādvaita.* So, *cidvilāsavāda* is said to be the expression of the *anvayī* aspect of *pūrṇādvaita,* and *māyāvāda* is the *vyatirekī* aspect of *pūruṇādvaita.* They are the two sides of *pūruṇādvaita,* two ways to propound the same thing, i.e. the Reality of *brahman* and the Unreality of the world. Whereas the approach of *māyāvāda* is explanatory, that of *cidvilāsavāda* is descriptive. In fact, *māyāvāda* is a *vāda* (school), but *cidvilāsa* is not a *vāda,* it is a *siddhānta* (theory). It is the expression of *aprokṣa anubhūti* (experience which is not perceptible to the senses).

Bhakti can be said to be *vilāsa* (enjoyment) of *advaita* with entire Universe as *viśvātmaka Īśvara,* which can be taken to be another name for *cidvilāsa.* It can be said that *cidvilāsa* is a statement of Reality, and *bhakti* is its enjoyment.

JÑĀNEŚVARA'S CONCEPTION OF GOD

The common view of *bhakti* is to treat it as a very personal affair, an intimate relationship between God and *bhakta.* This means that *bhakti* is based on accepting duality of God and *bhakta*: without accepting this duality, *bhakti* is not possible. Jñāneśvara's view is, however, different. In order to understand his view, we must understand his conception of God. Jñāneśvara uses various words such as *ātman, brahman, caitanya, vastu* (substance), *saṃvitti* (pure knowledge), and *īśvara,* and others to denote the Ultimate Reality.

He uses many similies to describe and explain the real character of *ātman*: "The glorious *ātman* is pure and perfect knowledge itself" (A. 6-87), "*ātman* is self-luminous" (A. 6-93).

The very first *ovi* of *Jñāneśvarī*, expresses the real nature of the Ultimate Reality:

> Om, the Primeval being, the very form of Supreme Self, the subject-matter of the Vedas, be bowed to. All glory to you. Oh you, the form of self who can be known from self-experience alone, I hail you.

Jñāneśvara clearly states that the world is not some independent entity apart from the *ātman.* It is the experience of the *ātman* beholding itself (A. 7-280). Bahirat points out, "In consonance with his healthy and optimistic world-view, Jñāneśvara fully brings out dignity and the real status of the individual soul" (1983: 64). Jñāneśvara asserts, "the light of the substance or *ātman* is the cause of the manifestation of the *ātman's* beauty that is enjoyed by *ātman* himself" (A. 7-291). *Ātman* vibrates in the form of the Universe. This is called *cidvilāsa* (J. 8-118, 119). According to Jñāneśvara, *ātman* expresses itself in the form of the world. The world is the sport of *ātman* and the expression of Divine Love and Joy. "Innumerable forms and sights arise but one pure intelligence (*cit*) underlies all" (A. 7-124). So, perceive that everything is *ātman.* According to Dandekar, "The world is neither a creation of *ātman* nor a real or illusory development of the *ātman. Ātman* and the world are one. The world is a '*Sphurti*', i.e. a luminous appearance of the *ātman*" (Dandekar 1969: 29).

JÑĀNEŚVARA'S APPROACH TO *BHAKTI*

According to Jñāneśvara, *bhakti* is not an external mode of approaching God, it forms the very essence of Reality, reality which is self-experienced (*svasaṃvedya*) and self-illuminated (*svasaṃvitti*).

According to orthodox Hindu philosophy a triad of the knower (*jñātā*), the known (*jñeya*), and knowledge (*jñāna*) is involved in cognition. Similarly, there is supposed to be the triad of *deva*, *bhakta*, and *bhakti*. The language in which we talk about the subject of *bhakti* is often that of *dvaita* (duality). All our transactions of knowledge, encompassing *jñāna* and *ajñāna*, are dependent on language. Jñāneśvara is fully aware of this fact. As he says, "Now the knowledge and ignorance whose very life pitiably depends upon the language" (A. 6-102). We tend to determine the nature of *bhakti* on the basis of "*bhakti*-language", where "*bhakti*-language" means that language which we use for talking about *bhakti*. If we are not alert enough, such language can easily mislead us. In the end it leads us to false knowledge. We must always be "alert about language". Jñāneśvara is aware of the defect of language as a "trap". He says, in *Amṛtānubhava*, "discharging the debt of language is necessary for all" (A. 3-1). He accepts language only as a reminder of *brahman* but nothing more than that. He praised the importance of language as follows: "When this is lost to us or to others in forgetfulness, it is regained by the word that reminds it to us. If the word thus glorifies itself as a reminder, it has no other merit beyond this" (A. 5-67, 68). According to Jñāneśvara, misunderstanding about *bhakti*, such as *dvaita* in *bhakti* is caused by language. He asserts that *bhakti* is very much there in *advaita*:

> In that way, although activism finds no place in non-dualistic spiritual principle, yet there is the devotion that finds a place in it, and this can be realized through personal experience alone, it being inexpressible in mere words. (J. 18-1151)

Not only *advaita-bhakti* is possible, but for true *bhakti*, *dvaita* cannot be even imagined. His clear view is that those who imagine the possibility of *dvaita-bhakti* do so due to ignorance:

> In that way this devotion operates, taking the support of ignorance and shows me the seer as the object to be seen. (J. 18-1121)

The language of *bhakti* anchors it in *dvaita*, using pairs such as *pūjya-pūjak* (worship-worshipper), *upāsya-upāsak* (worship-worshipper). Thus the notion of *dvaita* is reflected in the language itself. That is why we get misled, and believe that *bhakti* should be based on *dvaita*. This language of dualities creates a problem for a proper understanding of *bhakti*. This is the source of the difficulty that we have in understanding *advaita* between God and *bhakta.* It becomes impossible to get to the inner core of *advaita-bhakti* without renouncing this dualistic language.

According to Jñāneśvara, God and *bhakta* are not distinct but constitute an inseparable unity:

You have by now heard, that the devotee who gets absorbed in me through knowledge-cum-devotion is one with me. (J. 18-1130)

In this way, he knows me as unique truly through his reflexive devotion as part and parcel of his own self and also knows that he is that knowledge, viz., the realization of the self. (J. 18-1200)

According to Jñāneśvara, the removal of this ignorance, namely the belief that *bhakti* is based on *dvaita,* is called *jñāna-bhakti:*

As that ignorance has vanished now, the state of seeing inherent in the seeing agent merges into me, in this way the reflection merges itself into the original. (J. 18-1125)

Once in this state, there is no room for treating cognition as being threefold: as consisting of, the seer (the subject or agent), the seen (the object), and the process of seeing.

According to orthodox Hindu philosophy, especially Śaṅkarācārya's approach, *jñāna* and *bhakti* are two independent means to attain *mokṣa.* Jñāneśvara holds a different view. He uses the expression *jñāna-bhakti,* to indicate that *jñāna* and *bhakti* are one and the same saying "the devotee who gets absorbed in me through knowledge-cum-devotion is only myself" (J. 18-1130). The reason why it is difficult for us to understand the oneness of *bhakti* and *jñāna,* is that we start with a firm belief that *bhakti* is derived from emotion while *jñāna* is anchored in intellect. In Jñāneśvara's view of *bhakti,* there is no separation between *jñāna* and *bhakti.* They are not two distinct states, but only two names given to the same state of being. This very condition of unity can be said to be the "natural state of *ātman*" (J. 18-1205).

Hence we find it so clearly stated by Jñāneśvara: "Men of knowledge (*sāṃkhyas*) call it 'recognition of the self', while the devotees of God Śiva call it 'the power (*śakti*)', and we call it the Supreme Devotion (*parambhakti*)" (J.18-1133). He points out that we call the Ultimate Reality by many different names, but all of them refer to the same entity. It is not only the same; it is also the natural condition of *ātman* itself. "In fact, this is my own innate state of *brahman*, that is named *bhakti*" (J. 18-1113). In Jñāneśvara's understanding of *bhakti*, all actions are performed with the internal conviction that everything is *ātman*. He treats *svasaṃvitti* (self-illuminated knowledge), *jñāna*, and *advaita-bhakti* as synonyms. For him, there is no difference between *jñāna* and *bhakti*, they are one and the same. Needless to say, this oneness of *jñāna* and *bhakti* is equivalent to *advaita-bhakti*.

Jñāneśvara's understanding of *bhakti* can be summarized as a path of "differentiated unity". The experience of this unity is the outcome of *sādhanā* (practice of *bhakti*) in which the unity of *bhakti* and *jñāna* is experienced as knowledge.

As we have seen, Jñāneśvara's conception of God is that of *viśvātmaka deva*, or *sarvātmaka īśvara*. The definition of *bhakti-yoga* given by Jñāneśvara is very significant from that point of view. For him it means: "*je je bheṭe bhūta* | *te te mānije bhagvanta* | *hā bhakti yogu niścita* | *jāṇa mājhā* (Whomsoever you come across, you regard him as God. Know that this is my true *yoga* of devotion)" (J. 10-118).

This is in fact the founding principle of *bhāgavata sampradāya*, a principle that is also found in the Upaniṣads,[4] in *Bhagavadgītā*[5] and in *Bhāgavata Purāṇa*.[6]

This then is the philosophical foundation of *bhakti* for Jñāneśvara. It has some major social implications. It provides the foundation for a sound philosophy of social service. The principle of *advaita-bhakti* is the basis of social thought and human behavior. In the advaitic approach, the idea of *sarvabhūta* is very important. The concept of *bhūta* includes not only human beings but all beings, animate or inanimate. It embraces all creatures and encompasses not just humanity, but the entire universe. In this sense advaitic *Bhāgavata dharma* is wider than humanism. It is truly universal. *Advaita-vedānta* teaches us to identify ourselves with the entire universe. In Indian philosophy *viśva* is a name of God.[7] In other words, it is the expression of the advaitic realization through day-to-day life activity, which makes for *bhakti* or *dharma*. It is important to note that this kind of spiritual renaissance is badly required in the present world.

The vedantic approach conceives of *ātman* as identical with *brahman*. To attain *advaita-bhakti* is the culmination of a *bhakta's sādhanā*. This oneness with God must find its expression in a *bhakta's* day-to-day life. It guides us about what kind of attitude we should develop towards others, how to look upon others. This philosophy may be described as an "attitudinal philosophy". One who cultivates "*bhakti* attitude" is one who looks upon every being that is there in the world as a manifestation of God. And since there is *advaita* between God and *bhakta*, this is also an experience of *advaita* with the entire universe, which is *viśvātmaka īśvara*.

Svami Vivekananda, who translated advaitic philosophy into practical principles, says, "The highest form of worship that had been laid down for the *bhakta* was the worship of man. Really if there were to be any sort of worship, he (*bhakta*) would suggest getting a poor man, or six, or twelve, as his circumstance would permit, everyday to their homes, and serving them, thinking that they were *nārāyaṇas*."[8] This humanistic conception is the foundation of his practical goal of service of mankind, especially the poor. His concept of God is that of *daridra nārāyaṇas*, i.e. "God in the form of the poor." And he adds, "Look upon every man, woman and every one as God. You cannot help anyone, you can only serve."[9] This humility is the very core of *bhakti*. Svami Vivekananda shows us the way to a harmonious reconciliation of the good of oneself with the welfare of society.

Svami Vivekananda unites *karma* and *bhakti* together and brings it into practice. Jñāneśvara also says the same thing:

> If he (the seeker) worships such God pervading the hearts of all beings, by dedicating to him, the flowers in the form of performance of the prescribed duties . . . such worship propitiates Him very highly. (J. 18-917)

Jñāneśvara says that the worship of God does not mean only image worship, it involves performing one's own prescribed duty (*svadharma*) without expecting any fruit. As we have already seen, the conception of Universal God and the idea of serving every being are closely related to the principle of *naiṣkarmya* (exemption from action).

> His inner experience getting saturated with the realization that this entire universe is full with '*vāsdeva*', he proves to be the king among the devotees, and one of great knowledge (J. 7-136).

True *bhakta* must find God everywhere, within himself as well as without himself. In one word, the true *bhakta's* way of life is the life of harmony. The true *bhakta* is he who prays for universal happiness and harmony of the entire universe. We have clear reference to this in Jñāneśvara's *Pasāyadāna*:

In short, let all three worlds be perfectly happy and may everyone desire to offer perpetual worship to the Primeval person (*brahman*) and may those who live by the teachings of this work have perfect happiness in this and the next world.[10]

Bhakti can be said to be a basic principle of social philosophy. According to Jñāneśvara *bhakti* is not the worshipping of merely God, but the service of all beings as God. This notion provides us with a sound foundation of social philosophy. If we all follow the path of *parā-bhakti*, the world would be peaceful and full of bliss.

Bhakti can be a social force whatever works men undertake in the society, if they are inspired by the love of God, i.e. *bhakti*, there will be no conflict between men and the society.

Bhakti-yoga, especially *saguṇa-bhakti* is easy to have access to. Whenever we discuss *bhakti*, the discussion of *saguṇa* and *nirguṇa* is unavoidable. We conceive of God in the human form, that is because we are human beings. Our imagination is limited by our own experience and environment. Svami Vivekananda says that if the buffaloes want to worship God, they will, in keeping with their own nature, see God as a huge buffalo.

Basu (1990: 123) states, "the form of the object of worship, therefore, is immaterial. It is only an aid to train up the mind in the discipline of concentration so that it may eventually comprehend the abstract, formless spirit pervading the Universe." *Saguṇa-bhakti* can be said to be a gateway to *nirguṇa-bhakti*. *Saguṇa-bhakti* and *nirguṇa-bhakti* are never opposed to each other.

True *bhakti* totally depends on the urge and the faith, and the complete sense of surrender of the *bhakta* to God. The attainment of so-called *parā-bhakti* seems equivalent to *mokṣa*. In relation to this, Ranade refers to Jñāneśvara's doctrine of "asymtotism". Asymtote is a mathematical term. A curved line and an axis continually approaching each other and meeting at infinity is the meaning of this term. Similar is the relation between God and devotee (Ranade 1988: 127). According to Jñāneśvara:

When the devotee becomes one with me, he still continues to be a devotee. (J. 7-114-15)

When the devotee performs actions, he appears as a devotee, but internally he has attained identity with me. If a person works in full realization of his true state beyond his present life, can he, though in a separate body, remain separate from me? (J. 7-116-17)

Some little distance may still be left between God and a devotee. "So long as a devotee has a body and a mind and has to live in this world, to that extent and for that time he must fall short of complete divine attainment." This can be understood to mean that there is always a little room left for a devotee to worship God as long as he has a body. The state of *parā-bhakti* can be said to be almost identical with *mokṣa*, but still falls short of *mokṣa*, because room is still left for one's consciousness of love towards God.

NOTES

1. S.V. Dandekar puts the term *pūrṇādvaita* in his article, "Śrī Jñāneśvaramahārājāñce tattvajñāna", in *Śrī Jñāneśvaradarśan*, ed. N.B. Deshmukh.
2. *Cāṅgādeva pāsaṣṭi*, tr. Madhav.
3. *Amṛtānubhava*, tr. B.P. Bahirat.
4. *Yas tu sarvāṇi bhūtāni ātmani evānupaśyati | sarvabhūteṣu cātmānam tato na vijugupsate* || in *Īśā Upaniṣad*, 6.
5. *Sarvabhūtastham ātmānam sarvabhūtāni cātmani | īkṣate yogayuktātmā sarvatra samadarśanaḥ* || G. 6-29. *vāsudevaḥ sarvam iti* | G. 7-19.
6. *sarvabhūteṣu yaḥ paśyed bhagavadbhāvam ātmanaḥ | bhūtāni bhagavatyātmanyeśa bhāgavatottamaḥ* || BP XI. 2-45.
7. *Viṣṇusahāsuranāma*, 1.
8. Svami Vivekananda: *The Complete Works of Swami Vivekananda*, vol. 3, p. 391.
9. Ibid., p. 392.
10. *Jñāneśvarī*, tr. M.R. Yardi.
    Translations of *Jñāneśvarī* quoted in this article without references are done by Bhagawat, and *Amṛtānubhava* by R.D. Ranade in his *Mysticism in Maharashtra.*

REFERENCES

Bhagwat, R.K., 1989: *Bhavartha-dīpika Jñāneśvarī*, tr. into English. Madras: Samata Books.

Bahirat, B.P., 1984: *The Philosophy of Jñānadeva.* Delhi: Motilal Banarsidass.

Basu, D.D., 1990: *The Essence of Hinduism.* New Delhi: Prentice Hall of India.

Dandekar, S.V., 1969: *Dnyanadeo,* New Delhi: Maharashtra Information Centre.

Farquhar, J.N., 1984: *An Outline of the Religious Literature of India.* Delhi: Motilal Banarsidass.

Govt. of India, Publication Division, 1983: *Devotional Poets and Mystics.*

Macnicol, N., 1968: *Indian Theism.* Delhi: Munshiram Manoharlal.

Pande, S., 1993: *Medieval Bhakti Movement.* Meerut: Kusumanjali Prakashan.

Ranade, R.D., 1982: *The Bhagavadgītā as a Philosophy of God Realisation.* Bombay: Bharatiya Vidya Bhavan.

——, 1988: *Mysticism in Maharashtra.* Delhi: Motilal Banarsidass.

Svami Vivekananda: *The Complete Works of Swami Vivekananda,* vol. 3. Calcutta: Advaita Ashrama.

Talghatti, S.R. (tr.), 1996: *Cāṅgādeva pāsaṣṭi.* Pune: Maharashtra Academy of Engineering and Educational Researchs, Maharashtra Institute of Technology.

Tulpule, S.G., 1984: *Mysticism in Medieval India.* Wiesbaden: Otto Harassowitz.

Zelliot, E., 1976: "The Medieval Bhakti Movements in History: An Essay on the Literature in English", in *New Essays in the History of Religions,* ed. B.L. Smith. Leiden: E.J. Brill.

4

Hindu–Muslim Dialogue: A Rereading of Sant Eknath and Sant Shaikh Muhammad

VIDYUT BHAGWAT

Eknath (1532-99) and Shaikh Muhammad (1565-1660) were sixteenth-century figures born in the pre-modern Deccan. Eknath a Brahman from Paithan is well known for his scathing criticism of Brahmanism. Paithan was known for its Brahmanic orthodoxy. Eknath, right from his young age, kept challenging the orthodoxy by his action and by choosing to write not only in Marathi, the regional language, but in people's language which was a mixture of Marathi, Urdu, and at times he used Dakhni dialect with equal ease. Eknath was not alone in this people-oriented effort. There were many *sants,* their disciples sharing the life world of Eknath: e.g. Shaikh Muhammad Baba, born in Dhanur had links with Eknath as a disciple of Chand Bodhale and Janardan Swami (Eknath's *guru*). It seems that Shaikh Muhammad represented another branch of new thought that was emerging during that period, separated but connected with Janardan Swami's as well as Eknath's activities and work. There is ample evidence to show that he was also in touch with Sant Tukaram (1608-49). Shaikh Muhammad settled in Shrigonde, some 80-90 miles from Dehu. A collection of his writings as *Yogasangram,* edited by historian B.S. Bendre in 1959 notes that not much is known about this poet *sant* but his writing speaks for itself. His tomb in Shrigonde is worshipped by both Hindu and Muslim devotees separately, but on the same day (Bendre 1959: 14). *Yogasangram* consists of 2300 *ovis* and deals mainly with issues of going beyond this material world while living in it.

HINDU–TURK SAMVAD

In this paper I will try to translate most of the famous *Hindu–Turk Samvad* (Dialogue) of Eknath and some narratives from the texts of Shaikh Muhammad Baba, to understand and make meaning of the way of dialogue adopted by both these *sants*. How Hindu and Muslim communities and identities were trying to reach the abundance of life by going beyond their given frameworks will be evident through these translations.

Let us first look at the *Hindu–Turk Samvad* as it appears in the *Shri Sakal Sant Gatha* (vol. II, 123, 3970, pp. 583-6).

(Their) goal was one but *marg* was opposite.
Listen to the dialogue between these two.

The Turk calls the Hindu a *kafar* (non-believer). Hindu wards him off as a pollutant. This is how their cranky argument went on and a great debate took place.

TURK: Oh Brahman, Listen to my argument. Your religious knowledge deceives everyone. You say god has feet and hands. Is this how you worship him?

HINDU: Listen Oh Turk, you jerk! We look at God as residing in everyone. You ignore this expansive meaning and adopt nothingness or void.

TURK: Listen Oh Brahman. Eternally plunging into water, you are like a water cock. Anyone who reads your philosophy will be fooled. You have many stories which confuse people. Sometimes your god is made to beg, sometimes Bali traps him and turns him into a gatekeeper. Your *shastra* is totally slack. You even attack Allah. What sort of daring is this! All this affair is of those with little brains.

HINDU: You do not remember your own texts. You do not read them as a whole. Your Abdullah in the beginning preached begging. Begging is advised by your god. He attains salvation by giving up everything and taking pittance from begging. Your god passionately loves this. Every minute you remember Allah. . . .

For filling your belly you beg,
Allah give me *ghee*, bread and sweets,

Allah give me milk and rice,
Allah give me varied food,
Allah give me tasty food.

Brahman at least recites the *shlokas* while begging. His begging is not for collection. You are perpetually unsatiated. You are known to be sinful drunkards. Bali is a special disciple of *Khuda*. God is attracted by his devotion. God waits for him always. Why are you criticizing him?

TURK: Your Brahma fucks his daughter. He reads all false Veda. Your Vedas are your *shastra*. Brahma easily deceives by taking false form. Thieves can snatch *Khuda's* wife. Monkeys help your god. You have become silly and directionless reading these texts.

HINDU: Look at this Turk who finds faults with Brahman again and again. How did Baba Adam get his wife? Please read your holy book. You do not have knowledge of your own religion, and you fight with us? For Baba Adam, Maya became Eve. Since then the whole world became '*Admi*'. You call yourself by that name. You are deceived by your own language. For Baba Adam Maya became Eve. About her you tell us that she was tempted by the Satan. When Sita was snatched by Rawan why do you ridicule? At that time Firasta also took help and rescued Eve. Here Ram calls his own ancestors for purifying Sita.

TURK: Listen Oh Brahman whose thinking is on par with a donkey. Whatever you say gets reproduced. Anyone who reads your books will remain ignorant in a big way. Your god was ignorant, and hence brought in jail. Demon Kauns came to kill him. Your god was hidden by Devaki. This is how your books are a deception. Though he was hidden for a long time, still the god was given poison. Oh what a god! You are cheated by your own words. You call your god a cow herd; one cries listening to this because he calls an animal his God. You *kafar*, you have stopped thinking. You have brought down God. I feel like slapping you. . . .

HINDU: Your own people say that God is everywhere. Would he then not be in jail too? You see this dichotomy wrongly. Wherever your mind can imagine, there you can find your God. . . . If you imagine god is difficult, your heart will be filled with difficulties. But otherwise all closures will be opened by him. This is what your Paigambar says. If you listen carefully to Shahamodin, he treats a cow, an elephant and a monkey, all of them as protected by the god. These are the answers you will get from your book, but why don't you accept them? Dog, cow, rat, creatures all are looked after by god. Take your own *shastra* ahead. Why are you fighting with us?

TURK: You Brahmans are experts in spinning yarns. God has shaven your beard and head. You Hindus are purely evil. In your kingdom statues rule. God is given the names of statues. That place becomes a pilgrimage for you. Before these statues, masters become lusterless. Women, men all stand up before him and roll mindlessly. Are they not stupid? That stone which is painted with orange with *sindoor*, women stand before it in naked feet without cover and ask of it a child. Your Veda is totally loose. Every word of it is empty. Your god is inadvertent and unaware.

HINDU: God is everywhere; in water, land, woods, stone. This is what your own books say. Why don't you understand it yourself? Turk, you are completely lacking in understanding. Solidified or liquid, *ghee* is the same. You can see form and formlessness as one. You hate the statue. How mindless you are! God completes what humans leave uncompleted. This is what your own book holds. Why don't you accept this? We have shown your shortcomings. You send your god far away who is so near to you. Every time you call your Allah you experience disturbance. You have not met him yet. You need to call loudly one who is far away. To call who is near you, you only need to whisper. Your near one meets you but your '*Maulana*' shouts and wakes you up. You say '*Khuda*' is only to the East. Why are the other directions treated as empty? You must say that god is everywhere, and thus take your thinking ahead. You pray five times a day as these are god's times. What happens to all other times? Do they belong to a thief? You have deceived your own *shastra* by making it unidimensional. You accuse us of worshipping stones; why then do you keep stones on your dead bodies? You worship '*Haji*' with stones and treat him as '*Pir*'. You save the bones of a mere corpse; you dedicate sheets and flowers on stones and burn incense before it.

TURK: If all of you could purify yourselves by bathing in the Ganges, then why do you cook at separate hearths? You shout about 'pollution' and classify most people as 'impure'. You talk of god in every human being, yet you eat separately, you do not touch fellow human beings and keep human groups separated. You wish to throttle the one who grows grain for your food. You refuse to give up old habits and are left crying within your isolated communities. You declare as impure your own woman, whose cooking you eat. You sleep with her at night but banish her from the kitchen. Does this not make you 'impure'? You do not eat in homes where your daughter is married but delivers a girl child. You like the daughter but not the food in her house? So much for your great Brahman texts! You think your cooked food is the ultimate commitment but their food is the ultimate falsity! How come purity-impurity enters even father-daughter relationship? In building new relations you do not make people your own. Your *shastras* are fables. Therefore your religious texts will be reduced to ashes; Rites and rituals will go to hell. You will have to shake this world, Oh Brahman.

HINDU: You Turks are the height of stupidity! You have no sense of right and wrong. Despite being a living being yourself, you harm other living beings. The death conferred by '*Khuda*' makes the victim non-edible, but when you kill it you treat it as pure and edible. You treat yourselves as purer than '*Khuda*' himself. You *Yavans* have been proven to be of lowly order in both the worlds. You fall prey to the *maulana's* directives and follow the rituals of slaughtering the cock who flutters and struggles to escape. If salvation is in slaughtering the goat, then why do you pretend to do *namaaz* and keep the *roza*? The *maulana* who gives you directives is considered great while your sins keep growing and all your efforts are wasted. Oh Brother, God created both Hindus and Muslims. But if your commitment is only to the Turks, then you want to forcibly convert the Hindu to a Musalman. You think *Khuda* has made a mistake in creating a Hindu. What a brain you are! By converting a Hindu into a Musalman, you commit a crime to none other than your own *Khuda*!

TURK: Without *Khuda* humans cannot operate. Turk and Brahman both have only partial truth on their side but if they cut each other's throats then God is sure to punish them.

HINDU: We are all basically one. We fight in the name of caste and religion here but death does not recognize the discrimination.

TURK: God does not have a caste; *Khuda* does not discriminate us.

Hindu: I am delighted.

INTERPRETING *SAMVAD*

Let us see how this *Samvad* was received and interpreted by scholars. Romila Thapar has underlined in this imagined dialogue an undercurrent of satire, in the treatment of both the Brahman and the Muslim who seems to have been a *maulana*. "The language used by each for the other would today probably cause a riot. The crux of the debate states, 'You and I are alike, the confrontation is over *jati* and *dharma*.' The attempt is at pointing out the differences between facets of what were seen as Hindu and Muslim beliefs and worship, but arguing for adjustment" (Thapar 2000: 1008).

In her opinion, if we move away from the notion of monolithic communities, we will be able to see the historical potential of understanding how identities may actually have been perceived at points in time and their multiple manifestations and functions. Identities in history were neither stable nor permanent, hence the dialogue between Islam and other religions must always have been an ongoing process.

Shashi Joshi points out that the historical analysis of "religion" as a motif and "religious conflict" as a category for medieval India is focused on a wrong problem. These were not religious conflicts but very worldly confrontations, negotiating power relationships in culture and society, employing religion but more often, cultural symbolism. She sees *sufi bhakti* mixing and merging of cultures as a cultural contest for hegemony. The *sufis* were effectively the channels through which Islamic cultural hegemony penetrated the mass. The *bhakti sants* were the conduit forcing hegemonic ties (as opposed to dominant/subordinate) between Brahmanical culture and people. Though internal contest of *sufis* (who expressed knowledge as power), the *ulamas* (who expressed power as knowledge) and Sanskrit *pandits* and *bhaktas* was not insignificant, Joshi declares: "The anti-caste, anti-Brahman rhetoric of the *bhakti sants* was, in effect, a readjustment of relationships of power within non-Islamic caste society . . ." (Joshi 1994: 39-40). She concludes that though the form and content of both Islamic *sufi* and Brahmanic ideologues changed and adjusted accordingly changing the nature, but not the fact of power relations in society. *Sufi bhakti* adopted cultural strategies as modes of cultural integration and at the same time as channels of hegemony integral to the ideological influence of Islam and Brahmanism. This helped in locating them in the interplay of power between them.

Since 1980, Eleanor Zelliot has been writing on *sant* poets, translating their texts highlighting mainly caste and occasionally gender issues, explaining contemporary relevance of *bhakti* for the Dalit movement in India, particularly Maharashtra. She treats Eknath's writing as a mode of legitimacy for modern change. Eknath was not only a Brahman, but one from a famous family and lived in Paithan which was an ancient capital and a trading center of great importance even in the sixteenth century. Eknath's massive volume of work, varied influence on his writing, his training in the mainstream *shastric* tradition, his visit to Kashi but conscious choice of *bhakti* and devotion to Pandharpur, his knowledge of a very heterogeneous world in a religious center and market city crossed by several trade routes are noted in details by her. Eknath by birth experienced highly orthodox and closed Brahmanical world but in his adult life he was in contact with common struggling people from both Hindu and Islamic communities. Zelliot points out how Eknath's *bharuds* as a dialogue and performance are appreciated by many Dalit, Bahujan scholars (Zelliot 1981). In a way Eknath is seen by her as a model of modernization in relation to *bhakti*.

We need to address the question of how *bhakti* tradition was received and interpreted in the colonial period in Maharashtra. The arrival of colonialism marked the rise of print culture and in consequence, a new intelligentsia. The new rulers (Elphinstone for example) as well as a band of Christian missionaries needed to learn Marathi for the implementation of their desired projects. The evangelical missionaries began to distribute translated scriptures on a massive scale. The new intelligentsia's response appeared in the form of printed texts of the key *sants* like Dnyaneshwar and Tukaram. The process began in full vitality from 1844. Sadanand More points out that Tukaram's writings appealed to the religious as well as literary taste of the missionaries and colonial officials as his writings were direct and simple, lucid and trenchant in its critique of Brahmanism. A leading liberal British official like Alexander Grant confessed in the *Royal Asiatic Journal* that Tukaram's poetry revealed a high sense of morality and authentic spirituality based on *bhakti* (devotion) (More 1996: 225).

Missionaries treated *bhakti* as a bridge to Christ for commoners in Maharashtra. Eminent social thinkers like Justice M.G. Ranade turned to *bhakti* as an alternative to utilitarianism. He also argued that *bhakti* provided the energies which resulted in the rise of Maratha power under Shivaji. His own Prarthana Samaj initiative drew its sustenance from the *bhakti* tradition, and above all from Tukaram.

Mahatma Jotirao Phule had a complex relationship with *Varkari Sampraday*. He founded Satyashodhak Samaj (1873) as an alternative to Prarthana Samaj. But he knew the potential of *Varkari Sampraday* in resisting casteism and untouchability. More has demonstrated that while Phule kept himself aloof from the *varkari* tradition for reasons of his own, his *akhandas* are in fact organically linked with Tukaram's *abhangas.* Lokmanya Tilak's interpretation of *Geeta* is a confluence of *bhakti* and *karma.* Tilak stood against the rituals of *Varkari Sampraday* and followed Sant Tukaram in his forthright critique of hypocrisy.

Anthropologist Iravati Karve countered Rajwade's and Ketkar's denigration of the *varkari* endeavor as unscientific and backward. She in fact participated in the *vari* or pilgrimage to Pandharpur and then defined Maharashtra as that region where people visit Pandhari. G.B. Sardar refuted the charge of the *Varkari Sampraday* being non-intellectual and praised Tukaram for his honesty and transparent self-expression. D.K. Bedekar, an eminent and creative Marxist scholar, read Tukaram and *Varkari Sampraday* in a democratic, secular framework.

Jayant Lele argues that in order to understand the revolutionary potential of *Varkari Sampraday* one must enter the world-view of the peasant with gentle humility and alertness. He sees *Varkari Sampraday* as an example of an immanent critique of Brahmanism. "It rejects both counter culturalism and ritualism. As a discourse of the underprivileged, it penetrates the falsehood of an ideology through the eyes of suspicion but it does so in order to extract and expose the encrusted truth of that ideology through the sensitive ears of a believer" (Lele 1995: 80). For him the *sant* poets of medieval Maharashtra offer a most important methodological lesson of unmasking the hypocrisy and falsehood of the beliefs, and also developing the art of listening. Sadanand More considers the *varkari* tradition as the core of Maharashtrian culture and sees Tukaram as a social critic and a poet of a high order with matchless clarity of expression and an utter fidelity to his own integrity as a free and radical human being and *bhakta.*

Scholars and activists in Maharashtra have for several years sought to challenge the Ramdas-centric hegemonic discourse of *bhakti* and in doing so a Tukaram-centric counter hegemonic discourse on the *Varkari Sampraday* has emerged. This Tukaram discourse no doubt has been extremely significant to the rewriting of history of Maharashtra culture and society. However this paper by highlighting the rather sidelined discourse of Eknath, suggests opening up of plural voices and the connections between them in the counter hegemonic discourse.

The *Hindu–Turk Samvad* provides ample evidence of how local Hindu and Islamic traditions interacted and strengthened each other; how *bhakti* and *sufi sants*, despite their trenchant criticism of people's everyday life practices, were popular amongst them; how they created a new dialogical *marga* for India in combining varied traditions, particularly Hindu-Islamic confluence and how they make it possible for us to search for the gray areas between the communal and the secular.

SITUATING EKNATH

In this context a brief review of Marathi reception of Eknath may help us in making meaning of the texts translated in this paper. Eknath's writings were studied mainly as literary expression. Many scholars studied Eknath's life, work and writing emphasizing the many genres he adapted. I will stick only to one study which was used as a textbook by many generations of students of Marathi literature since the 1950s.

N.R. Phatak's book *Shri Eknath: Vangmay ani Karya* (Shri Eknath's Literature and Work) was first published in 1950 and was revised several times. While contextualizing the *Hindu–Turk Samvad*, Phatak mentions Narsi Mehta from Junagadh and uses Meerabai from Udaipur. He uses the term "Hindu Community" and its efforts to organize itself through stories of Ram, Krishna from fourteenth-fifteenth century. Phatak notes that both the Hindu and Muslim communities were in a mood to rethink about the aggression around the sixteenth century. Phatak narrates a story. Under the rule of Sikandar Lodi (r. 1489-1517), a Brahman made a claim that Hindu and Islam, both these religions have claims towards truth and have equal merit. Sikandar Lodi then asked the Brahman to convert to Islam and of course after the Brahman's refusal, killed him. This story is narrated by the author to prove how the Brahmans were open and ready to give equal status to Islam. Phatak, while reporting the dialogue omits an extremely crucial part of the dialogue where the Turk points out sharply the injustice and irrationality that was inherent in Brahmanical patriarchal practices. While reporting Eknath's Hindu-Turk dialogue Phatak gives two examples of Muslim religious leaders (*dharma pracharaks*) Sayyad Shah Muhammad Sadik Sir Mastan Hussaini (1568) and Khusuja Khunmir Hussaini (1520) who traveled from Madina to Paithan to Nasik, and who forcibly converted Hindus to Islam. This is mentioned as necessary background for Eknath's Hindu–Turk dialogue, but we find no reference to Shaikh Muhammad Baba's *Yogasangram* in Phatak's writing.

Phatak has historically reviewed Eknath's period and admitted that local Muslims in southern India were neither dogmatic nor aggressive. Eknath had been born in an affluent family and left his comfortable home in his young age. He was made to return home to marry and to accept family life. Phatak has noted that Eknath went beyond his caste and challenged all those conservatives who tried to outcast him. Eknath's son Hari Pandit was unhappy with his father's popularity and people-orientedness. But Eknath's time was such that under Islamic rule Hindus had space to bring about a change in their plight. In Phatak's opinion *sufis* were also outwardly Islamic but had seeds of Hindu philosophy in them. Islam had in it freedom of thought and *sufi sants* were prompt enough to criticize rigidity and conservatism of both Hindus and Muslims. Hindu *bhakti* borrowed a lot from *sufis*. But Phatak, while summing up the dialogue between Hindu and Turk tells us that Hindu's sharp question "Does god have caste?" was immediately accepted by the Turk, saying "*Khuda* does not have caste, he does not need to discriminate."

N.R. Phatak has also noted that Islam and Hindu religions in Eknath's time were becoming more people-oriented and less rigid. But Hindu caste system was turning to be more tight as self-defense. Brahmans taking lead in torturing other religious groups made Eknath to be so openly harsh on Brahman community. Huge, well-known Hindu temples were attacked by Muslim rulers for tremendous wealth but small villages had Bhairav, Vetal (folk deities) and *pir* supporting each other. In Phatak's view neither *sufis* nor *sants* were successful in stopping their practices and rituals. Eknath was good in writing Sanskritized Marathi as well as using Persian Arabic language. Phatak noted many dialogues written by Eknath like "Child and an adult Brahman", "Dog and a Brahman", "A Mahar and Brahman", etc. Every dialogue tells us about how so-called powerlessness of these figures was compensated by their real knowledge. While ending his book on Eknath, Phatak appreciatively highlights some part of Eknath's dialogue between a dog and a Brahman.

BRAHMAN: How do you call a Brahman as devoid of knowledge ?

DOG : Can any one be a Brahman only as a body ?

BRAHMAN: Vedas tell us that by birth Brahman is superior.

DOG: If Brahmans are so great why do they also die? Why *bhaktas* become immortal?

BRAHMAN: How to make meaning of it ?

DOG: One must become like them. *Bhakta* has no caste or kinship.

BRAHMAN: How did you achieve this knowledge?

DOG: I was blessed by Guru Eka and Janardan.

The translated texts written in a mixed form of Marathi and Dakhni suggest that in the Deccan region during the sixteenth century there was an official patronage to the production of vernacular literatures and encouragement and space for people's language.

Phatak has noted that the languages used by both Eknath and Shaikh Muhammad exhibit confidence of their own language without seeking any sanction from outside authority, without feeling the need to fall back upon either Sanskrit or Arabic expressions.

Hindus during this period were practicing diverse kinds of worships and rituals in Vedic, Non-vedic, Purana traditions. But they were all bound by the caste system which basically provided them with their specific occupation and skill. There are many stories about Eknath which tell us that Eknath did not observe rules and restrictions of purity-pollution but the stories also tell us that even Eknath had to go through penance for feeding Mahars at the occasion of his father's *shradha*.

Phatak also tells us about Eknath writing nearly 300 *bharuds* which reflect his close association with people from Dhangar, Gosavi communities who were of course a part of village economy and culture. Eknath wrote sometimes becoming Marie aie, Satwai or Khandoba, leaving consciously his caste and his Brahmanic training. This is how he was able to become people's organic representative. Historians like Mate, G.T. Kulkarni note that we do not get any information of ruling Sultans, their officials, their behavior or overall torture suffered by people, issues of conversion wars, truce in Eknath's writing. Janardan Swami was employed in Devgiri as an inspector, Eknath himself was well versed with trade and accounts but he has not at all directly addressed the political issues of his time. Instead he preached a life world where every human being had to go beyond self or body but every day hard work had to continue with commitment. In this period Burhan Nizamshah organized open discussion of philosophers from different religious background. Shah Tahir presented his view on "Shia" sect and Nizam accepted to convert to Shia sect. Phatak notes that this must have produced intellectual openness amongst Maharashtrian Muslim thinkers. Mrutyunjay (1565-1650), Shaikh Muhammad (1560-1660) were two prominent Muslim *sant* poets and many others like Hussein Amberkhan, Muntoji, Latif Shah also wrote on similar themes. Eknath's *bharuds* are particularly appreciated by many contemporary scholars like Dr Dhande and highlighted Eknath's specificity as writing for and becoming marginalized (Dhande 2003).

DIALOGUE AS A FORM OF EXPRESSION

Eknath wrote several dialogues. These dialogues were invariably written between two polar opposite existences or beings, e.g. a child and a Brahman or a Mahar and a Brahman or a dog and a Brahman and a Hindu–Turk dialogue. What was he trying to achieve through these dialogues? Eknath had observed his people and society around him all through his life. He saw them fragmenting, suffering and searching for answers to their crisis by creating their own small gods and their own small answers. Eknath learnt a lot from these toiling people. His method of reaching people was by internally examining, critically looking at himself, his own location, his training. Eknath gave up many privileges as a Brahman who was trained properly in Veda, Vedanta, Upanishad, Geeta, Bhagvat. He faced wrath from his own community. There are many stories about him of being excommunicated, hated by his community even by his son as noted earlier.

Eknath's choice of writing in the form of a dialogue needs a sensitive understanding. He was trying to capture many worlds of experience and knowledge through it. His language in these dialogues at one level was disclosing world around him and also making sense of things, e.g. a dialogue between 'Hindu–Turk' begins with confrontations, they accuse each other but this debate historically makes sense when both of them realize that their seeing each other was at once superfluous but pertinent. Eknath in a way adopts a genre of play or game. The dialogue has a performative quality. Eknath himself is outside this dialogue. Hindu and Turk are imagined characters. Turk is an outsider who looks at the Hindu scrutinisingly as a dominating Brahman; Hindu also has skepticism about Turk and his knowledge. Through this imaginary dialogue many things are said harshly, mockingly. Points, counterpoints carried out in their dialogue reveal normative structures disclosing worlds which were forming their self, e.g. rituals which were making them blind towards the larger reality and goal. All dialogues written by Eknath make all speaking subjects capable of knowing and acting, taking responsibility for their knowledge and action, e.g. Hindu and Turk both raise truth claims, pursue their truths and at the end when they accept a common ground they create validity of each other. They reach a consensual agreement but avoid power or coercion and reach an agreement on truth as part of its meaning. In every dialogue Eknath makes speaker to raise claims to validity. Turk when accuses Hindu texts, Purana stories as a deception gives concrete examples and proves his point. The Hindu partially has to accept it in order to create shared meaning. Slowly they in the course of dialogue create life world, the social space inhabited in common. Both Hindu-Turk are made to represent the dogmas initially but both of them are depicted to be in search of real cooperative truth which is capable of self-criticism and criticism of others. The language as is evident even in the English translation as is used by Hindu-Turk is dynamic. It flows like a stream, carries many possibilities and it is not a standard sophisticated expression. It has its own power rooted in its context, circumstance and its specific cultural, social context in which it operates.

In short I would like to suggest that *sufis* and *sants* both were very much a part of the early modernity of India. Eknath and Shaikh Muhammad, were struggling, negotiating within their context. We must see, understand and interpret them as part of the emancipatory cultural histories. Drawing them out solely as "*sant* poets" often excludes their agency in challenging the political priesthood of their times and blurs their historical relevance as early voices against violence, power and coercion. These voices are expressions of freedom and equality emerging from their lived experiences as members of specific communities. These texts are a demand for a new world to be realized not in the next life through *karma* but in their empirical world. This nascent modernity has several clues for today. The Hindu–Turk dialogue was not only a plea for adjustment but an attempt and locate unity and commonality between the two religious groups.

SHAIKH MUHAMMAD

Let us now turn to Shaikh Muhammad Baba and read some select texts in translation. Shaikh Muhammad writes as a local Musalman. He is not an outsider in his region. He does not adopt a dramatic mode of dialogue, but his writing is in tune with what Eknath was trying to achieve. In a way there is an unsaid dialogic relationship between Eknath and Shaikh Muhammad. Both of them belonged to one and the same *guru*-disciple tradition. In this text Shaikh Muhammad has redefined and conceptualized in a new emancipatory way all the basic terms used by both the communities.

(Why the need of a *guru*?)
One who has the skill of singing is known as a singer.
One who knows dancing may have the capacity to hypnotize the whole world.
But they (the experts) help you go beyond this world. For that you need a real *guru*.
Who is a real *qazi*, *maulana*, *fakir*?

The *qazi* is one who understands everything without telling, while practicing justice he will not allow his mind to be unstable.
'Equal' and 'unequal' both will be weighed by him in a perfect balance.
As a principle he will not take a bribe.
He will blame or reward a person as he deserves it.
He becomes one with God and cleanses his mind from inside and expresses it from the outside.
One must recognize such a person as *qazi.*
Maulana is the one who knows his roots. He treats others' pains as his own.
His silent prayer creates a bang in the world.
He is one with the ultimate spirit.
He cuts with the knife of wisdom the buffalo of ego and eats it.
His *namaz* in the *masjid* is done in a trance. This is what a *maulana* is like.
A *fakir* is one whose sensory pleasure splits.
With every breath he remembers Allah.
He runs away from vulgar gossip and enjoys solitude.
He does not boast about being a *fakir.*
His natural meditative posture is ruled by love.
This is how the true live *fakir* is. (Bendre 1959: 88-9)

Who is a Musalman?
Only one feature allows anyone to be called a Musalman.
Everyone resides in the womb for nine months. If you markedly recognize where you were, you are a real 'pure' being.
But when you take birth by detaching yourself from the womb, I do not know anyone remembering this process. Everyone holds onto their opinion desperately.
See as many people as you want—they have all been nurtured in a womb. Without the womb this animate/inanimate world cannot have occurred. *Sants* and *bhaktas* alike must experience this truth. All had a Sunni Musalman name. But hiding it as Vaishya (trader), Kshatriya (warrior), Brahman (priest—highest in the *varna* hierarchy) they identify themselves by different surnames and talk loosely, giving untrue ideas. If you call a Brahman a Sunni Musalman, he will be furious. This is how he hides the truth and celebrates falsity. It is like hiding your body by exhibiting clothes. Those who hide the weapon by brandishing only the scabbard. This is the ritual of Vedas which hides the original birth place. (Bendre 1959: 93).

. . . while you utter the word Allah if you also call him Hari, what do you lose?

Those who do not talk about either Allah or Hari are to be recognized as barbarians, rouges. Listen, if Allah and Hari were two, they would have fought and finished each other. They would not have kept trace of each other. (Bendre 1959: 142)

Creatures residing in water never thank water, until they are out of it and are tormented by lack of it. The same happens to people towards the end of their life.
Sunlight keeps the animate and inanimate world going, but never gets thanked or saluted. But when the sun sets (in the twilight) all crazy people become perplexed. (Bendre 1959: 180-1)

SHAIKH MUHAMMAD'S REQUEST

Shaikh Muhammad has answered with love. He says:

I do not know etymology. I am unskilled. Those learned sages (*pundits*) laugh at me because I do not speak a pure language. I was born a '*Mlechha*'. I am not socialized in Marathi. This is how all these knowledgeables criticize our language. I have not learnt the old texts (*shastra-puranas*). I have also not learnt to use pure language. I have taught myself with the help of God. Then Goddess Saraswati told me that I am at the root, fallen from *yoga*. But that is how God has decided to reside in my speech. (Bendre 1959: 195)

In short both Eknath and Shaikh Muhammad Baba were trying to democratize the social discourse around them and empower people to go beyond their caste community boundaries, e.g. Eknath's dialogue between a Brahman and a Mahar shows how a Mahar has the strength, wisdom, knowledge making capacity when he redefines *nirguna* (abstraction-formlessness) and spells out a new theory of "selfhood" in the *bhakti marga*. Eknath redefines his own identity along with Mahar identity and suggests that rebirth was a problem only for those who lived the life of conservation and psudo purity.

One needs to note that this text *Yogasangram* was selected as an important signpost of Muslim Marathi writing by the Muslim Other Backward Classes organization in Maharashtra as a secular, democratic voice immediately after the Babri Masjid and the riots that followed (1993). The last two decades, Mandal, Masjid and the World Bank years, have created a need for a new language, new visions to address the complexity faced by the intellectual and political world of India. Different camps—socialist, Marxist, radicals—are not so certain about their standpoint. Post-modernism which challenged all meta or grand narratives has also rejected the "dialectic of spirit". Some scholars suggest a *marg* of secularization of cultural commonsense as an answer to Hindu nationalist bigotry in contemporary India. They suggest that this would help in avoiding falling in the trap of populist movements, which contribute to reactionary modernism. Many look at the gloomy presence of the twenty-first century as a result of our being in the transitional period of experiment and exploration. If the dream of a secular, democratic modern India is to be realized, a re-reading of the pre-modern medieval *bhakti* texts with more sensitivity seems to be one of the possible *margs*.

PRIMARY TEXTS

"Hindu–Turk Samvad", in R.R. Gosavi, ed., *Shri Sakal Sant Gatha*, vol. II, Pune: Sarathi Prakashan, 2000.

Bendre, B.S., 1959: *Yogasangram, Shaikh Muhammad Baba Krut.* Pune: PPH Bookstall.

REFERENCES

Dhande, Chandrakant, 2003: "Sant Eknath ani Dalit Samvedan" (Sant Eknath and Dalit Sensitivity), in R.T. Bhagat, ed., *Sant Sahitya ani Dalit Samvedan.* Kolhapur: Chaitanya Prakashan.

Joshi, Shashi, 1994: *Composite Culture and Cultural Fault Line.* Nehru Memorial Monograph Second Series, No. LXXXVIII.

Lele, Jayant, 1995: *Hindutva: The Emergence of the Right.* Madras: Earthworm Books.

More, Sadanand, 1996: *Tukaram Darshan.* Pune: Gaaj Prakashan.

——, 2004: "Varkari Sahitya: Bhumika ani Swarup" (Varkari Literature: Content and Form) in Special Issue of *Varkari Tradition and Marathi Culture.* Pune: Satyashodhak Sanghatak, November 2004, pp. 32-39.

Phatak, N.R., 1950: *Shri Eknath: Vangmay ani Karya* (Shri Eknath: Literature and Work). Bombay: Manoj Printing.

Thapar, Romila, 2000: "The Tyranny of Labels", in Romila Thapar, *Cultural Pasts: Essays in Early Indian History.* New Delhi: Oxford University Press.

Tulpule, S.G., 1962: *Pach Sant Kavi* (Five Sant Poets). Pune: Sangam Anand.

Zelliot, Eleanor, 1981: "Chokhamela and Eknath: Two Bhakti Modes of Legitimacy for Modern Change", in Jayant Lele, ed., *Tradition and Modernity in Bhakti Movements.* Leiden: E.J. Brill.

5

Dr. Ambedkar's Path to Buddhism: A *Mārg* to *Navayāna*?

ELEANOR ZELLIOT

I also take refuge in the words of the Buddha to be your own guide. Take refuge in your own reason. Do not listen to the advice of others. Do not succumb to others. Be truthful and take refuge in the truth. Never surrender to anything. If you keep in mind this message of Lord Buddha at this juncture, I am sure, your decision will not be wrong. (Babasaheb in 1936 at Dadar, Mumbai)

These words of Dr. B.R. Ambedkar at the time of the announcement that he would convert and that his followers should also think about conversion are printed at the end of every message in the e-mail of the Buddhist Circle, a group of Buddhists, often young and always technically knowledgeable, who are followers of Dr. Ambedkar. It is reflective of the independent thinking of the "new Buddhists". It is related to a term that some are beginning to apply to Ambedkar Buddhism, *navayāna*, the new vehicle. *Navayāna* is in contrast to *mahāyāna*, the great vehicle; *hīnayāna*, the lesser vehicle, a term Theravāda (the way of the elders) Buddhists do not like; and *vajrayāna*, the vehicle of the thunderbolt. Dr. Ambedkar's Buddhist teaching, found chiefly in *The Buddha and His Dhamma*,[1] was primarily founded on Theravāda texts, but its departure from what is generally thought of as classical Buddhism prompts the new term.

There are other schemes for organizing the groups of Buddhists. H. Saddhatissa notes four main Buddhist traditions: Theravāda in South and South-East Asia; Tibetan, which includes

Nepal, Bhutan, Sikkim, Mongolia and Siberia; and Zen and Pure Land, found in Japan, Korea, China, Vietnam, Malaysia and Singapore.[2] The idea of "Engaged Buddhism" reaches across the older forms of division and includes Dr. Ambedkar's Buddhism; the TBMSG (Trailokya Bauddha Mahāsāṅgha Sahayāka Gāṇā), which is the Indian offshoot of the Friends of the Western Buddhist Order in England; the Sārvodāya Shrāmadāna movement in Sri Lanka of A.T. Ariyaratne; Buddhadasa Bhikkhu and Sulak Sivaraksa of Thailand; Thich Nhat Hanh of Vietnam, now exiled in France; and the Soka Gakkai in Japan.[3]

Most of the Buddhists in the Ambedkar movement reject the term "Neo Buddhism", often applied to them since the mass conversion in 1956. It seems to them an indication that somehow the Buddhist conversion was not an authentic part of Buddhism. And while the terms "Harijan", and "Untouchable" have been largely displaced by Dalit, a word meaning oppressed, no one would dare to use the term Dalit Buddhists if he or she wanted to be an acceptable journalist or critic since "oppressed Buddhism" is a contradiction in terms even though its adherents may be oppressed. This essay hopes to explore how Ambedkar Buddhism or *Navayāna* Buddhism relates to older Buddhism and innovates within the Buddhist tradition.

AMBEDKAR'S FOUR PROBLEMS

Ambedkar was introduced to Buddhism as a young student, and in his lifetime read widely in Buddhist literature. Before accepting the Buddhist religion, however, he had to work through the difficulty he had in accepting standard interpretations of Buddhism. In his Introduction to *The Buddha and His Dhamma,* Ambedkar noted four problems in the traditional view of Buddhism. As we consider these, it must be remembered that Ambedkar was an Untouchable and in much of Hindu society, it would be thought that some previous sin had brought him (and all others like him) to his despised place. It must also be remembered that Ambedkar was very highly educated, with a M.A., a Ph.D., a D.DS in Economics and admission to the bar.

His religion was important to him but devoid of myth, totally rational. Meera Nanda calls it "Deweyana Buddhism", after the great American educator, rationalist and promoter of democracy, John Dewey, who was Ambedkar's teacher at Columbia University.[4]

According to the Introduction of *The Buddha and His Dhamma*, the first problem in Ambedkar's mind was the idea that the Buddha went on his search for *nirvāṇa* because he saw for the first time a dead person, a sick person and an old person. "This answer is absurd on the face of it," wrote Ambedkar, since Gautama was 29 when he left his home. The second problem is more difficult for Ambedkar to deal with since the four noble truths, "Āryan Truths", writes Ambedkar, are part and parcel of every introduction to Buddhism of any kind. But in Ambedkar's mind, the formula "cuts at the root of Buddhism. If life is sorrow, death is sorrow and rebirth is sorrow, then there is an end of everything". Ambedkar questions the four truths as original teachings and wonders if they are a later accretion added by the monks.

The third problem for Ambedkar was old deeply held Hindu idea of *karma*. "The Buddha denied the existence of the soul. But he is also said to have affirmed the doctrine of *karma* and rebirth. . . . In what sense did the Buddha use the words *karma* and rebirth? Did he use them in a different sense than the sense in which they were used by the Brahmins of his day?" Ambedkar put the problem in terms of the impossibility of rebirth if there is no soul, but clearly he challenged the very idea that untouchability came from a previous life's bad actions.

And the last problem: "What was the object of the Buddha in creating the Bhikkhu?" To create a perfect man? or to create a social servant? Ambedkar clearly felt that the *bhikkhu* should devote his life to the service of the people as their friend, guide and philosopher.

Before noting the sources which inspired Ambedkar or backed up his beliefs, we should note that the entire text of *The Buddha and His Dhamma* is cast as teachings of the Buddha. The verses are numbered and arranged in Biblical fashion. The teaching *mudrā* of the Buddha's hand is on each page. And behind all of it is the firm conviction that the Buddha was entirely rational, and none of his teachings can be seen as superstitious or mythic or illogical.

KELUSKAR AND KOSAMBI

The legend of the gift of a biography of the Buddha to Ambedkar in his youth is important in establishing his early exposure to Buddhism but also indicates ideas about Buddhism current among Indian intellectuals in the late nineteenth and the twentieth centuries.[5] Krishnaji Arjun Keluskar, principal of Wilson High School in Bombay and author of biographies of Shivaji and the Buddha, gave a copy of *Bhagwan Gautam Buddha* in Marathi (published in 1898) to Ambedkar to celebrate his passing the Matriculation examination in 1907. In that biography, which is still in print, Keluskar referred to a dispute over the waters of the Rohini River and Siddharth Gautama's intervention to prevent war between the Śākyas and the Koliyas, and Ambedkar took this as the rationale for the Buddha's leaving home to seek a path to peace and his own fulfilment. The Sanskrit scholar Dharmanand Kosambi (1876-1948) in his biography of the Buddha, published in 1940 and also still in print, also gives the frequent quarrels between Śākyas and Koliyas as the reason for Gautama's leaving home to find the way to peace.[6]

It is probable that these two sources were sufficient proof for Dr. Ambedkar's solution to the first problem, the reason for Gautama's leaving his home. But the ideas of these two scholars are also important because of who they were. Keluskar was not only principal of the very prestigious Wilson High School, he was a very early biographer of the seventeenth-century king Shivaji Maharaj, seen as the founder of Maharashtra and still all important in the ideology of the Marathi speaking area. One could make a leap of faith and assume that Keluskar's dual interests brought Buddhism into the realm of national or at least regional legitimacy.

The role of Dharmanand Kosambi in Ambedkar's thinking may be very important, although we know of no direct meeting. Kosambi traveled to Buddhist holy places, studied in what was then Ceylon, became a *sramanera* and at times a *bhikkhu*, taught Pali, worked on Buddhist texts at Harvard, and founded an *ashram* in 1936 in Parel in Bombay "with the avowed intention of destroying untouchability through Buddhist philosophy".[7] The date of this Buddhist enterprise is the same as Ambedkar's declaration for mass conversion, but Kosambi's identification with the Gandhian movement, which was opposed to Ambedkar at the time, may have prevented direct contact. We do know that his biography of the Buddha was important to Ambedkar Buddhists and has been kept in print by their support.

FOUR ĀRYAN TRUTHS

The conventional presentation of the Four Noble (or Āryan) Truths was a problem for Ambedkar, as the idea that suffering is caused by greed would be for anyone suffering at the hands of society. Actually, the Truths in Buddhist scripture are more subtle than that, but here is a commonly accepted version found in *Webster's New International Dictionary of the English Language*, 2nd edition, 1947:

> Four Āryan Truths
> 1. that all life is subject to suffering
> 2. that desire or the will to live is the cause of repeated existences in which sorrow is inevitable
> 3. that only the annihilation of desire (that is, yearning, craving, ambition, as distinct from will) can give release
> 4. that the way of escape is the Eightfold Path: right belief, right resolve, right word, right act, right life, right effort, right thinking, right meditation.

Christopher Queen has done much research to trace the sources of Ambedkar's thought. He has visited Ambedkar's library at Siddharth College in Mumbai many times, and notes that of more than 20,000 volumes, 250 volumes treat Buddhist history and literature in addition to translations. The volumes were marked heavily and clearly read and studied. Queen quotes a telling passage from James Bissett Pratt's *The Pilgrimage of Buddhism* (New York: Macmillan, 1928: 15-17 passim):

The central theme of the Buddha's teaching is the moral life. . . . And if one takes the teachings of the Buddha as a whole, noting the actual emphasis of the Nikayas, *it becomes very difficult to give the Four Noble Truths the all-dominating position that our Western convention assigns them.* The Buddha recognizes sorrow in the world, but he also recognizes joy. (The italics are Ambedkar's emphasis, marked in red.)

Ambedkar in many places clearly defines the term *dukkha* in very physical terms. "Poverty gives rise to sorrow. But removal of poverty does not necessarily give rise to happiness." "Hunger is the worst of diseases." (Book IV, Part III, section 10, p. 369)

A poem by the late Daya Pawar illustrates the way in which Ambedkar Buddhism has interpreted the concept of *dukkha.*[8]

I never see you
in Jeta's garden
sitting with eyes closed
in meditation, in the lotus position
or
in the caves of Ajanta and Ellora
with stony lips sewn shut
sleeping the last sleep of your life.

I see you
walking, talking,
breathing softly, healingly,
on the sorrow of the poor, the weak, going from hut to hut
in the life-destroying darkness,
torch in hand
giving the sorrow
that drains the blood
like a contagious disease
a new meaning.

The problem of *karma,* or the sins of one life determining the status and welfare of the next, is of great importance. It has been shown that while the idea of *karma* is widely accepted among Indians, and is seen as the justification for untouchability by many, it is often not accepted by Untouchables.[9] Indeed the number of myths of origin which indicate that some cosmic mistake brought a caste to the level of untouchability would indicate that traditional ideas of *karma* have never been widely accepted by the lower castes. Ambedkar posed the problem as a question in his introduction. "The Buddha denied the existence of the soul. But he is also said to have affirmed the doctrine of *karma* and rebirth. At once a question arises. If there is no soul, how can there be *karma*? If there is no soul, how can there be rebirth?"

In a section in *The Buddha and His Dhamma* on what the Buddha modified, Ambedkar puts the Buddha's theory of *karma* this way:

> He discarded the theory that all deeds committed in some former birth have the potency to produce suffering, making present activity impotent. He denied the fatalistic view of Karma. He replaced the view of Karma by a much more scientific view of Karma. He put new wine in old bottles. (Book I, Part VII, section 2, p. 104)

The fourth problem, that of the role of the *bhikkhu*, was settled firmly in Ambedkar's mind in that he felt the *bhikkhu* must take on the needs of society. He could be compared to some Christian missionaries in that respect. Ambedkar was not impressed by the *saṅgha* which he visited in Ceylon in 1950. He seems to have had more respect for the Burmese *bhikkhus* during a visit in the same year. He spoke to the Buddhist Sasana Council while he was there, beginning with the advice that spreading Buddhism outside Burma to India would yield much to their effort. He cautioned them against regarding the Indian converts as lower class, noting that Christianity entered Rome first among the "poor and despised". "Religion if it is of the right type ennobles people and elevates them. People do not degrade religion." The steps that must be taken to revive Buddhism in India, Ambedkar told the Burmese Council, are these: 1. The preparation of a Buddhist Gospel. 2. A ceremony like baptism which would make a "person feel that he is ceasing to be a Hindu and becoming a new man". 3. The appointment of lay preachers. 4. "The establishment of a Buddhist Religious Seminary where persons who wish to become preachers could be taught Buddhism and also comparative study of other Religions. 5. The introduction of congregational worship in the *vihāra* every Sunday followed by a sermon." In addition big temples and *vihāras* should be built in Madras, Bombay, Nagpur and Delhi, and high schools and colleges in Madras, Nagpur, Calcutta and Delhi. Essays on

Buddhist topics should be written by anyone interested and awarded prizes.[10]

NARASU'S INFLUENCE

As Ambedkar thought through the kind of Buddhism he envisioned for India, he probably most relied on a book on Buddhism by P. Lakshmi Narasu (1861-1934), whose *The Essence of Buddhism* was published first in 1907, reprinted in 1912, and given new life by Ambedkar in 1948 with his own introduction (Bombay: Thacker and Company). Ambedkar felt Narasu's book was the "best book on Buddhism that has appeared so far" and recommended it to all those wanting to learn about the *dhamma.*[11] Another book by Narasu, *Religion of the Modern Buddhist,* seems not to have been published during his lifetime but was preserved in manuscript form by Vasant Moon, editor of the *Dr. Babasaheb Ambedkar Writings and Speeches* volumes and his wife Meenakshi Moon. Edited and introduced by G. Aloysius, it was published in 2002 in Delhi by Wordsmiths. Much of Narasu's thought is similar to Ambedkar's. Narasu was part of a Buddhist movement in Tamil Nadu led by Iyothee Thass (born 1845) which at times attracted a mass following,[12] but was no longer a vital force by the time Ambedkar began to consider conversion.

THE REJECTION OF HINDUISM

There are other aspects of Ambedkar's Buddhism which set it apart from other forms. In contrast to the way in which Buddhism spread north, east and south-east outside of India, combining Buddhist ideas and images with previously important religious ideas or symbols, *Navayāna* Buddhism discarded almost all elements of Hinduism in its effort to shake off both caste and any irrational practice or belief. It would be as if Tibetan Buddhism totally rejected Bon, Buddhism in Thailand and Vietnam rejected the houses of the spirits and ancestor worship, Buddhism in Sri Lanka refused all influence from the Hindu Gods. The way in which Buddhism had been absorbed in Hinduism through the assumption that the Buddha was an *avatār* of Vishnu, one brought to earth to mislead the evil, also had to be denied. The twenty-two oaths which are part of a conversion ceremony make this abundantly clear. Quoted in full from a pamphlet issued by the Buddhist Society of India, New Delhi, without corrections of the translation from the Marathi, one can see the balance of rejection and acceptance asked of the new converts:

BUDDHIST'S OATHS

1. I will not regard Brahma, Vishnu and Mahesh as Gods nor will I worship them.
2. I will not regard Rama and Krishna as Gods nor will I worship them.
3. I will not accept Hindu Deities like Gauri, Ganapati, etc. nor will I worship them.
4. I do not believe that God had taken birth or incarnation in any form.
5. I do not believe that Lord Buddha was the Incarnation of Vishnu. I believe this propaganda as mischievous and false.
6. I will never perform any Sharaadha nor will I offer any Pinda.
7. I will never act against the tenets of Buddhism.
8. I will never get any SAMSKAAR performed by Brahmins.
9. I believe in the principle that all are equal.
10. I will try to establish equality.
11. I will follow the Eight Fold Path of Lord Buddha.
12. I will follow all the ten Paramitas of the Dhamma.
13. I will have compassion on all living beings and will try to look after them.
14. I will not lie.
15. I will not commit theft.
16. I will not indulge in lust or sexual transgression.
17. I will not take any liquor or drink that causes intoxication.
18. I will try to mould my life in accordance with the Buddhist preachings, based on Enlightenment, Precept and Compassion.
19. I embrace today the Bauddha Dhamma discarding the Hindu Religion which is detrimental to the emancipation of human beings and which believes in inequality and regards human beings other than the Brahmins as low born.
20. This is my firm belief that the Bauddha Dhamma is the best religion.
21. I believe that today I am taking New-birth.
22. I solemnly take oath that from today onwards I will act according to the Bauddha DHAMMA.

Sabbe Satta Sukhnee Hontu

There was one aspect of Hinduism which was not totally rejected, and that was the *bhakti* movement, the medieval religion which was based on experience, open to all, and often radical in its beliefs. Ambedkar himself was fond of Tukārām, a seventeenth-century Marathi saint-poet, and quoted him all his life. His book on the *Untouchables* (Delhi: Amrit Book Company, 1948) was dedicated to Chokhameḷa, Ravidās and Nandnār, three Untouchable saints who "by their piety and virtue won the esteem of all". Ambedkar also congratulated the Eknāth Research Society in Aurangabad, noting "how great a contribution the reading of this Saint's literature can make to the moral rearmament of man".[13] Eknāth was a Brahmin saint-poet of the sixteenth century who ate with Untouchables and wrote as if he were a Mahar. But the Mahar saint, Chokhameḷa, believed his Untouchable status was his *karma* and the temple that was the focus of his devotion was closed to Untouchables until 1950, and the meaning of Cokhameḷa to the followers of Ambedkar was dissipated by the time of conversion.

INNOVATIONS IN *NAVAYĀNA* BUDDHISM

Developments since the Conversion in 1956 also add to the new quality of *Navayāna*. For one thing, activity is not centered around some huge *vihāra* or temple or decided upon from a central organization. There are active organizations: the Trilokya Bauddha Mahāsāṅgha Sahayāka Gāṇā (TBMSG)[14] centered in Pune with many branches; the newly established Jambudvipa and Manuski, also in Pune; the All India Bhikkhu Sangha;[15] the Nagaloka center in Nagpur and Wamanrao Meshram's institution just outside the city; and the large scale organized march to Bodh Gaya led by Surai Sasai in the 1990s to reclaim all of the Bodh Gaya temple for Buddhism. But there is no overall effective center, and there is a surprising amount of activity on the part of local Buddhists in urban localities. For instance, my recent visit brought me to two *vihāras* in Pune where women wanted me to participate in a service, and the *vihāras* were ones I had never heard of before, built and maintained totally locally. For another, a group of younger Buddhists maintain an e-mail contact through the "Buddhist Circle" which calls forth constant discussion of Buddhist principles, announcements of activities, and since all are highly qualified in technology, possible new employment opportunities. A few *bhikkhus* participate in the discussion, but it is primarily a very creative method for "digital *Dalits*" (my term) to communicate with each other.

A rather unusual feature of the conversion is that, according to the well-known writer Baburao Bagul,[16] it freed the *Dalit* from the psychological imprisonment of untouchability, releasing him to write, to create poetry and short stories and autobiography and to enter the world of literature to such a degree that it literally changed the face of Marathi literature. Little of this *Dalit Sāhitya* directly concerns Buddhism, although when it does it is very striking. Daya Pawar's image of the Buddha in the slums is given above. In another poem, *Jhāḍ* (tree), he writes:

This tree I saw mangled with sorrow
had roots as deep down as the Bodhi-tree's.
But the Bodhi-tree flowered,
and this tree through all seasons was barren.[17]

Another reference to the Bodhi-tree is in Mina Gajbhiye's poem *Piṃpaḷvṛkṣa.* She ends her poem of skepticism about the traditionalism and hypocrisy of Hinduism (or the middle class) with the note that she has shown some seeds. "Will at least one seed sprout? Bodhi tree. . . ."[18]

An innovative approach to Buddhism by a *Dalit* writer is the poem to *Yaśodharā*, the Buddha's wife, by Hira Bansode, in which she combines feminist sympathy for the wife left behind with a belief that perhaps Yaśodharā is "behind the closed eyelids of the Buddha".[19]

At times, figures from Buddhist legends are made the subject of modern poetry. Daya Pawar in a poem called *Siddhārthanagar*, a slum in which he actually lived, ends with the idea that the cruel society around the settlement is Angulimal, the tyrant robber the Buddha converted, and he asks:

How should we confront
this ferocious Angulimal?
O Siddhartha,

If we fight tooth and claw
Try to understand us.
Try to understand us.[20]

A completely different use of the image of Angulimal is in Tryambak Sapkale's poem with that title. The poem begins, "When I came into this world I was crying, the world was laughing . . ." and then "As I ran through this bounteous, plentiful land my feet burned, I ran yelling for life, hoping to meet some saint like Eknāth. I met quite a few who reverenced Eknāth. They were engrossed in their *kirtan.* My cry did not enter their hearts. . . ." And then in a use of the image of the fingers that Angulimal cut-off and wore as a garland, Sapkale writes:

I tried to catch hold of this turning world.
My hands were brushed off. I fell.
The world laughed
pointing its fingers at me. Tears dried.
Feet froze.
Gathering all my strength
I laughed at this world
Ha . . . ha . . . ha . . . ha . . . .
The world trembled at my laugh.

He, I said, how come
you rabbits' spawn aren't laughing anymore?
Those fingers that were pointed at me
will become fingers in the garland around my neck.

Angulimal.
I am Angulimal . . .
I am Angulimal. . . .[21]

A very interesting use of the image of the Buddha is in Arjun Dangle's *Āṇi Buddha mārun paḍlā* (and the Buddha died).[22] In this story, a young Buddhist student attempts to get his fellow Buddhists formerly from the Mahar caste to let the Untouchable Mangs, traditional enemies of the Mahars and supposedly beneath them, to use their well. He refuses to give money to help build a Buddhist temple when they will not accept the Mang's needs. But when his father dies, he must have help with the funeral and he agrees to contribute. He looks down at his dead father's face, and he sees "the Buddha has died".

INTERNATIONAL ASPECTS

There are efforts to broaden the scope of Ambedkar Buddhism, or *Navayāna*, in many ways, to make it known to other Buddhists and other Dalits. In England, Buddhists attempt to cooperate with Vālmiki and Ravidāsi groups, Untouchable castes formerly Bhangi or Chuhra and Chamar, which have found in Hinduism heroes and saints to give them self-respect and to be objects of devotion. In Canada, Ambedkar Buddhists also attempt to integrate Ravidāsi Sikhs into their Ambedkar celebrations. In a very ambitious program, the newly formed Manuski (humanity or human-ness, a Marathi word much used by Ambedkar) group in Pune and the Nagaloka retreat center at Nagpur called an international Buddhist conference in October 2005. Some 120 delegates from the United States, United Kingdom, South Korea, Sri Lanka, Taiwan, Japan, Thailand, Cambodia, Indonesia, Laos, Tibet, Bangladesh, Myanmar and India participated in an eight day event. Included was a pre-conference workshop on Dr. Ambedkar's life and beliefs before the main conference on the theme of "Buddhism and Social Equality" began. Speakers included Lokamitra, a long time English Buddhist leader in India, on Dr. Babasaheb Ambedkar and a number of Indian Buddhists on their ideas and experiences. It was noted that due to a lack of information on Dr. Ambedkar's peaceful revolution for social change, some people brand the entire movement as a political move, and the conference effectively presented Dr. Ambedkar as a Buddhist leader. The pre-conference ended with a visit to the Diksha Bhumi, the land where conversion took place and now the site of a tremendous *stūpa*. Hundreds of thousands of Buddhists from all over India had gathered there, as they do every October, to reaffirm their faith.

Speakers during the conference included Samdhong Rimpoche of Tibet and the Dalai Lama; Sulak Sivaraksha, one of the proponents of Engaged Buddhism in Thailand; and representatives from Taiwan, the United Kingdom and Korea. After the conference, some delegates went on pilgrimage to Ajanta,

Ellora, Pitalkhora, and the Aurangabad Buddhist caves and also saw Milind College, which Ambedkar had established near there. Reports indicate the conference was successful in establishing the Ambedkar Buddhist movement as genuine and important Buddhism.

KĀLAMA SŪTRA

The word *Navayāna* was not used at the conference, and it is possible it will never come into worldwide currency. Nevertheless it is a useful concept. There is now a Navayāna Publishing House in Pondicherry. Gary Tartakov writes of the "*Navayāna* Creation of the Buddha Image", in *Reconstructing the World: B.R. Ambedkar and Buddhism in India* and Gail Omvedt and Eugenia Yurlova use the term in their articles.[23] Many orthodox Buddhists in the beginning of his movement were affronted by Dr. Ambedkar's interpretation of Buddhism and now others may take objection to the term. Yet it indicates that there are many facets to Buddhism, and this latest of movements may be one of the most important modern developments.

It is clear that the Kālama Sūtra guided Ambedkar's reading of the Buddha's teaching. Ambedkar quotes the Buddha's speaking to the Kālamas this way: "What I have said is 'do not go merely by what you hear; do not go merely by what has been handed down from one to another; do not go merely by subtleties of reasoning; do not go by subtleties of logic; do not go by considerations based upon mere appearances; do not go merely by agreeable beliefs and views; do not go merely by the word of some ascetic or superior'." And then Ambedkar summarizes the argument in his own words "But consider whether the beliefs and views sought to be inculcated are salutary or insalutary, blameworthy or blameless, lead to well-being or ill-being. It is only on these grounds that one can accept the teachings of anybody."

NOTES

1. *The Buddha and His Dhamma,* written in English by B.R. Ambedkar, was published in 1957 as Siddharth College Publication: I in Bombay. It was reprinted as vol. 11 in the *Dr. Babasaheb Ambedkar Writings and*

Speeches series by the Education Department of the Government of Maharashtra in 1992. A Supplement to vol. 11, *Pali and Other Sources of the Buddha and His Dhamma,* by Vasant Moon, was published in the same series in 1995. "The Use of Buddhist Scriptures in B.R. Ambedkar's *The Buddha and His Dhamma*" by Adele Fiske and Christoph Emmrich appears in *Reconstructing the World: B.R. Ambedkar and Buddhism in India,* edited by Surendra Jondhale and Johannes Beltz. New Delhi: Oxford University Press, 2004.

2. H. Saddhatissa, *The Buddha's Way.* London: George Allen and Unwin, 1971: 121.
3. See *Engaged Buddhism: Buddhist Liberation Movements in Asia,* edited by Christopher S. Queen and Sallie B. King. Albany: State University of New York Press, 1996.
4. "A 'Broken' People's Defend Science: Reconstructing the Deweyan Buddha of India's Dalits", in *Breaking the Spell of Dharma and other Essays,* by Meera Nanda. New Delhi: Three Essays Press, 2002.
5. See my "The Indian Rediscovery of Buddhism, 1855-1956", in *Studies in Pali and Buddhism,* edited by A.K. Narain. Delhi: B.R. Publishing Corporation, 1979, and D.C. Ahir, *The Pioneers of the Buddhist Revival in India.* Delhi: Sri Satguru Publications, 1989.
6. See *Pali and Other Sources* by Vasant Moon, pp. ix-xi.
7. Zelliot 1979: 393. The best source in English on Kosambi's life is P.V. Bapat, "Professor Dharmanand Kosambi", *Modern Review* 83 (1948), 134-7.
8. From Daya Pawar's introduction to his *Kondwāḍa* (cattle pen). Pune: Magowa Prakashan, 1974. Translated by Vidyut Bhagwat, Jayant Karve and Eleanor Zelliot.
9. See Pauline Mahar Kolenda, "Religious Anxiety and Hindu Fate", *Journal of Asian Studies* XXXIII (1964): 71-81.
10. Typescript of "Record of my talk to the Buddhist Sasana Council of Burma: An Enlarged Version".
11. G. Aloysius in the introduction to P. Lakshmi Narasu's *Religion of the Modern Buddhist.* Delhi: Wordsmiths, 2002: p. xviii.
12. See *Religion as Emancipatory Identity: A Buddhist Movement among the Tamils under Colonialism,* by G. Aloysius. New Delhi: New Age International Publishers for the Christian Institute for the Study of Religion and Society, 1998. By the 1950s, however, when Ambedkar began to visit Buddhist places, the only large number of Buddhists were in the Kolar Gold Fields. He attempted to visit them in 1954 but was turned away by their overwhelming devotion to him.
13. *Dr. Babasaheb Ambedkar Writings and Speeches,* vol. 17, *Dr. B.R. Ambedkar and His Egalitarian Revolution: Part Two: Socio-Political, Religious Activities.* Mumbai: Government of Maharashtra, 2003: 130.
14. Alan Sponberg, "TBMSG: A Dhamma Revolution in Contemporary India", in *Engaged Buddhism* 1996: 73-120.

15. See Detlef Kantowsky, *Buddhists in India Today: Descriptions, Pictures, and Documents.* New Delhi: Manohar, 2003: 150-9.
16. See Eleanor Zelliot, *From Untouchable to Dalit: Essays on the Ambedkar Movement.* New Delhi: Manohar, 1992 (1996): 288.
17. Daya Pawar, op. cit.: 35.
18. See Eleanor Zelliot, "Shri Dalit Sahitya: The New Voice of Women Poets", in *Images of Women in Maharashtrian Literature and Religion,* edited by Anne Feldhaus. Albany: State University of New York Press, 1996: 69-70.
19. See Hira Bansode's poem in Eleanor Zelliot, 1996: 71-3.
20. The poem in full is reproduced in Zelliot, 1992: 294-5. The translators are Vidya Dixit, Jayant Karve, Eleanor Zelliot.
21. The poem in full is reproduced in Zelliot, 1992: 295-6. The translators are Jayant Karve and Eleanor Zelliot. This is an unusual poem for Tryambak Sapkale, whose usual poems are gentle and optimistic. See the *Journal of South Asian Literature* XVII: 1 (Winter-Spring 1982): 100.
22. The story is in Arjun Dangle's collection *Hi bamdhavaraci manasa.* Pune: Magova, 1979.
23. *Reconstructing the World* was edited by Surendra Jondhale and Johannes Beltz. New Delhi: Oxford University Press, 2004.

PART II

LITERARY CULTURE AND SOCIAL REFORM

6

No *Mārga* to *Svarga*?: The Sati Failure Case in Late Eighteenth-Century North Deccan[1]

HIROYUKI KOTANI

INTRODUCTION

On a day in July 1782, the widowed wife of Bapurao Deshpande of Jalnapur in the north Deccan decided to become a Sati. Having gone through the prescribed rites of self-immolation in the funeral ground, she began climbing the burning funeral pyre of her deceased husband, when several Englishmen from a cantonment of the English East India Company passed by and rescued her from self-sacrifice. They carried her to the cantonment and made her live there. After a month had passed, the Englishmen summoned learned Brahmans from Jalnapur and asked them to purify her and readmit her to her caste.

This posed two difficult legal problems. One problem was whether the woman, who had failed to become a Sati because she had been prevented from doing so by infidels (Englishmen), could be purified of her sin of failing to become a Sati by purificatory ritual (*prāyaścitta*) and readmitted to her caste. The other was whether the woman, who had had social contact (*saṃsarga*) with infidels through having lived in the cantonment of the East India Company, could be purified of the sin of social contact (in medieval Marathi, *saṃsarga doṣa*) with infidels by *prāyaścitta*.

This Sati failure case propounds important problems in regard to the relationship between the brahmanical tradition of jurisprudence and the socio-political reality of India just before the beginning of British colonial rule.

CIRCUMSTANCES SURROUNDING THE SATI FAILURE CASE

Jalnapur (or simply Jalna) is a town in the north Deccan on a branch of the Godavari River, situated some 40 miles east of Aurangabad. Jalnapur was then in the territories of the Nizams of Hyderabad, the successor state of the Mughals in the Deccan. In 1766, the Nizam government concluded a Treaty of Perpetual Honour, Favour, Alliance, and Attachment with the English East India Company, by which the Nizam government ceded the five districts along the Bengal Bay, later collectively known as the Northern Circars (Aitchison 1931: IX-X, 22-5). Thus cantonments of the East India Company began to be constructed in the Nizams' territories in the Deccan including the area around Jalnapur. The Englishmen who intervened in the self-immolation of the widowed wife of the Deshpande of Jalnapur were officers or soldiers of the East India Company stationed at one of the cantonments in the Deccan.

The Brahmans who had been asked by the Englishmen to purify the woman in question must have been greatly embarrassed over whether it was lawful to perform *prāyaścitta* on her, as they had never experienced this sort of thing. One of them consequently sent the following letter of inquiry dated 28 August 1782 to the Dharmādhikārī of Nasik who was respected as the authority on such legal matters:[2]

Śrī svasti śrīmat sakala muni gaṇa labhya karuṇā maya naṃ(>n)da nam(n)dana pada araviṃdạ rasa āsvāda medurī bhūta maṇaḥ ṣaṭpadeṣu / muni traya vihita karma ācaraṇa prasanna mānasa ānīta pavitra kīrt<t>i kathā śravana kṛta arthī kṛta nija nikhila gotrodbhaveṣu (gotra udbhaveṣu) / kṛta atiśaya puṇya parilabdha bhūdeva śarīra vidhi(>ī) yamāna tapaḥ puṃja prakāśa dedīpyamāna anala daṃ(>saṃ?) dahyamāna pātaka samūheṣu / Śrī Godā tīra virājamāna rāghava ādhya gaṇita sura gaṇa maṃdita Śrī Janaschāna (=Janasthāna, another name of Nasik) nivāsi bhūsura varyeṣu (indicating the addressee) / Jālnāpur vāsi śākhā traya brāhmaṇa (indicating the addresser) viracita avirata aneka sa aṣṭa aṃga praṇipāta śatāni samullasaṃ(>n)tu / śubhakṛta saṃvatsara nabho'sita pakṣa pañcāmī bhṛgu vārāv / adhikam asmādīya bhāukam(>bhāvukam) avabudhya bhavadīya bhavyaṃ boddhum āśāsmahe viśeṣastu /[3]

Bapurao Deshpande of this place, a Ṛgvedī Brahman, died. His wife decided to do *sahagamana* (going with the husband to *svarga*) and went to the crematory. After having performed the rites ending with the worship of stone (*śilāpūjanāṃta karma*), she immediately began to climb the funeral pyre (*citā*) of her husband, when some Sahebs (*sāheb loka*) of a chāvanī (cantonment of the English East India Company) came along and prevented her from doing *sahagamana*. They took her to the cantonment and made her live there. One month passed in this state. On the second day of the dark half of Śrāvaṇa, they summoned learned Brahmans (*śiṣṭa Brāhmaṇa*) and asked them to purify her and then readmit her to her caste (*jñāti*). There is a provision in such law codes (*dharmaśāstrāce graṃtha*) as the *Nirṇayasindhu*, *Smṛtyarthasāra*, *Dinakaradyota*, *Nārāyaṇabhaṭṭī* and others to the effect that *satīparigraha* (acceptance of a chaste woman) should be done by performing *prāyaścitta* (purificatory ritual) on her as follows: "A woman, who fell down from *citta* (a normal state of mind) (*cittabhraṣṭā*), if she did so when unconscious (*moha*), shall purify (herself) of the sinful deed by *prājāpatya*." There is also an alternative reading (in place of "*cittabhraṣṭā*"): "a woman, who fell down from *citi* (a funeral pyre) (*citibraṣṭā*)". These are the Sahebs' orders and have the support of *śāstra* (for accepting the woman). I myself, however, have never seen or heard of such a matter, so I have had doubts about it and have written this letter to you, as Janaschāna (Nasik) is a sacred place comparable to Varanasi (*avimuktakṣetratulya*) in this part of the country. So, please let me know if there is any provision in the law codes that is contrary to the purport of the above-cited text, or otherwise inform me that you are agreed to *satīparigraha* (acceptance of a chaste woman). According to your instructions I will conduct myself.

P.S. (*tāzā kalam*)

Up to this day, the woman has been observing the prescribed norms (*ācāranvita*). Her good conduct (*sadācaraṇa*) is unquestionable. (ASS I-201)

The Brahman who wrote the letter must have been a leading member of the Brahman caste, to which the woman belonged. He thus, as the representative of the "learned Brahmans" who had been asked by the Sahebs to purify her, wrote the letter of inquiry to the Dharmādhikārī of Nasik.

From the letter and the reply of the Dharmādhikārī, that will be examined later, the circumstances in which the woman was prevented from completing *sahagamana* by the Sahebs appear to be as follows:

The funeral rites of her deceased husband were performed. The last rite was the "worship of stone" performed by the relatives. In the *Antyeṣṭipaddhati* (treatise on funeral rites) written by Nārāyaṇabhaṭṭa, the procedure of the "worship of stone" is prescribed in detail. Nārāyaṇabhaṭṭa (b. 1513) was a well-known *śāstrī* or law-code writer belonging to the Bhaṭṭa family whose ancestor migrated to Varanasi in the fifteenth century from Paithan (Pratiṣṭhāna), a large sacred place in the north Deccan on the Godavari River. According to P.V. Kane, even in the twentieth century the majority of Ṛgvedī Brahmans of western India performed the funeral rites in accordance with the procedures prescribed in the *Antyeṣṭipaddhati* (Kane 1968-77: IV 212). The law code referred to as the *Nārāyaṇabhaṭṭī* in the above-cited lettter of inquiry is nothing other than the *Antyeṣṭipaddhati* (Kane 1968-77: I 1054). Kane summarizes the procedure of "worship of stone" prescribed in the *Antyeṣṭipaddhati* as follows:

He [the performer of the funeral rites] makes a *saṅkalpa* that he would wait upon (or worship) the dead, takes two fuel sticks and offers them to the fire and performs the worship of Agni, Kāma, Loka and Anumati by offering clarified butter with the appropriate formula. . . . Then he makes the fire flame up with the mantra Ṛg. X. 16. 9. . . . Then the performer should take a jar (full of water) on his left shoulder and make a hole in it on the back of the jar with a broken but smooth stone. He should go round thrice with his leftside towards the burning body from the spot where the feet of the corpse lie and utter certain mantras. The jar is struck thrice. All the *sagotra* relatives go round the burning corpse. Then the jar is completely broken near that part of the funeral pyre where the head rests. The relatives without looking back turn to the left and come out of the cemetery with the youngest members first. The relatives repair to a spot where water is flowing, wearing only one garment and with their faces to the south and hair dishevelled, plunge into the water once, sip water, place on the bank that stone (*aśman*) with which holes were made in the jar, offer water mixed with sesame on that stone with folded hands with the words "O departed, of such a gotra and of such a name! May this water mixed with sesame reach you". The performer offers water with the uttariya for allaying the thirst (of the departed) due to the burning. (Kane 1968-77: IV 213-14)

The funeral rites of a deceased husband having thus been completed, the rites of *sahagamana* of his widowed wife commenced. After making *saṅkalpa,* she performed several rites such as uttering *mantras,* offering clarified butter, and going round the burning pyre. Then she performed the "worship of stone" (*śilāpūjana*) in which the same stone, with which a hole had been made in the jar used in the funeral of her husband, was worshipped (vide Müller 1992). In the *Nirṇayasindhu* (written by Kamalākarabhaṭṭa in 1612), the following provisions regarding the "worship of stone" are cited, though their sources are not named.

> When a (widowed) wife performed *anvāroha* (climbing the funeral pyre of her husband), the offering of *piṇḍa* and water mixed with sesame with folded hands (*tilāñjali*) should be severally done (to the husband and wife). (The funeral rite to be done) by using a stone should be separately performed (to the husband and wife). Likewise, an offering should be made to the same stone. (*Nirṇayasindhu:* 1055. The author's tentative translation)

The last sentence, "Likewise, an offering should be made to the same stone (*dadyād ekaśile tathā*)", means that in the "worship of the stone", a widowed wife makes an offering to the same stone used to make a hole in the jar at the funeral ritual of her husband.[4]

In the letter of inquiry, the widowed wife of the Deshpande of Jalnapur was said to have performed "the rites (of *sahagamana*) ending with the worship of stone (*śilāpūjanāṃta karma*)". This means that she finished the various rites of *sahagamana* up to the "worship of stone". Immediately after that, she set about climbing the funeral pyre of her deceased husband but exactly at that moment the Sahebs appeared to prevent her from self-immolation and carried her to the cantonment.

PROVISIONS OF LAW CODES RELATING TO THE SATI FAILURE CASE

As indicated earlier, one of the legal problems involved in this Sati failure case was whether or not a woman who failed to complete *sahagamana* could be purified of her sin by *prāyaścitta* (purificatory ritual). The woman did not stop *sahagamana* of her own free will, but the very fact that she could not complete the *sahagamana* was assumed to have made her a sinner.

The Brahman who wrote the letter to the Dharmādhikārī of Nasik knew that there was a provision in the law codes prescribing that a woman who fell down from *citta* (the normal state of mind), or in another reading, from *citi* (a funeral pyre), could be purified of her sin by performing the purificatory rite known as *prājāpatya*, provided that she had fallen when uncousious. The Sanskrit verses cited by the Brahman in his letter of inquiry are reproduced here with their English translation.

cittabhraṣṭā tu yā nārī mohad vicalitā bhavet | prājāpatyena śuddhyeta tasmād vai pāpakarmaṇaḥ || iti || citibhraṣṭeti vā pāṭhaḥ ||[5]

A woman, who fell down from *citta* (a normal state of mind) (*cittabhraṣṭā*), if she did so when unconscious, shall purify (herself) of the sinful deed by *prājāpatya*. There is also an alternative reading (in place of *cittabhraṣṭā*): a woman, who fell down from *citi* (a funeral pyre) (*citibhraṣṭā*).

This appears to be a provision of the *Āpastambasmṛti* (written ca. 600-900) quoted in the *Nirṇayasindhu*, one of the *dharmaśāstras* referred to in the letter of inquiry cited above, with an alternative reading of the first verse. The relevant portion of the *Nirṇayasindhu* reads as follows:

citibhraṣṭā tu yā nārī mohad vicalitā bhavet | prājāpatyena śuddhyeta tasmād vai pāpakarmaṇaḥ || (*Nirṇayasindhu*: 1054-5)

A woman, who fell down from a funeral pyre (*citibhraṣṭā*), if she did so when unconscious, shall purify (herself) of the sinful deed by *prājāpatya*.

It is apparent from this that *citibhraṣṭā* (falling down from a funeral pyre), not *cittabhraṣṭā* (falling down from a normal state of mind), is the correct reading. Thus, the provision of the *Āpastambasmṛti* quoted in the *Nirṇayasindhu* is, without doubt, a prescription for a woman who failed to complete *sahagamana*.

As mentioned earlier, the *Nirṇayasindhu* was written by Kamalākarabhaṭṭa in 1612. He was also a well-known *śāstrī* as was his grandfather, Nārāyaṇabhaṭṭa, the author of the *Antyeṣṭipaddhati*. The *Nirṇayasindhu* was popularly relied upon as an authoritative work for making legal decisions (*nirṇaya*) among the Brahmans of the Deccan. Thus, the Brahmans of Jalnapur also knew that the provison of the *Āpastambasmṛti* regarding a woman who failed to complete *sahagamana* was quoted in the *Nirṇayasindhu.*

The *Nārāyaṇabhaṭṭī* referred to in the letter of inquiry is, as indicated earlier, the *Antyeṣṭipaddhati* written by Nārāyaṇabhaṭṭa, in which the provision of the *Āpastambasmṛti* on a woman who failed to complete *sahagamana* is also quoted (Müller 1992: 207).[6]

Further, this same provision of the *Āpastambasmṛti* is quoted in the Aparārka's commentary on the *Yājñavalkyasmṛti* (citibhraṣṭā tu yā nārī mohad vicalitā tataḥ | prājāpatyena śudhyet tu tasmād vai pāpakarmaṇaḥ || Kane 1968-77: II 633, n. 1483). The text quoted by Aparārka is slightly different from the text in the *Nirṇayasindhu,* but the meaning is almost same. Aparārka was a minor king who reigned over part of the north Konkan along the Arabian Sea in the twelfth century (Kane 1968-77: I 713-23). Brahmans of the north Deccan must also have known the provision of the *Āpastambasmṛti* regarding a woman who failed to complete *sahagamana* through Aparārka's commentary on the *Yājña-valkyasmṛti.*

Thus, the custom of *sahagamana* appears to have been observed in the north Deccan in the eighteenth century, and Brahmans of this part of the country were well acquainted with the fact that the provision of the *Āpastambasmṛti* regarding a woman who failed to complete *sahagamana* was quoted in many medieval law codes and commentaries. This might mean that there were actually women who fell unconscious from the funeral pyre.

If the term "falling down from a funeral pyre" (*citibhraṣṭā*) is understood as a figurative expression meaning the failure to complete *sahagamana* in general, the above-mentioned provision of the *Āpastambasmṛti* could be applied to the woman whom the Englishmen prevented from completing *sahagamana.* The remaining problem was whether or not she was unconscious when she was "rescued" from self-immolation. There is no mention of this in the letter of inquiry, but from the reply of the Dharmādhikārī of Nasik, it appears that she was understood to have been absent-minded when she was "saved" from self-immolation by the Englishmen.

SAMSARGA DOṢA WITH CHRISTIANS

Another legal problem involved in this incident pertains to the purport of the P.S. as follows: "Up to this day, the woman has been observing the prescribed norms (*ācāranvita*). Her good conduct (*sadācaraṇa*) is unquestionable." In fact, what does this mean?

In Indian culture, the concept of sin continued to develop over time. A sinner who died without performing *prāyaścitta* to purify himself of his sin was assumed to wander around various hells, and then be reborn again and again as inferior creatures, and in the last stage as a man with handicaps (cf. *Yājñavalkyasmṛti*: III 206-10). Further, the sin of an unpurified sinner was assumed to have been transmitted to a man who had *saṃsarga* (social contact) with him. In medieval times, this idea of transmission or chain-transmission of sin through *saṃsarga* with an unpurified sinner was highly developed. Kane comments on the point as follows:

> [M]edieval writers gradually extended the scope of *saṃsarga* in a spirit of exclusiveness and of over-emphasis on ideas of ceremonial purity. For example, the Smṛtyarthasāra (p. 112) remarks that he who associates with a person who associates with a *mahāpātakin* has to undergo half the expiation that the first associator has to undergo. But that work does not go beyond this. The Mit[ākṣarā] (on Yāj[ñavalkyasmṛti] III. 261) appears to hold that the associator, even though he does not become patita, is liable to undergo expiation and that even 4th and 5th associators in a series are liable to undergo expiation though it is lesser and lesser. (Kane 1968-77: IV 27-8)

Further, in medieval times, *saṃsarga* with a man of different religion itself began to be looked upon as a sin. In the early part of the eighth century, the army of the Umayyads under Muḥammad bin al-Qasim invaded and occupied most parts of Sindhu. This widened the chance of social contact (*saṃsarga*) with Muslims, through which the idea that *saṃsarga* with Muslims was a sin began to develop. Kane points out: "The *Devalasmṛti* (written by 900) opens with a question by the sages put to Devala who was sitting on the banks of the Sindhu (Indus) at ease as to how brāhmaṇas and members of the other varṇas when carried off by Mlecchas were to be purified and restored to caste" (Kane

1968-77: II 389-90). *Mlecchas* in the *Devalasmṛti* meant, without doubt, Muslims. Thus, after the eighth century, law-code writers had to deal with the question of purification of a man who committed the sin of *saṃsarga* (*saṃsarga doṣa*) with a Muslim.

From the sixteenth century, when the Portuguese and then the English began to frequent India, *saṃsarga* with Christians was also looked upon as a sin along the line of the sin of *saṃsarga* with Muslims.

In this Sati failure case, the woman in question must have been assumed to have committed the sin of *saṃsarga* (*saṃsarga doṣa*) with Christians, merely because she was "rescued" from self-immolation by Englishmen and taken to the cantonment to live there. *Saṃsarga*, however, commonly meant *lagnavyavahāra* (relationship through marriage) and *annavyavahāra* (relationship through food and drink). In this Sati failure case, it is unlikely that the woman in question had a relationship of marriage with an Englishman, so that the relevant problem was over relationship through food and drink. To take the food and drink of infidels such as Christians was looked upon as the grave sin of taking forbidden food and drink. Thus, the P.S. of the letter of inquiry (Up to this day, the woman has been observing the prescribed norms; Her good conduct is unquestionable), meant that she did not take the food and drink of Englishmen, though she was living in the East India Company cantonment. There must have been Hindu families living there who served the English. She must have lived in such a Hindu home where she continued to observe the prescribed norms of her caste. People around her knew this and the Brahman writer of the letter of inquiry informed the Dharmādhikārī of this fact, as it made a great difference whether she merely lived in the cantonment, or took the food and drink of Englishmen. Generally speaking, a man who merely lived with infidels could be purified of his sin of *saṃsarga* with infidels by undergoing *prāyaścitta*, but it was difficult to purify a man of the sin of having taken the food and drink of infidels while living with them. Thus, the Brahman writer of the P.S. made it known to the Dharmādhikārī that so long as the sin of *saṃsarga* (*saṃsarga doṣa*) with Englishmen was concerned, she was not disqualified for purification by *prāyaścitta*. Therefore the only remaining legal problem concerning the woman was over the matter of whether a woman who failed to complete *sahagamana* could be purified of her sin by *prāyaścitta.*

PROVISIONS OF *DHARMAŚĀSTRAS* AND PRACTICES OF THE LEARNED (*ŚIṢṬĀCĀRA*)

Thus, the Brahman writer of the letter of inquiry knew well that various medieval law codes quoted the provision of the *Āpastambasmṛti* prescribing for a woman who failed to complete *sahagamana* to be purified of her sin by the purificatory rite of *prājāpatya,* and that the woman in question was observing the prescribed norm of her caste, even though she was living in the cantonment of the East India Company. In spite of this, he had doubts about the provision quoted in the medieval law codes, saying he himself had never seen or heard of such a thing as purifying a woman who failed to complete *sahagamana.* He must have been irritated by the fact that this Sati failure case was caused by the intervention of Englishmen. What he wished to say might be that he knew of no precedent relating to the purifying of a woman who had been "rescued" from self-immolation by infidels.

The Dharmādhikārī of Nasik sent the following reply to the inquiry (dated 2 October 1782) to the effect that the woman's readmission to the caste could not be approved:[7]

(The long greetings in Sanskrit are omitted.) You sent me a letter, the purpose of which is as follows: The woman, who had decided to do *sahagamana,* performed the rites (of *sahagamana*) beginning with *saṅkalpa* and ending with the worship of stone (*saṅkalpapūrvaka śilāpūjanāṃta vidhi*); Just at that time, the Sahebs prevented her from doing *sahagamana* and took her to the cantonment to make her live there; One month passed in this state. In the succeeding parts (of the letter), the order of the Sahebs (to purify her) and the provision of *śāstras* (regarding a woman who fell down from a funeral pyre) were written. Thus, intervention (in *sahagamana*) was done after she had performed *śilāpūjana.* From what I heard from the leading person among the learned (indicating the writer of the letter of inquiry), such a sort of thing as what was actually seen had never been experienced before (*śiṣṭamukhā pāsūn śrutvā pratyakṣa dṛṣṭa hā prakāra ananubhūta*). When the circumstances are examined from some angles in relation to the provision regarding a woman who fell down from a funeral pyre (*citibhraṣṭā vākya*), the woman in question had no idea in her mind of intentionally falling down from *citta* (a normal state of mind) (*cittabhraṣṭatva*), nor of intentionally falling down from a funeral pyre (*citibhraṣṭatva*). Therefore, her case does not deviate from the basic purport of the provision of the law codes (*graṃtādhāra yāhūn anyatar nāhīṃ*). Thus, there is the support (of law codes for purification of her sin). However, according to an axiom (*nyāya*) that "an act which does not lead (the performer) to heaven or an act which is not liked by people should not be done, even though the act would have been admitted as *dharma* (*asvargyaṃ lokavidviṣṭaṃ dharmyaṃ api ācāren na tu*)",[8] (*satī*)*parigraha* (acceptance of a chaste woman) cannot be agreed for the sake of showing that there does not exist the practices of the learned on this issue (*śiṣṭācāra abhāva nidarśane karūn*). (ASS I 202)

The Dharmādhikārī of Nasik admitted that the provision of law codes regarding a woman who fell down from a funeral pyre could be applied to the widowed wife of the Deshpande of Jalnapur. He understood the term "falling down from a funeral pyre (*citibhraṣṭā*)" as a figurative expression meaning the failure to complete *sahagamana* in general, and further he acknowledged that the woman in question was unconscious when she was "rescued" from self-immolation. In spite of this, he replied to the Brahman of Jalnapur that he could not agree with purification of her sin. He based his judgement on an axiom (*nyāya*) that "an act which does not lead (the performer) to heaven or an act which is not liked by people should not be done, even though the act would have been admitted as *dharma* (*asvargyaṃ lokavidviṣṭaṃ dharmyaṃ api ācāren na tu*)". This Sanskrit verse is the latter half of the following provision of the *Yājñavalkyasmṛti* in the *Mitākṣarā* I 155:

karmaṇā manasā vācā yatnāddharmaṃ samācaret | asvargyaṃ lokavidviṣṭaṃ dharmyaṃ api ācāren na tu ||[9]

By actions, the mind and words, diligently do *dharma*. But an act which does not lead (the performer) to heaven or an act which is not liked by people should not be done, even though the act would have been admitted as *dharma*. (The author's tentative translation)

Thus, the Dharmādhikārī judged either that the woman who fell down from the funeral pyre (failed to complete *sahagamana*) could no longer be led to heaven (*svarga*), even though her sin be purified by *prājāpatya*; or, alternatively, that the readmission to her caste of the woman who fell down from the funeral pyre was not liked by people. In either case, he did not agree with the purification and readmission of the woman to her caste. Further, he judged that the practices of the learned (*śiṣṭācāra*) on this issue not yet having been established, the provision of *śāstras* regarding a woman who fell from a funeral pyre should be suspended from enforcement.[10]

Though the Dharmādhikārī admitted that the provision of law codes regarding the purification of a woman who fell from a funeral pyre was applicable to the woman in question, he must have been reluctant to agree to her purification. In this state of mind, he remembered there was a relevant provision in the *Yājñavalkyasmṛti* (*Mitākṣarā*) that "an act which does not lead (the performer) to heaven or an act which is not liked by people should not be done, even though the act would have been admitted as *dharma*". To the Dharmādhikārī, this provision appeared to provide suitable grounds for disagreeing with the performance of *prāyaścitta* on the woman in question.

The Dharmādhikārī's state of mind must have been influenced by the circumstance that the woman in question was "rescued" from self-immolation by the Englishmen, exactly when she set about climbing the funeral pyre of her husband. This point aroused in the mind of the Dharmādhikārī a feeling either of reluctance or disgust about the performance of *prāyaścitta* on her so as to readmit her to her caste. That men of India, particularly the so-called Sanatanists, became bigoted whenever Englishmen intervened in the practice of Sati was amply experienced later in the nineteenth century under British colonial rule. The Dharmādhikārī as well as the Brahman writer of the letter of inquiry might have had a similar mentality as that of Sanatanists in the nineteenth century.

CONCLUSION

Thus, this Sati failure case included two legal problems: first, whether or not a woman who had failed to become a Sati could be purified of her sin by *prāyaścitta*, and second, whether or not *saṃsarga doṣa* (the sin of social contact) with Christians could be purified by *prāyaścitta.* While judging these legal problems, the Dharmādhikārī of Nasik did not observe the provisions of *dharmaśāstras* verbatim. He knew of provisions in the *dharmaśāstras* to the effect that even an act which had long been observed as *dharma* should not be done in changed social conditions.[11] He followed this normative principle of brahmanical jurisprudence in disagreeing with the performance of *prāyaścitta* on the woman. He must have thought that the appearance of Englishmen in the Indian sub-continent changed the social conditions hitherto prevalent, and therefore that the provision of the *Āpastambasmṛti* regarding a woman who fell down from a funeral pyre had to be suspended from enforcement.

It is another matter that his judgement following the normative principle of brahmanical jurisprudence must have caused hardship in the life of the woman in question. She must have been ex-communicated from her caste for the remainder of her life.

NOTES

1. While preparing this paper, I have been greatly helped by Dr. Yasuke Ikari (Professor Emeritus of the Kyoto University), the outstanding Indologist of Japan, in reading the Sanskrit texts such as the *Nirṇayasindhu* and the medieval Marathi documents mixed with Sanskrit verses.
2. Dharmādhikārī (*dharma+adhikārī*) meaning law-officer, however, was not an officer of a state (government). He was a hereditary law-officer in the local society independent of a state, whose office was a *vatan,* that is, a hereditary patrimonial right in combination of the office and perquisites therefrom. Dharmādhikārī existed in such sacred places as Nasik and Kolhapur (Karvir) and big cities like Pune. He was the representative of all the Brahmans of such places belonging to various castes and brahmanical schools. His main duty was the performance of the purificatory rituals known collectively as *prāyaścitta* on persons (sinners) who wished to be purified of their sins (in medieval Marathi, *doṣa*). See, for more details, Kotani 2002: Chapters 9 and 10.
3. In transliterating the long greetings in Sanskrit at the beginning of the letter of inquiry, I have been helped by Dr. Shingo Einoo. The character in < > is omitted from the printed text and the character(s) before > in the printed text should be replaced by character(s) after >.

4. The printed text of the last two verses of the *Nirṇayasindhu* goes without break as follows:

   pṛthakśilenakuruvītadadyādekaśiletathā

   The Hindi translation of this portion reads: "pṛthak śilāke ūpar na karai kintu ekahi śilāpai karai", rendering the Sanskrit text as follows: "pṛthak śile na kuruvīta | dadyād ekaśile tathā". My translation is based on the following reading of the Sanskrit text by Dr. Yasuke Ikari: "pṛthak śilena kuruvīta | dadyād ekaśile tathā".
5. The printed text of the Sanskrit verses cited by the Brahman of Jalnapur in his letter of inquiry to the Dharmādhikārī of Nasik is slightly corrupted as follows:

   cittabhraṣṭā tu yā nāri mohādvicalitā bhavet || prājāpatyena śudhyeta tasmād vai pāpakarmaṇa iti || cittibhraṣṭeti vā pāṭhaḥ ||

   I have made a necessary correction of the corrupted portions of this printed text.
6. The *Dinakaradyota* referred to in the letter of inquiry of the Brahman of Jalnapur is, in fact, the *Dinakarodyota* written by Dinakara, an elder brother of Kamalākarabhaṭṭa, the author of the *Nirṇayasindhu.* (Kane 1968-77: I 1045; Sardesai 1946: 209). Thus, three of four law codes mentioned in the letter of inquiry are works written by members of the Bhaṭṭa family whose ancestor migrated to Varanasi from Paithan in the fifteenth century. Further, Gāgabhaṭṭa, who performed the *rājasūya* (coronation) on Shivaji in 1674, is a son of Dinakara (Kane 1968-77: I 906, n. 1365; Sardesai 1946: 209-10). Thus, the Bhaṭṭa family continued to have close relationships with people of the Deccan even after their migration to Varanasi, and therefore, their works were well known among the Brahmans of the Deccan. The family tree of the Bhaṭṭas is shown in Kane 1968-77: I 906.
7. This reply of the Dharmādhikārī is written in Marathi mixed with Sanskrit terms and verses. Besides, the printed text of this letter of reply contains many corrupted or questionable portions as well. I have corrected them as far as possible.
8. The printed text of this axiom (*nyāya*) in the letter of reply of the Dharmādhikārī is very badly corrupted as follows:

   asvargya lokavidhi (dvi) ṣṭhaṃ dhamamapyācaret tv iti |

   Dr. Y. Ikari deciphered this corrupted text as the verse of the *Yājñavalkyasmṛti* in *Mitākṣarā* I 155 and helped me in making an extensive correction of the corrupted portions.
9. A provision of similar purport can be found in the *Manusmṛti* IV 176.

   parityajedarthakāmau yau syātāṃ dharmavarjitau | dharmaṃ ca api asukhodarkaṃ lokasaṃkruṣṭam eva ca ||

Let him avoid (the acquisition of) wealth and (the gratification of his) desires, if they are opposed to the sacred law, and even lawful acts which may cause pain in the future or are offensive to men. (Bühler's translation)

The *Viṣṇupurāṇa* (III. 11. 7) also states as follows:

parityajedarthakāmau dharmapīḍākarau nṛpa | dharmam api asukhodarkaṃ lokavidviṣṭaṃ eva ca ||

Let him (prince) avoid wealth and desire, if they give uneasiness to virtue; and abstain from virtuous or religious acts if they involve misery or are censured by the world. (*Viṣṇupurāṇa*: 258)

10. As regards more general problems of the relationships between provisions of law codes and the practices of the learned, see Kane1968-77: III Chapter XXXIII Customs and Dharmaśāstra Works.
11. Kane points out as follows:

The above discussion illustrates how practices once recognized by Vedic passages and by the people gradually fell into disuetude [correctly, desuetude—the author] and how reason and the common sense of ordinary people asserted themselves even against Vedic and smṛti texts. The Mit[ākṣarā] is very clear in its statement that whatever comes to be hated by the people in general should not be practised, even though it was once practised and has the support and authority of Vedic and smṛti texts behind it. Those who desire change in social customs and the practices of the people in various directions rely on this text of Yāj[ñavalkyasmṛti] and on similar texts of Manu IV.176 and Viṣṇu Dh[arma] S[mṛti] 71, 85 and on the Mit[ākṣarā] for authority. (Kane 1968-77: III 630)

REFERENCES

MARATHI SOURCE BOOK (Abbreviation)

ASS: Bhārat Itihās Saṃśodak Maṇḍal ed., *Aitihāsik Saṃkīrṇa Sāhitya,* 13 vols., Puṇeṃ, 1934-67.

SANSKRIT WORKS

Manusmṛti: Manusmṛti with the Manubhāṣya of Medhātithi, ed. G. Jha, 2 vols., Delhi: Parimal Publications, 1992.

Nirṇayasindhu: Nirṇayasindhu of Kamalākarabhaṭṭa, ed. with Hindi translation by Vrajaratna Bhattacharya, Varanasi: Chaukhamba Vidyabhavan, 1991.

Viṣṇupurāṇa: The *Viṣṇupurāṇam*, Sanskrit text and English translation by H.H. Wilson, Delhi: Parimal Publications, 2002.

Yājñavalkyasmṛti: *Yājñavalkyasmṛti by Yogīśvara Yājñavalkya with the Mitākṣarā commentary of Vijñāneśvara*, ed. with the Prakasa Hindi commentary by Umesacandra Pandeya, 5th edn., Varanasi: Chaukhambha Sanskrit Sansthan, 1994.

Antyeṣṭipaddhati: Klaus-Werner Müller, *Das Brahmanische Totenritual nach der Antyeṣṭipaddhati des Nārāyaṇabhaṭṭa*, Stuttgart, 1992. (German translation of the *Antyeṣṭipaddhati* with explanatory notes.)

English Works

The Laws of Manu: English translation of the *Manusmṛti* by G. Bühler, Sacred Books of the East, vol. 25, Oxford: Oxford University Press, 1886.

Aitchison, C.U., ed., 1931: *A Collection of Treaties, Engagements and Sanads relating to India and Neighbouring Countries*, 14 vols. Calcutta: Government of India General Publication Branch.

Kane, P.V., 1968-77: *History of Dharmaśāstra*, 5 vols., 2nd edn. Poona: Bhandarkar Oriental Research Institute (original edn., 1930-62).

Kotani, H., 2002: *Western India in Historical Transition: Seventeenth to Early Twentieth Centuries*. New Delhi: Manohar.

Sardesai, G.S., 1946: *New History of the Marathas*, vol. I. Bombay: Phoenix Publications.

7

Mārgī, *Deśī* and *Yāvanī*: High Language and Ethnic Speech in Maharashtra

SUMIT GUHA

INTRODUCTION

The analysis of speech variation should form an integral part of the study of South Asian civilization. (Gumperz, 1961)[1]

In 1996, Jan Houben edited an important collection of essays on the historical status of Sanskrit up to the thirteenth century C.E.[2] An essay by Ashok Aklujkar pointed to an important feature of the socio-linguistic history of Sanskrit: that it has, until recently, "served as a frame for positioning other Indian languages, current as well as classical, and has regained prominence in India, probably several times, after receiving setbacks".[3] The present paper will consider an episode in that long history. It focuses on how an emerging Indic vernacular 'Marathi' that had hitherto oriented itself to Sanskrit developed from the fourteenth to the eighteenth centuries. This was period when Marathi-speakers were still attracted to the long-standing cultural power of Sanskrit, but also impacted by the heavily Arabized Persian and Dakhni that dominated administration and urban life. An examination of the socio-linguistic impact of these divergent forces is (I feel) important in order to understand how speech communities and identities interacted in the long centuries before modern institutions of governance brought language and script to the center of the political stage in India and elsewhere.

Linguistic anthropologists have, since at least the 1950s, been exploring the verbal micro interactions that aggregate up to the big and seemingly "natural" entities we call ethnicities, castes, tribes or nationalities. They have also investigated the processes by which minority languages and dialects have for long periods of time resisted the attritional processes of modern media and education. John Gumperz was a leader in this field, and it is hardly surprising that much of his early research focused on India, a stably multilingual country where linguistic coexistence has created innumerable polyglots. In 1982, Gumperz summed up decades of work on these issues:

> Language differences play an important role in signalling information as well as in creating and maintaining the subtle boundaries of power, status, role and occupational specialization that make up the fabric of our social life. Assumptions about value differences associated with these boundaries in fact form the very basis for the indirect communicative strategies employed in key gatekeeping encounters . . . which have come to be crucial in determining the quality of an individual's life. . . .[4]

It must be evident that this holds even more strongly for the past, before the current availability of personal data in written (files, dossiers, resumes), electronic (database holdings, governmental and corporate) and impersonal graphic (surveillance videotapes, webcams, etc.) forms. Before the eighteenth-century, on the other hand, the audible, visual and perhaps olfactory presence of individuals provided most of the information that pre-structured their social reception. Classifications of language and genre were themselves historically shaped and reshaped. Sheldon Pollock recently pointed to the historicity of "boundaries of languages, cultures, societies, and polities that were created after the fact and in some cases very recently—boundaries that literary and linguistic processes in large part helped to create have been taken as the condition of emergence and understanding of these processes themselves".[5]

The closing centuries of the first millennium C.E. witnessed the emergence of local languages into the epigraphic record of South Asia, even as Sanskrit continued to remain prominent as a language of high culture and statecraft from the Hindukush to the Java Sea. A decade ago, this period was magisterially surveyed by Pollock, who described a 'Sanskrit cosmopolis' extending well beyond the frontiers of South Asia. Yet as he points out, it was not associated with any imperial power elite or trading diaspora. Even in its heartland of northern India, he argues that it did not function as a language of the chancery, of practical imperium. By the later fourth century C.E., he argues, "Prakrit continues here to execute documentary functions, Sanskrit has emerged from its sacral domain with a very different kind of public work to do." So for example, in a Pallava inscription of the sixth century, Prakrit records the everyday—boundaries, rights, duties, etc.[6]

Such a division continued even as regional languages such as Kannada, Telugu and Marathi emerged. In 1050 C.E., the Brahmans of Dive in coastal Maharashtra, deposited the copper-plate title deeds to their tax-free village as security for a loan. The mortgagee, also a Brahman, acknowledged this transaction in a copper-plate written in recognizable Marathi. As the mortgagee was titled "one learned in the six branches" but wrote the receipt in Marathi, we may assume that the mortgagor Brahmans did not know Sanskrit, and likely harbored a justifiable suspicion of documents that they could not read.[7] Meanwhile, scholarly literati began composing important Marathi texts by that time, a process that accelerated in the next century, under the Yādavas of Devagiri (modern Daulatābād).

POLITICAL CHANGE AND LINGUISTIC SEPARATION

By the first quarter of the fourteenth century the Kākatīya of Warangal and Yādava of Devagiri were swept away by the Sultans of Delhi, who briefly unified almost the entire sub-continent under their rule. Persian and Turkish were established in north-western India by the twelfth century. Refugees from greater Iran flooded into India in the thirteenth century, as urban centers throughout the Eastern Islamic world reeled under the impact of steppe peoples like the Oghuz Turks and the Mongols. Furthermore, the immigration of Persianized Sufi holy men was patronized by the new regimes which saw their settlement as a legitimizing force.

In addition, we should also bear in mind that great poets like Amir Khusro and *Ma'sud Sa'd Salman* existed alongside a much more numerous body of humbler Persianized literati whose training qualified them for little more than clerical employment around the courts and camps of the new rulers. It is likely that they would quickly seek to establish control over the slowly expanding chanceries of the emerging sultanates of northern and southern India. A model for this process may be found in the well-documented study of the Kāyasths of Hyderabad by Karen Leonard. She finds that there was no indication that senior officials of former Qutb Shahi secretariat passed into Mughal service after the conquest of 1687. As the breach between the Nizam of Hyderabad and the Delhi court widened, three enterprising family founders quickly took control over important offices and recruited dependents, often as sons-in-law, from north India.[8]

Specialized or insufficiently lucrative state functions might be contracted out to local functionaries who only occasionally appear in the surviving historical record. Thus only that fact of his writing a treatise on coinage has allowed us to discover that the Khalji mint was operated by a Jain, the Thākkura Pheru.[9] The tax revenues of entire provinces were farmed out: Ibn Battuta tells us that a Hindu merchant farmed the entire tax revenue of the old Yādava kingdom under Muhammad bin Tughlaq.[10] If this was a widespread practice, then the Persian-speaking elite needed little contact with commoners.

Thus I suggest that a working arrangement soon crystallized, by which high prestige and public functions were controlled by a Persianate elite, which dealt with outsiders through the emerging camp dialects such as Urdu and Dakhni. This select body of officials would soon form a "caste-like" body, endowed with special skills and practices and recruited by patronage and co-option. This elite would use Dakhni with outsiders and inferiors and Persian for government business purposes. This would create a linguistic situation that Gumperz has described:

> one where networks of relationships reflect long term, interpersonal cooperation in the performance of regular tasks and the pursuit of shared goals, they favor the creation of behavioral routines and

communicative conventions that become conventionally associated with and serve to mark component activities. Many of the special argots, trade languages, caste dialects and other special parlances cited in the sociolinguistic literature have survived pressures for assimilation precisely because of their function in marking institutionalized activities and craft skills whose practitioners all came from similar home and ethnic backgrounds.[11]

People whose business obliged them to deal with government functionaries probably developed a rough and ready bilingualism on the pattern observed by Della Valle in Khambāyat in 1623.

> Indians who talked with us and made themselves understood in Portuguese or Persian, being all factors or merchants, and therefore unlearned, could not give us an account of these things [whether Mahāvīra and Mahādeva were the same deity]. Moreover, they speak these languages badly and save for buying and selling, are not very intelligible. We could not, for lack of the languages discourse with other learned gentiles, who were familiar only with their Indian tongue.[12]

The earliest impact was clearly felt by the old high language of ceremony and government: Sanskrit. The number of Sanskrit inscriptions in the core areas of the Delhi-Agra and Bahmani sultanates fell, while Arabic and Persian inscriptions appeared in unprecedented numbers. The number of Arabic and Persian inscriptions then increased until the seventeenth century. On the other hand, bilingual inscriptions were limited. A few Sanskrit-Persian records from Gujarat and a handful of post-1500 Marathi-Persian and Gujarati-Persian records can be found in Bendrey's compendium.[13]

The kingdoms of southern India that preceded the southern incursion of the Delhi sultans pioneered the development of their regional vernaculars into literary tongues. The regional sultanates of southern India similarly supported the development of the new vernacular: Urdu or Dakhni. Holy men began to use this emerging *lingua franca* to render religious discourse accessible to the common folk.[14] Ibrāhim Ādilshāh II of Bijapur (r. 1580-1627) actually composed a set of songs in this language.[15] The early modern era was also a period of commercialization as the opening of the sea-route from Europe impacted the coasts of the Indian Ocean.

RETURN TO THE VERNACULARS

An important phase of linguistic change began when the Nizamshahi and Adilshahi sultanates pioneered the administrative use of local vernaculars. The earliest surviving examples date no earlier than the first decades of the sixteenth century. I suggest that their appearance signals the effort by central authority to penetrate more deeply into local society and correspondingly, perhaps the greater interest of at least the local elites in knowing about and communicating with the state. S.A.I. Tirmizi mentions a similar practice from the contemporary Lodi and Sur sultanates of northern India, citing an order of Sikandar Lodi from 1519. "The document is written in *tāliq* with transliteration in *Kaithi* script. This Afghan practice of biscriptual documents continued under Sher Shah and is discernible in some documents of the early part of the reign of Akbar."[16] Let us visualize the social logic of the "biscriptual" situation. There clearly existed a class of functionaries, whether *zamīndārs* or *kārkuns*, who were literate in their own specialized script.[17] They did not read Persian but had frequently heard the stereotyped Persian of official writing. They could therefore grasp the import of a written order provided it was in a script they knew. Hence, as rulers drew more deeply on local resources and information, it was necessary to generate these *Kaithi* documents. We may then ask why Persian was retained and indeed given pride of place at the head of the document? It seems likely that this was because its retention symbolized the cultural and political dominance of the ruling elite—a sentiment echoed in Hyderabad by its powerful premier, Sir Salar Jung in the nineteenth century. When a north Indian official proposed replacing Persian with Urdu in the Nizam's administration, Salar Jang exploded:

> You Hindustani [northern Indian] people have little practice in Persian speech and writing. Persian language is the symbol of the victory of the Muslims. We have conquered this land with the sword. Having destroyed this symbol in your own country [north India] you people want darkness here too.[18]

Southern India took a further step towards a higher degree of polyglossia. But these early texts, however, signal the hold that

Persian had acquired in the central administration. The "translations" are close to being transcriptions from Persian into Marathi. Consider an early bilingual Adilshahi *farmān* from 1540. The Persian runs:

Kārkunān pargane Terdal m'alum dānad ke harchah zamīn yak Chāvar dar savād kasbeh mazkūr kird bandeh Lakkodi va Pirand az kasbah va karyāt. . . .

The Marathi version is:

Da [space][19] *Kārkunāni paa [pargane] Terdal mālum dānad hāci zamīn cāvar 1 yak dar savād kasbe ma[jkur] kirdi bande Lakod va Piran kasbe va karyāti*. . . .

The ceremonial portions at the beginning of the "Marathi" text are direct transcriptions from Persian, preserving the prepositions, the Persian plural forms, etc. The common nouns (excepting, perhaps, the land-measure *cāhur*) are all Persian. Other than the Modi script, the only features that enable us to identify the target language as Marathi are the 50th, 51st and 52nd words *cālile āhe taiseci*, followed by the 61st *āhe* again and the 64th *kīje*. The letter has a total of 73 words; as may be seen Marathi is only represented by three verbs, one adverb and possibly a noun.[20]

Another example is the longer "Marathi" letter from deputy minister Malik Sarq [*sic*] granting Babuji Mudgal certain offices in Nalgonda region.

D [space] Phurmān Humāiyunu sharfe niphād yāpht bajānib Malik Sark Khoj nyamātul naib gaibat va kārkunani hāl va istakbāl kile Syādurg va mokadmāni va reyā va barayā kasbe va karyāti va mujāfati kile majkūr a ki marhāmati Alampanha. . . .

The first recognizable Marathi word is the gerund *karuhūn/karūn* used twice, and then the stative verb *āse*. Only after the towns and villages affected have been listed do we find a significant infusion of Marathi, as we come to the functionally important part of the order. This directs local gentry and officials to attend on and submit to the new hereditary officer and cooperate with him. Even here, the pattern previously noted is maintained: Marathi words are almost all verbs and possessive pronouns.[21] As I have suggested in the context of the northern biscriptual texts, it seems likely that the target audience would be minor officials or gentry, persons who frequented the Court, the *thāna* and the *kacehri*, and thus acquired a considerable familiarity with the terminology of Persian administrative practice. This would be all the easier because important people (though literate), usually had documents read to them and then dictated responses. (The practice also enabled a court official to maintain a record of the transactions and orders given—a *rojkird* or *rojnishi*.)

So it would seem that at some point around the end of the fifteenth century, the sultanates increased the involvement of vernacular elites in state functions. This made it necessary for the Persianate elite to unbend and communicate with them, even if in highly Persianized forms of the current vernaculars. We may connect this with the break-up of the Bahmani sultanate into five regional kingdoms, all of which were initially threatened by the southern kingdom of Vijayanagara, and then slowly subverted by the power of the Mughals. So states needed to draw more intensively and regularly on local fiscal and military resources. This meant more frequent and intensive communication with autochthonous gentry and intermediary literati. It is also possible that Portuguese harassment at sea reduced the supply of the West Asian immigrants who had staffed the upper echelons of the sultanates in the fourteenth and fifteenth centuries, and this also increased these regimes' dependence on local gentry and officials. These connections would also bring ambitious and quarrelsome sprigs of the gentry to the courts and the camps of the rival sultans and Mughal viceroys and commanders.[22] Finally, Malik Ambar, the Ethiopian slave who rose to be regent of the Ahmednagar sultanate is usually credited with successfully using Maratha light cavalry to harass and defeat his better equipped enemies, both Mughal and Dakhni. Thus a range of opportunities encouraged linguistic mixing, at least at the functional level described by Della Valle.

That the local horses and their riders had previously been viewed with some contempt by Persianate men-at-arms is reflected in the name *bār-gīr* (literally, load-bearer, i.e. inferior servant) that continued to be applied to them. The name was then unselfconsciously adopted by these troopers: incidental evidence of their ignorance of Persian. The higher status *silahdār* (man-at-arms) came to mean a free-lance who owned his horse and weapons.

As *watandārs* and aspirants to *watan* began to flock to the courts, the various royal and viceregal courts would need more clerks and officials competent in local languages and (at least) able to follow the established terminology of their respective chancelleries. We may assume that many of those who made the effort needed to become literate were or hoped to be, employed in some capacity by the state. The linguistic flexibility thus acquired would carry over into other fields. It might also become a mark of social distinction via what linguists have termed "prestige imitation". All this would ultimately flow into popular speech. Thus devotee-poet Eknath's *guru*, Janardana (1504-75) was employed by a Muslim fort commandant under the Nizamshahi sultanate in the early sixteenth century. Eknath (1533-99) was clearly educated for state employment, though he did not choose that career. He composed a number of poems that essentially play on the officialese of his early years to present an elaborate metaphor for the frail and corrupt body inhabited by the wise but feeble soul. The titles of these works reflect their parodic origins: *Arzdast* (petition), *Tākidpatra* (stern admonition), *Jābcithi* (in this context, distraint-letter), *Kaul* (agreement, assurance) and others. I translate a *Jābcithi* below:

(To) Jivājīpant [wise soul] endowed with all capacities: tax arrears were found due from you and so you were sent to Body-ville. While in Body-ville you were misled by the ideas of the Merchant Dissipation and Chieftain Greed. Therefore the Banker Desire and Count Jewel-lover joined you and ruined your property. Village Headman Intellect separated himself (from you) and began to say "Ear-valley and Mouth-city are important places—hearing (pious words) and singing religious songs are their autumn (*kharīf*) and spring (*rabi*) harvests. But Mother Covetousness has prevented access to them. This needs to be resolved." Close to the Master is Bhagavat [purana] rao, the finance minister, son of the Lady [Bhagvad] Gita—an intermediary to approach him needs to be found. He is in the hands of the Lord Detachment. First (we must) approach the Pandit Remorse: he is under our control. He will take charge of your speech. Then you can go to Bhagavatrao, the minister.

He will free you. After that you will not return to Body-ville or Womb-town again. You were warned that you would soon suffer confiscation of property (*talaph*) by Yamaji Pant (Death); his confiscations are never returned. This Edict (*sanad*) is from the Presence (*Hujūr*). Therefore do as you are commanded. Not otherwise. The only shelter is Janardana (Krishna, also Eknath's *guru*). With this blessing, the Distraint-letter.[23]

Eknath was immensely popular in Maharashtra: if we grant that it is unlikely that he would compose poems that were wholly incomprehensible to his audience, it follows that many ordinary folk could catch the parodic allusions that structure these poems. That would, in turn, demonstrate a widespread acquaintance with official terminology and genre in sixteenth-century Maharashtra. Indeed, such songs might well have led many rustics and women to seek the meanings of the official terms used, and perhaps ultimately incorporate them into their own speech. The poem also alludes realistically to the fact that powerful people could not be directly approached: one had to find a suitable intermediaries. Such men would be functionally multilingual and might signal their closeness to power by liberally sprinkling their speech with loan-words from the language of the powerful.

LINGUISTIC IDENTITY AND DIFFERENCE

The high languages nonetheless seem to have maintained separate traditions to at least the end of the sixteenth century. Akbar was keenly interested in having Persian renditions of important Sanskrit texts. But, as A.A. Rizvi has established, these translations were via the intermediate medium of Hindi. Rizvi quotes the concluding passage from the *Mahabharata* translation titled the *Razm-nama.* "Some Brahmans . . . read the book and explained it to this sinful author in Hindi, and the author wrote it down in Persian."[24] But as Gumperz pointed out, linguistic codes are also identity markers. The constant presence of new immigrant speakers of Persian (and sometimes Arabic) would reinforce the foreignness of their languages and scripts. A devotee of the *bhakta* saint Tukaram wrote a stylized lament of the state of things prevailing in the current Dark Age (*kaliyuga*).

Alongside the upsetting of social mores of appropriate familial behavior, the poet complains that people were too proud to salute the servants of Hari, but that they worshiped even the slippers of *mlecchas* in order to fill their stomachs. Such devotion also corrupted their speech: even Brahmans taking up the betel-leaf bundle (he continued), begin to use *avindhavāṇī*.[25]

The trend continued, and Sanskrit literati even began to cultivate a range of vernaculars. In the early 1650s, Jayarama Pindye, polylingual poet from Maharashtra composed the *Rādhāmādhavavilāsa campu*. The core of this text is in Sanskrit, as are the opening cantos. But the poet's real claim to distinction was his ability to versify (he claims, extempore) in twelve languages. One of these was Persian, which he simply calls *Yāvanī*, i.e. Muslim; another is *Dākṣiṇātya* (southern) *Yāvanī*, which is clearly Dakhni. A variety of Urdu, or Hindustani, written in what seems to be a feminine voice appears under the name "Rekhtā". All this is occurring, we must remember, at the court of a Maratha ruler moving to establish a dominion in the Andhra-Karnataka-Tamil Nadu tri-junction. Elements of language-identity are found in this work. An important noble, for example, calls on the poet to compose in Marathi *thor he bhāṣā āprā*, noble is this our language.[26]

A multi-lingual milieu generates a new awareness of language identity. But important people needed to communicate in various languages, and were usually accompanied by specialists in these. Thus when Shivaji was imprisoned after coming to the Mughal court in 1666, he sent most of his followers back but retained a Sanskrit poet and a Saksena Kāyastha even during his imprisonment.[27] Thus he would be in a position to communicate formally in both the prestige languages of the subcontinent.[28] Shivaji himself seems to have consciously deployed language as an instrument in state-building. In 1674, he was formally anointed as *Chatrapati* or sovereign monarch, and introduced a marked change in official titles and epistolary styles. The two letters below will illustrate the change. I have emboldened Persian terms in both texts. Both are official order concerning Brahmans: the first reassures those living in Trimbak (Nasik) that they would not be harassed by the Maratha armies; the second is an order addressed to one of his commanders (but likely given to the beneficiary) telling him not to cause any trouble to the Brahmans during military operations.

1670-1671

kaulnāma aj rakhtkhāne Rājśrī Shivājīrāje Sāheb dāmdaulat-hu taa[amām] bhaṭāni va samast bhikshuk bhaṭāni Tri[bak] kaa[asbe] Tribak suhur san ihide sabain alaph . . . Tumhi sukhe rahane kone goṣṭicā śak na dharne daribāb kaul āse mortab sud

1674

Svastiśrī Rājyabhiṣeka Śak [1596] Ānandanāma saṃvatsare Āśāḍh śudh pratipada Saumyavasar Kṣatriyakulavataṃsa Śrīrāja Śivachatrapati yāni Rājmānya Rājśrī Cāndjī Kaḍam yānsi ājñā kelī yesije. . . tumhi ***svārisikārimule*** *yetānjatā Bhatgosāviyās upsarga dyāl tari yekandar na deṇe . . . koṇhivisi upasarg na deṇe. Jānije [seal] bahut kāy lihiṇe.*
suru sud bar

The second letter is also noteworthy in the amount of Sanskrit *tatsama* introduced into the Marathi text. The change in vocabulary is obvious, though we may notice that the officials of the secretariat still used their old Persian abbreviated endorsements at the foot of the document. Changing the stereotyped terminology and structure of official correspondence may have proved difficult and inefficient. This is suggested by letters in which old Persianate terms slip back in the later portions of the text, when (we may presume) dictation was in full flow, and the speaker focused on substantive matters. Thus safe-conducts were usually termed *kaul*; after the coronation the new term was *abhayapatra*. In a letter written in his third regnal year, Shivaji sought to reassure a hereditary official who had gone over to the Mughals, and induce him to return. It opens in a highly Sanskritized form: it is likely that these standard headings were inserted by a clerk, and the monarch only dictated the substantive part of the message. If so, the concluding portion shows how hard it was to shake established forms of speech, with several Persian terms cropping up, unselfconsciously indigenized with Marathi suffixes.

Svastiśrī Rājyabhiṣeka Śake 3 Nala Saṃvatsara Māgh vadi Aṣṭami, Guruvāsre Kṣatriyakulavataṃsa Śrīrājā Śivachatrapati yāni Rājśrī Bābājī Rām deśkulkarṇi ***paa[rgana]*** *Puṇa yānsi dilhe abhayapatra yaiseje. . . .*

tumcā haklawājima va ināmat vagaire amānat *kele hote te tumce* ***dubāle*** *kele āse varkad* ***mirāsadārāpramāṇe*** *tumcehi cālau* ***mukāsāhevisi*** *kāhi* ***andeshā*** *na karṇe* ***kaul*** *āse jānije lekhansīmā.*[29]

Long usage was clearly difficult to overcome. Thus a letter of the fifth regnal year (C.E. 1679) opens with the "reformed" regnal year and date, but is addressed to Tuk Parbhu the *mazamdar*, even though that title should have been replaced by *amātya.*[30] Once again, the substance of the message introduces the Persianate officialese and abbreviations: *ni*[*sbat*], *bāki, bābat, vajai, hujūr, badal,* etc. Tuk Parbhu's clerks had not changed their dating practices: they endorsed the letter "received (day) 7 (month) Muharram (*pau*[*paivasti*] 7 *maharama*)".[31]

Shivaji's oldest son, Sambhaji briefly defected to the Mughals in 1679 before returning to the fold. He won a contested succession the following year, imprisoned the younger brother who had been raised against him, executed some conspirators and perhaps felt the need for a stronger assertion of legitimacy. Shortly after his accession, he issued an elaborate grant-deed on the occasion of his pilgrimage to the family shrine at Śikhara Śingnāpur. His knowledge of Sanskrit was exhibited at the beginning of the document "Know that by me, Śrī Śambhurāja Chatrapati son of Śrī Śivarāj this is written at the top." The document is dated in the seventh year after Shivaji's coronation. Sambhaji's decision to make the grant is written out in a form comprehensible only to the very learned. But these forms were clearly thought to be still unfamiliar to less accomplished officials. Beneath the Sanskrit endorsement by the minister Raghunatha Narayana come the notations of the record office. "11th day of the moon month Bhādrapad—*urf* (is known as) Sabān, Year *ihide samānin alaph* (Arabic: Eleven hundred eighty one, i.e. 1181 or C.E. 1680)."[32] Four Sanskrit grants made by Sambhaji's younger brother, and successor, Rajaram (1689-1700) have been printed. All of them are grants to Brahmans, and are shorter and less elaborate than the self-exculpatory one just cited.[33]

MARATHI LANGUAGE AND MARATHA POLITICS

On the other hand, the Marathi language was tenaciously retained, even though Persian was, at the time, the major language of diplomacy in South and West Asia. Unlike the Mughal official abandonment of Turkish after Babur, the Marathi language, much changed by loan-words, was retained. This occurred though the Peśvās and other leading Maratha dynasts pursued a policy aimed at a protectorate over remnants of the Mughal empire in north India. It is significant therefore, that unlike the Sanskrit *Śivabhārata/Śivacarita* composed under the patronage of the first *Chatrapati*, when a verse history of the Peśvās was composed around 1772, it should be in Marathi in the *ovi* meter, though evidently written by a Sanskrit-knowing literatus, deeply immersed in the traditions of the Purāṇa and Kāvya literature.[34] Clearly, the Maratha linguistic identity had assumed a new significance in the politics of South Asia. It was strongest among the Marathas. As Warren Hastings, returning disgraced after Wadgaon and Salbai, wrote in 1785:

> Having mentioned the different interests which seem to divide the present members of the Marattah State, I should leave the subject imperfect, were I not to add, that the Marattahs possess alone, of all the people of Indostan and Decan, a principle of national attachment, which is strongly impressed on the minds of all individuals of the nation.[35]

The Maratha courts increasingly came to depend on their own language, but ornamented it with many Persian and Hindustani loan-words. An extreme example is Nana Phadnis' letter to King George III which contains sentences like "*Hī goṣṭa Hinduce mahzabāt bahut na-munāsab.*"[36] As English officials who learned Indian languages usually studied Persian, communication had to be mediated by extempore translators, much as in Akbar's day. We get a glimpse of this process at work in the heading to a diplomatic dispatch from the English ambassador to the Peśvā:

> Translation of a paper taken in Persian 4th Septr. 1794, by M.N.D. [Maulvi Nuruddin] Sir C.W.M.'s Moonshy from a Marratta paper read to him by Behroo Pundit as to the Durbar's answer to the verbal representations of of Sir C[harles] W. M[alet]. . . .[37]

The Pune courts indubitably employed writers skilled in Persian—perhaps Bhairon Pandit himself knew a little. But the decision was nonetheless made to respond to an English envoy in Marathi—incomprehensible to him, but understood by others around the Darbar. May we infer that a direct Persian answer would be incomprehensible to many and might lead to suspicion? The decline of Persian and rise of Marathi was also evident at Nagpur in 1804. Sridhar Pandit, a senior minister of Raghoji Bhosle of Nagpur visited the British Resident Elphinstone on 9 January 1804. "I told him that I had something to say to him in private if he would accompany me to another Tent. He answered that nobody present understood Persian and that if I would speak to him in that language our conversation would be secret enough."

A few months later, Elphinstone had another audience with Raghoji (16 May 1804).

> 3rd. On my presenting the list, the Rajah *examined it and after hearing it read,* gave it to Sireedur Pundit whom he desired to keep it.
> 4th . . . . Sireedur Pundit then read the Draft aloud and I explained your Excellency's Motives in proposing it. . . .
>
> I may not have been exact in stating what was said in this Conversation by the Rajah and what by his Minister—in general his *Highness spoke himself in Mahrattas (sic), and what he said was repeated by Sireedur Pundit.*[38]

This cultural power inherent in Marathi was also in evidence at the Thanjavur Court, where the descendants of the seventeenth-century conquerors spoke their own version of Marathi. By about 1800, linguistic drift alarmed some of the community, and led Ramkavi to compose a metrical Marathi dictionary-thesaurus, the *Bhāṣāprakāśa.* It was to aid the recollection of Desasthas living outside the (Maratha) Desa (*deśāntarīcyā deśastham smaraṇārtha upegahi*) if they were to attempt the composition of correct Marathi prose and verse. The first regular chapter addresses determining the gender of nouns: always one of the most difficult areas for non-native learners. But the text is not purist. The effort to oust Persian is generally absent from this work, except in priestly contexts. For example, in the section on gifts and exchanges, where things given to Vaidika scholars and mendicants are termed *dāna,* but if given in trade *moḷa* or *kimti.* Sometimes terms current in the region are given Marathi-Persian alternatives: *sarvamānya mhanije nām tyānce inām hi.*[39]

As his dominions slipped inextricably in the hands of the East India Company, the last Maratha ruler at Thanjavur, Sarfoji Bhosle read the writing on the wall and added some of his own. In 1803, the great patron of Sanskrit learning and Karnatak music had a long narrative history of the family written and carved on the walls of the Sri Brihadisvarasvami temple in their former capital. Surrounded with examples of literary Sanskrit and Tamil epigraphs, the last "*Coladeśādhipati Śrīmant Rājśrī Mahārāja Kṣatrapati Sarfoji Rāje Sāheb*" had his personal Ciṭnis, Baburāya compose and inscribe a family history in unadorned Marathi prose.[40]

ABBREVIATIONS

SCS: *Śivacaritra Sāhitya*
BISM: Bhārata Itihāsa Saṃśodhak Maṇḍala
T: *Traimāsika*

NOTES

1. John J. Gumperz, "Speech Variation and the Study of Indian Civilization" 1st pub. 1961; reprinted in *Language in Social Groups.* Stanford: Stanford University Press, 1971, 77-96; citation p. 91.
2. E.M. Houben, "Socio-linguistic Attitudes reflected in the work of Bhartrhari and later grammarians", in Jan E.M. Houben, ed., *Ideology and Status of Sanskrit: Contributions to the History of the Sanskrit Language.* Leiden: E.J. Brill (1996), 159-60.
3. Ashok Aklujkar, "Sanskrit as Supreme Language", in Houben, ed., *Ideology and Status of Sanskrit,* 60.
4. John J. Gumperz, *Discourse Strategies.* Cambridge: Cambridge University Press, 1982, "Introduction", 6-7.
5. "Introduction", to Sheldon Pollock, ed., *Literary Cultures in History: Reconstructions from South Asia.* Berkeley: University of California Press 2003, 12.
6. Sheldon Pollock, "The Sanskrit Cosmopolis, 300-1300: Transculturation, Vernacularization, and the Question of Ideology", in Houben ed., *Ideology and Status of Sanskrit,* 197-8, 209, 213.
7. Published by Mo. G. Dikshita "Dive Āgār yethīl Marathi Tāmrapaṭ Sake 972", in Dikshita, ed., *Dakṣiṇcyā Madhyayugina Itihāsacīn Sādhanen,* vol. 4. Pune: Bhārata Itihāsa Saṃśodhak Maṇḍala, 1951, 44.
8. Karen I. Leonard, *Social History of Indian Caste: The Kayasths of Hyderabad.* Berkeley: University of California Press, 1978, 26-8, 39-43, and letter cited on 175.
9. Thakkura Pheru, *Dravyapariksa aura Dhātulpatti,* ed. Nagendra Prasad and Bhamvaralala Nahata. Vaisali: Prakrta Jainasastra Sodha Samsthana, 1976.

10. *The Travels of Ibn Battuta A.D. 1325-1354*, trans. H.A.R. Gibb, completed by C.F. Beckingham, vol. 4. London: The Hakluyt Society, 1994, 795.
11. Gumperz, *Discourse Strategies*, 42.
12. *Pilgrim: The Travels of Pietro Della Valle*, abridged and translated by George Bull. London: Hutchinson, 1989, 225.
13. This is evident in V.S. Bendrey, *A Study of Muslim Inscriptions*. Bombay: Karnataka Publishing House, 1945, 22.
14. Richard M. Eaton, *Sufis of Bijapur 1300-1700: Social Roles of Sufis in Medieval India*. Princeton: Princeton University Press, 1978, 133-42.
15. Nagari edition, edited by Pandhrinath Ranade, Preface by M.B. Shaha, *Ibrāhīm Ādilshāh dvitīya likhita Navarasa Rāgmālā*. Dhule: I.Vi.Ka. Rajvade Samshodhana Mandala, 1987.
16. S.A.I. Tirmizi, ed., *Mughal Documents 1526-1627*. Delhi: Manohar, 1989, 9.
17. Kaithi is a scribal derivation of the Nagari script: exactly analogous to the Modi current in Maharashtra.
18. Cited in Muzaffar Alam, "Language in Mughal Politics", *Modern Asian Studies*, 32, 2 (1998), 331.
19. Writing 'da' at the beginning of a letter was a Marathi epistolary form used in letters sent to subordinates. Madhukar R. Kulkarni, *Modi Lipi Paricaya ani Aitihasika Namunā Patren*. Pune: Bharatiya Itihasa Samkalana Samiti, 1991, 37.
20. "Sankirna Patren", in BISMT 61, 2-4; SCS 14, 52ff.
21. G.H. Khare, ed., *Śivacaritrasāhitya*. Part 11, 34-5. Pune: BISM, 1957-8.
22. Sumit Guha, "The Family Feud as a Political Resource in Eighteenth Century India", in Indrani Chatterjee, ed., *Unfamiliar Relations: Family and History in South Asia*. Rutgers: Rutgers University Press, 2004.
23. R.R. Gosavi, ed., *Sakalasantagatha*. Pune: Savathi Prakashan, 2000, vol. 2, 530-1.
24. Athar Abbas Rizvi, "Translations of Sanskrit Works at Akbar's Court", in Iqtidar Alam Khan, ed., *Akbar and His Age*. Delhi: Indian Council of Historical Research, 1999, 174-5.
25. *Sakalasantagatha*, 2: 1023.
26. Jayaram Pindye, *Rādhāmādhavavilāsa campu*, ed. V.K. Rajwade, 1924; reprint. Pune: Varda Books, 1991, 262. It is possible that Durg Thakur's elision of the r/l distinction in "apra" reflects the influence of Avadhi or some northern variant of Bhakha on his speech.
27. M.P. Singh, *Shivaji: Bhakha Sources and Nationalism*. Delhi: Books International, 2001, 272. The title "*Kavisur Kavikalasa*" [*kavisvara kavikalasa*] indicates that the Brahman was retained for his literary skills.
28. Singh, *Bhakha Sources*, 263.
29. "Sankirna Patren" in BISMT 61, nos. 2-4 (1982-3), 58-9.
30. *Rājavyavahārakośa*, ed. Kailash N. Sane in *Śivacaritrapradīpa*. Pune:

Bharata Itihasa Samshodhak Mandala, 1925, 144-77, citation from 144. One of the most unsatisfactory neologisms in the text: the functionary was an auditor-accountant. The Sanskrit term would mean confidential companion or minister.

31. "Sankirna Patren", 59-60.
32. The full Sanskrit text, with a facsimile of the first page is in "Sankirna Patren", 64-9. The original is 3 meters long and 23.5 cm. wide. Six sheets had to be joined to produce it. In the text, *yugmavyomarasendu* gives the year Ṣaka 1602. I owe this reading of the date to the editor's note, 62. Translations mine.
33. *Sanads and Letters,* Selected by Ganesh Chimnaji Vad, ed. Purshotam Vishram Mawjee and Dattatreya Balvant Parasnis. Poona: Jagadhitechu Press, 1913, 211-18.
34. Narendra Wagle and Ananta R. Kulkarni, eds. and trans., *Vallabha's Paraśrāma caritra.* Bombay: Popular Prakashan, 1976 (text and translation).
35. Warren Hastings, *Memoirs Relative to the State of India.* London, 1786, New edition, Calcutta: K.P. Bagchi (1978), 49.
36. Cited in Madhava T. Patwardhan, Introduction to *Pharsi-Marathi Kośa,* 2nd edn. Pune: Varda Books, 1997, 7.
37. V.G. Dighe, ed., *British Records of Maratha History: Poona Residency Correspondence: Maratha-Nizam Relations,* vol. 4. Bombay: Government Central Press 1937, 145.
38. R.M. Sinha and A. Avasthi, eds., *Elphinstone Correspondence 1804-08.* Nagpur: Nagpur University Historical Society, 1961, 1, 40-2. Emphasis added.
39. Ramkavi, *Bhāṣāprakāśa,* ed. Shankara G. Tulpule. Pune: University of Pune, 1962, text, 1-6.
40. T. Sambamurti Row transcribed and published, *The Marathi Historical Inscription at the Sri Brihadeswaraswami Temple at Tanjore.* Tanjore: Sri Krishna Vilasa Press, 1907, passim and 119. It is interesting that the 'ch' of 'chatrapati' is replaced by 'Kṣ', perhaps in an effort at Sanskritization!

8

Locality and Universality of Vernaculars: A Study of Language Learning among the East India Company's Civil Servants

KYOSUKE ADACHI

INTRODUCTION

For the East India Company's civil service, the ability to converse fluently in vernacular languages was an essential qualification. The East India College was established to provide two year's general and vocational education for youths of sixteen to eighteen nominated by directors to writerships in the overseas service. The company personnel were expected to master Hindustani as well as Sanskrit and Persian as normative high languages through the curriculum. Europeans had observed that a language that was used in *bunders* and *bazaars* functioned as the *lingua franca.* Toward the end of the eighteenth century, they termed the unknown but widely spoken language as Hindustani based on the regional notion of India in the Persian language. This appellation led to the assumption of a universal "language of India"—a common language that accorded with the economic and pragmatic understanding represented by John Borthwick Gilchrist.[1] Meanwhile, district officers gradually had to perceive a distinct linguistic phenomenon—the diversity of vernaculars in India. Hindustani is a language that is chiefly spoken only in north India; on the other hand, the company's servants had to contend with various local vernacular languages and letters. In western India, earlier traders and missionaries had already "discovered" the Marathi, Gujarati and Canarese languages spoken, and *Balbodh* (i.e. *Devanagari*), *Modi* and Persian letters used, consequently, the pursuit of commercial and political activities in the districts further urged the company's servants to vest these languages with a new administrative status.

The purpose of this paper is to prove that the government of the Bombay Presidency delineated the elastic domain of the colonial vernacular. The author interprets this process in terms of the fluctuation between the universality and locality of colonial vernacular language in the early nineteenth century. Vernaculars, as local and county languages, were confined to each district as they emerged on each district's map of linguistic recognition. Pinge scrupulously surveys this issue and traces the development of Marathi learning by Europeans through an in-depth examination of the records of the state archives, English and Portuguese materials, and Marathi incunabula (Pinge 1960: 81-118). Nonetheless, since Pinge's work is chiefly concerned with the formative phase of the Marathi language, the manner in which the status of vernacular languages are interrelated within the recognition of the East India Company's servant is still open to debate. The primary consideration of this paper, therefore, should be to complement Pinge's argument in order to articulate the hierarchical category and status of vernaculars in western India under the Bombay bureaucracy.

This paper's standpoint revolves around the attempt to illustrate the early colonial representation and reproduction of vernaculars in western India, however, vernacular languages and literatures were undoubtedly not simple fabrication of colonialism. In fact, Marathi literary expression appeared in various inscriptions was flourished among religious sect such as Mahanubhav and Varkari after the thirteenth century and expanded the variety in late Peshwa's court in the eighteenth century (Government of Maharashtra 1971). It is beyond the scope of this paper to argue long history of vernacular language in detail, but it is important to consider the argument that variations of relation between Sanskrit and non-Sanskrit can be seen as varying ways and degrees of naturalizing of high standard language (Houben 1996: 181-93). The Marathi literary practice, more or less, developed between indigenous vernacular idiom and the transregional "high" language such as Sanskrit and Persian. Relating to the medieval Sanskrit and vernacularization in Kannada region, Pollock uses the terms of cultural practice, "Way" and "Place" (*marga* and *desha*) and insightfully highlighted constitutive relationship between literature and the local community (Pollock 1998: 17-25, 2000. 597). If this approach is anywhere near the truth of vernacularization, then, it is imperative that we should examine the central to this issue, that is the various historical aspects of "philologies of contact" and "philologies of community". For such conjectures, we will provide an evidence of it by tracing and verifying the system of oriental language learning among the Company's civil servants and partly extend the argument on the command of language and language of command (Cohn 1985) to examine the domain of colonial vernacular communication under the Company Raj. The data to be discussed below were collected through the historical analysis of the Board's Collection and the departmental proceedings/ consultations in the India Office Records and the departmental compilations of oriental literature in the Maharashtra State Archives from 1820s to 1850s.

ORIENTAL LEARNING IN THE BOMBAY BUREAUCRACY

Mountstuart Elphinstone and his followers' policies exhibited the preservation of native customs in the opening of the Poona Sanskrit College in 1821 to promote indigenous learning. However, there is limited information with regard to another plan running parallel with that of Poona College. The other plan was aimed at establishing a college in a presidency town. The presidency college was designed to offer the servants of the East India Company courses in the oriental languages of India, in a manner similar to Fort William College in Calcutta. The expansion of the government of Bombay Presidency accelerated the demand to establish colonial administration. The East India

Company was anxious to assign civil servants to the newly acquired territory especially for revenue collection, and they urged the Bombay Government to provide the servants with 'the means to teach them native languages on their arrival in Bombay'.[2] In order to pursue this proposition, Elphinstone issued an important minute dated 2 June 1820 to nominate a committee to procure teachers and courses of study and to encourage proficiency in native languages.[3] They submitted a plan for the establishment of the college in Bombay on 13 November, after consulting with an outline of the constitution of the Fort William College, the statement of duties performed by the professors and examiners, the list of the class books being used and the memorandum of the establishment in Madras.[4]

This college had the potential to be a center of oriental learning on the west coast of India. The constitution of the college had three comprehensive branches that combined the servants' training and native instruction: (1) a college to teach eastern languages to gentlemen in the civil and military establishments; (2) a college to instruct the Hindus in their own sciences and (3) a college to teach languages and laws to the natives. These establishments would be administered by a college council and assisted by a secretary who was an examiner and a librarian. Of these branches, the college for instructing Europeans in eastern languages was estimated to have from 30 to 40 students with oriental lectures of four courses. The course of study in Bombay college plan shows the nature of curriculum. Two first courses were obligatory and two last courses were optional. The first course aimed at acquaintance with Persian or Arabic alphabet in various modes and Gujarati or Marathi alphabets and at the study of the grammar of these languages and some conversancy with the colloquial part of them. The second course was to develop the study of the selected languages to translate and converse with facility and propriety and to transmit without assistance in any ordinary business such as the forms of epistolary correspondence and petition. The third course comprised the study of Oriental literature in general, namely the grammar, prosody and rhetoric of the Sanskrit, Arabic and Persian and the various compositions in these languages as well as in the Marathi,

Gujarati and Hindustani. The fourth course was to embrace the study of Hindu and Muslim law in English translation and in the original language.[5]

Unfortunately, the scheme was stranded during the discussion of the governor's council. According to the records, the reasons for this were financial matter as well as the problem of educating natives in Bombay. The council opposed it as they believed that the natives in the presidency town would quickly loose their peculiar habits.[6] The committee was requested to refer to William Chaplin's proposition for the establishment of a college in Poona. An expense of two lakh rupees per year was sanctioned by the supreme government to set up this college to support native literature in the Deccan. The source of this arrangement was the *dakshina*, a distribution of prizes among learned Brahmans for which the Peshwa's government allotted grants annually.[7] Instead of a large college, the Bombay Government facilitated oriental learning for civil servants by procuring a sufficient number of natives who were qualified to teach native languages to young Englishmen as their *munshis* and alternated college plan by constituting an organ of superintendence to examine the students.

In spite of its miscarriage, the Bombay college plan influenced subsequent oriental learning. What is significant in the instructions provided to the framing committee is that Elphinstone proposed the acquisition of two native languages—one was "Hindustanee", which was "indispensable to every civil servant", and the other was "Maharatta" or "Guzerattee", which was considered "essential in the education of the civil servants", while they were also encouraged to learn advantageous additions such as Persian, Sanskrit and Arabic. What needs to be emphasized at this juncture is that these ideas initiated the learning of Marathi and Gujarati in Bombay bureaucracy, while these mandatory clauses in the selection of languages fell into the linguistic hierarchy.

Hitherto, the East India Company had occasionally examined its servants in Hindustani, but it was not necessarily conducted on the basis of a uniformed criteria. In the presidency town the examination committee was set up and examiners were appointed, on the other hand, the provincial examination was usually conducted by superior officers at that post. For instance, the examination in Satara on 2 December 1820 was as follows:

> The first was to give the corresponding Hindoostanee to 130 or 140 words, taken indiscriminately from the Dictionary. The second was to translate a Hindoostanee paper on business into English and the third was to render into Hindoostanee two English extracts of moderate difficulty.[8]

Meanwhile, the examination report of 19 January 1821 shows the following:

> The gentleman examined is allowed to retire into an adjoining room, and to perform these exercises at his leisure. But the other exercises are performed extempore, and consist in reading and translating into English two dialogues, three common stories, and a page or two of one of the prose class books of the college of Calcutta; in translating into Hindoostanee questions on various subjects proposed viva voce by the committee, and in conversing with a moonshee. During these different exercises we have also paid attention to the gentleman's acquaintance with the general rules of Hindoostanee grammar.[9]

On 19 April 1821, according to the recommendation of the examination committee, the Bombay Government decided to set up periodical examinations of civil servants in native languages three times a year and they promulgated a notification to that effect. The Bombay Government clarified the exact degree of proficiency in the native languages that they considered as a requisite qualification of employment.[10] It was evident from the dispatch of the Court of Directors dated 1 June 1823 that this system hierarchized Hindustani as a primary language and Marathi or Gujarati as secondary languages. Instead of using the expensive apparatus of a college, in their dispatch, the Court of Directors advised the Bombay Government to provide writers who arrived in Bombay with practical knowledge of the country's languages to intercourse with the natives through the second language examination system.

> Hindustanee as the language almost universal throughout India, is of primary importance, and as your civil servants are to be employed either in Guzerat or among the Mahratta, the Guzerat languages for those who are to be employed in Guzerat, that of Mahratta, for those

who are to be employed among the Mahratta, in addition to the Hindustanee, must fully qualify them for all that intercourse which the native of their duties requires.[11]

SECOND LANGUAGE PROMOTION SYSTEM

These ideas were crystallized in the circular dated 16 September 1824 in which oriental learning was dexterously linked with personnel management by making the acquaintance of certain languages as the condition for promotion. The main argument on the relationship among languages is as follows: (1) None of the higher appointments in the judicial or revenue departments can ever be conferred upon gentlemen who have not acquired a certain proficiency in one or more of them; (2) Hindustani shall be considered as an indispensable qualification for official employment; (3) Marathi or Gujarati are those languages in the next level that are useful in this establishment, one of which is essential and should be acquired by every writer—in addition to Hindustani—before his promotion to the second step in any line and (4) The acquisition of Persian, Sanskrit or Arabic, in addition to Hindustani and Gujarati, or Marathi, cannot fail to strengthen the claims of a servant in his consideration by the government. Under this system, the junior civil servant was forced to learn oriental languages for the purpose of promotion. Thus, without passing the examination, promotion and salary were not permitted en principe.[12]

In 1821, the examination committee assumed that "the gentlemen examined should be fully competent to transact all magisterial, judicial and revenue duties without the aid of an interpreter". However, at the same time, they conceived that the existing examination system would be inadequate. A critical review by the committee revealed that Fort William College in Bengal required a degree of proficiency "greater than what is indispensable for the transaction of public business in inferior situations" and being directed more to "a literary than a practical knowledge of language".[13]

It is reasonable to assume that this policy attached importance to practical aspects, to the distinct factors that influenced language and colonial vernaculars in the Bombay Presidency. The examination committee observed that the "poetry in Hindoostane, Mahratta and Guzeratte being in a style perfectly distinct from prose, it does not appear to us that its knowledge is necessary nor do we think that any written translation into English is a requisite; as the examiner can best judge for proficiency in this respect by the viva voce examination". This position led to the following subjects being included in the civil servant's examination: (1) oral translations from prose, letters and petitions, (2) written translations of a tale or a similar style of narration, a letter, petition or government resolution, with premeditation but without any assistance from English into the native languages, (3) viva voce translation of a dialogue or questions and answers proposed by the examiners from English into the native languages, (4) conversations with the examiners in the native languages, (5) knowledge of the grammatical rules and principles of the native languages demonstrated by parsing quickly and correctly any passage or by immediately answering any question on a subject proposed by the examiners.

The examination committee had functioned as an important organ for oriental study and interchanged personnel with other institutions such as the Literary Society of Bombay established in 1804.[14] Especially, it is notable that Vans Kennedy (1784-1846) played an important role in the language examination at this phase. It seems that under these circumstances, he configured the domain and standard of Marathi language. In the preface of the "Dictionary of the Marat,ha[*sic*] Language", Kennedy described the Marathi language region as "being bounded on the North by the Satpura mountains, and by a line drawn from their West from Daman to Goa by the Sea, and on the South and East by a line drawn from Goa to the Warda near Chanda, and thence along that river to the Satpura mountains". At the same time he posited Marathi has three distinct level or styles which vary considerably from each other:

> The first, or Pracrit, is employed in books only, and abounds in Sanscrit words. The second is the language spoken by all well educated natives, and particularly by such as are employed in any situation Civil or Military under Government. It admits less frequently of Sanscrit words but adopts freely such as belong to Arabic, Persian or Hindi. The third style is

peculiar to the cultivators and lower classes; In this foreign words are introduced more sparingly and though it perhaps possesses few common terms unknown to the second style, yet there must be in it may colloquial and technical terms which scarcely ever occur in general intercourse with those who do not belong to the same class or trade.[15]

He avoided the first style to overcome the defect of William Carey's dictionary in which "the words actually used by the Marattas are so buried under Sanscrit ones that the student can never ascertain the precise word which he ought to use" and students were expected to read the works in the first style with the assistance of Wilson's Sanskrit Dictionary. With regard to the third style, its peculiarities was nothing other than "using particular words in the place of other employed in the second style, or in expressing the implements and operations of a particular occupation or trade" and could be substituted by the second style.[16]

In addition to the examination committee's right of personal management through second language promotion and the fixture of a standard for proficiency in native languages, the Bombay Government assigned the examination committee with the most important duty that is the superintendence of all the branches of education among the natives engaged in the promotion of oriental literature. In its order, the government prescribed that the secretary should formulate a plan to provide them with well-educated natives and prepare the necessary elementary books in the languages of the presidency. The Court of Directors sanctioned the establishment of a regular committee for the examination of the junior civil servants that comprised three members, namely, the government's Persian secretary, a second who was to be nominated by the government at each examination and the third who was to be a salaried permanent junior member and secretary to the committee. The native officers were Mirza Hussun of Shiraz as the Persian *munshi*, Jugunnath Shastree as the Maratha *shastri*, Bapoo Shastree from Ahmedabad as the Gujarati *shastri* and Mohummud Ibrahim Mukba as the Hindustani *munshi*. They were occupied in the critical examination of all the translations, original compositions and lithography of oriental literature with the help of notable orientalists such as V. Kennedy and George Jervis. Their services were indispensable in formulating the principles of two languages such as Marathi and Gujarati, whose study was then still in the formative phase.[17]

EXPANSION OF TERRITORY AND ELABORATION OF VERNACULARS

The command over vernacular languages and the knowledge of revenue and criminal regulations for civil servants became *sine qua non*. With the expansion of the company's territory, the government was required to promote the vernacular language of the newly acquired territories. In the 1830s, the principal collector of Dharwar informed the Bombay Government that all assistants appointed to his collectorates should learn Canarese. Canarese was assumed to be "the language spoken by three-fourths of the inhabitants of southern Mahratta"; therefore, its knowledge was "infinitely more valuable than that of any other language".[18] The report of the sub-collector of Hooblee of the Dharwar collectorate illustrates the linguistic conditions of that district. The practice in the Madras Presidency of using Marathi as the language of accounts in districts where there was no language of intercourse was followed in the Dharwar district, which had been subject to Maratha power and comprised *jagheerdars* and Brahmin functionaries from the Deccan. However, the report insisted that "in the cutcherry everyone speaks Canarese to communicate with each other and with hereditary village officers who rarely understand Marathi, and the use of Marathi excludes from our service the Lingayats who write and speak in Canarese".[19] Canarese had the potential to become the district language since most of the documents during Tipu's reign were written in Canarese and Marathi. The Governor in Council entirely concurred with the sub-collector's opinion that Canarese should be regarded and adopted as a language of the district, and the use of Marathi should gradually decline into disuse. For this purpose, the Governor in Council coerced the government of India to prepare a Canarese version of a general code of laws that was to be promulgated thereafter.

As the functions of the language and locality began to merge, local languages had to be elaborated in the bureaucratic system of Bombay. Hindustani was regarded as barely understood except in large towns in Gujarat and especially in the Deccan and the Konkan and considered to be unknown except to the local authorities. The government's resolution on the learning of a second language was passed on 16 September 1824; however, it fell into disuse after a few years. Under these circumstances, the rule in question had to be renewed and strictly enforced. On 16 February 1836, the Governor in Council, issued a notification for the selection of a second language as regional vernacular by the place of his appointment.

> The vernacular language of the Carnatic or the main portion of the zilla of Dharwar is Canarese and the government on deciding on the gradual adoption of that language as the medium for transacting all public businesses in that province, the writers . . . will not in the future be entitled to promotion in that zilla, unless they have previously passed an examination in Canarese as well as in Mahratta.[20]

The knowledge of two languages became the prerequisite for public employment in all presidencies by this time. Due to the discontinuance of Persian in the courts,[21] the servants in Bengal should learn Persian and Hindi or Bengali or Urdu and Bengali. In the Madras government, the two languages to be studied were Tamil and Telugu or Canarese. The affairs thus depended on the circumstances of each presidency, and the East India Company's home authority could not overlook the inconsistency of the examination system in terms of personal management. The Court of Directors desired to communicate with Fort William and Fort St. George in order to secure uniformity in the rules existing in the different presidencies for writers to qualify to enter public service.[22]

After comparing the systems, the Bombay Government analyzed the differences prevailing between the Bengal and Bombay systems in the letter dated 3 August 1841. The Bengal examination system, which was being assisted by the Fort William College with the establishment of secretaries and *munshis* and auxiliary materials, was more focused on the literary than was Bombay's practical system. At the time, in contrast to the Bombay examination that was more practical or more colloquial in the above-mentioned five sub-heads, the Bengal examination was more literarily conducted on the basis of the following four sub-heads: (1) oral translation of certain specified works, (2) translation into English of the extracts of the same works, (3) translation of a narration from English into the language in which the examination is held and (4) translation of sentences from English. The examination books in Bengal were *Anwaree Soheilee* and *Goolistan* in Persian, *Prem Sagur* in "Hindee" [Hindustani] and *Hitopadesh* in Bengali.[23]

Based on these communications, the Court of Directors proposed the unification of the examination systems in three presidencies in their dispatch dated 26 April 1843 as follows: (1) A system that was exercised in Bengal and Madras to control the writers on the plans of the superintendence was introduced. (2) The restriction of tuition to native teachers in Bombay whose competency should be determined based on their examination by competent authorities. (3) The invariable institution of an initiatory examination as soon as a writer arrives in Bombay. (4) The allowances made to students while preparing for examinations in Calcutta and Bombay, the highest allowance being the same as that of an assistant who first enters the public service. (5) A graduated scale of rewards in Madras and a greater uniformity in the criteria for which they are bestowed in the three presidencies. (6) An enforcement for proficiency in two languages on the basis of the penalty of a transfer to England after a certain period. (7) The commitment of the writer's time to his studies in Madras and Bombay with permission to reside in the province.[24]

The most crucial difference was the facility and period allocated for a student to qualify for the public service. In Bengal, a student was given 12 months along with the assistance of college teachers, and a further extension of three months was provided to complete his studies. They were sent back to England on the expiry of the period. On the other hand, in Bombay, no definite deadline was prescribed within which a student had to qualify in either of the languages. If a student did not pass the Hindustani examination in four months, his only recourse was to be employed as a supernumerary assistant in the interior station. If a student did not pass the Marathi or Gujarati examination, he would only be precluded from being promoted. It was in the office that he learned the second language, namely, a vernacular language of the district that was used in the courts and offices of the station, more quickly and precisely than he could by merely studying with the help of a teacher.[25]

COMMAND OF VERNACULAR LANGUAGES

On 12 March 1845, the Bombay Government issued a new examination rule in coordination with other presidencies. The examination rule was expected to prescribe a certain mould for the study of each vernacular language. For Hindustani, the characters required to be known were the printed *Nushk*, and written *Taleek* and the books such as *Aklag-i-Hindee, Bagh O'Buhar, Khird Afroj* and *Tota Kuhanee* were to be read. For Marathi and Gujarati, the characters required to be known were the *Balbodh* and also the *Modi* and Gujarati in running hand, the books such as the *Singhasun Butteeshee, Punchonakhyan,* and Aesop's fables. For Canarese, the character required to be known was that ordinarily written in Mysore and Bellary and the books such as Aesop's fables, and the catechism of the History of the Maharashtra. The style of examination was as follows:

(1) Translations viva voce, and without premeditation into English from a prose, particularly from letters and petitions.
(2) Written translations with premeditation, but without any kind of assistance from English, of a tale or similar kind of narratory style, and of a letter, or petition, or section of a government regulation.
(3) Translations viva voce, from English, of a dialogue, or of questions and answers proposed by the examiners.
(4) Conversation on all common, commercial, revenue and judicial subjects, and a tolerable degree of fluency in replying.
(5) Knowledge of the grammatical rules and principles in any passage by answering any questions on the subject by the examiners.

In addition to the above proficiency, higher proficiency would entitle a student to a certificate, and a prize of Rs. 800 and extraordinary proficiency would entitle a student to a degree of honor and a donation of Rs. 1,600. Eminent knowledge of Hindu and Muslim law, Arabic or Sanskrit and of the regulations would entitle the young civilians to a degree of honor, Rs. 300, a medal and a prize of oriental books.[26]

The problem is how far the examination rule accomplished its aim. The Court of Directors assumed that the civil servants in the Bombay Presidency had sufficient knowledge in Marathi and Gujarati as well as Hindustani, since Hindustani is obligatory subject at Haileybury, and the study of Marathi and Gujarati is comparatively easy by previous acquaintance with Sanskrit. The Bombay Government confirmed the list of civil servants who had not passed the second language examination, and in December 1843, they circulated a questionnaire to more than 80 civil servants throughout the Bombay Presidency. According to my research conducted in the State Archives, at least 77 answers to this query are available. We suggest that these data depict the malfunctions of oriental learning in the Bombay bureaucracy. A glance at the answers to questions (Table 1), illustrates the convergence to Marathi in district administration as well as the complimentary use of Hindustani.

However, at the same time, the answers show that 21 servants

TABLE 1: COMPARISON BETWEEN THE LANGUAGE OF THE DISTRICT AND THE LANGUAGE USED FOR BUSINESS IN THE OFFICE

Language of the district	*Language of business in the office*
Marathi (45)	Marathi (41)
Gujarati (24)	Hindustani (21)
Canarese (17)	Gujarati (15)
Hindustani (13)	English (9)
English (6)	Canarese (8)
Persian (1)	NA (6)
Arabic (1)	
Portuguese (1)	
All languages (2)	
NA (7)	

Source: By the author, based on the answers to circular no. 4033 of General Department 1843. In case more than one language is stated, it is counted in the respective language.

confessed that they were unable to read papers. Most of the papers that came to the office were not read by the Company's servant himself, and they had to depend on the *cutcherry's carcoons.* Although the Company's servants did not require translations in Hindustani, approximately half of them required third-party intervention when they spoke to native *zamindars* and *ryots.*[27]

At Haileybury, the youth entering college were obliged to study Sanskrit in the first term, Persian in the second term and Hindustani in the third term. Meanwhile, Edward Backhouse Eastwick officiated as a professor of Hindustani and Marathi in the oriental department and James Ballantyne lithographed *A Grammar of the Mahratta Language* for the use of the East India College written in Devanagari and Modi.[28] Notwithstanding that, their vernacular education did not meet growing demand of the servants of the Bombay Presidency any longer and it led them to reconsider oriental learning in the light of linguistic diversity.

In fact, district officer's opinions on vernaculars were manifold. For instance, A.N. Shaw, the revenue commissioner of the Northern Division, issued circular to all collectors[29] inviting opinions with regard to the East India College problem. He considered that it would be preferable to commence the teaching of Hindustani from the first term and either Marathi or Gujarati in the second term instead of Sanskrit and Persian as these were considered "dead languages". At the same time, the correspondence was referred to Townsend, the revenue commissioner of the Southern Division and his subordinate servants. The opinions were in favor of the study of Persian (nine servants), Sanskrit (seven), Hindustani (fourteen), Marathi (sixteen), Gujarati (five) and European literature (eight). Townsend opined that Hindustani was of great use all over India, he objected to the study of provincial languages like Marathi or Gujarati at Haileybury, since they could be acquired in the country, especially by students who had a good foundation of the mother tongues —Sanskrit and Persian.

Colonial administrators were required to systematically direct the attention of their servants to the knowledge of vernaculars. When Richardson's *Hints on Examinations in the Vernacular Languages* is published in 1853, within 130 Covenanted Civil Service, there are three men who have passed in four or more languages; there are eleven who have passed in more than two languages, there are ninety-three who have passed in two languages; there are twenty-three who have passed in only one language. From 1823 to 1842 one hundred and eight persons joined the service and sixty were within the last ten years.[30]

CONCLUSION

Thus far, we have outlined the history of oriental learning in Bombay Presidency. The Bombay Government linked the civil servants' training system with oriental languages. This resulted in the emergence of the examination committee as an important organ of oriental learning. It must be reiterated that the promotion of a second language assumed Hindustani, the first language, as the national language of India, and considered Marathi and Gujarati to be local languages. In accordance with the expansion of the Company's territory, the Bombay Government had to place vernacular languages of each region under this system. The examination systems and the command of vernacular language of civil servants exposed the limits of the training system in the East India Company to accommodate growing demand and recognition of vernaculars. It is not sufficient to show the administrative framework of language learning among the Company's civil servants. We need to incorporate other factors in order to argue universality and locality of vernaculars. From this point we might go on to an even more detailed examination of the linguistic recognition of colonial officers as well as missionaries and native intellectuals.[31] While the rise of bourgeoisie lent an impetus to reform of public service in England, the struggle against patronage in the East India Company was bearing the fruit. The system of appointment of East India Company's servant by patronage was replaced by an open competitive examination and in January 1858, the East India College, old Haileybury was closed down. Nevertheless, the training of vernaculars once established did not lessen its importance as national question,[32] or rather accelerated the desire of language instruction among colonial elite and native intellectuals to dominate colonial communication.

NOTES

* The archival research for this paper was supported by the grant from the Research Fellowships of the Japan Society for Promotion of Science for Young Scientists.

1. John Borthwick Gilchrist (1759-1841), took the office of Professor of "Hindoostanee" in the College of Fort William established in 1800. Gilchrist tackled the project defining what language as common language with native *pundits.* In 1804 he returned to Edinburgh due to ill health. From 1818 to 1826 he served as Professor of Hindustani for East India Company in London. Relating to his theory on "Hinduwee", "Sanskrit" and "Hindoostanee", see Sadiqur-Rahman Kidwai, *Gilchrist and the 'Language of Hindoostan'*, New Delhi: Rachna Prakashan, 1972, pp. 89-96.
2. Letter dated 17 April 1816, "Introduction of Aumani management into the Pergunnah of Nerriad, in consequence of the refractory conduct of the Patells" quoted from Extract of Revenue Letter to Bombay dated 14 July 1819 in IOR F/4/667/18622: Establishment of a College for the Junior Civil Servant at Bombay, and of a Hindoo College at Poona, pp. 18-20.
3. Minute by the Honorable Mountstuart Elphinstone dated 2 June 1820, ibid., pp. 21-46.
4. Letter from the college committee dated 8 July 1820 in Extract Bombay Public Consultations 11 October 1820. ibid., pp. 51-7. F. Warden, T. Goodwin, V. Kennedy, Dr. J. Taylor and W. Erskine were the members of the committee. In this letter the committee proposed the importance of rigid and impartial examination into the qualifications of the junior civil servant. They supposed the promotion of civil servant should not be permitted according to seniority but to the good conduct and proficiency. As to the details of Fort William College, see Sisir Kumar Das, *Sahibs and Munshis: An Account of the College of Fort William,* New Delhi: Orion Publications, 1978 and Constitution of Fort William College, originally dated 21 May 1806, revised on 3 June 1814 and 16 November 1816, ibid., pp. 59-96.
5. Letter from the college committee dated 13 November with a revised code of rules for the college of Bombay in Extract Bombay Public Consultations, 17 January 1821. ibid., pp. 103-71.
6. Minute by Prendergast, ibid., p. 172, Extract Bombay Public Consultations dated 28 February 1821, ibid., pp. 187-92 and Extract Bombay Public Consultations dated 15 August 1821, ibid., pp. 207-22.
7. For the details of *dakshina* and establishment of Poona college, see Adachi, "Dakshina Rules of Bombay Presidency (1836-1851): Its Constitution and Principles", *Journal of Japanese Association for South Asian Studies,* vol. 13, 2001, pp. 24-51.

8. Letter from the commissioner in the Deccan to the chief secretary dated 2 December 1820 quoted from Extract Bombay Public Consultation in IOR F/4/19245: Papers regarding the Examination of Junior Bombay Civil Servants in the Vernacular Language, pp. 63-70.
9. Letter from the committee for the examination of junior civil servants in the country language, to the chief secretary, dated 19 January 1821 in Extract Bombay Public Consultations, 24 January 1821. ibid., pp. 77-82.
10. Government notification dated 19 April 1821, ibid., pp. 89-96. The notification announced for the information of junior civil servants the examination of the proficiency in the native languages would be periodically conducted on May, September, and January in each year.
11. Extract Public Letter to Bombay dated 11 June 1823, ibid., pp. 7-21. Interestingly, the so-called "classical language" was given slight consideration and the focus was shifting to vernaculars from the viewpoint of training of officers after disembarkation. Sanskrit and Persian were regarded as recommendatory as affording a preference, but it was nothing more than "ornamental" and should be acquired at the option of individual at their own expense.
12. Circulars to writers dated 16 September 1824, IOR P/346/09, Consultation of 22 September 1824, nos. 5206-8.
13. Letter from the Committee proposing a plan of the examination of the junior civil servants and rewards for proficiency in the native language dated 20 November 1824 in IOR P/346/12, Consultation of 22 December 1824, nos. 6902-3.
14. The Literary Society of Bombay originated from the meeting held on 26 November 1804 at the government house at Parel, where Sir James Mackintosh lived. The original members were Jonathan Duncan, the governor, James Mackintosh and William Erskine. In 1819 three volumes' Transactions were published. It should be noted that Vans Kennedy of examination committee played an important role of the society. He fulfilled the secretaryship and afterwards became the president in 1831.
15. Vans Kennedy, *A Dictionary of the Maral,ha Language*, Bombay: Courier Press, 1824. See also Manuscript of a Mahratta Dictionary annexing a copy of the preface, dated 7 July 1823 in IOR P/346/01, nos. 2258-77. Due to limitation of space, a detailed discussion of Kennedy's theory is not possible here. According to Rocher, Kennedy leveled caustic criticism at the Marathi translation of Bible by Serampore Mission to be 'fit for worms' in anonymous article, 'Oriental Translations of the Scriptures' *Asiatic Journal*, 28, 1829 (Rocher 1989). His attack led to the controversy with supporters of Serampore version of Marathi bibles. See, William Greenfield, *A Defence of the Serampore Mahratta Version of the New Testament in Reply to Animadversions of an*

Anonymous Writer in Asiatic Journal, September, 1829, London: Samuel Bagster, 1830. In the meantime, it should be noted that he developed his theory on the affinity of Indian languages, in *Researches into the Nature and Affinity of the Principal Languages of Asia and Europe*, 1828.

16. Marathi learning at Fort William College and Serampore Mission and their influence upon Bombay should be further re-examined. Das states that Carey recommended one Vaidyanath as Marathi scholar at Fort William College on 23 January 1804. He was formerly a *pundit* of J.K. Lovett and helped Carey's translation of Bible from Bengali into Marathi. On the other hand, during the period between 1801 and 1828, no more than 5 persons (C.W. Gardner, C.R. Martin, S.J. Moor, in 1802, C. Chapman in 1803, and H. Sergent in 1806) studied Marathi at Fort William College and it led to discontinuance of the course there (Das 1978: 46-7 and 56).
17. Minute by John Malcolm dated 27 May 1828, IOR P/346/46, Consultation of 9 July 1828, no. 137.
18. Letter to the Government of Bombay from J. Nisbet, Principal Collector of Dharwar dated 19 October 1833, in MSA GD 1833, vol. 11 (282), pp. 32-3.
19. Revenue extract from the annual report of the sub collector of Hooblee dated 9 September 1835 in Extract from the proceedings in Territorial Department, MSA GD 1836, vol. 19 (351), pp. 43-6. Memorandum by W.H. Wathen dated 8 February 1836, ibid., pp. 73-4.
20. Government notification dated 16 February 1836, ibid., pp. 75-6.
21. Act XXIX of 1837 passed by the President of the Council of India on 20 November 1837, Section I enacted to dispense the use of Persian language in Bengal, in judicial and revenue proceeding. See IOR V/8/31. In Bombay Presidency chiefly by the Act III of 1827 Section X and XI the language of Decrees, Orders, and process in courts to be written was prescribed, and by Act IV of 1827 Article XXXIV the language of depositions to be taken was defined (IOR V/8/24). These arrangements were complemented by the introduction of vernacular language in Act XII of 1843 (IOR V/8/32).
22. Extract of a letter from the Court of Directors dated 21 October 1840, no. 25, paragraph 74: in MSA GD 1841, vol. 23 (594), p. 243. Letter from the secretary to the government of Bengal on the resolution for revision of statute of College of Fort William dated 23 June, ibid., pp. 245-52 and Rules for the College of Fort St. George dated 13 July 1827, MSA GD 1840, vol. 22 (539), pp. 172-89.
23. Letter to the secretary to the Government of India, no. 2503 of 1841, MSA GD 1841, op. cit., p. 256.
24. Consultation at Court of Directors dated 26 April 1843 in MSA GD 1843, vol. 39 (764), pp. 93-111. Letter no. 78 from officiating secretary to the Government of India to the secretary to the Government of

Bombay dated 29 July 1843, ibid., pp. 87-92 and Minute read 2 November 1843, ibid., pp. 113-20.

25. It seems that this arrangement was due to the misapplication of the government notification dated 25 January 1839, which declared that civil servants who had not passed second language were not permitted to draw full salary. Order of the Government of Bombay dated 25 January 1839, MSA GD 1839, vol. 27 (496), p. 36. See also List of Junior Civil Servants, MSA GD 1842, vol. 46 (671), pp. 53-9, and Circular to collectors dated 8 March 1842, ibid. pp. 107-10.

26. MSA GD 1845, vol. 50 (956), pp. 178-86.

27. MSA GD 1843, vol. 40 (765), pp. 1-27. The questions in the questionnaire were as follows:

    [1] What is the language of the district in which you are employed?; [2] In which language do you conduct the business of your office?; [3] Are you able to read all the papers, including accounts, etc. that come before you in the common language?; [4] Do you read such papers as your ordinary mode of conducting business or are they read to you?; [5] If they are read to you, are they translated as the reader proceeds into Hindoostanee or any other language?; [6] Do you directly speak to natives who come to you for business or do you use an interpreter?; [7] Are you able to converse with any native to acquire information that he may have in the language of your district without the intervention of a third party?; [8] Are you in the habit of conversing with Jumeendars and Ryuts of the country?; [9] Are you capable of dictating orders, decrees, etc. in the language of the district?; [10] Are you in the habit of dictating these orders, or do you merely explain the meaning to a Karkoon who puts those ideas into a structured form?; [11] In the event of an emergency, can you yourself write an order in the district's language without another's assistance?

    Answers are available in ibid., pp. 28-344 and MSA GD 1847, vol. 45, pp. 121-5.

28. J. Ballantyne, *A Grammar of the Mahratta Language for the Use of the East India College at Haileybury*, Edinburgh: J. Hall. According to the preface dated 20 May 1839 Marathi class had been recently formed at the college. Carey's grammar was a target of criticism once more.

29. Circular no. 2034 of 1850 to all the collectors of the Northern Division in MSA GD 1850, vol. 66, p. 179. Shaw's opinion was concurred by 21 servants of the revenue department in his division. Four servants suggested that only Persian should be abandoned and one servant recommended teaching Hindustani in the first term followed by Persian, omitting Sanskrit and Arabic. The summary is available in MSA GD 1852, vol. 13, Comp. no. 625.

30. Arthur St. John Richardson, *Hints on Examinations in the Vernacular*

Languages of Western India, Bombay: Messrs. Thacker & Co., 1853, pp. 4-5. We must draw attention to the difference of qualification by the kinds of service. Military officers qualified themselves for employment by passing one or more vernacular language, and interpreters must pass Hindustani and Marathi. Hindustani, Persian, Arabic, Malay and Sindhi were the language in which Naval officers were qualified for the office of interpreter. Medical officers should pass Hindustani to be nominated for the office of Civil Surgeon or Vaccinator. Vaccinators were required to pass in the vernacular language of the district within a reasonable time. Uncovenanted servants had to pass in Hindustani and undergo an examination in the language of the country, ibid., pp. 1-14.

31. At the meeting of the General Education Committee, several of the native teachers of the Marathi language filed a petition asking to allow them taking part in the examinations. In reply to the petition, Stevenson tested on Marathi grammar, but only one Brahmin, out of twenty or thirty candidates succeeded to answer to his satisfaction, ibid., p. vii. This is an interesting case where language examination became a contested terrain.
32. For instance, regarding the discussion on the oriental language education of this period, see W. Nassau Lees, *Instruction in the Oriental Languages Considered, Especially as Regards the Education of Candidates for the East India Civil Service, and as a National Question,* London: Williams and Norgate, 1857.

ABBREVIATIONS

IOR F/4: Board of Control General Records in the British Library.

IOR P: Proceedings and Consultations particularly, Bombay General Department (1823-59) in the British Library.

MSA GD: Proceedings of the General Department of the Government of Bombay (1821-60) in the Maharashtra State Archives.

REFERENCES

Adachi, K., 2001: "Dakshina Rules of Bombay Presidency (1836-1851): Its Constitution and Principles", *Journal of Japanese Association for South Asian Studies,* 13, pp. 24-51.

Ballantyne, J., 1839: *A Grammar of the Mahratta Language for the Use of the East India College at Haileybury.* Edinburgh: J. Hall.

Cohn, B., 1985: "The Command of Language and the Language of Command", in *Subaltern Studies IV: Writing on South Asian History and Society,* ed. R. Guha. Delhi: Oxford University Press, 1985, pp. 276-329.

Das, S.K., 1978: *Sahibs and Munshis: An Account of the College of Fort William.* New Delhi: Orion Publication.

Government of Maharashtra, 1971: *Language and Literature.* Bombay: Directorate of Govt. Printing, Stationery and Publications.

Greenfield, W., 1830: *A Defence of the Serampore Mahratta Version of the New Testament in Reply to Animadversions of an Anonymous Writer in Asiatic Journal,* September 1829. London: Samuel Bagster.

Houben, J.E.M., 1996: "Socio-linguistic Attitudes Reflected in the Work of Bhartrhari and Later Grammarians", in *Ideology and Status of Sanskrit: Contributions to the History of the Sanskrit Language,* ed. J.E.M. Houben. Leiden: E.J. Brill.

Kennedy, V., 1824: *A Dictionary of the Marat,ha Language.* Bombay: Courier Press.

Kidwai, S.R., 1972: *Gilchrist and the 'Language of Hindoostan'.* New Delhi: Rachna Prakashan.

Lees, W.N., 1857: *Instruction in the Oriental Languages considered, Especially as regards the Education of Candidates for the East India Civil Service, and as a National Question.* London: Williams and Norgate.

Naregal, V., 2001 *Language Politics, Elites, and the Public Sphere: Western India under Colonialism.* New Delhi: Permanent Black.

Pinge, S.M., 1960: *Yuropiyananca Marathica Abhyasa va Seva.* Pune: Sadhana Press.

Pollock, S., 1998: "The Cosmopolitan Vernacular", *The Journal of Asian Studies,* 57(1), pp. 6-37.

Pollock, S., 2000: "Cosmopolitan and Vernacular in History", *Public Culture,* Society for Transnational Cultural Studies, 12(3). Durham: Duke University Press.

Richardson, A. St.J., 1853: *Hints on Examinations in the Vernacular Languages of Western India.* Bombay: Thacker & Co.

Rocher, L., 1989: "Kennedy, Vans (1784-1846): A Preliminary Bibliography", *Journal of the American Oriental Society.* 109(4), pp. 621-5.

9

Paths to Progress: Gender and Social Reform in Nineteenth-Century Maharashtra

MEERA KOSAMBI

Shortly after her meteoric arrival from Bengal, Pandita Ramabai established her Arya Mahila Samaj in Pune in 1882. Its stated objective of mobilizing women for the social reform measures that concerned them closely incurred the wrath of the social conservatives. Reporting on a meeting of the Samaj that discussed child marriage and disfigurement of widows, *Kesari* offered a few words of advice to the "learned Ramabai and the entire Arya Mahila Samaj":

> It is true that these customs are evil, and the Lion [*kesari*] has often roared, demanding that they be abolished. But our roars have not penetrated the ears of our countrymen. Who then is going to listen to the noise made by a few weak females [*abala*]? In reality, it is the task of men to eradicate these and several other evil customs that prevail among our people. Women will not be able to interfere in it for many years to come, no matter if they are great *panditas* and have reached the ultimate stage of reform. (*Kesari*, 8 August 1882; my translation)

At the same time, the Pandita also had support—from liberal social reformers such as M.G. Ranade and R.G. Bhandarkar—for the Arya Mahila Samaj that was in fact created on the foundation of a rudimentary women's club that their Prarthana Samaj had organized. But there was a normative convergence between the social reformers and the conservatives, across the ideological divide—the liberals too had their own ideas about the "woman's place" in family and society. Even after educating his wife Ramabai at home and grooming her as a public speaker, Ranade demanded total obedience from her and discouraged independent thinking. Ramabai Ranade innocently reveals that:

> I never failed to do what Himself [Ranade] wanted, because I knew very well that Himself would otherwise be angry. . . . Himself had a firm expectation that I should follow his thinking without his having to tell or instruct me explicitly. (Ranade 1953: 83-4; my translation)

Thus the difference between the conservatives and the liberals was one only of degree within an overarching agreement on patriarchal essentials, such as women's total dependence on men. The result—or even the objective—of such reform efforts could not be other than what Sumit Sarkar describes, in the context of Bengal, as "the limited and controlled emancipation of wives" (Sarkar 1994: 106).

Late nineteenth-century Maharashtra constructed its social reform project of "emancipating" women, like the project of liberating the nation, as a solely male enterprise. However, whereas it was clear that the nation was to be liberated from colonial domination, the source of women's oppression remained unclear and was identified only in generalized and disembodied terms, such as "evil customs" and "ignorance". The patriarchal social structure that institutionalized this oppression, and the construction of women as permanent "others" in need of male help, remained unexamined. Thus, while male reformers framed the issues for social reform pertaining to women, women themselves articulated different priorities, problems and solutions. This dissonance forms the core of my paper.

This paper essentially "engenders" the Brahman-dominated reform movement. It is an exercise in "rethinking social reform from a gender-sensitive perspective" and subjecting it to feminist "critical scrutiny, which has rendered past certainties increasingly uncertain", in the words of Patricia Uberoi (1996: xi, xiv). It first discusses the differential masculine and feminine perceptions of goals and paths to social progress. My implicit argument is that the success of the social reform initiatives would have been considerably heightened and expedited had women's voices been heard and their concerns addressed. It then spells out my own version of the analytical framework of public/private spheres that explains when and how women could enter the reform arena; and attempts to trace the path women had to traverse in order to participate in public life. The essay ends with a discussion of women's voice and visibility—that is, their emergence in the public sphere and its implications as regards their agency.

SOCIAL REFORM: GENDERED PERCEPTIONS OF GOALS AND PATHS

Throughout the nineteenth century, Maharashtrian society exhibited a hegemony of Brahmans, that was derived from the century-long precolonial, dynastic reign of the powerful Peshwas of Pune. They were prime ministers to the Maratha Chhatrapatis, who turned into the region's de facto rulers, and led the Maratha Confederacy, spanning western and central India, to challenge the English East India Company's territorial march across the subcontinent. Under the subsequent British Raj, the dominance of Brahmans, especially Chitpavans like the former Peshwa, was not only perpetuated but even consolidated throughout Maharashtra, although Jayant Lele argues that the community's influence was "coercive rather than hegemonic even within the caste" (Lele 1998: 177).[1]

The only exception to this rule was the city of Mumbai, the East India Company's stronghold whose social stratification was realigned broadly along class rather than caste lines to suit its commercial needs. It was dominated by European merchants, followed by the influential Gujarati mercantile communities—the relatively Anglicized Parsis, as well as Hindus and Muslims—who built up its trade. Maharashtrians rarely figured in commerce, but their traditionally literate castes took to Western education and found a niche in the burgeoning white-collar and professional sector, and retained social leadership. Mumbai's crystallization into "self-conscious groups" occurred along the lines of "occupation and status, not caste" (Masselos 1974: 1-

11). In contrast, Pune, still the cultural capital of Maharashtra, remained deeply caste-conscious and imbued with the spirit of the *shastras.*

Thus the mainstream reform discourse remained an upper caste, middle class and male project, whose preoccupation with gender issues was dictated primarily by the Brahman community's oppressive marriage-related customs and increasingly also by the British official policy of making political rights contingent upon social reform. The Brahman self-absorption not only inserted the Hindu scriptures into the reform discourse as its mainstay, but also disregarded the customs of the majority of the region's population. As D.D. Kosambi points out:

> When the question of Hindu widow remarriage was being violently argued by the reformers . . ., even the most scholarly (like R.G. Bhandarkar) looked only to correct interpretation of the sacred texts, from the *Ṛgveda* down. That 85 per cent of the population in their immediate locality allowed widows to remarry (and permitted divorce when either party felt aggrieved) made no impression upon the scholars nor upon the authorities of Hindu law. (Kosambi 2002: 4)

Under the influence of the traditional thinking derived from the *shastras,* a majority of the Brahman community insisted with *Kesari* that "Our women will have to submit themselves to male control for a long time to come" (*Kesari,* 8 August 1882: my translation). The most popular literary specimen of conservative retaliation against the reform effort was *Taruni-Shikshana-Natika* (A Short Play about Young Women's Education, 1886) by Narayan Bapuji Kanitkar (Kashibai's uncle-in-law), that paints a dire scenario of the near future by parodying all "modern" *bêtes noires.* Its central character is a barely disguised caricature of Rakhmabai whose controversial court case for the Restitution of Conjugal Rights was then in progress—a rich young woman with "ornamental" rather than useful education, whose conversation is liberally sprinkled with English words and whose addiction to English Romantic literature leads her to first repudiate and then divorce her husband to woo her teacher (who "sensibly" spurns her). In the background are a rich, young, Westernized man who has drunk himself almost to death; an eager young widow who rushes into remarriage with a man who turns out to be much older than he claimed; and a school taught partly by Englishwomen, called the Arya Mahila Hotel. In the preface Kanitkar sketches in a breathlessly long list the ominous effects of women's education, linked in the popular mind to "women's freedom" or emancipation:

> Society can be said to be thoroughly ruined when [women] start wearing glasses for short sight caused by studies, when their cheekbones become visible, when they become weak and their progeny short-lived, when their religious restrictions are loosened, when they deride the Hindu religion and develop a wish to accept an alien religion or become atheists, when their pure and simple Maharashtrian speech becomes adulterated with a mixture of English words, when they get access to vulgar books like Reynold and Boccacio which turn their naturally tender minds wayward, when they develop contempt for Hindu customs and caste practices and feel like imitating the foreigners' customs and manners in their entirety, when they drink alcohol to their hearts' content along with men and develop a taste for forbidden foods, when they desire to indulge in English ballroom dancing, when they start to insult their parents-in-law, husbands and other kith and kin at every step, when they begin to like love marriages, when they enter courts of law to break their marriage bonds because their husbands are stupid, ignorant, illiterate, poor and therefore unlovable, when they abandon their homes to act on the stage, when they begin to believe that love is blind and the path of elopement sweet! (Kanitkar 1890: 14-15; my translation)

At the same time, liberal ideas made inroads into reformist thinking essentially through Western education and an acquaintance with British thinkers. The late nineteenth-century social leaders had to pick their way through the strands of indigenous androcentrism of *Manusmriti* and the newly imported social liberalism of J.S. Mill. The impact of *On the Subjection of Women* was felt long before its Marathi translation was published in 1902 by Govindrao Kanitkar (Kashibai's husband). Perhaps Mill's most loyal adherent was G.G. Agarkar who consistently promoted his ideology through his journalistic writings upholding women's right to education and spouse selection:

> Women and men may engage independently in whichever profession they choose, obtain whatever education they want, give examinations and win degrees as they wish, and marry whenever they choose in order to conduct their married life according to their wishes—we have no

doubt that such freedom will be available to all in due course of time. (Agarkar 1984: 198-9; my translation)

The Brahman community was deeply conflicted about the impact of Westernization and about social reform that pivoted on the issues of women's education, abolition of child marriage and raising the age of consent within marriage, and a humane treatment of widows (including remarriage when possible). These interventions were ameliorative rather than radical, and circumscribed by a shared patriarchal paradigm that retained the perception of woman as primarily a wife-mother-homemaker while improving only the conditions for her functioning. Thus the slight postponement of the consummation of marriage was tied to the birth of healthier progeny; the wife's education was intended to make her a better companion for her educated husband and also an efficient housewife and enlightened mother; the widow's education was viewed as a means for making her a useful member of society (usually as a teacher in a girls' school) without contesting her marginal role within the family. Women's own attempts to exercise agency, enter the public sphere, and shape their own destinies was met with both implicit and explicit resistance.

In this social milieu, the first gendered epistemological dissonance arose because the mainstream, male discursive construction of women remained anchored to the *shastras*, especially *Manusmriti.* In fact, a key actor and leader of the conservative faction, V.N. Mandlik, had himself published an edition of *Manusmriti* in 1886 (Doniger 1991: xlix). Manu constructed women solely as wives, mothers and homemakers ("Women were created to bear children, and men to carry on the line"), denying them selfhood and subjectivity, and asserted the derogatory need to exercise strict control over women ("a woman is not fit for independence"; "unguarded women would bring sorrow upon both families"; "It is the very nature of women to corrupt men here on earth") because of their innate lascivious tendencies (*Laws of Manu*: 209, 197, 115). Running through the normative treatment of women was the belief even of the reformers that women themselves were incapable of deciding what they wanted or needed, because "a woman's understanding is unreliable" (*Laws of Manu*: 159).

Articulate women were not slow to contest the *shastras*' damage to their self-image. Rakhmabai wrote in 1885:

Our law-givers (i.e. the writers of Shastras) being men have painted themselves . . . noble and pure, and have laid every conceivable sin and impurity at our door. If these worthies are to be trusted, we are a set of unclean animals, created by god for the special service and gratification of man who by right divine can treat or maltreat us at his sweet will. Reduced to this state of degradation by the dictum of the Shastras, looked down upon for ages by men, we have naturally come to look down upon ourselves. (*Times of India*, 26 June 1885)

Having made a similar complaint in her *Stri Dharma Niti* (1882), Pandita Ramabai wrote in *The High-Caste Hindu Woman* (1887):

Those who diligently and impartially read Sanskrit literature in the original, cannot fail to recognize the law-giver Manu as one of the hundreds who have done their best to make woman a hateful being in the world's eye. . . . She, the loving mother of the nation, the devoted wife, the tender sister and affectionate daughter is never fit for independence, and is 'as impure as falsehood itself'. She is never to be trusted; matters of importance are never to be committed to her. (Ramabai 1981: 29)

Years later Kashibai Kanitkar joined the battle against Manu:

Manusmriti contains sayings which are both favorable and unfavorable to women. No one gives a thought to the favorable opinion, but the sayings which are unfavorable to us are widely prevalent. The injunction that "women should never be independent" is observed to the letter; but the injunction that "a woman is the goddess of the house and should be revered" is thought of once in a while, during leisure time chats. . . . Manu opines that women are attached to the bed (indicating love of sleep), the seat (indolence), ornaments, and given to passions, harassment of others and immorality. So much disrespect for the female sex! Since ancient times, the people of our country have never harbored a charitable opinion about us. Manu has said in a couple of places that women should be honored and given ornaments and adornments. But why? So that the family should prosper. Women should be made happy so that the house will be filled with food grains, cattle and children; and one's social status will rise. This is the only reason to make women happy. If they are unhappy and disgruntled, the home will be visited by calamity—this is the reason to make women happy. There is no feeling that they are fellow creatures like ourselves, that they are as useful to

> the world as we are, that their rights are the same as ours, and that they should therefore be treated as equals. (Kanitkar 1911: 553-4; my translation)

The second area of disagreement was women's education. The kind of meaningful education that the socially aware women wanted for themselves did not appeal to the pervasive, patriarchal image of women shared by both the social reformers and the conservatives. Partha Chatterjee has argued persuasively that in Bengal the nationalists first constructed women as bearers of the "Eastern" tradition, and then allowed them to educate and modernize themselves in order to promote society's modernization (Chatterjee 1999). But in Maharashtra the East-West binary was repeatedly deployed rather to contain women within the home to preserve their purity and subservience. The "Western woman" was deployed as a deterrent trope of education, individualism and independence, to avert the danger of the Eastern woman stepping outside the bounds of domesticity, following her Western counterpart. The persistent fear was that under the Western influence, Indian women would develop an independent existence instead of submerging their identity in their husbands'—that they would become "women" instead of "wives".

This moral anxiety extended to women's education, centering around four issues: that the educated wives would become their husbands' equals; even worse, that they would become professionally qualified and compete with men for jobs; that they would neglect their domestic duties; and lastly that they would develop the Western women's addiction to pursuing their own independent interests through a study of literature and music. The first three fears were universal when women's education was first introduced, as shown by Pandita Ramabai's review of American women's education (Kosambi, tr. and ed. 2003). The fourth seems to have been specific to colonized India, and was symbolized by Shakespeare, Milton, and the piano as deterrent emblems of literary and artistic pursuits—but only in connection with women. Witness Dr. K.R. Kirtikar's outburst against Rakhmabai whom he believed to be too highly educated to look after her ailing husband:

Banish all education if it so hardens a Hindu girl's heart as to force her to leave her husband to the aches and pains of disease, herself flying to her piano for the enjoyment of pleasure or to her Milton and Shakespeare for the enlightenment of her mind! It would not do to kill that sweet love which is a woman's instinctive virtue, by uncontrolled or misguided education and unrestrained freedom when the character of the individual is forming in his or her younger days. (*Mahratta*, 17 April 1887)

Of the basic patriarchal position on education, there were many variants. Tilak's conservative position was that home-making was the only education a woman needed:

Every educated, middle class man wants his wife to be literate and well-trained in household duties, to spend her leisure hours in reading religious texts in order to improve her mind, and to help him in domestic duties. Just as a trade is of primary importance to a craftsman and training is secondary, so are household duties generally primary for women and education incidental. . . . By the age of 15 or 16, a woman should be well-trained in housework, and this training will never be available in a school as much as at home. The marital home is the "workshop" of female education. (Tilak 1976: 219-20; my translation)

This position was further buttressed by the *Mahratta's* insistence that girls needed an education adapted to the "female nature" and the "weaker sex", and that such education could be imparted most suitably by male relatives at home rather than in a school which posed numerous moral dangers through the freedom it afforded from the strict controls imposed at home (*Mahratta*, 26 July 1891). The new Female High School at Pune that these conservatives vehemently opposed was defended by Bhandarkar, one of its founders, with the following assurance:

We do not propose in this institution to make our women learned and teach them to neglect their household duties and take to books. What we intend to do is make them more fit to discharge those duties and open a window in the prison-house of a social system through which they may look into the modern world. (*Mahratta*, 11 October 1891)

That education was not to inspire women to think independently was also implicit in Ranade's instruction to his wife to understand and obey his wishes at all times. Cast in the same mould was G.K. Gokhale, Ranade's political disciple and heir, who declared Ramabai Ranade to be the ideal "educated wife" because she "devoted herself to the service of her husband and considered herself blessed in doing so . . . in spite of the new education, novel ideas and changing circumstances which have provided a new direction to her thoughts and way of life" (Gokhale 1953: 7-8; my translation). The success of a woman's education was obviously to be measured by her enlightened deference to her husband's authority.

There was no discursive space for women's own longing for a meaningful education—a longing that came across in Rakhmabai's lament that the "wicked practice" of child marriage "comes between me and the thing which I prize above all others—study and mental cultivation. Without the least fault of mine . . . every aspiration of mine to rise above my ignorant sisters is looked down upon with suspicion and is interpreted in the most uncharitable manner" (*Times of India*, 26 June 1885). For Pandita Ramabai, education was a crucial component of women's emancipation, which led her to open her Sharada Sadan in 1889 as the first residential school for women in Maharashtra, and perhaps in India. Kashibai Kanitkar, speaking for herself and for Anandibai Joshee, valorized the "gift" of education to the extent of most abjectly conceding their indebtedness to their husbands for the next seven lives (Kanitkar 1912: x). For Kashibai this gift had meant literary self-expression; on Anandibai it had bestowed the opportunity to serve Indian women as a medical doctor.

The issue of women's health care revealed perhaps most explicitly the deep chasm between masculine and feminine epistemologies. In 1880 Anandibai Joshee complained to an American friend about the high "mortality among Indian women", claiming that "fifty per cent die in the prime of their youth". She added a bitterly sarcastic comment on the perceived dispensability of women: "It is not a calamity if a father loses a daughter or two as he is thereby spared much trouble and embarrassment to which he is exposed by abominable customs and manners".[2] Anandibai's public assertion in 1883 that "there is a growing need for Hindu lady doctors in India" (Dall 1888: 84), reiterated a demand registered a year earlier by Pandita Ramabai's testimony before the Hunter Commission for

Education. Ramabai had argued that because of Indian women's unwillingness to consult male doctors and lack of rapport with European women doctors, "The want of lady doctors is . . . the cause of hundreds of thousands of women dying premature deaths" (Bodley 1981: xiv).

But *Native Opinion* (17 September 1882) immediately retorted that the urgent need was for not women doctors, but trained midwives, because patriarchy's stake was in women's reproductive health, not in their general health. Subsequently the publicity given by Dr. W.W. Hunter to Pandita Ramabai's arguments in Britain contributed to the formation of "The National Association for Supplying Female Medical Aid to the Women of India", known popularly as the Dufferin Fund, after the vicereine of India who was its president (Bodley 1981: xiv). Its objectives were to send British women doctors and nurses to India, and to open new hospitals for women or women's wards in existing hospitals. But *Kesari* (27 April 1886) opposed the scheme as a Christian wedge into Hindu society that would pose danger to the very foundation of Hinduism. With heavy sarcasm it painted a vivid picture of British lady doctors and trained midwives putting a stop to infant deaths and also to the "ignorant practices" of "our sweaty wives" at the time of delivery. It added:

> If English lady doctors gain entry into our homes, our women will discard their superstitiousness and lose their fear of eating foods and drinking drinks forbidden by religion. A close proximity will spring up between us and our rulers, and our homes will come under the influence of the Christian religion which is a hundred times superior to our Hindu religion! (my translation).

Why only female patients were susceptible to the "corrupting" influence of Christian medical personnel was never explained. But *Kesari* perhaps feared the charge of callousness regarding women's health problems, and hastened to suggest that Anandibai Joshee ("who is proud of her caste and her people", in a pointed jab at Pandita Ramabai) should be requested, upon her return to India, to open medical classes in Marathi for women of respectable families. *Kesari*'s casually framed plans ended with Anandibai's early death, and were never revived.

PUBLIC AND PRIVATE SPHERES

By articulating through their writings and speeches, their thoughts on their own location within family, society and the reform movement, some women registered their presence in the public sphere. But how was this transition accomplished and what were its implications?

The public/private dichotomy has had a long and chequered career in feminist literature. The once popular dichotomy, corresponding to the male/female spheres of activity, with social transition being marked by women crossing from the private into the public sphere, began to be questioned by some feminist scholars more than a decade ago. To cite just one influential example, Gisela Bock counted among the discarded conceptual frameworks of women's history, "the relation between the public and the private, or the political and the personal, or the sphere of power and the domestic sphere", because of the realization that "the personal is political" (Bock 1991: 4). But more recently the public/private distinction has regained popularity. Mary Ryan concludes, on the basis of some historically plotted cross-cultural studies, that "Empirical discoveries . . . leave no doubt that the concepts of public and private have proven to be very useful in historical research". However, she also adds the rider that "We certainly cannot apply the quartet of public and private, male and female, in some simplistic fashion across time, place, and human experience" (Ryan 2003: 14, 24).

The challenge thrown by my material on Maharashtra demands a new conceptual framework with both analytic and empirical relevance, and has led me to develop and hone the private/public dichotomy further to suit my own purposes. To begin with, I view these two as not dichotomous but simply distinct spheres, with a porous boundary. Further, both spheres are subdivided. The public sphere is naturally split into socio-cultural, political and economic domains. The political domain—or the political public sphere—is the domain of political power; it is inhabited by Indian as well as British men and dominated by the latter. The socio-cultural domain subsumes social customs and institutions related to the family (including marriage), as well as health care, education and literature. This domain is inhabited by Indian men and women, and dominated by the former.

This divide was implicit also in the colonial state's perception of its legitimate sphere of domination being the political one, while social and religious matters remained the exclusive purview of the various Indian religious and caste communities. The demarcation was further reinforced by Queen Victoria's proclamation in the aftermath of the great uprising of 1857 to guarantee non-interference by the state in the socio-cultural arena. Both the political and the socio-cultural public spheres are defined by a gender bias and a caste bias: its Indian occupants are men of the upper castes. The economic domain and its transformation under the evolving phases of colonialism and imperialism in a way undergirded both these, and have been subjected to extensive scholarly analysis. The present discussion, however, focuses only on the socio-cultural and political domains.

The private/public distinction in Maharashtra emerged as a distinctly colonial phenomenon; the distinction had little relevance in the precolonial Peshwa period. In fact, the conceptual boundary between the "public" and "private" spheres was as blurred as was their spatial anchoring. During the Peshwai, Pune and other cities in the region had no public buildings, for example, and all activities were located within residential buildings. Political activity was based in the Peshwa's palace or the mansions (*wadas*) of his *sardars*; the standing army was housed in forts; the penal institution of the jail did not exist separately, offenders being incarcerated either in the *kotwal chavdi* (part of the residence of the *kotwal* or magistrate) or in hill forts which were military encampments. Socio-cultural activity was also bounded within the residence: education was home-based, the sick were nursed at home, and entertainment was also arranged at home. Not only were the public and private spheres enmeshed together, but so were political and socio-cultural domains. With the coming of the British, a whole spectrum of public structures appeared on the cityscape: the secretariat, council hall, town hall, jails, schools, hospitals, as well as theaters. (Also, separately demarcated and planned military cantonments housed troops permanently.) Thus the urban landscape changed in tune with the new institutional structure. It was after the creation by the British of the physical "public" space that Indian public leaders created meeting places for the number of organizations that were rapidly set up—both those that formed part of civil society (like the Sarvajanik Sabha), and those that had a more cultural—at least ostensibly cultural—function (like the Elocution Society or Vakrittvotejak Sabha).

In the precolonial scenario, the family itself had no separation of spheres other than the male and female spaces. As the new social and political organizations shaped the public sphere, so did the social tensions within the family caused by the reform discourse create fissures within the new private sphere. Other regions of Asia also show the colonial connection in this regard. As Elizabeth Thompson points out on the basis of historical studies of women in the Middle East, "Dichotomous conceptions of public and private . . . emerged out of the colonial encounter" (Thompson 2003: 53).

In my framework, the traditional, male-dominated, private sphere is subdivided into the "male zone" and the "female zone" (often referred to as the domestic sphere). The female zone is location-based and confined to a specific part of the house, and sealed by a rigid though invisible boundary; it is sacrosanct in that men in the family rarely have entry there (Kosambi 1998). Even the patriarch who wants to have a word with one of the women would stand outside the women's common room (*majghar*) and try to attract the attention—by clearing his throat, for example—of one of the senior women through whom the message would be routed. The male zone was traditionally homogeneous; but the coming of British rule and the consequent social changes led to its bifurcation into the "traditional" and the "modern" male zone. This is not a locational distinction but one of social space within the men's area of the house. The boundary between the two is not dense but is nevertheless uneasy. Women cannot enter the social space of the traditional male zone which is conservative and rigidly enforces gender segregation. But these women can access the social space of the modern male zone at the behest of their progressive husbands, especially in temporary situations of nuclear family living.

The distinction between the public and the private sphere was porous, as already indicated. Men's reformist or anti-reformist activities in the political and socio-cultural public spheres were after all the offshoots of their meetings and discussions within the modern or traditional male zones: Justice M.G. Ranade's drawing room was a hub of social and political reform; the reception hall of the Tilak *wada* was an informal club of anti-reformers. These were among the prominent places where incursions into the public sphere were planned.

For women, entry into the modern male zone was relatively easy in temporary nuclear family situations. When Ranade took along his wife Ramabai on his extensive tours of the districts, she was able to spend a considerable amount of time with him, listening to his exposition of various topics of current interest, reading the newspaper to him, and even managing his correspondence. She so enjoyed these excursions that she describes them with excitement (Ranade 1953: 91-2). Kashibai Kanitkar recounts as a memorable period in her life the couple's stay at Nevase where Govindrao Kanitkar was posted. The two would read together, discuss books, go horseback riding and have picnics with their children. Once they were visited by Hari Narayan Apte, the famous novelist, who would join them in nightlong discussions on literature and other topics (Kanitkar 1929: 9). These were the periods that enabled Ramabai's later leadership of the women's cause and Kashibai's literary contribution. Anandibai Joshee's ideas and career plans were shaped by her married life within a nuclear family, that is, the modern male zone. My contention thus is that women could enter the public sphere only if they could first access the modern male zone as a stepping-stone.

The public/private distinction proposed here differs from Partha Chatterjee's (1999) dichotomy of the "home" and the "outside" in his study of colonial Bengal, where the home symbolizes the spiritual East as also the domestic domain inhabited by women who are constituted as bearers of Indian culture and tradition, and the outside world constitutes the public space politically colonized by the materialistic West. For the Bengali nationalists of the late nineteenth century, according to

Chatterjee, the "home" represented a non-negotiable Indian space, while the "outside" was the space of political negotiation with the colonial state. A reading of Maharashtra's social past suggests that well into the twentieth century, many aspects of the "home"—especially marriage-related institutions—were brought by the social reformers from the socio-cultural domain to the purview of negotiation with the colonial state, and thus within the political domain. Nor was the home simply a "private" sphere, as I have already argued.

Women's activities in the public sphere were their occasional writings (books or newspaper articles), public speeches, and management of women's institutions. The general reaction to these varied according to the then current male perceptions of the activity and the person who initiated them.

Pandita Ramabai's Arya Mahila Samaj was opposed as encroachment on male territory by the social conservatives, as already mentioned. But at about the same time, her Marathi debut, *Stri Dharma Niti* (Morals for Women, 1882) was reviewed approvingly by *Kesari* for its surrogate male stance in advising women: "It is additionally commendable that the task of championing the women's cause and of speaking or writing on their behalf, which used to fall to the lot of men so far, has now been undertaken by one belonging to the female sex herself" (*Kesari,* 1 August 1882; my translation). Her later book, *United Stateschi Lokasthiti ani Pravasavritta* (The Peoples of the United States, 1889), however, met with stiff resistance from the same paper for its pervasive feminism: "It is not surprising that Panditabai has lashed out at the male sex; that is a bad habit she has formed. Who knows how she intends to fulfil her object without the help of men!" (*Kesari,* 7 January 1890; my translation). One of the Pandita's public speeches describing her experiences in the USA was disrupted in Pune in 1889 with vulgar heckling and obscene comments (Agarkar 1984: 267-9). In 1889 Pandita Ramabai also opened her Sharada Sadan, a residential school for women (primarily for widows) in Mumbai. Surprisingly the conservatives welcomed it, and Ramabai herself, warmly:

> It is a wondrous deed to collect a few thousand rupees in a foreign land, by begging on behalf of people of an alien religion and alien traditions and customs. The fact that this was accomplished by a destitute member

of the weaker sex, through her firm resolve, courteousness, and other laudable traits makes us pity our menfolk and feel proud that such an extraordinary woman was born in our midst. (*Kesari*, 12 February 1889; my translation)

Only two years later, when Ramabai was suspected of carrying on indirect proselytization there, the Sadan was labeled as "the widows' mission house" (*Kesari*, 14 July 1891) and later, Ramabai herself as "a deceitful tigress in a sheep's clothing" (*Kesari*, 12 January 1904).

Anandibai Joshee's public speech in Bengal on "My future visit to America, and public inquiries regarding it" was printed in Mumbai (Dall 1888: 82-3), but what reactions it evoked is not known. Excerpts from Anandibai's letters were publicized by her husband Gopalrao through *Kesari*, and were very much admired as markers of her pride in her Maharashtrian identity, her adherence to Maharashtrian customs and the occasional, small Maharashtrian cultural incursions into American society. Ramabai Ranade, in her initial, fumbling speeches, functioned so obviously as her husband's mouthpiece that she escaped criticism. But Kashibai Kanitkar was less fortunate when she gave a talk in the public library of Dahanu on the Indian National Congress in 1889 (shortly before she was to attend its meetings as one of a handful of women delegates). *Kesari* charitably supported the attempt by any woman "who lives in her husband's shadow and does not transgress the boundary of the world that is appropriate for the female community, to offer a few words of advice to others in the light of her own understanding". But it offered Kashibai some advice of its own:

We think that Mrs. Kashibai should not pounce upon political topics just yet. It would be more beneficial if she speaks a few words about women's education, domestic conditions, the interaction between men and women, etc. (*Kesari*, 26 November 1889; my translation)

Ramabai Ranade's autobiography, more in the nature of an almost hagiographical biography of her husband, published a few years after his death, was universally valorized as a sign of her true *pativrata dharma*. By the same token, Rakhmabai who repudiated her child marriage was heavily attacked by the conservatives, and supported only partially by the liberals who used her court case as a weapon in the struggle to abolish the custom of child marriage.

Some women thus made their voices heard, and gained visibility in the public sphere. But their initiatives in the socio-cultural domain of the public sphere were generally treated as "domestic" private interventions and occluded from the historical archive because of the discursive marginality of the domestic sphere. A telling case in point is the Rakhmabai court case of 1884-9 which fed into the public agitation for social reform focusing on the bride's consent to marriage.[3] It was located at the imbrication of the social-cultural and the political public spheres, inviting as it did action from the colonial government in terms of legislative reform of an Indian social custom. The agitation was rooted in Rakhmabai's personal protest—in terms of her "Hindu Lady" letters to *The Times of India* and her part in the judicial trial itself—which was very much in the public sphere. But it served merely as an "excuse" for the agitation and continued to be regarded as a highly publicized "private" act, or rather, a "domestic" private act—it remained a pretext and not even a premise for the discourse. Nowhere were Lata Mani's oft-quoted words more apt, that in the context of the sati debates in Bengal, "women are neither subjects nor objects, but rather the ground of the discourse" (Mani 1997: 117).

Thus the relationship between voice, visibility and agency is far from a simple one. This is best illustrated by A.K. Ramanujan's discussion of folklore where he makes the point that "agency in . . . women's tales is connected with their being able to tell their own story and with its being heard", because "speech is an indication of power" (Ramanujan 1997: 224-5). But the fact that speech is a necessary though not sufficient condition for exercising agency or acquiring power is demonstrated by his own analysis of folk stories. In his "male-centered" tales, women are secondary to the male protagonists and sometimes help the hero in his quest. "These stories end in marriage—for they speak of the emancipation of the hero from the parental yoke and the setting up of a new family, as he comes into his own". In the "women-centered" tales, "the heroine is either already married or she is married early in the tale, and then the woman's troubles begin". She has to overcome marital harassment, and sometimes reform her husband, to be able to achieve a happy married life. "A woman's culturally constructed life-forms, her meaning-universe, is different from a man's" (Ramanujan 1997: 218). Leaving aside the irony that the institution of marriage that signifies the male protagonist's "emancipation" also signals the female protagonist's oppression, we see the woman's "voice" frequently employed only to express her grievances. We may see this as the first step, but only the first step, towards exercising her agency. Possession of a voice does not by itself empower a woman.

Going even further, it is possible to see the female voice sometimes employed as a male proxy in the Marathi women's early autobiographies that form the core of my primary source material. Ramabai Ranade's reminiscences (1953, first published in 1910) speak not of her agency or empowerment but of her total and willing surrender of agency to her husband whose personality and actions she describes almost hagiographically. Her narrative begins with Justice Ranade's birth and ends with his death, and she apologizes for dwelling even briefly on her own family history. Significantly, she never recorded her own considerable achievements after she came into her own after Ranade's death, to run the Seva Sadan to educate women and to agitate for women's compulsory education and enfranchisement in the Bombay Provincial Council. Also Kashibai Kanitkar is so self-effacing in her sporadically written memoirs (Vaidya 1991) that she omits to mention either her creative writing or her contribution to the Seva Sadan. If agency cannot be experienced by those who are denied a voice, possession of a voice does not necessarily translate automatically into agency either.

Again, women's voices were heard mostly through their writings that were disregarded within the frame of social reform, although the reformers made occasional gestures in their direction. Telang mooted the idea of enlisting "the help and cooperation of our ladies" as "absolutely essential" in implementing social reforms, at the Third Social Conference in December 1889 (Chintamani 1901: 136). A year later, at the height of the Age of Consent controversy, Ranade suggested, with a paternalism that seems to have been characteristic (judging by his wife's memoirs), that women should organize their own public meetings to consider their problems: "No matter what they resolve, in the light of their own understanding, I will consider that to be a historic, golden day" (*Sudharak*, 15 September 1890; my translation). Only Agarkar explicitly sought to correct the discursive power imbalance by suggesting that "we should follow the inclination of women" who were the ones to suffer from the custom of early cohabitation. The clarification obtained by a few men of his acquaintance from their wives showed that:

> in order to escape the unbearable pain due to premature cohabitation, women are ready to accept any kind of preventive measures! But we selfish and impatient men do not pay any attention to their condition, and do not even think of listening to their views! (*Sudharak*, 8 December 1889; my translation)

Agarkar's obvious implication was that "It takes a special kind of deafness not to hear such clear enunciation", as Chris Healy says in a different context (Healy 1997: 45).[4]

The idea of inducting women into the reform effort, or even consulting them about their problems and preferred solutions, never formed an integral part of the social reform movement of the late nineteenth and early twentieth centuries. But women themselves appropriated agency in public life from the 1920s when they began to agitate for their educational and political rights.

NOTES

* This paper is based on part of the 'Introduction' in M. Kosambi 2007. It generally uses current place names (e.g. Mumbai, Pune) except in terms like the "Bombay Presidency".

1. One may add that this influence was coercive even within the Chitpavan subcaste; the orthodox Chitpavans harassed the less conventional members of their subcaste as much as they harassed other Brahman subcastes. I am thankful to Sarojini Vaidya for this suggestion.

   The phenomenal ascendance of the originally poor community of Chitpavans was caused by the selective patronage extended by the Chitpavan Peshwas, denied to other Brahman subcastes. Deshasthas frequently owned lands in the Deccan plateau and the Saraswats in Goa, but the latter had migrated to Mumbai in large numbers. Thus it was the Chitpavans and Saraswats who took to Western education and participated in the reform movement in a significant measure.
2. Anandibai Joshee's letter to Mrs. Theodocia Carpenter dated 1 November 1880; The Carpenter Family Archive.

3. The Rakhmabai case is analyzed in 'Resisting Conjugality: Rakhmabai's Protest' in M. Kosambi, 2007.
4. Healy's context is the Australian aboriginal perceptions of Captain Cook's "discovery" of the island continent.

REFERENCES

Agarkar, Gopal Ganesh, 1984: *Agarkar-Vangmaya, Khanda 1 (Sudharana-vibhag-Purvardha)*, ed. M.G. Natu and D.Y. Deshpande. Mumbai: Maharashtra Rajya Sahitya ani Sanskriti Mandal.

Bock, Gisela, 1991: "Challenging Dichotomies: Perspectives on Women's History", in *Writings Women's History: International Perspectives*, ed. Karen Offen et al. Bloomington: Indiana University Press, pp. 1-23.

Bodley, Rachel L., 1981 (1887): "Introduction", in Pandita Ramabai, *The High-Caste Hindu Woman*, rpt. Bombay: Maharashtra State Board for Literature and Culture, pp. i-xix.

Chatterjee, Partha, 1999: *The Nation and Its Fragments: Colonial and Postcolonial Histories.* New Delhi: Oxford University Press.

Chintamani, C. Yajnesvara, ed., 1901: *Indian Social Reform, in Four Parts being a Collection of Essays, Addresses, Speeches, etc. with an Appendix.* Madras: Thompson & Co.

Dall, Caroline Healy, 1888: *The Life of Mrs. Anandabai* [*sic*] *Joshee.* Boston: Roberts Brothers.

Doniger, Wendy, 1991: "Introduction", in *The Laws of Manu*, translated by Wendy Doniger and Brian K. Smith. New Delhi: Penguin Books India.

Gokhale, Gopal Krishna, "Prastavana", in Ramabai Ranade (1953).

Healy, Chris, 1997: *From the Ruins of Colonialism: History as Social Memory.* Cambridge: Cambridge University Press.

Kanitkar, Kashibai, 1911: "Samrajya-sattekhali Stri-shikshanachi Pragati" (The Progress of Women's Education under Imperial Rule), *Vividha Jnana Vistara*, November-December, Darbar Anka, pp. 152-61.

———, 1912; *Dr. Anandibai Joshee Yanche Charitra va Patre* (The Life and Letters of the late Dr. Anandibai Joshee), 2nd end., Mumbai: Manoranjan Grantha Prasarak Mandali.

———, 1929: "Don Shabda", in H.N. Apte, *Haribhaunchi Patre.* Satara: Aikya-sampadan Mandal, pp. 9-14.

Kanitkar, Narayan Bapuji, 1890 (1886): *Taruni-Shikshan-Natika athava Adhunik Taruni-Shikshan va Stri-Swatantrya Yanche Bhavishya-Kathan* (A Short Play about Young Women's Education, or Predicting the Future of Young Women's Modern Education and Women's Freedom), rev. 2nd edn. Pune: N.B. Kanitkar.

Kesari (Marathi weekly, Pune), selected issues.

Kosambi, D.D., 2002: *Combined Methods in Indology and Other Writings*, ed. Brajdulal Chattopadhyaya. New Delhi: Oxford University Press.

Kosambi, Meera, 1998: "Home as Social Universe", in *The House and Home in Maharashtra*, ed. Irina Glushkova and Anne Feldhaus. New Delhi: Oxford University Press.

———, tr. and ed., 2003: *Returning the American Gaze: Pandita Ramabai's "The Peoples of the United States* (1889)". New Delhi: Permanent Black.

———, 2007: *Crossing Thresholds: Feminist Essays in Social History*. New Delhi: Permanent Black.

The Laws of Manu, translated by Wendy Doniger and Brian K. Smith. New Delhi: Penguin Books India, 1991.

Lele, Jayant, 1998: "Gender Consciousness in Mid-Nineteenth-Century Maharashtra", in *Images of Women in Maharashtrian Society*, ed. Anne Feldhaus. Albany: State University of New York Press, pp. 163-91.

The Mahratta (English weekly, Poona), selected issues.

Mani, Lata, 1997 (1989): "Contentious Traditions: The Debate on Sati in Colonial India", in *Recasting Women: Essays in Colonial History*, ed. Kumkum Sangari and Sudesh Vaid. New Delhi: Kali for Women, pp. 88-126.

Masselos, J.C. 1974: *Towards Nationalism: Group Affiliations and the Politics of Public Associations in Nineteenth Century Western India*. Bombay: Popular Prakashan.

Native Opinion (Anglo-Marathi weekly, Mumbai), selected issues.

Ramabai, Pandita, 1981 (1887): *The High-Caste Hindu Woman*, rpt. Bombay: Maharashtra State Board for Literature and Culture.

Ramanujan, A.K., 1997: *The Flowering Tree And Other Oral Tales from India*, ed. Stuart Blackburn and Alan Dundes. New Delhi: Viking.

Ranade, Ramabai, 1953 (1910): *Amachya Ayushyatil Kahi Athavani*, 7th edn. Pune: K.G. Sharangpani.

Ryan, Mary P., 2003: "The Public and the Private Good: Across the Great Divide in Women's History", *Journal of Women's History*, vol. 15, no. 2, pp. 10-27.

Sarkar, Sumit, 1994 (1985): "The Women's Question in Nineteenth Century Bengal", in *Women and Culture*, ed. Kumkum Sangari and Sudesh Vaid. Bombay: Research Centre for Women's Studies, SNDT Women's University, rpt., pp. 103-12.

Sudharak (Anglo-Marathi weekly, Pune), selected issues.

Thompson, Elizabeth, 2003: "Public and Private in Middle Eastern Women's History", *Journal of Women's History*, vol. 15, no. 1, pp. 52-69.

Tilak, Bal Gangadhar, 1976: *Samagra Tilak Vangmaya*, vol. 5. Pune: Kesari Prakashan.

The Times of India (English daily, Bombay), selected issues.

Uberoi, Patricia, 1996: "Introduction: Problematising social reform, engaging sexuality, interrogating the state", in *Social Reform, Sexuality and the State*, ed. Patricia Uberoi. New Delhi: Sage Publications, pp. ix-xxvi.

Vaidya, Sarojini, 1991: *Shrimati Kashibai Kanitkar: Atmacharitra ani Charitra* (1861-1948), 2nd edn. Mumbai: Popular Prakashan.

10

Naoroji Furdoonji and the "Young Bombay Party": Reflections on the Early Debate on Reform in Western India

AROON TIKEKAR

It is commonly known that the modern Indian Renaissance was first started and consummated in the nineteenth-century Bengal and then spread to the rest of the parts of India. This is true to a large extent but with a difference. The introduction and growth of Western liberal education in India through the instrumentality of the British rule brought about a cultural resurgence by "cultural induction", taken to mean a direct transfer of ideas. The expression "renaissance" being taken to mean a socio-economic reconstruction depended on the degree and duration of the contact with English education and Western ideas.[1] Since Bengal came in contact with the English education early, the newly educated Bengali elite's response came early. The Bengal Renaissance started through serious debates both over the Hindu religion and its corrupted tenets, and its outward manifestations such as idolatry, outdated social taboos and customs, and the iniquitous and unjust caste system that increased social inequality. Hence the major thrust of their early activities revolved around primarily religious reform. Without undermining the importance and merits of the achievements of Bengal reformers an attempt is made in this paper to establish that the seeds of an equally significant Renaissance were sown almost independently and concurrently in Bombay around the same time. The Bombay reformers, on the other hand, surely took a different path—that of social reformation. They believed that destroying one's religion without substituting another is of no use and, therefore, it is difficult to reform religion in the first place, and that an early social reform movement would mentally prepare the society to gradually accept reforms in religious matters. The Bombay reformers believed that any attempt at wholesale religious reform could be counter-productive if the society was not ready for such a radical change. This early view is reflected in a letter published in the *Bombay Gazette* of 4 April 1864: "I think we are rather in the Fourteenth century of England than in the Sixteenth of Europe. Who could choose to be in the position of Wickliffe than in that of Luther?" The English educated early Maharashtrian intellectuals regarded the English language as a window to the secular scientific world and made a distinction between the ethos of English society and the ethos of modern science and the liberal Western thought. While they admitted that there was much to be learnt from the English, they rejected the Englishman and his culture. Hence the ambivalence in their attitude. For they had a sneaking admiration for qualities of the Englishman such as industry, adventure and inquisitiveness. They, however, still openly despised him for the ruination their policies brought about in India. The slowness of the religious reform in western India was much compensated by attempts at social reform such as opening schools for both boys and girls; starting anti-caste movement such as Paramhansa Sabha, though it worked much in secrecy; seeking amelioration of the condition of women; attacking superstitious beliefs and inculcating scientific knowledge and temper through the publication of newspapers, and such other activities. On the one hand they made a severe critique of the decadent Hindu society and on the other, made serious attempts at restructuring it on just principles. It would not be an exaggeration to argue that early serious attempts at social reform facilitated the western India reformers to create an all powerful urge for political reforms in the later decades of the nineteenth century. The fact that the renaissance movement saw the emergence of a galaxy of leaders from western India in the second half of the nineteenth century explains this phenomenon.

True, that the Bombay reformers did not give precedence to religious reform over the social as was done by the Bengal reformers, in fact, they advocated simultaneous reforms in all directions—social, religious, educational, economic, cultural and political. For them it was a matter of tactical retreat, namely to lie low regarding the loss of political power after 1818 until the society regained its normal social health by getting rid of social ills. Therefore, the early movements for social protest and religious dissent in the early nineteenth-century Maharashtra gradually outgrew into protest movements against the oppressive foreign rule. This transition from socio-religious reform to assertive movements for political freedom was, thus, a natural corollary.

The scope of this paper is restricted to the beginnings of social reform in Bombay, now called Mumbai, and seeks to establish how a group of radical enthusiastic youngsters, the early recipients of liberal Western education in this part of India, initiated a process of social change. It also tries to identify these reformers who were derisively referred to by the older generation as "the Young Bombay Party" drawing a parallel with the radical and supposedly impetuous "Young Bengal" movement. An attempt is also made to locate what was cohesive in them as to group them together under one epithet. The nucleus to this band of young radicals was provided by the professors and students of the Elphinstone College. It is in this regard an attempt is made to evaluate the contribution of Naoroji Furdoonji (1817-85) who took up the mantle of leadership of this group after the premature death of Professor Balshastri Jambhekar (1812-46). The paper also makes an appraisal of the Young Bombay Party as a conduit between the two different types of leadership, viz., the early leadership of the Bombay merchant or Shetia class and the latter one of the urbanized, Western educated liberal elite.

The paper is based on the contemporary Indian literature and seeks to analyze, perhaps for the first time, how Keshab Chunder Sen's pleas to break caste system head-on during his visit to Bombay in 1864 had a catalytic effect on the debate among the

Young Bombay Party. Their response reveals the inner complications and fractures that differentiated between the Bengal and the Bombay reformers.

The role of Bombay's merchant princes like Sir Jamshetji Jejeebhoy (1783-1859), Framji Cowasji (1767-1851), Jagannath Shankershet (1802-65) and others, in the development of modern Bombay in its nascent days has, by and large, been well investigated and their contributions to the socio-politico-cultural ethos elaborately evaluated. In the early decades of the nineteenth century, these self-educated successful businessmen provided leadership not only to their respective communities but also to the entire city which was growing at a bewildering speed.[2] Equally well-researched are the various reform movements and the biographies of reformers which present a spectacle of a society in turmoil in the middle of nineteenth-century Bombay. In sharp contrast with the earlier generations of leaders, the members of the Young Bombay Party who formed the new intelligentsia were much exposed to English education and Western culture. It was not just a difference in generational approach to the issues of the day but the latter group was more radical in social restructuring.

THE TRANSITION OF LEADERSHIP

The transition of leadership from the earlier generation to the members of the Young Bombay radicals, was not straight and easy. It had to pass through the hands of the "noble band of early reformers—touched by the very first rays of the rising sun of education" as Sir Pherozeshah Mehta referred to them.[3] In fact, a great deal of credit for instilling the reformist zeal in the rising intelligentsia goes to this "noble band" of early reformers who were exposed to the Western socio-political ideas, introduced to them by their European teachers and professors. These teachers and professors and the students were associated with either Elphinstone Institution (est. 1828) or the Elphinstone College (est. 1835). This group of the earlier generations of Elphistonians —referred to as the "Young Bombay Party"—was a conduit between the two types of leaderships mentioned earlier.

These were "noble band of early reformers" referred to by Sir Pherozeshah, chief among whom were two of the earliest Indians to become assistant professors at the Elphinstone College—Balshastri Jambhekar and Naoroji Furdoonji. It is argued here that these two Indian assistant professors, who taught their students beyond the curriculum and successfully created a band of genuine and ardent social reformers, were ably guided by some of their European professors such as A.M. Paton, Henry T. Green, R.T. Reid, R.S. Sinclair, L. Hulings, Alexander Grant and Dr. John Harkness. Neither these young radicals desired to show disregard to tradition which their elders respected most nor did they ever think of hurting the sensibilities of the elder generation but they were convinced of the express need for a change in the existing social structure. It is their fervent advocacy of reform that earned them the epithet "Young Bombay Party" by the earlier generation in a rather derisive way, making an oblique comparison with the "Young Bengal" movement.[4] This derisive epithet, in due course of time, the young reformists held in pride. "The Young Bombay Party" was a term loosely applied and was never a well-knit group similar to the "Young Bengal" under the tutelage of Henry Louis Vivian Derozio (1809-31),[5] who taught at the Hindoo College in Calcutta, from 1826 to 1831.

One may be tempted to consider the Young Bombay Party as a mirror image of the Young Bengal group. However, except the name and almost identical period of existence, there are hardly any common reference points. Derozio's students—Ram Gopal Ghosh, Dakshinaranjan Mukherjee, Rashik Krishna Mallick, the Rev. K.M. Bannerjee, Radhanath Sikdar, Ramtanu Lahiry and Peary Chandra Mitra—were members of the Young Bengal group who prided in their atheism and libertine attitude. Thomas Edward describes about the meetings of the Young Bengal Movement:

> The principles and practices of the Hindu religion were openly ridiculed and condemned and angry disputes were held on usual subjects. The Hindu religion was denounced as vile and corrupt and unworthy of the regard of rational human beings. The degraded state of the Hindu formed the topic of many debates.[6]

There are quite a few direct references to the phrase "Young Bombay Party" in the life-sketches of its leader Naoroji Furdoonji and other reformers.[7] But for Jim Masselos who in his *Towards*

Nationalism: Group Affiliations and the Politics of Public Associations in Nineteenth Century Western India[8] makes a discrete mention to "The Young Bombay Party", scholars have hardly paid adequate attention to the contribution of these early radical reformers to the renaissance movement in Maharashtra.

BALSHASTRI: THE PIONEER OF RENAISSANCE IN WESTERN INDIA

Balshastri Jambhekar, the first brilliant product of the liberal Western education, who showed extraordinary potential of leadership and scholarship, died unexpectedly and prematurely at the young age of 34, to the great grief of his disciples. His European teachers and the contemporary leaders of Hindu society such as Jagannath Shankerseth, had admired Jambhekar's scholastic achievements, and expected him to play a greater role as facilitator between the new rulers and the "native" populace. His contemporary, Dr. John Wilson, aptly called him as "one of the most learned natives who has yet appeared in western India".[9] Balshastri, when barely 20, was appointed Deputy Native Secretary of the Bombay Native Education Society, only to be promoted within two years as the Native Secretary of the society. After being away in Akkalkote, a small Princely State in southern Maharashtra, where he was tutor to the Prince for over a year, Balshastri returned to Bombay as the first "native" assistant professor at the Elphinstone College in 1835. When Professor A.B. Orlebar was on furlough, Balshastri was deservedly appointed Acting Professor of Mathematics, the first Indian again to hold such position.[10] Besides his academic excellence, Balshastri is regarded as a "pioneer of the Renaissance in western India and Father of Modern Maharashtra" for his all-round contribution to social rejuvenation.[11] A pioneer in Marathi journalism by starting the newspaper, *Bombay Durpun* and monthly, *Dig-Durshan* for disseminating scientific knowledge, he was also an ardent advocate of social reforms such as widow-marriage, reconversion and upliftment of the socially depressed. The role played by him in the Narayan and Sripat Sheshadri Conversion episode is noteworthy for two reasons, firstly,

Balshastri's attempt to reconvert laid the foundation of the future *Shuddhi* movement of the Arya Samajists, and secondly, by seeking shastric sanctions he sought legitimacy from the traditional section of the society. This method of reform became the main strand of social change for most of the reformers in the nineteenth century. Besides, he was one of the earliest Indologists in western India and his research papers were read in absentia in the Bombay Branch of the Royal Asiatic Society.[12] Also, he was an active member of the Bombay Geographical Society which was formed in 1831. Despite his social engagements, he found time to produce voluminous useful literature and historical works. This brilliant career was cut short by his untimely death in 1846. His short though very fruitful career certainly provided the necessary inspiration to his students and associates, chief among them were: Dadoba Pandurang Tarkhadkar (1814-82), Govind Narayan Madgaonkar (1815-65), Naoroji Furdoonji (1817-85), Bhogilal Pranvallabhdas (1818-89), Ram Balkrishna Jayakar (d. 1866), Narayan Dinanathji Velkar (d. 1870), Raghunath Narayan Khote (1821-91), Nana Moroji Trilokekar (1822-95), Dr. Bhau Daji Lad (1822-74), Atmaram Pandurang Tarkhadkar (1823-89), Kero Laxman Chhatre (1824-84), Dadabhoy Naoroji (1825-1917). This galaxy of youngsters who not only excelled in their chosen field of activity but also helped to shape the future of modern Maharashtra is a proof enough of how Balshastri Jambhekar became a beacon light to them.

Soon after Balshastri's untimely death, Naoroji Furdoonji came to bear the mantle of leadership. In him, the students of the Elphinstone College found a worthy successor to Balshastri Jambhekar. Naoroji Furdoonji, one of Balshastri's earliest and brightest students at the Elphinstone Institution became his associate from 1839. Naoroji taught at the Elphinstone College between 1839 and 1845. Balshastri and Naoroji were, thus, colleagues for nearly six years. For over a decade, Naoroji had occasions to closely follow Balshastri's benevolent efforts.

A.K. Priyolkar, the doyen among Bombay researchers, has complained that, in the absence of a single, authoritative biography of Naoroji Furdoonji, much of his life and works have remained little known or forgotten.[13] Priyolkar, perhaps, relied for Naoroji's life and work on the information provided by some contemporary accounts. However, there is enough reliable information to construct a biographical account of Naoroji Furdoonji.

NAOROJI MASTER

Born at Broach (today's Bhadoch) in March 1817, Naoroji Furdoonji was five years junior to Balshastri Jambhekar and eight years senior to Dadabhoy Naoroji. At the Elphinstone College, Balshastri and Naoroji worked as colleagues and this made them have a vision of a new society. Naoroji Furdoonji received his early education at Broach and was indebted to Vallubram, a school-teacher of that place. He was then sent to Surat to receive higher education under the Rev. Thomas Salman of the Surat London Missionary Society. Naoroji's father Furdoonji was in the employment of James Sutherland who subsequently was appointed a member of the Executive Council of Bombay. It was Sutherland who took keen interest in Naoroji's education and on his advice was brought to Bombay for education at the Native Education Society's school. Naoroji made excellent progress there in English and other subjects under the well-known teacher the Rev. Mainwaring, winning many prizes and scholarships. He was presented with a silver medal at the hands of the Earl of Clare, the then Governor of Bombay, for his proficiency in English and History. After completing his school education Naoroji was employed as a teacher in the Native Education Society's school which was his alma mater, a rare honor in those days!

When Naoroji was barely 19, he accepted the position of the native Secretary and translator to Sir Alexander Burns (1805-41), the famed traveler known for his missions to Afghanistan, Bokhara, Persia. In 1836, Burns was sent on a mission, apparently commercial but really political, to Dost Mohammad, the Amir of Kabul and was later made political agent at Kabul. In 1841, the relationships between Afghanistan and Britain were particularly sore and Sir Alexander was assassinated along with his entire party. Naoroji Furdoonji, however, escaped the calamity as he had returned to India just before the attack, to take care of the family hard pressed by the unexpected death of his father who was drowned in the Bombay harbor while returning by boat from Panvel.[14]

Naoroji was extremely popular with his students at the Native Education Society's school as well as the Elphinstone Institution, which became college in 1835. Fondly called by his students as "Naoroji Master", he soon rose to the position of Assistant Professor, five years after Balshastri. The Elphinstone Institution, where both Balshastri Jambhekar and Naoroji Furdoonji instilled in the spirit of reform among their students, became the nucleus that ultimately crystallized into the "Young Bombay Party". Among their students were Dadabhoy Naoroji, Bhau Daji, Kero Laxman Chhatre, Sorabji Shapurji Bengallee, Dadoba and Bhaskar Pandurang Tarkhadkar, Vishwanath Narayan Mandlik, Vinayak Jagannath and others. Their watchword was—Reform, an all-pervading reform, since they believed in efflorescence and not piecemeal reform.

In a reply to a public address accorded to him, at Bombay on 20 December 1895, Pherozeshah Mehta made a direct reference to this group of youngsters. "The spirit and influence of these young men, penetrating in a hundred directions," he said, "have left an abiding mark in the aims, thoughts and aspirations of the people of this Presidency who will always cherish with pride and affection the names of Naoroji Furdoonji, Dadabhoy Naoroji, Sorabji Bengallee, Vishwanath Narayan Mandlik and many others, the first fruits of the growth of the Elphinstone Institution."[15] Naoroji Furdoonji remained for the Young Bombay reformers their "Naoroji Master" even in their later life.

THE NATIVE IMPROVEMENT SOCIETY

In 1845, Naoroji Furdoonji was appointed as an interpreter at the Supreme Court of Bombay. In that capacity he served the Government until his retirement in 1864. Balshastri Jambhekar had founded the Native Improvement Society in 1845 and was its first President. Here the young educated men of the day read papers and discussed various questions related to general improvement. The offshoot of this activity was the Students' Literary and Scientific Society, established in June 1848.[16] This Society was established on the initiative of two English professors—A.M. Patton and R.T. Reid—shortly after their arrival in Bombay. Initially, its membership was restricted to the students of Elphinstone Institution only. Their initial activities were confined to the presentation and discussion of papers on a variety of subjects concerning the Indian society, though the discussions excluded religious and political issues. Soon their activities expanded into starting of schools and until proper teachers could be employed these young Elphinstonians worked themselves as teachers. The membership of the society expanded rapidly from 24 (18 of whom were students) in 1848 to 106 in 1852 (26 of whom were students). It can be observed from the available annual reports, that since 1852, membership was thrown open to all educated persons but not to Shetias or other men of commerce, a decision that speaks much about the Young Bombay spirit.

Surprisingly Naoroji Furdoonji's name does not appear in the list of the Society's founder-members. He joined the Society in 1851. In the very next year, he became Secretary of the Gujarati-Hindu Schools along with Mohunlal Runchhoddas. Naoroji Furdoonji, it appears, did not stay with the Students Literary and Scientific Society for long. But the Society was surely a good training ground for young Elphinstonians in their future endeavors in social reform. A cursory glance at the reports of the Society which mentions the subjects of papers read in its proceedings, gives a fair idea of the zeal these young reformers bore to bring about an all-round enlightenment in society.

Being Elphinstonians, the Young Bombay group possessed a corporate sense of identity. It is their cohesiveness and their common interest in public activity that earned for them the epithet of Young Bombay.

> Behind the activities of Young Bombay lay an acceptance of the intrinsic value of a liberal Western education and the knowledge which is imparted, an attitude that despite the increasing spread of education was still not common. Their role was to provide the link of communication between the active and the ever-advancing intellect of Europe and the hitherto inert and dormant mind of India.[17]

It is interesting to note that Balshastri Jambhekar who, in 1832, started the Anglo-Marathi newspaper the *Bombay Durpun* had similar objective: to diffuse European knowledge and provide a forum for discussion of the methods by which prosperity and happiness of the people might be ensured.[18]

In 1851 Naoroji Furdoonji entered the fray with full gusto when he established the Rahanoomai Mazdiasin Sabha, a religious society, the first of its kind, of which he remained President till his death. Aware as he was, of the fact that, like Hindus, the Parsees too were subject to numerous religious prejudices, Naoroji realized that no improvement could be possible as long as the Parsee community continued to be enmeshed in religious shackles. By dint of perseverance and courage, and with the co-operation of a few progressive Parsees such as Sorabji Shapurji Bengallee, he was able to correct many a social aberration that had been hampering the progress of the Parsee community. Of course, he had to meet with great opposition from the orthodox sections of the Parsee community. Naoroji and other Parsees of the Young Bombay Party were, however, dauntless. Naoroji had started as early as 1840 a magazine called *Vidyasagar* to help diffusion of knowledge similar to the *Durpun* of Balshastri Jambhekar. However, it is only after the establishment of the *Rast Goftar* by Dadabhoy Naoroji that the Young Bombay Party got recognition of sorts and, within some years, it became an influential organ to voice their views on religious and social reform among the Zoroastrians in particular and the Hindu society in general. Through this newspaper, Naoroji Furdoonji and Sorabji Shapurji, consistently attacked outdated religious practices and fervently appealed for reform. Besides, Naoroji was also engaged in theological discussions with Dr. John Wilson and other missionaries, and published numerous tracts and also *Rahnoomaee-e-Zarthosti.* Naoroji was widely acclaimed to be the reformer who secured for Parsees a Matrimonial and Succession Act. He was the guiding spirit behind the Parsee Law Association and was often consulted by the courts of law on customs followed by Parsees.

Bengal's aristocratic zamindars came together in October 1851 to form the British Indian Association, with the express object of sending memorials and petitions enlisting their demands on the eve of the Charter to be granted in 1853. Bombay too similarly responded. Dr. George Buist, editor of the *Bombay Times,* however, urged the Young Bombay, in the persons of Naoroji

Furdoonji, Narayan Dinanathji, and Dr. Bhau Daji to form an association for a similar purpose. Naoroji Furdoonji and Narayan Dinanathji were among the Indian shareholders of the *Bombay Times*. However, the Bombay Association could not be established without the support of the leaders of the earlier generation. That explains the presence of Jagannath Shankershet and Sir Jamshetji Jejeebhoy in the body. Perhaps this association, the first political association in western India, was the last platform where both the old guards and the young radicals came together. The Bombay Association sent two petitions to the British Parliament in 1852 and 1853 respectively demanding commercial and educational reforms. The presence of both generations of leaders in the drafting of the petitions delayed the process and a lot of time was spent in the choice of words, the radical members wanting to be more critical, and the conservative members trying to check the over-enthusiastic progressiveness of the radicals. After a few years of good work, the Bombay Association became defunct. Dr. Bhau Daji and Naoroji Furdoonji tried to revive it but in vain. However hard the duo tried to resuscitate the Bombay Association, it could never get back to its original status.

In 1885, yet another association was formed entitled the Bombay Presidency Association. Although this association achieved some level of success, the days had changed and the Young Bombay Party leaders of the earlier times had to take a backseat since the new generation of leaders were more articulate, more radical and more vociferous than them.

DR. BUIST'S TIRADE

Dr. George Buist, editor of the *Bombay Times* during the period 1840-58, was a strong supporter of the Young Bombay Party. When, in 1850, it was decided to increase the share capital of the *Bombay Times* by allowing more Indians to become shareholders of the proprietary concern, Dr. Buist induced Naoroji Furdoonji, Narayan Dinanathji and others to buy shares. It was an irony of fate that Dr. Buist who was with these Young Bombay men in all their adventures, became their *bête noire* for his anti-Indian vituperations during the Revolt of 1857. The Indian shareholders successfully rallied under the leadership of Naoroji

Furdoonji and Narayan Dinanathji to unseat him from the editorship. Naoroji Furdoonji, who spearheaded the attack on Dr. Buist, became a staunch enemy for the deposed editor. Through the *Bombay Standard*, which Dr. Buist's Scottish friends helped him to start after he lost the position with the *Bombay Times*, the learned doctor attacked Naoroji like a wounded lion. He even went to the extent of seeking removal of Naoroji from government service, but failed. Dr. Buist died in 1860. Naoroji continued to be in government service until his retirement in 1864.[19] Although Dr. Buist continued his tirade against educated Indians, derided their associations, much to the liking of his Anglo-Indian conservative diatribe but with no consequence.

In the changed situation, political reform was to gain more importance *vis-à-vis* social reforms. Its echoes were found in the Municipal Corporation of which Naoroji had been a member and was already enrolled as a clever debater on the Indian side. After his retirement from government service, Naoroji Furdoonji visited England thrice and during these visits he labored hard to enlist the sympathy of Englishmen in the cause of the Indians. He gave evidence before the Indian Famine Committee, delivered numerous speeches before the East India Association and endeavored to influence the various Chambers of Commerce in England in favor of India. He spoke before the British Parliament Committee, as the representative of the Bombay Association and the Poona Sarvajanik Sabha. It is there that he struck friendship with John Bright and Henry Fawcett and others who were greatly impressed by his intimacy with Indian problems.

In 1873, Naoroji visited Gujarat and conducted a careful enquiry into the condition of farmers and published it. At the time of the disastrous floods at Surat, Naoroji Furdoonji was appointed Honorary Secretary to the Relief Fund. In 1884, for his valuable contribution to public services, he was decorated with the title of CIE. In reply to the felicitation that was given to him at the residence of Sir Dinshaw Maneckjee Petit, Naoroji Furdonji said:

> I have worked hard and have taken an active part in measures having for their object the amelioration of the social, intellectual and political condition of the community to which we all belong; I have persevered in this labour of love through good report and bad report, and have

> encountered formidable difficulties, and have many times made considerable personal sacrifices. Not infrequently have I been denounced as disloyal to the rule of our beneficent sovereign, and threatened with ignominious dismissal from the public service. But having chalked out a course of action for myself, and having calculated all the risks, I have continued firm and steadfast in my path, and have, by dint of perseverance, overcome many of the difficulties which I have encountered. . . . Let me assure you, gentlemen, that in rendering the services I have referred to, I have not conferred any obligation or favour on my countrymen. I have simply done my duty as a member of society.[20]

And what a member of the society he was. His example was worthy of emulation. It was little wonder that Sir Richard Temple, the then Governor of Bombay, called him "the tribune of the city people". Apart from the public work at the Bombay Municipality, if Naoroji Furdoonji had the credit of establishing the first girls' school, the first native library, the literary society, the first body for improving the condition of women, the first institution for social and religious reforms, the first law association and first educational periodicals, his disciples too were no less deserving. And who were they? Dadoba Pandurang, the famed Panini of Marathi grammar, co-founder of Manav Dharma Sabha and Paramhansa Sabha,[21] and author of *Dharmavivechan* which became the philosophical basis of both Prarthana Samaj and the later Jyotiba Phule's Satyashodhak Samaj[22]; Bhaskar Pandurang Tarkhadkar whose eight letters published in the *Bombay Gazette* proved to be "the first open letters of revolt against the British Colonial Policy"[23] and one who was forerunner of Dadabhoy Naoroji's Drain Theory; Dr. Atmaram Pandurang, Dadoba's younger brother and one of the founders of the Bombay Association as well as of the Prarthana Samaj; social thinkers like Ram Balkrishna Jayakar who was the first President of the Paramhansa Sabha, the earliest anti-caste movement in western India; Professor Kero Laxman Chhatre, whose mathematical postulates were much appreciated in Germany and who was the teacher of B.G. Tilak and G.G. Agarkar; social reformers such as Dr. Bhau Daji Lad and Sorabji Shapurji Bengallee; activists such as Vinayak Jagannath, one of the founders of the Bombay Presidency Association; Bhogilal Pranvallabhdas, eminent Gujarati educationist and pioneer reformer; Govind Narayan

Madgaonkar, the celebrated author of *Mumbaiche Varnan* and one of the earliest to write on local history of Bombay; Vishwanath Narayan Mandlik, the eminent legal authority, author of *Hindu Law Digest* and translator of Mountstuart Elphinstone's work on Indian history and who edited in three volumes the transactions of the Bombay Literary Association established in 1804; and these are only a few of them. The members of the Young Bombay Party were not radicals in the mould of Jyotiba Phule and later day Gopal Ganesh Agarkar, but wanted social change along the tradition-modernity continuum. In matters political, they believed in constitutional form of agitation and generally believed that the spread of liberal education would eventually dissolve all social prejudices and rejuvenate the Hindu society by eliminating redundant social practices, and that such a social progress would ultimately lead to political demands.

The members of the "Young Bombay Party" seemed to have initially vacillated between two positions—"whether religious reform should precede social reform or vice versa". Such vacillation invited criticism both from the orthodox section of the society as well as the progressive radicals. The orthodoxy—status quoists as they were—criticized them for their new fangled ideas, which in their opinion were half-digested imports from the Western education. On the other hand, the progressives derided them as *Bolke Sudharak* (reformers only in speech) for their lack of courage to translate their high sounding ideas into action. The contemporary newspapers obviously did not spare in condemning their failure to practice what they preached. This apparent weakness and also the social limitations from which the members of "Young Bombay Party" lumbered, prominently surfaced during the two visits to Bombay in 1864 and 1868 of Babu Keshab Chunder Sen, the Apostle of Brahmo Samaj.

KESHAB CHUNDER'S DISCOURSE IN BOMBAY

Keshab Chunder during his first public discourse to Bombay inhabitants on Thursday, 1 March 1864, had exhorted the reformers to revolt openly against the rigid and ossified caste system that had promoted inquisitions and socially baneful effects, one that hindered social cohesion. The members of the

"Young Bombay Party" instead of hailing him as their new inspirational fountainhead, somehow responded in extreme caution. To quote from the *Bombay Gazette* "the talented Baboo said that he had arrived at Bombay at a critical moment, when the question of caste had stirred up the native community to its inmost depth. To a certain extent the natives of this country animadversions of their enemies when they declared that an educated Hindoo had no respect for his conscience but followed a time-serving and compromising policy. . . ." Dr. Bhau Daji who presided over the well-attended function chose to ignore the speaker's appeal however forcefully made. To the editor of the *Bombay Gazette*, this was perplexing. The editor wrote on 19 March 1864:

> We had expected that Dr. Bhawoo would seize the opportunity to declare himself once for all the leader of the uncompromising reformers of Bombay, by accepting the Baboo's invitation. It was a disappointment to us when his cold measured sentences fell on our ears, and when we heard him asking,—What is Truth? and admitting that he and his friends were unwilling to make any move until they had ascertained whether the Deism preached by the Baboo or the Christianity preached by the Missionaries was the truth they searched for. The lecturer, it seemed to us, did not ask more than this: that men who, like Dr. Bhawoo Daji, deplore the evils of caste and renounce idolatry, should form themselves into an alliance or friendly brotherhood, of which the members might be either Deists or Christians, for protesting by speech and example against the absurd customs and degrading superstitions which have caused India to sink so low a level among the nations of the earth. Surely, this is a little thing to ask of earnest, conscientious thoughtful men. If Dr. Bhawoo Daji would not allow that the time has now come when the reformers of Bombay should take this first step towards ascertaining the truth, when does he think that a favourable opportunity will arrive? If he intends to sit waiting on the bank till the river has run itself out, before he attempts to cross, we fear his eyes will grow dim and his senses fail him ere he reaches the further shore.

Dr. Bhau Daji's behavior at the meeting though irked many well-meaning Europeans and especially the missionaries, but the editor of the *Bombay Gazette* was neither surprised nor did he consider his response as cold-shouldered and cowardly. The missionaries seized this as an opportunity to lambast the caste-ridden iniquitous Hindu society. Many Europeans who sympathized with the missionaries joined their diatribe in condemning the educated Hindu leaders. Some attributed the cold response of Dr. Bhau Daji and the Young Bombay to the materialistic spirit that had pervaded Bombay life at that time due to cotton export boom as a result of American Civil War.[24] But Dr. Bhau Daji like other members of the Young Bombay Party did not believe that the radical religious reform could be easily palatable to the society and that the effect of such untimely introduction could be counter-productive. Perhaps they had the experience of the first anti-caste movement, namely, Paramhansa Sabha in mind. This earliest effort at removing caste barriers, though had worked in secrecy for fear of ridicule and social ostracism, could not really hold water. At the most, it just left its impressions on members such as Dadoba Pandurang and others.

Also, Dr. Bhau Daji during an earlier visit to Calcutta had rebuked the Brahmo Samaj for emphasizing contemplation at the expense of practical social work. He had commended the work of the Bethune Society and had called upon the Brahmos to imitate it.

A letter to the editor, written under the pseudonym "A Paramhans", obviously by a member of the erstwhile Paramhansa Sabha, in *The Times of India* on 24 March, 1864 said:

> This difference of opinion arises from the different lights in which this movement is viewed. The Baboo thinks this to be a religious movement, others invest it with greater importance than it deserves; I think it to be a more social movement and not a religious one. The abolition of caste throughout India will no doubt do good to society, but will it in any way effect our religious state? If it will not, is eating and drinking whatever, and with anybody I like, a sufficient inducement to estrange myself from dear parent, my beloved wife, my bossom friend, and my fellow countrymen? . . . will renunciation of caste by a few persons in the present state of our society improve our social status? In my humble opinion instead of doing any good, it will injure the cause of reform. These reformers will be excommunicated; and no one will follow them; with orthodox Hindus they will be worse than converts, whom they will not hate so much as they will followers of Baboo Keshub Chunder Sen. This is the fate of all reformerers. It may be said, it was the fate of Luther and Wickliffe . . . why were the attempts of Wickliffe frustrated, and those of

Luther crowned with success? Because the fourteenth century was not prepared for the change, while sixteenth was.

In a way, it was a statement which suggested that time had still not come for an open repudiation of caste system as desired by the Brahmo leader. Before the din and dust raised by Keshab Chunder's lectures was yet to be settled the Bombay reformers met at Dr. John Wilson's house to decide further course of action. The assembly included men like Dr. Bhau Daji, Dadoba Pandurang, Dr. Atmaram Pandurang, Karsondas Mulji, Ardeshir Framji, Sorabjee Shapurji where Keshab Chunder Sen himself was also present. The discussion again revolved around the form of protest against idolatry and caste. Several reformers spoke with warmth, vehemence and bitterness and denounced all the educated young men as cowards and hypocrites. So was Karsondas Madhavdas' speech. Karsondas Mulji, who had suffered a great deal for his progressive views till then declared that he was prepared for a sacrifice and would not compromise even at the risk of his exclusion from the caste. Many of those present agreed with him. Prominent among them was Dadoba Pandurang who had started the first anti-caste movement in the form of Paramhansa Sabha in 1847. It was agreed that those who had gathered there should form an association or alliance of reformers. Five members, viz., Dadoba Pandurang, Atmaram Pandurang, Rao Bahadur Ramachandra Moroba Venoba and Karsandas Mulji himself signed a declaration on oath. Karsandas Madhavdas who had earlier waxed eloquence against reformers, however, did not sign the pledge. Dr. Bhau Daji on the other hand said that he "would not adhere to any such alliance as long as he was not convinced of the unreasonableness of following either Christianity or Theism".[25] Dr. Bhau Daji and some others excused themselves from the second meeting also. Some came two hours after the scheduled time. Sorabji Shapurji proposed four conditions as binding upon all members:

1. that they renounce and hate idolatry,
2. that they break caste,
3. that they perform other funeral and marriage ceremony, and

4. that they maintain intercourse with each other without distinction of caste.

Dadoba Pandurang, having heard the conditions, declared that he was for none of them. In fact, none of those who had signed the pledge in the first meeting came forward to declare whether he was for or against these conditions or whether he was going to fulfill the moral obligation. Even as time passed and midnight approached, no conclusion could be arrived at. Dr. Wilson then proposed that the reformers should hold a meeting among themselves and invite those, only those, to participate who hate caste and idolatry.

Notwithstanding the criticism of the radicals of the Young Bombay Party in many quarters, a detailed justification of the cautious approach of the Bombay reformers in contrast to the one exhorted eloquently by Baboo Keshab, appeared in the leader of the *Indu Prakash.* Not only did it refute the charges leveled against Dr. Bhau Daji and his compatriots but it also showed precisely the relative differences between the approaches of the reformers of Bombay and the "radical" Brahmos of Calcutta. The analysis of the reform movement is not only forthright in criticizing the reformers but also it makes clear the public ignominy these reformers suffered from the social limitations they had to live with. The arguments advanced in it are worthy of quoting *in extenso* (The syntax and grammar as per the original.) :

> Our reformers have however themselves in a measure to blame for the treatment they have received. At the same time that they have been quietly doing immense good. They have been noisily crying out for some tangible sign of the progress they have made. They have cried out for someone to break caste, for some one to marry a widow and but a month or two ago they subjected a native gentleman to something like persecution because he would not risk the loss of caste. All this clamour for a sign, itself the mark of faithlessness, has tended to obscure the real and truly great work which they have accomplished; and so it has happened that when they were called upon to swear that they hated caste and idolatry, and they refused, that they are taunted as empty talkers, and hypocrites and trimmers. We can safely say, however, that it was not the oath, but the manner, and time of it, that they objected to. For ourselves, we will go further, for we would refuse an oath altogether. It could not bind us if our convictions were not defined, and if we really

hate caste and idolatry, what is the use of oath? Can it enable us to impose our convictions on the mass of our countrymen, or to give us a whit more liberty in our social relations? Our belief is that in so far as it would cast on our Reformers the imputation of secret society, a common oath between them would prove injurious to progress, and would certainly destroy their own happiness. This demand for organization proves that the mass of the Hindus are not prepared for radical reforms. If they were, they would come spontaneously, in the course of nature as it were. The very demand for organization betrays the rash design of a minority impatient to force its policy prematurely. Could they have their way, social revolution with all its anarchy, and sufferings, and hatreds and not reformation would be the result. In the political world we have already seen the results of the tyranny of minorities in the successive Governments of France and the present subjection of Italy to Piedmont. The leaders of Young Bombay were therefore in our opinion quite right to refuse to subscribe to an officious and barren oath. They hate caste and idolatry, but they refuse to make their hatred of it the instrument of universal discard and confusion in Hindu society. And if we turn, from what they refuse to *talk* about and *say*, to what they have silently *done*; how favourable a contrast this despised, benighted Bombay, present to self-conceited, babbling Calcutta, which sets itself up to teach India progress. Calcutta can talk, a couple of hundred young men in Calcutta can drink Champagne and eat beef in secret, and know all the ins and outs of the Lal Bazar, but where are its Schools, and Colleges, its University and College buildings, its Museums and Halls, and Gardens, above all its Girls' schools, and public native Libraries? What practical good citizens can Calcutta show like our Jamsedji Jejeebhoys, Jugunnath Sunkerseths, Dr. Bhau Dajis, Cowasji Jehanghiers and the Camajees? We will allow that in the region of abstract ideas Calcutta is ahead of Bombay. But we are not mercurial Bengalees—we are solid Parsees and solid Guzerathis, and slow, hard headed shrewd Maharattas, and we as naturally prefer the sober and sure ways of the English and plenty of Rupees to pave our way comfortably, and handsomely, as our countrymen in their out of the way region in the corner of the Bay of Bengal prefer the hysterical programme of Frenchmen, content to starve in a decaying capital for an idea, if only they may talk, talk, talk. We are not however despising the Young Baboo's teachings, who so recently electrified us out of our five senses, by his fervid eloquence in the Town Hall. Let us lay his burning words to hearts and let then these rekindle our convictions of truths, moral and spiritual, so that we can take no rest until we realize them in our lives individually and so far as *practicable* socially. Let us examine ourselves, conscientiously that we may make certain of the sincerity of our convictions that we may make certain that we are not restrained by moral cowardice, but by the just sense only of what is safe and practicable in the glorious cause of social and religious reform. We must allow that there is something deficient in the progress of Bombay. We abound in wealth, in philanthropy, and in public spirit; education has spread widely, and the educated exert great influence, some indeed of our educated fellow citizens who have only their brains to depend on, enjoy greater influence in Bombay than the greatest wealth can by itself command; above all there is a wide-spread hatred of caste and yet it is clear that we must still despair of any wide-spread movement against caste and idolatry. This *must* be due to some weakness in our convictions. This is proved also by the very anxiety we exhibit to make the anti-caste movement general, and social, rather than a personal movement. We will not move unless others move with us. Now if our convictions were stronger they would be the only support we should require: Our consciences would then force us to throw up caste regardless of consequences; and acting for ourselves alone, and not forcing a social change on our fellow countrymen against their wishes, no mischief would result to the community. Very strangely too we daily see Hindus of every caste becoming Christians, and devoted "Missionaries of the Cross". They make an infinitely greater personal sacrifice than we as Hindu reformers are called upon to make. They give up Hinduism, and their lives to protesting against it without any compromise; and they do it in spite of every family tie, and the active hatred sure to be excited against themselves for their *apostasy*. But they cannot help themselves: truth, or what they believe to be the truth, is dearer to them than all the tender sanctities of parent, husband, wife and child, than all the happiness of life, than very life itself. Strange that there should be such a difference between men of the same race, tongue, and caste! We begin to recognize this difference and to enquire anxiously for its cause. It is evident that these men who are so brave and single-minded for what they believe to be truth, receive a new faith, for the faith which education has destroyed within them. On the other hand the education provided by the State simply destroys Hinduism, it gives nothing in its place. It is founded on the benevolent principle of non-interference with religion, but in practice it is the negation of God in life. It is forgotten that while interference in Christian countries would be a tyranny, that in an idolatrous country *education itself is interference* with the established religion. Christians holding a faith pure and rational in its essentials, may receive the highest education and be only the more confirmed in their faith, and more tolerant of each other's minor differences. But education must destroy idolatry, and the State education of India, benevolent in its idea, practically teaches atheism. It leaves its victims faithless. Our young men are many of them forced by it into the unhappy position of the skeptics and infidels of Europe. Well may be the re-organization of society seem impossible under such circumstances. As soon as this is generally perceived and felt the cry will go up to England "Father, Father, give us Faith!". Knowledge alone does not suffice for men, nor material prosperity, nor good government: the things of this light are fleeting, the life to come is eternal, and men and nations can only be happy in reorganizing and acting righteously on this divine fact. Without Faith life is without an aim, death without hope, and there can be neither individual happiness nor national greatness. If England will not hear our cry and indeed anticipate it, then will the shriek go up to our Father in the Heaven, "Father, Father, give us Faith!"

Although it is difficult to ascertain the authorship of this editorial, one could certainly conclude that it came from a deep and contemplative mind who knew that any supplanting of social institutions without providing an alternative system would eventually produce social anarchy. Justice Ranade was later so very successfully, to catch this in appropriate words. "National mind" he said, "cannot rest in agnosticism",[26] for "agnosticism is a paralysis of thought".[27] Besides, their cautious approach makes it clear that they totally ruled out any attempt to make reformism a different sect similar to Brahmo Samaj. Perhaps, for the reasons above cited they worked secretly for Paramhansa Sabha, being disinclined to form a different sect; and even in the later times defeated all attempts to make Prarthana Samaj a body similar to Brahmo Samaj.

VIEWS ON RELIGIOUS REFORM

The detailed and clear-cut argument about the debate on the preference to social reform over religious reform by the editor of *Indu Prakash*[28] is enough to show the views on the matter of reform the Young Bombay Party had. The refusal of its members to accept the pleas of Baboo Keshab Chunder regarding religious reforms was also a confirmation of their own view on social reform, which ultimately manifested in concrete shape in the form the establishment in December 1867 of the Prarthana Samaj under the leadership of Dr. Atmaram Pandurang, and with Dr.

R.G. Bhandarkar and Justice M.G. Ranade, both who joining a year after its establishment and becoming its chief ideologues the direction of social reform was determined in unambiguous terms. That part of social history is all too known. Baboo Keshab Chunder's discourses in Bombay, however, helped them to remove cobwebs of doubt and surprisingly strengthened their earlier commitments to social reform in terms of method and contents.

In conclusion, this paper, thus, argues that there was a group of young Elphinstonians who, under the tutelage initially of Balshastri Jambhekar and later, after the unexpected demise of Balshastri, of Naoroji Furdoonji, avowed to bring about reform in almost all walks of life in western India in general and Bombay in particular. This group, known as the Young Bombay Party, and obviously compared with the members of the Young Bengal Movement under the leadership of Henry Derozio, differed with its Bengal counterpart and gave preference to socio-economic reforms rather than religious reform. Unlike the Bengali reformers the Bombay preformers showed more sobriety in religious matters, as was seen in their apparently cold reaction to Baboo Keshab Chunder Sen's fervent appeals in Bombay for initiating religious reform. The Bombay reformers showed greater maturity in their opposition to quick religious reform as their experience had taught them that the principle of "Two steps forward and if need be, one step backwards" alone can bring about changes in matters religious. Radicalism in religious matters, being counter-productive, by and large, was shunned as a method of social change. Perhaps, it is due to the preference to the socio-cultural change rather than the religious, directly or indirectly, resulted in the large number of political leaders that Bombay gave to the national movement. Moreover, it could be seen that Indian enterprise and technical skills were far more evident in Bombay's rather than Bengal's renaissance. The most noteworthy fact was that while the Bengal renaissance was almost entirely brought about by the Bengalis, the Bombay renaissance, true to the cosmopolitan nature of its social fabric, was brought about by Marathis, Parsees, Gujratis, and even some of the lower castes like Kamatis and Bhandaris substantially contributing to it.[29]

NOTES

* I am thankful to Dr. Aravind Ganachari for his suggestions and inputs from which I have greatly benefited.

1. K. Mukherji, "The Renaissance in Bengal and Maharashtrian Thought from 1850 to 1920", *Arth Vijnan*, December 1962, pp. 331-41.
2. Christine Dobbin, *Urban Leadership in Western India: Politics and Communities in Bombay City 1840-1855*, New Delhi: Oxford University Press, 1971.
3. C.Y. Chintamani (ed.), *Speeches and Writings of Honourable Sir Pherozeshah Mehta*, K.C.I.E., Allahabad: The Indian Press, 1905, p. 277.
4. "Derozio and Young Bengal", in Sushobhan Sarkar, *Bengal Renaissance and Other Essays*, New Delhi: People's Publishing House, 1970, pp. 108-22. Also see, Thomas Edwards, *Henry Derozio*, New Delhi: Rupa, 2002.
5. Derozians are the student followers of Henry Louis Derozio. He was a lecturer at the Hindu College, Calcutta, from 1826 to 1831. During that short period this young gifted teacher moulded the entire life of a number of brilliant students and made a deep impression on them. Under his influence, the students drew their inspiration from Voltaire, Locke, Bacon, Hume, and Tom Paine, among others. His views were too radical for the age and the authorities of Hindu College dispensed with his services. He died at the age of twenty-three. R.C. Majumdar (Gen. ed.), *The History and Culture of the Indian People: British Paramountcy and Indian Renaissance*, Mumbai: Bharatiya Vidya Bhavan, 3rd edn., 1991, pp. 38-40.
6. Thomas Edwards, op. cit., p. 64.
7. C.E. Buckland, *Dictionary of English Biography*, 1906, p. 157; G. Parameswaran Pillai, *Representative Indians*, London: George, Routledge & Sons, 1897, p. 237; R.H. Jalbhoy, *The Portrait Gallery of Western India*, Bombay: Education Society's Press, 1886, n.p. The contemporary newspaper, the *Bombay Gazette* of 19 March 1864 makes the following reference: "Few young men there could have listened to the address unmoved; and none who heard the applause with which the Baboo's [Keshab Chunder Sen] invitation to his Bombay's fellow countrymen to be up and doing was received . . . could help conceiving a hope of the regeneration of India. The temper of the audience, we must own, was much more enthusiastic than that of Dr. Bhavoo Dajee, who, when the lecturer had sat down, rose to speak in the name of Young Bombay. . . ."
8. J.C. Masselos, *Towards Nationalism: Group Affiliation and the Politics of Public Association in Nineteenth Century Western India*, Bombay: Popular Prakashan, 1974, pp. 28-33, 37-40, 43-6, 54-5.
9. John Wilson, *Indian Caste*, vol. II, Bombay, 1877, p. 24.

10. It was Balshastri's student Dadabhoy Naoroji to whom goes the honor of being the first Indian to be a full-fledged professor at the Elphinstone College.
11. G.G. Jambhekar (edited and compiled), *Memoirs and Writings of Acharya Balshashtri Jambhekar (1812-1846)*, vols. 1 to 3, Centenary Memorial Volumes, Poona, 1950, vol. 1, p. 40. (The cover page shows that there are four volumes (I-IV) but actually only three volumes were published)
12. He was not made a member of the Bombay Branch of the Royal Asiatic Society for being an Indian but his papers were read and published in its transactions.
13. A.K. Priyolkar, *Doktar Bhau Daji: Vyakti, Kaal va Kartrutva* (Marathi), Mumbai: Marathi Sahitya Sangh, 1974, p. 485.
14. *The Times of India*, 28 September 1885.
15. C.Y. Chintamani, op. cit., p. 480.
16. The reports of this Society's first four years of activities were not available to me.
17. The *Bombay Quarterly Magazine and Review*, vol. 1. no. 2, January 1851, pp. 128-9: quoted in Masselos 1974, p. 28.
18. G.G. Jambhekar (ed.), op. cit., vol. 2, p. 2.
19. Aroon Tikekar, "Dr. George Buist of the *Bombay Times*: A Study of the Self-proclaimed Messianism of an Anglo-Indian Editor, 1840-1857", in *Writers, Editors and Reformers: Social and Political Transformation of Maharashtra 1830-1930*, ed. N.K. Wagle, New Delhi: Manohar, 1999.
20. G. Parameswaran Pillai, op. cit., 1897, pp. 242-4.
21. Anant Kakba Priyolkar, *Paramhansa Sabha va Tiche Addhyaksh Ramchandra Balkrishna*, Mumbai: Mumbai Marathi Granth Sangrahalaya, 1966, pp. 1-62. Also see for more details, J.V. Naik, "Early Anti-Caste Movement in Western India: The Paramhansa Sabha", *Journal of the Asiatic Society of Bombay*, vols. 49-51, 1979, pp. 136-62.
22. Prior to founding Paramhansa Sabha, Dadoba along with Durgaram Mancharam and Dinmani Shankar, founded Manav Dharma Sabha in Surat on 22 June 1844. Anant Kakba Priyolkar (editor and biographer), *Rao Bahaddur Dadoba Pandurang—Purvardh: Atmacharitra, Uttarardh: Charitra*, Mumbai: Keshav Bhikaji Davale, 1st edn., 1947, pp. 243-5. Dadoba Pandurang also wrote in 1843, a rationalist treatise entitled *Dharmavivechan* under the pseudonym Ek Jagadwasi Arya. It is published in Anant Kakba Priyolkar, *Paramhansa Sabha va Tiche Addhyaksh Ramchandra Balkrishna*, Mumbai: Mumbai Marathi Granth Sangrahalaya, 1966, pp. 63-122. This work was later closely followed by the followers of Prarthana Samaj and Satyashodhak Samaj of Jyotiba Phule.
23. Dadoba Pandurang Tarkhadkar makes first mention of these letters written by his brother Bhaskar in his autobiography-cum-biography

published by A.K. Priyolkar (editor and biographer), *Rao Bahaddur Dadoba Pandurang—Purvardh: Atmacharitra, Uttarardh: Charitra*, Mumbai: Keshav Bhikaji Davale, 1st edn., 1947, p. 198. For a proper analysis of Bhaskar Tarkhadkar's letters see J.V. Naik, "An Early Appraisal of the British Colonial Policy", *Journal of the University of Bombay*, vols. XLIV-XLV, 1975-6, pp. 243-70.

24. N.R. Phatak, *Nyayamurthi Mahadev Govind Ranade Yanche Charitra*, Pune: Nilakanth Prakashan, 2nd enl. edn., 1966, pp. 104-5.
25. The detailed report of this meeting at the residence of Dr. John Wilson appeared in the letter "ABC" in the *Bombay Gazette*, 31 March 1864. However, some members present at that meeting felt that publishing such a report of a private meeting was an infringement on their privacy.
26. M.G. Ranade, "Butler's Method of Ethics", in *Miscellaneous Writings of the Late Hon'ble Justice M.G. Ranade*. Bombay: The Manoranjan Press, 1915, p. 69.
27. M.G. Ranade, "Philosophy of Indian Theism", in *Religious and Social Reform*, collected and compiled by M.B. Kolaskar. Bombay: G. Claridge & Co., 1902, p. 14.
28. This paper was reproduced in *The Times of India*, dated 29 April 1864. It is the first direct exposition of the reformist approach of the contemporary Maharashtrian intellectuals.
29. Tikekar, Foreword to Gangadhar Gadgil's *Prarambh: The Beginning*, an epic novel on early nineteenth-century Bombay, translated by Arvind Dixit, New Delhi: NBT, 2006.

11

Way of Making Writer's Own Literary World: With Special Reference to Prof. Keshav Meshram and Dalit Literature

HIDEAKI ISHIDA

DALIT LITERATURE AND DALIT AUTOBIOGRAPHY

The late M.B. Citnis said during a seminar on Dalit Literature in November 1967 that, "Now there can be two kinds of approaches for Neo-Buddhist writers (in order to write literary works); one is that your (upper-caste Hindus) society is responsible for bringing us to the present-day condition, therefore we write revolutionary literature against the society which exists before our eyes, the other is that my life is different from that of others and it is worth writing. Perhaps more excellent works will be produced through the second approach." This statement was published in the first issue of *Asmita* (presently *Asmitadarsh*) and heralded a new era in Dalit Literature (Dangle 1978).

Dalit Literature first became popular in the 1960s through the works of Baburao Bagul. His literature in those days was full of fighting spirit and accused caste-ridden Indian society of social injustice. During the 1970s, Dalit Literature became more popular owing to the monthly *Asmitadarsh* and the protest movements of Dalit Panther. Some leaders of Dalit Panther, such as Namdeo Dhasal, Raja Dhare, Prahlad Cendwankar, Arjun Dangle, were aggressive writers and poets. They wrote revolutionary literature as a whole.

In the decade of the 1970s Dalit Literature began to show a remarkable change. Dalit writers began to look at themselves and write of their own lives. They began to portray their lives, which were different from those of others, in their own style. This was the very approach recommended in the above statement of M.B. Citnis. Now they began to have confidence in their new writings. Most discussed among them was *Balute* (1978) of Daya Pawar. Some of the other important works were *Athwanince Pakshi* (1972) of P.I. Sonkamble, *Mukkam Post Dewace Gothne* (1979) of Madhav Kondvilkar, and *Upra* (1980) of Lakshman Mane.

In these autobiographies Dalit writers showed how their lives were different from those of ordinary Indian people and how they were forced to live miserable lives about which higher caste people hardly knew anything. Miserable and humiliating situations took place in every nook and corner of their lives. Dalit writers tried to describe such scenes as honestly as they could. Many of those situations were caused by higher caste people, but here we should note the fact that they were not always caused by only higher caste people but sometimes also by people of their own caste or other "nearby" depressed communities. When Dalit writers revealed such facts, they had to face severe criticism hurled upon them by people of their own community. This problem is associated with Dalit writers even today whenever they write some story or fiction tinged with a critical tone.

Keshav Meshram, a prominent Dalit writer of many successful works, has written a lot of stories tinged with such a critical tone. This paper is intended to examine how Keshav Meshram made up his own literary world in which he boldly criticized even Dalit people when it was necessary.

KESHAV MESHRAM AND *HAKIKAT ANI JATAYU*

Keshav Meshram (born in 1937) started writing regularly in the 1960s. His autobiographical novel *Hakikat* was published in 1972. This was his first published book. He wrote his autobiography in the form of a novel, which was a rare case in Marathi Dalit literature. He wrote this "novel" in the years from 1964 to 1968 ("foreword" of the novel). I think the time when he wrote it was one of the reasons why Meshram produced his "autobiography" in the form of a novel, as Dalit autobiography was still rare in those days. *Athwanince Pakshi* was published in the same year, 1972, and that was in a sense the first Dalit autobiography which won a distinguished reputation in Marathi literature.

Hakikat may give an impression as a novel of reserved expression for a piece of Dalit literature. In *Hakikat* we don't see such horrible scenes of discrimination, insult or humiliation as we see in the works such as *Athwanince Pakshi* or *Upra.* The hero of *Hakikat* also has to live a hard life as a Dalit boy. He has to work in many places, but he doesn't face, except for one example, severe scenes of humiliation. We notice in the novel that the hero is rather annoyed by the deeds of his own caste people. (A similar situation is found in Madhav Kondvilkar's *Mukkam Post Devace Gothne.*) In the hometown of the hero boy, where Mahar and Mang people mainly live, there are three groups of people. First is the group of the older generation. They are uneducated and superstitious. Many of them work in the mill. Second is the group of young, willing people who go to school. The hero boy belongs to this group. Third is the group in question. They are, "the people who know only extirpation, destruction and hatred. They bear hatred from generation to generation. They are insulted by higher caste people at every step and satisfy their grudge by revenging on me who is one of their caste fellows intentionally with increased hatred" (p. 25). They stealthily frustrate young willing boys in their various plans which those young boys made for the sake of their community. Who do such things? "It is they who are whore-mongers, drinkers and beef-eaters. They are rich people who live extravagantly submerged in every luxury" (p. 29). But the hero boy does not accuse those people loudly. His tone is reserved.

Jatayu is a short novel which was published in the same volume combined with *Hakikat.* This is a story of a young Mang boy, Abhiman, whose life and future is devastated in the surroundings which are the result of poverty, lack of education and bigoted convention. The author's motive in writing this novel was to show how a young man of promising ability is destroyed by the evils of Indian society. Abhiman lives in an area called Siddharth Nagar, where there are about 200 houses (huts). Almost all the huts belong to Mahar people, while about 10 huts belong to Mang people. Here it is worth noting that in some places the author described malicious doings of the majority Mahar people against minority Mang people. It is remarkable as Abhiman's higher caste school mates don't behave in such a discriminative manner.

Abhiman's tragedy was mainly caused by his family affairs, though all the surrounding factors, including Mahar people's behavior, overlapping each other, gradually drove Abhiman into the dead-end road. If his parents had been more thoughtful and well-advised, Abhiman would not have fallen into such an entrapment as to serve as an assistant to the murdering bogus charmer. On the whole this story does not have a protesting tone, though it depicts incessant hardships brought upon an honest young Dalit boy.

The above-mentioned may be summed up as follows; in his first two novels Keshav Meshram described two hard-toiling young Dalit boys, one successful in life, the other collapsing. At first glance these two boys may give opposite impressions, but there are some points common between them. These boys have normal relations with higher caste people, or it should be said that such scenes alluding to poor relations with higher caste people, except for a few examples, were not provided in these novels. On the contrary we rather notice that these boys are often troubled by people of their own caste or some "nearby" caste. They realize that the Dalit problem is not so simple as to be finished off simply by criticizing higher caste people. They find it necessary to have critical eyes on their own Dalit society in order to understand the Dalit problem in total. This critical standpoint continued to be the basic attitude of Keshav Meshram as a writer ever afterward.

CORRUPT LEADERS, CORRUPT PEOPLE

Now we are going to see how his critical standpoint was realized in his later works (mainly short stories). To begin with I take up those stories in which the author's critical eyes observe the negative side of Dalit society.

Hatkananglekar correctly pointed out that Keshav Meshram

described a wide range of characters who belong to the low strata of the society of Mumbai (Hatkananglekar 1996: xviii-xix). Many of them hail from the countryside of Maharashtra and are now living in some slum of Mumbai. Some of them are related to the underworld. Some others get involved in some crime or other though they have a strong wish to live a safe life. Keshav Meshram takes a warm-hearted look at poor people who succumb to hard luck in the end, while he takes a stern and merciless look at corrupt and hypocritical people whoever they may be.

In *Morca* (1-1) corrupt Dalit activists are described who exploit honest activists engaged in the Namantar movement. They are from Nagpur and travel to Mumbai by train without tickets. Mumbai activists collect contributions with great difficulty for the sake of their Nagpuri counterparts, but the Nagpuris waste the money on food and drink and laugh at the honest Mumbai activists.

Bandgul (2-12) is a story of Ajabrao, a corrupt Dalit politician who, pretending to be a servant of the Dalit public, abuses the Dalit cause and makes money illegally. If someone suspects him to be corrupt, that person will be killed or lured into a trap from which he shall never be freed.

Agnicakra (6-2) gives a picture of two corrupt young Dalit leaders of Yuvak Aghadi (Young Front). They have been abusing the Dalit cause and living extravagantly with the money they made illegally. This time they got a large sum of Rs. 35,000 by working for an underworld don who runs many "pleasure clubs" in Mumbai. At present the most harassing anxiety for them is if they are suffering from AIDS.

The realities of corrupt Dalit leaders are well known to the general Dalit people. Keshav Meshram shows the limits of confidence which Dalit people repose in their leaders. *Beduk* (2-11) is a story of a Dalit man whose son was killed by the son of the village head like a frog in a well. The boy, eleven years old, was helping his father in sweeping the well which was supposed to be "freed" for neo-Buddhists and Harijans in the ceremony by the hands of the District officers. The son of the village head, a college student, was aware of "liberation" of the well and with a repulsive feeling threw stones into the well to amuse himself, knowing fully well that someone was in the well, and killed the boy. A Dalit leader of the village tried to persuade the boy's father to complain to the police about the incident, but the boy's father wouldn't agree to the suggestion made by the Dalit leader. He receives 100 Rupees for compensation from the village head and goes away. The reason is not made clear in the story why the boy's father did not complain to the police but received money. This man may be too cowardly. One thing is clear that the boy's father does not have the least bit of trust in the Dalit leader of the village just as he does not have in the police. In *Gosht Hote Kay Bagha* (6-8) a boy of seven years old lost some of his fingers when he was operating a machine at the sugarcane juice stall. The owner of the stall made him operate the machine against the agreement on the boy's duty. The boy's mother complains to the police. A Dalit leader who was arbitrating between the two parties takes money from the stall owner secretly and walks off. Now the boy's mother cannot believe anybody. Life has become utterly meaningless for her.

Corruption, of course, is not limited only to leaders. Keshav Meshram wrote many stories in which people, not only Dalit, of various occupations are shown to be entangled with corruption. In *Pasaydan* (5-1) a corrupt PWD officer has to face denunciation hurled against him by his own younger brother. In *Tartud* (4-1) a literary scholar (Dalit) who obtained a Ph.D. degree in USA and now is a commissioner at some governmental office makes money utilizing his position. He declared in his testament that he has been a perfect Brahmacari, but in reality he had a child by a so-called common-law wife. In *Binhadryacya Dharnikamp* (8-4) the RMO of the governmental hospital in an Adivasi area is a corrupt doctor. He tries to entrap his accuser using his own wife by fabricating an illicit affair between the accuser and his wife. In *Gutanda* (6-1) a young railway engineer (Dalit) witnesses how an engineer in charge of a construction site is surrounded by sugary temptations. In *Kadelot* (3-1) a railway worker in charge of the carriage depot at night runs a carriage brothel. One day he finds a prostitute woman lying in the carriage. It was his daughter who has been missing after her marriage. She must have been sold off to some human traffic syndicate. The grieving father declares in regret that he will stop this business today.

Human traffic is one of the horrible crimes tenaciously repeated in the underworld of Mumbai. Keshav Meshram describes how the crime is carried out in such a detail as you may not come across easily in Marathi literature (Hatkananglekar 1996: vii). In *Pathawani* (1-2) a Dalit woman ostensibly manages a girls' hostel in Mumbai and collects poor Dalit girls from remote villages. She is respected like a living goddess by credulous villagers, but in reality she sells off those girls.

Similarly in *Anukampa* (5-8) a doctor, non-Dalit, collects women who are found on the streets or in the dirtiest places in the city in utterly forlorn conditions. The doctor gives these women a good treatment in his hospital which is equipped with the latest medical machines and the qualified nursing attendants. When the women recover their good health they are secretly transferred to some unknown place and the doctor gets an enormous amount of money in return. This time he prepared four women and got 25 lakh rupees.

Keshav Meshram wrote many stories showing how women are forcibly, but easily, drawn into the world of sex business. In *Sapla* (1-10) a pregnant girl goes to see her lover at his hut in a slum area to persuade him to marry her. His hut was locked. An old woman living in an opposite hut kindly invites her to have a rest in her hut. Soon after having tea, in which a sleeping drug was dissolved, she fell asleep. When she got up she was raped by some men related to the underworld. She understands in a desperate despair that she will be definitely sold off to the prostitution syndicate. In *Gargar Phirki* (4-5) Partap, a driver, happens to see his sister at a secret club a decade after she disappeared abruptly. He learns that she was abducted and sold off. In *Bhartad* (6-5) Jubi runs away with a Muslim man after she was raped by her cousin whom she has been taking care of. The Muslim man promises to marry her and she is converted to Islam. After that she is gang-raped and sold off to Kamathipura. In *Warul* (5-7) Nayna runs away with her lover and her two little nieces. In Mumbai her lover tries to sell her off, so she runs away with her nieces. After some time of hardships she voluntarily prostitutes herself to give food and shelter to her little nieces. In *Pathpurawa* (3-11) Sulki, a Hindu girl, marries into a rich family, but her husband turns out to be impotent. Her husband invites his friend to have sexual relationship with his wife. Later she is sold off.

Recruiting beggars is also a part of human traffic business. *Khadakhadi* (8-8) is a story of Dolly, a woman beggar. She is handicapped by both legs and when she was a child she was thrown away near the front gate of the criminal children's rehabilitation home. A teacher of the home handed her over to a man who manages a group of beggars. In another story *Kicat* (8-9) a widow is living a poor life with her son in a slum in Mumbai. Recently her son got a job to her joy, but her happiness did not last long. One day her son was hit by a train and seriously injured. Nazhir is a well-wisher and has been kind to the widow and her son. Nazhir introduces a Muslim welfare organization to her. The organization takes charge of her son and takes him away. The mother simply believes that her son was transferred to a hospital somewhere. What happened actually is that her son was sold off to Gujarat as a beggar and Nazhir got 15,000 rupees for that.

SEXUAL CRIME ON WOMEN

As I pointed earlier, when Keshav Meshram observes Dalit society he observes it totally, therefore he does not hesitate to point out even the evil side of Dalit society. At the same time as a writer, needless to say, Keshav Mehram also observes other weaker sections of Indian society. One example is women. In his stories we come across a number of criminal scenes. In many of those crimes women are sexually abused and often degraded to the status of prostitute. It is natural for Keshav Meshram, as a writer of accusation of social injustice, to describe sexual crimes against women. Some examples were already given above. Some more will be added here.

In *Jhadap* (2-6) high caste college students from the city rape Adivasi girls in a village temple. Later they are killed by the angry Adivasi people. Similar things happen in *Vikhar* (8-7) in which similar college students from the city rape a village woman. Later they get heavily drunk and are killed by the angry honeybees. In *Gili Apula Ugav* (4-6) a high school girl and her younger brother are rescued in the flood by their kind neighbors, who take them to a remote dairy farm. But at night a gang of cowherds rape both the girl and her brother. In *Wakhwakh* (5-4) a girl who is looking for some taxi to go home in front of the station late at night catches a rickshaw at last. The rickshaw man entices her into his den and rapes her with his playfellows.

There are some other cases of sexual crime or abuse. In *Pani Khol Manace* (8-6) Vidya marries a man who is sexually impotent, but she does not perceive that because the younger brother of her husband replaces him in the dark room at night. After some months she is informed of the reality. Upset and angry, Vidya protests furiously and she is killed by her husband and in-laws in the end. *Patrawal* (2-10) is a story of a Dalit landlord who had a snake charmer kill his pregnant concubine and her mother.

Sometimes the enemy of a woman is found in her house. In *Gosht Hote Kay Bagha* (6-8) the heroine is raped by her own brother when she was still a little girl of eleven years old. In *Bhartad* (6-5), as mentioned before, the heroine was raped by her cousin and that made a beginning of her fallen life. In *Shosh* (4-10) the step-father bears in mind that he is entitled to make his step-daughter work as a prostitute when she comes of age.

Keshav Meshram has sometimes encountered criticism that his stories only arouse the low passion in readers. Devendra Khandare cites an instance of criticism made by P.S. Nerurkar. Khandare justifies Meshram's standpoint saying that Meshram described a sufferer's feeling. A sufferer often nourishes a crooked emotion of retaliation. Meshram showed in his stories the mechanism how morals of a suffering person collapse and he commits a crime (Khandare 1994: 26-7). Khandare's explanation is correct but not sufficient. I would like to add some words, that is, if someone misreads Meshram's intention it is because Meshram sometimes does not describe the mental mechanism of the sexual criminal in enough detail as Khandare vindicates it. In many cases the focus is on the victim or on the incident but not on the assaulter. The assaulter appears suddenly and commits a crime as if sexual crime was his inborn privilege. This may have given a wrong impression to some readers that Meshram is interested in only showing the scenes of sexual crime. Even when the focus is on the assaulter, the frame of his mind is not sufficiently illustrated. In many of the stories I mentioned in this section this weak point is found more or less. It is not, needless to say, that Meshram wrote only such stories. He has many stories in which assaulter's frame of mind is well described. I think they are among the best stories of Keshav Meshram. I will mention about them later.

HARSH REALITY OF DALIT PEOPLE

Keshav Meshram wrote these stories of sexual abuse on women because he, as a Dalit writer, wanted to draw attention of the readers to the weaker sections of Indian society. His sympathy is always with those people who are deprived of rights for a happy life. But at the same time he never abandons his standpoint as a realist. His eyes do not overlook the hard luck which people of weaker sections often cannot avert.

In *Unca Ubhi Mati* (4-2) an old woman lives with her grandson who has recently started working regularly. Now she is happy after long years of hardships and begins to look for a bride for her grandson. But very suddenly her grandson is killed in an accident at his job site. Thus the woman's short-term happy life comes to an abrupt end. In *Tada* (4-3) Cokha's happy life is terminated by a sudden visit of his sister who, after running away from home, became a prostitute and is now suffering from an incurable disease. In *Awatan* (5-2) Sidram loses his son as his son dropped to his death from the top of a human pyramid playing Govinda in the Janmashtami festival. The boy was his only son. After the death of his wife he has been bringing up his son alone. In *Galsal* (6-6) after some shameful years Maina was helped out of the dishonorable surroundings by a Muslim man. She was converted to Islam and had a happy married life with him. But when she was in the hospital with her new born baby, a communal riot breaks out and her husband is killed. She runs away from the hospital with her baby, but in the end she throws her baby away into a well in her village. *Kalti Dupar* (3-3) is a story of an old manual laborer who was buried to death under the coal he was unloading from the wagon. He had to work alone because it was the very day of mass conversion which Babasaheb Ambedkar presided over and all the manual laborers of his area were out to Nagpur.

These stories tell us how fragile Dalit life really is. In some stories readers may get an impression that it is too merciless of the author to force such hard luck on his Dalit characters. But Keshav Meshram holds that we should not avert our eyes from the harsh reality of weaker Dalit people. Meshram does not abstain from showing us more tragic scenes which take place when these vulnerable people wound each other in their desperate endeavor to seize whatever small chance they believe will open a way to a better life.

For example, *Asra* (1-4) is a story of Nagorao, a young Dalit, who is bringing up his brother's son, a five year old boy. A girl, daughter of a widow living in the opposite hut of Nagorao, falls in love with him. Girl's mother contrives a plan and puts out the eyes of Nagorao's nephew. When the boy became totally blind Nagorao makes a beggar of his nephew and marries with the girl. The widow's intention to put out the boy's eyes is almost beyond reader's understanding. *Catka* (2-7) depicts a father who is at a loss to bring up his two little children after his wife's death. At last one day he takes his children to the busy city center and leaves them there while they are sleeping. In *Amnesamne* (5-9) Santosh, a young promising store owner, helps in full measure his friend from the same countryside open his own store. But his friend betrays him saying to his fellows that Santosh swindled substantial money out of him. Furthermore the betrayer started trading in narcotic drugs and tried to destroy Santosh's honest business under the patronage of a degraded politician. Santosh determines to retaliate against the ingrate and sets fire to the betrayer's store.

DEATH AND DEFECTIVE FAMILY

In many stories of Keshav Meshram we notice that "death" plays an important role. In many cases the miserable life of the main character starts with the death of some near relation, mostly a parent, in his or her family. If no one dies, someone is seriously ill or a good-for-nothing or drunkard. *Maranmala*, title of the collection of short stories (No. 4), gives a hint that "death" has a special place in the literary world of Keshav Meshram.

In *Asra* (1-4) Nagorao is rearing his nephew, whose father is an orderly of a colonel and is now with his master stationed at far away in the Himalayan mountains. The boy's mother died during his delivery. In *Velhal* (1-5) Raghunath Desai's father was arrested as a murderer. In reality he was not a murderer but a substitute, but Raghunath does not know that. In *Bohni* (1-6) the delinquent hero, a boy of around twelve to thirteen years old, does not know anything about his parents. In *Andharkhai* (3-2) too Kalidas, a young snatcher, does not know about his parents. In *Damchak* (1-6) hero boy lives with his mother. His father died when he was a little child. The same situation is found in *Rakti* (2-4) in which the hero boy lives with his mother. His father died three years before. In *Utara* (2-9) Manju's father, after the death of his first wife, marries his second wife, who teases Manju. Now Manju is working as a maid in a rich family and she has almost forgotten her father and step-mother. In *Kalawant* (3-12) a singer girl lost her parents when she was a little girl and was reared by her maternal uncle. In *Unca Ubhi Mati* (4-2) a widow lives with her grandson who lost both parents and siblings in a traffic accident.

I curtail other examples otherwise they will continue endlessly. These frequent deaths and defective families show the fragility of Dalit life. It may be said that we don't come across many of such stories of Keshav Meshram as would encourage or fill reader's heart with a positive mood toward life. If some character, especially Dalit, becomes favored with some happiness, we begin to feel a fear that something bad may happen to the character at any moment. If you want to read stories with a happy ending you have only a few of them. In *Dhagada,* the collection of short stories (No. 3), there are two stories written for juvenile readers. In *Chalang* (3-8) a diligent boy of about fifteen years old is held up in a dark jungle and attacked by wild beasts. He is rescued by his father and brother. In *Shakkal* (3-9) the hero boy makes up with his elder sister by assisting her in breaking off a marriage offer from an immoral man. There are some other examples, one of which is *Tobra* (8-5) in which Nisha, a bar girl, meets Campak, a guest of the bar, who seems to be honest and trustworthy and is far different from her ordinary guests whose only desire is a woman's body. Both of them have a favorable impression with each other and there is a hint that the impression will soon change to a mutual love. Another example is *Na Sampnara Ujed* (4-8) in which a school peon has acid poured on his face by gangsters and loses his eyesight. His wife sells off his hut and runs away, leaving him alone, with someone taking her children and the gift money presented by the teachers of his school. Informed of this his friends support him so that he can live by himself.

VARIOUS CHARACTERS

Keshav Meshram, as a Dalit writer, wrote stories which raise voices of protest against discrimination. *Modta* (2-1) is a story of Narayan, a Dalit high school boy, whom the principal of the school treats harshly. The principal works him as a menial servant and tries to prevent him from studying on any pretext. On learning that the principal tried to get him arrested by the police, Narayan determines to set fire to the principal's house on Saturday night when the principal is dead drunk and asleep in bed with his concubine. In *Katakati* (1-8) a primary school teacher teases a fourth year Dalit boy. On the morning of the inspection day Dalit people stick a paper on the high wall of the school. On the paper are written all the immoral conducts of the teacher. In *Patrawal* (2-10) a Mang woman says that her husband and children were not rescued in the flood because villagers didn't want to touch Mang people.

It is often pointed out that there are few Marathi writers who pictured such various characters as Keshav Meshram did. It is true that we meet a variety of characters, especially those from the lower strata of the Indian society, in the stories of Keshav Meshram. Black magic or black magicians are described in the stories such as *Ilam* (1-12), *Bhuk* (3-10, title is different, story is same as *Ilam*), *Basmati* (2-3) and *Thunka* (7-20). *Damchak* (1-7) shows the preparation process of marriage food of the Bhangi caste. In *Kurghodi* (5-5) a washerman's world is depicted. In *Atlya At* (3-4) the hero boy works as a cycle rickshaw man. (A similar situation is found in *Hakikat.*) In *Bewaras* (5-3) the hero boy works at the municipal dog asylum and kills forty to fifty dogs in a day operating some electric machine. In *Nadi! Nadi, Candi De . . .* (6-9) a potter's son finds out a secret place of best quality clay for pottery only to meet a tragic end. *Kalawant* (3-12) is a story of the singers in an itinerant troupe.

Some stories give us rough idea of the underworld. *Andharkhai* (3-2) and *Badlaw* (8-2) give a picture of the severe reality of street criminals, such as snatchers, pickpockets, lifters, luggage thieves, etc. Their world has their own stringent rules. *Ghasaran* (8-3) depicts in detail the method of multiple arsons committed by a young gangster under directions from the underworld land shark to eject the hut dwellers of the slum. *Adwata* (5-10) describes a man in politics who hires professional killers to kill powerful opponents of his boss for the coming election.

Musalmans also have an important place in some stories of Keshav Meshram. In *Pathpurawa* (3-11) a Hindu woman in origin, after a wretched married life with an impotent husband, was sold off to the prostitution syndicate. She was redeemed by a Muslim man and is now living happily with him. Similarly in *Galsal* (6-6), as mentioned earlier, a Dalit girl is helped out by a Muslim man and has a happy married life with him. An opposite case to these is found in *Bhartad* (6-5) in which a sexually abused Hindu girl elopes with a Muslim man only to be sold off by him. In *Kicat* (8-9), as mentioned earlier, a self-styled Muslim welfare organization is shown to be engaged in human traffic. *Sanadi Tethe . . .* (8-1) depicts a terrorist camp in Kashmir, where abducted children are gathered to do the miscellaneous chores for the terrorists in the camp. If any child turns out useless he will be killed and thrown away.

Anathayi (6-4) is an important work. A Muslim driver Aftab wants to have a third wife. Ashfak, leader of Muslim fundamentalists, encourages Aftab saying that to have plural wives up to four is a fundamental right of orthodox Musalmans. There is an organization for the human rights in the city. Mumtaz, a college lecturer, is an activist of the organization. A few months ago the organization offered to support a woman who had been divorced recently. That is the very woman Aftab wants to make his third wife. Mumtaz's father once saved Aftab when he was surrounded by angry people because he was driving drunk. Ashfak's group regards Mumtaz's organization with enmity and has already attacked it several times. One day Mumtaz comes to see Aftab and asks him to tell Ashfak to abstain from attacking her organization. A few weeks later Aftab learns that the woman he wanted to make his third wife married the person he trusted and that Mumtaz was killed by Ashfak's group under the pretense of a traffic accident. Aftab cannot stop shedding tears of regret, but it is too late now. Readers feel relieved with the tears Aftab sheds over the death of Mumtaz and his own thoughtless acts.

I would like to mention briefly about his novel *Pokharan*, which is an historical novel and very different from the author's other works. Set in an ancient age, when Aryans began to mix with the original inhabitants of India, this novel describes how these original inhabitants protected their natural life and labor-based culture against the Aryan Brahmanism. This is a unique novel.

Talking of historical stories, Keshav Meshram wrote a story titled *Samarpan* (3-14) in 1961. This story is about the ideal chastity of a medieval Rajput woman. The style is old. This is a piece of work written before Keshav Meshram became a solid Dalit writer.

NOTEWORTHY STORIES

In this section I will deal with the noteworthy stories of Keshav Meshram. I argued earlier that in the stories of Meshram scene descriptions sometimes exceeds character portrayal and this has often led to the criticism that his stories are not so profound as expected. The reason why character portrayal becomes insufficient is that in the many stories of Meshram the focus is placed on the victim of the incident or on the incident itself. Those stories depict how the incident happens on the victim. They often give an impression that a horrifying incident or a sexual crime takes place as if it was destined to be. Meshram's intention is to emphasize the fragility of Dalit life or the vulnerability of women. But readers do not always react as the author hopes and think that describing a sexual crime or a horrifying incident itself is the main theme of the author. This leads to the criticism mentioned above. If Meshram had centralized his focus more on the assaulter or on the frame of mind of the assaulter or the main character, things would have been different. Of course Meshram has written many stories whose focus is on the assaulter or on the frame of mind of the assaulter or the main character. I think those are the most noteworthy of Keshav Meshram's stories.

First of all I would like to comment on the story *Bohni* (1-6). Kisna is a street child of about thirteen years old. He does not know anything about his parents. He does various risky "jobs" which bring him money to live. One of the "jobs" is to carry a parcel of the hospital refuse to the refuse dump and throw it away. He was told that the parcel contains the wastes of the secret medical experiment conducted by the doctor of the hospital. It should be thrown away without being noticed by anybody else otherwise the secret experiment will become useless. One day he was hit by a cycle-rickshaw. Passengers of the rickshaw were a boy of about ten years old and his sister of about six. They are children of a rich family. The girl is a frank speaker and says that this boy (Kisna) is dirty as a black bear. On that afternoon when he was carrying the parcel of the hospital, unable to restrain himself in disconsolation, he opened the parcel and found a dead fetus. In the confusion of mind he comes back to the city center, where he happens to see the frank speaking girl. He successfully entices her to ride on the bicycle in front of him. When it gets dark and the girl begins to be fractious Kisna hits her on the head to shut her up. Her head hits against the handle of the bicycle and she dies. Kisna throws her away at the refuse damp. This story has several things common to many other stories of Keshav Meshram. There are deaths (death of the girl and dead fetus), a defective family (of Kisna who is living alone), criminal jobs and miserable Dalit life. But this story is written from the standpoint of the assaulter, therefore readers do not misunderstand the author's intention. This story has become an excellent story of juvenile delinquency.

Bandgul (2-12) is also a representative story of the author. This story, as I mentioned earlier, accused the corruption of Dalit politician through the character Ajabrao. Ajabrao's scandals, his method of crime, his idea of corruption, all these things gave this story a conspicuous place in Dalit literature in the early 1980s when self-criticism on Dalit society itself was still rare. There is hardly any room left on the readers' side for misunderstanding the author's intention in this story. The same thing can be said about stories such as *Morca* (1-1) and *Pathawni* (1-2).

Velhal (1-5) is an exceptional story for Keshav Meshram, because the main character, Raghunath Desai, is not from the Dalit community. He is a son of Konkanasta Brahman. His family used to be rich landlords but was ruined in the days of his grandfather. His father could keep the least prestige of being a landlord by favor of a Marwari moneylender. One day the Marwari's son, Hansraj, killed a dancing girl. Raghunath's father took the guilt of murder in place of Hansraj, got himself arrested and got his debt written off as a reward. Little Raghunath did not know that. He and his mother got the protection of the Marwari. He had to bear slanderous remarks of village people while he lived in the village. Now he is working for Hansraj's sari store in Mumbai. When new saris arrive he dresses up mannequin dolls with them. He does this work all alone at midnight. While dressing up the dolls, he talks with them. Dolls are the only consolation to his soul. Now he almost cannot have a normal relationship with living girls. This story shows how a wounded heart hinders normal growth of mentality. And this is the very problem which Dalit people have been facing in the caste-ridden Indian society.

Mozmap (6-10) is another noteworthy story whose ending is different from other stories. Namabai, after the death of her elder son and the disappearance of her drunkard husband, worked as a vegetable hawker and raised her second son, the only blood relative left will her. Now her son has grown up and married. Her daughter-in-law is a ninth grade pass-out but she is awkward and poor at housekeeping. Her son is rather weak-hearted and henpecked. In the end Namabai makes up her mind and begins to live alone separate from her son and his wife. The ending of this story may look rather simple, but this story is noteworthy because it depicts an attitude of an old woman toward life. After ups and downs in her hitherto life Namabai selects her own style of life, which gives a fresh impression to readers. A similar situation can be seen in another story *Padjhad* (5-6), in which, contrary to Namabai, Jayabai selects a life to live with her son's family only to regret it. This story also gives readers a chance to think over how to live a life in total.

Lastly I refer to the story *Hadra* (3-7), in which a Dalit lawyer Samadhan Shende's unsuccessful married life is described. Samadhan married Mukta, a Gujarati Jain woman, for love. On the occasion of her first delivery her relatives, who had almost severed relations with this couple, came over suddenly and took her away to her relative's house for the delivery. After that Mukta changes gradually and their relations grow cold. Now they have three children but Mukta gives her affection only to her children and takes a contemptuous attitude toward Samadhan because of his caste and his dark complexion. Some years previously Samadhan came to know Maya who was a relative of his client. Wounded and troubled by his wife's vicious attitude, he had illicit relations with Maya and it continued until recently. His conduct became known to his wife and her relatives. This led to the complete collapse of their relations. At last Samadhan decides to break up his own family. This story is noteworthy because this story may have some relations with the author's personal life. Keshav Meshram wrote an autobiographical novel *Hakikat,* in which the author's school days were pictured, while in *Hadra* author described a married life and its collapse. Needless to say, *Hadra* is a fiction, but this story seems to be as important as *Hakikat* when we study the literature of Keshav Meshram.

CONCLUSION

I would like to conclude my points as follows. Keshav Meshram, as a Dalit writer, has been creating his literature for the Dalit cause, but his literature covers the whole of human society. His sympathy definitely lies with Dalit people, but this is not always guaranteed as indisputable. He has very critical eyes which see deep inside men and society and reveal mercilessly the dark side of them. He has boldly accused Dalit leaders and even poor Dalit people if they betrayed his trust in them. This attitude of his has been maintained in his literature from the very beginning of his career as a creative writer.

Among many important themes Keshav Meshram especially placed the focus on the problems of fragility of Dalit life and vulnerability of women. These themes were often realized through the sudden death of some person in a Dalit family or by sexual crimes on women. Stories of this type were sometimes misread and caused criticism that Meshram is interested in describing only the scenes of sexual violence or horrifying incidents. Of course Meshram did not mean that at all. He simply intended to give voice to the harsh reality of Dalit life and weaker sections of Indian society. Many of his stories have been given a high evaluation, especially the stories in which the background of the incident and mental frame of the characters are well described.

REFERENCES

The rule of numbering short stories is as follows: for example *Bandgul* (2-12) means that the short story *Bandgul* is the 12th story in the collection of short stories No. 2. The numbering of the collection of short stories is as follows:

No. 1: *Kharwad* 1980. Aurangabad: Dhara Prakashan.
No. 2: *Patrawal* 1981. Mumbai: Dinpushpa Prakashan.
No. 3: *Dhagada* 1984. Pune: Shri Vishakha Prakashan.
No. 4: *Maranmala* 1988. Pune: Suresh Ejensi.
No. 5: *Amnesamne* 1989. Pune: Suresh Ejensi.
No. 6: *Kolishtake* 1990. Aurangabad: Saket Prakashan.
No. 7: M.D. Hatkananglekar, ed., *Jwala-Kallol* 1996. Wasai: Dimpal Publication.
No. 8: *Asudwal* 2005. Wasai: Dimpal Publication.

Numbers above correspond with the publication order of the collections of short stories of Prof. Keshav Meshram.

Dangle, Arjun, ed., 1978: *Dalit Sahitya: Ek Abhyas.* Mumbai: Maharashtra Rajya Sahitya-Sanskriti Mandal.

Khandare, Devendra, 1994: *Keshav Meshramance Kathavishva.* Mumbai: Sambodhi Prakashan.

Meshram, Keshav, ed., 1978: *Vidrohi Kavita.* Pune: Continental Prakashan.

Meshram, Keshav, 1979: *Pokharan.* Mumbai: Popular Prakashan.

——, 1981: *Hakikat ani Jatayu.* Mumbai: Lokwangmay Griha Prakashan.

PART III

POLITICS, POLITICAL CULTURE AND RELIGIOSITY

12

The Ways of *Satyagraha* in Bombay, 1930

JIM MASSELOS

PATHWAYS AND SPACE

The apparently simple notion of *marga* or pathway assumes considerable complexity when considered in the context of the politics of resistance and of mobilization against dominant power structures. Apart from metaphorical usage in phrases like the path to freedom or the path of *satyagraha,* the path has played, as will be seen, a critical role in nationalist protest against the *raj.* Before proceeding to specific discussion I want first to unpick some of the complexities which surround the term.

At its simplest, the path is an arrow through space. Even in this there are two inherent and interconnected ideas, direction in and through space. One involves tracking through terrain and the other heading towards an objective. One privileges traversal, the other conclusion—but both presuppose direction towards an objective, and imply closure when it is attained. Both also, in this conquest of space, imply difference, a sense of proceeding from here and there. It is a relationship that is apparently dialectical or polar in structure.

But, in suggesting opposed states, the path then goes on to confound the implicit polarity, for the path equally mediates transition, from here to there, from the outer to the inner, from outside to inside (Bachelard 1969: Chapter 9). The path in its track through terrain has a notion of achievement, or even of conquest, over the space through which the traversal occurs and over the objective, the destination. In bringing together the here and there, it connects and unites, rather than separates. In doing so, the path may impose new characteristics on what is being traversed and it may create something new at its destination. What they might be, what characteristics might attach to that space vary according to circumstance and situation.

In terms of political action such unaltered space bears a relationship to the prevailing power of the state. Whether public or private, space is regulated and comes under the control of the state. It is regulated space (the phrase is from Dodgshon 1987: passim). Examples abound of progression through regulated space and the attempt to alter its character. When mutinous soldiers rushed from Meerut on 11 May 1857 and headed the 40 miles to Delhi to get the emperor, Bahadur Shah II, to lead their uprising, they were reinstating an earlier notion of Mughal regulated space over the prevailing regulated space of British rule. Similarly, when the initial revolutionaries of 1789 marched on the Bastille and forced open its doors, their path through Paris challenged the regulated space of the Bourbon state, and defied it when they occupied the Bastille. Both paths, that of the sepoys and the Parisians, had much the same trajectory—where what was important was reaching an objective and ending the journey. It was an objective which required the traversal of territory that was hostile and which represented or signified what was being opposed, territory that was part of the regulated space of the institutions under challenge just as much as was the destination. In proceeding through the space, along their path of resistance, both groups were altering the nature of what they traversed. They changed its connotations.

The procession of sepoys out of Meerut through to Delhi signaled that the territory was no longer regulated by British power; the overthrow of the Bastille had the same effect in relation to the Bourbons. The path of resistance changed the nature of the space which it traversed. It thus transmuted the apparent dialectic of here/there, the apparent polarity of inside/outside, and brought them together in unity. In these instances it was through reaching the endpoint, the emperor's palace in the Red Fort, or the Bastille in Paris, which changed the nature of the space and reinforced the teleology of the path, the closure of reaching an end.

Another kind of track, and another kind of relationship with traversed space, occurs when the focus is less on the trajectory of the path, less on the consequent closure and more upon the path itself. Here it is the journeying through space, rather than the arrival that has primacy. The destination itself becomes incidental; it is the space that is important, the terrain traversed. The terrain thus becomes a field for interaction, a space open for incursion, intrusion, exploration and contact. The path opens up space, makes it available and accessible to gaze, conversion, colonization.

It is time now to see how these reflections apply to the politics of protest in western India in 1930 as inaugurated by Gandhi's salt march to Dandi, and then its echoing in Bombay where protest developed its own urban particularity.

THE SALT MARCH

When Mahatma Gandhi set out from Sabarmati Ashram in Ahmedabad early in March 1930 and walked through the villages of Gujarat to reach the seaside at Dandi a month later, he did so with the specific objective of breaking the salt laws. His action turned the salt tax into a symbol of all that was iniquitous about the British *raj* and enabled a direct confrontation with British rule. This one specific act was made to objectify all that was wrong with British rule and in turn provided the exemplar for the wide and popular movement that followed. Such use of delimited targets to represent wider issues was an inherent part of Gandhi's style of non-violent resistance, and of overall strategies he had developed in earlier campaigns. He turned specific issues into symbols of the wider national malaise; the particular became the general, and highlighted the opposition to the realities of subordination under the British imperialism.

The climax of the march to Dandi was the moment when he stooped down on 6 April, picked up a handful of mud from the seaside and in token fashion manufactured the salt that symbolized opposition to the *raj*. The action, the moment of his breaking the laws, justified the long march and emphasized the end point, the ritual manufacture of salt. It was easily imitated and provided the signal for much making of salt throughout a great deal of India. For the next few months seemingly everywhere *satyagrahis* took water from the sea or from local rivers and ponds, boiled it and made salt. In doing so they asserted their resistance to the government and its laws, and their unity with other protestors and of course with the Mahatma.

In all this, it was Gandhi's arrival at Dandi and what he did there that assumed prime importance. Yet the journey itself had an importance whatever the outcome. His progression is seen as an example of his astute ability to maximize the impact of whatever he was doing. In this instance the month of marching enabled media coverage to build up and the apparently chimerical and quixotic objective acquired mythic proportions courtesy of a press coverage that had grown exponentially by the time he reached Dandi. The march then has won attention as a stage-managed event, even including specific discussion of the route and of which villages Gandhi chose to walk through and which ones he by-passed (Weber 1997; Brown 1977; Bakshi 1981).

Just as the act of picking up a handful of mud represented much more than what was actually happening, so too was the march more than a public relations exercise. The journey itself, the progression, had importance beyond the objectives of reaching an end point and providing a model for others to imitate. Though limited to a single region of India, his traversal through the Gujarati countryside established a wider idea of the commonality of all of India, and equally of its re-occupation by a purified India. During this time the British government did not contest that space and did not ban the procession; it watched carefully but did not stop what was happening. In consequence, the *satyagrahis* were enabled symbolically to re-occupy the space of the nation and bring it under the umbrella of a campaign that asserted the primacy of the nation. As Gandhi put it at Dandi on the night before he made that historic stoop to pick up salt:

> For the present Dandi is our destination but our real destination is no other than the temple of the goddess of *swaraj*. Our minds will not be at peace till we have her *darshan*, nor will we allow the government any peace. (reprinted in Weber 1997: 334-8)

From the beginning of the campaign there were at least two key elements. One was the destination, the specific act of breaking the salt laws and establishing easily understood symbolism of opposition to the British *raj*. Another was changing the attributes of regulated space—the march signifying spatial re-occupation, the assertion of the country's space as being unequivocally that of the nation. The march itself contained within itself both elements, uniting them seamlessly. It was therefore both elements that were contained in the widespread movement that followed Gandhi's taking up in his hands the mud of the Dandi coast. However, at the beginning of the movement, as protests were repeated elsewhere, it was the manufacture of salt that was the prime objective rather than the assertion of space. Yet, as the campaign progressed over time, it was the second element that assumed importance and became as significant as the actual acts of boiling down the water and selling the resulting dried powder. It was the traversal rather than the ostensible objective, the manufacture of salt, that became critical as demonstrated in Bombay in the months following the Dandi march.

SALT LINES

During March the Bombay Congress Committee had been planning what it should do once Gandhi had manufactured salt on 6 April.[1] The day itself was part of the panoply of nationalist festivals that Congress had been developing over its years of struggle. The 6 April date was the anniversary of Gandhi's first major campaign in India eleven years earlier, the Rowlatt Satyagraha of 1919. The Congress high command had established a National Week which commenced on that day and concluded a week later with the commemoration of those killed in the 1919 Jallianwala Bagh massacres in Amritsar. So there was a plethora of events that the Bombay committee was planning (*Bombay Chronicle,* 7 April 1930). The first day set the tone for much of what followed and had two main elements, a morning and an evening program.

The morning program was inaugurated at 6.30 a.m. on Monday, 7 April at Congress House in Girgaum, then a predominantly middle class, largely Marathi speaking part of the city. Bugles sounded, ten volunteers, under the joint leadership of a Parsi, K.F. Nariman, and a Muslim, Ali Bahadur Khan, were garlanded and honored, national songs were sung and the national flag saluted. The compound filled with people who moved out with the volunteers in an orderly procession through Girgaum and Tardeo, heading towards the sea (see Map 1). At its starting point the procession was reported to be a quarter of a mile long (*Bombay Chronicle*, 8 April 1930). There was also a large audience on the pavements urging on the procession with cries of *Mahatma Gandhi ki jai.* The procession reached the sea face between the Mahalaxmi Temple and the Haji Ali *dargah* where people collected seawater and took it to the nearby *maidan.* There, they lit fires in *sigris* they had carried from Congress House, boiled the seawater, and manufactured salt. To much cheering the announcement was made that the volunteers had broken the salt laws (*Times of India,* 8 April 1930). The police watched, and waited, but did nothing. The meeting finished around 8.15 a.m. There were similar, but smaller, ceremonies in the suburbs of Bombay, including Vile Parle, Santa Cruz, Khar and Bandra.

The evening program had a different trajectory. There was again a march from Congress House, but to a different and nearby site, to Chowpatty Beach, where it had been customary for years to hold public meetings. Perhaps over 50,000 people attended the meeting which began at 6.30, a number sufficiently great for the gathering to be addressed from two platforms simultaneously (*Bombay Chronicle,* 8 April 1930). At the meeting people expressed their hostility to foreign cloth, chanted boycott slogans, and tossed foreign caps and cloth in the direction of the platforms. The items were gathered and burnt on a bonfire. As well there was further token manufacture of salt.

Thereafter, over the next few days and weeks the movement developed a momentum of its own, as a range of other kinds of protest emerged—bonfires of foreign cloth, *hartals,* closure of shops and schools, *swadeshi bazaars,* picketing of liquor shops and so on. The extent of resistance was considerable and gave to Bombay a key role as a center of opposition to the British authorities during the Salt Satyagraha and Civil Disobedience

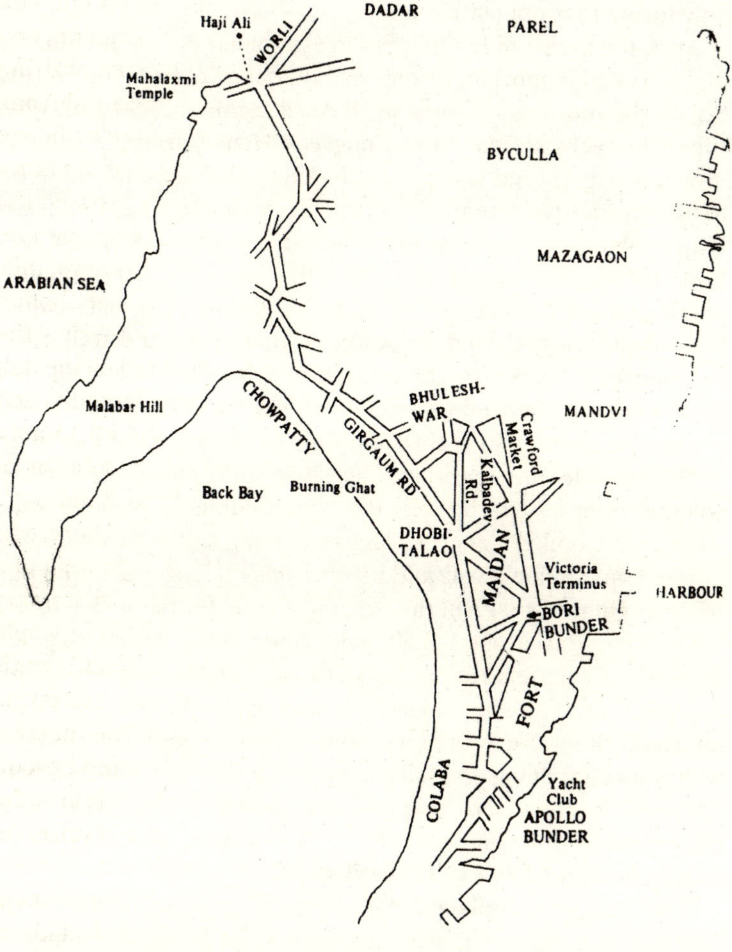

MAP 1: BOMBAY, *c.* 1930, reprinted from Masselos 1991, p. 85.

during 1930 (for a fuller discussion see Masselos 1987: 71-86). Providing a core element in all the resistance was salt-making and processions, though of course they were by no means the only forms that opposition took.

After the arrest of leading Congress volunteers on the Monday night/Tuesday morning, Congress declared a *hartal* of protest. So, on the morning of Tuesday, 8 April, again at 6.30 a.m. when fifty volunteers set out from Congress House to make salt, the crowd that gathered was persuaded not to accompany them but to observe *hartal* instead. This time the volunteers headed not to Haji Ali but to Chowpatty, much nearer to Congress House (see Map 1). Another crowd was there to join in the ceremonial of singing national songs and saluting the national flag, after which the volunteers gathered seawater in their *lotas* and took them to Congress House to manufacture salt. The following day, Wednesday, a hundred volunteers sallied out of Congress House in small groups walking through different parts of the city to get to the seaside; the next day, Thursday, there were two hundred volunteers in 20 batches. By this stage some 32 pans of water were on the boil in Congress House making salt—the compound had become a factory. It and its environs no longer seemed part of the regulated space of the *raj*. It was time for the police to act.

On Thursday around 6.30 p.m. some three hundred police arrived at Congress House, broke through cordons of *satyagrahis*, arrested three Muslim volunteers, and broke the pans and *sigris* on which the water was being boiled. People gathered to watch what was happening and followed the three people who had been arrested as they were taken to the police station. They were described as forming "literally . . . a crowd of admirers a mile long" (*Bombay Chronicle*, 11 April 1930).

The Congress replaced the salt-making equipment and the next day sent out even more volunteers, some four or five hundred, who marched out in ten batches to make salt in various parts of the city. The day after, more *satyagrahis* went out in the morning to make salt. On Sunday, 13 April, a *hartal* was observed in the afternoon followed by a large meeting on the sands of Chowpatty in the evening when over 200,000 people attended to listen to speakers on three different platforms. In the morning there had been what had become the usual departure of volunteers from Congress House as well as from other wards in the city to Chowpatty and other seaside locations. At Chowpatty itself there had been an early morning meeting attended by some 50,000 people, and during the morning people crowded for about a mile along the seafront from every possible vantage point watching first the meeting and later small groups of people going to the seashore for salt water. One newspaper reported that "thousands" of women marched to the seaside celebrating the occasion like a marriage festival and noted that they then filled their *lotas* with water and took it home, there to manufacture salt (*Bombay Chronicle*, 14 April 1930). The campaign had thus moved away from the specific Congress organization to broaden its mass base and incorporate ordinary individuals. Thereafter, morning excursions to make salt became a regular feature of city life and they continued to be so despite the fact that on the following Sunday the police began to make concerted attacks on salt-making premises by raiding salt makers in four different parts of the city. On the same night the police also began stopping meetings such as one held on Esplanade Maidan.

Before I discuss their *bundobast*, I want to summarize some of the implications of what had been happening over the first two weeks. Over this time a pattern had developed and the forms of opposition had become routine.

As we have seen, in order to collect seawater the volunteers had to go out from wherever they were and get to the seaside. Initially there was a single procession that tracked through residential and retail areas of the city. Subsequently, smaller groups fanned out, taking their own tracks through different parts but coming together at the end to collect the water and at different locations to boil it down to salt. The initial path became a number of paths going in different directions, so the effect was that the tracks of the salt makers created a web which spanned various city localities. The path was no longer a single line through these areas but a sweep of criss-crossing tracks, and so established a sense of a composite space under the umbrella of resistance and lawbreaking. The paths joined together as a web, net or network and thus defined a field and became a field, though the prime objective was still very much the critical act of making salt.

The volunteers as they moved in the early morning through the localities achieved other affects. Their movement publicized the campaign and its activities, and directed attention to what was happening and to the issues, symbolic and actual, much as Gandhi had done during the course of his much longer march. The volunteers promoted the Congress position and persuaded people to participate. Perhaps subliminally, their presence did something more: it asserted that the urban space was the nation's space, that the streets of Bombay were the people's and the nation's, whatever the role of the police as the law enforcement arm of the British government.

There was another way in which the first two weeks' activity linked in with city life. The timing of the salt making, the processions and even the evening meetings were located within the context of the rhythms of urban life in that the morning processions were over before offices, stores, markets and other retail outlets opened at 10 or 10.30 in the morning. People could participate in the processions or the salt making in the morning and still be able to get to work. Similarly, the evening meetings were held after work finished, as people made their way home, or even after they had returned home. There was still enough time for them to attend the meetings, which were often held near to where they lived, and get home in time for dinner, after 8 p.m. The campaign functioned so well because it conjoined political objective, urban space, and city time rhythms seamlessly within the national protest and within the symbolic structure of opposition.

SONG LINES

Another expression of resistance surfaced later during 1930 that equally relied for effectiveness on the conjoining of time-rhythm, traversal of space, and nationalist objective. This was an entirely novel feature, the *prabhat pheri* (for a fuller discussion see Masselos 1999a: 94-114). The *prabhat pheris* were small bands of people who went around the streets very early in the morning, starting from between 4.30 and 5.30 a.m. in the twilight of the false dawn, singing songs welcoming the dawn. The singers greeted the beginning of the new day and urged people to open their eyes, wake up and realize what was happening. They had an extensive repertoire of songs, some of which the government later banned as seditious. All had a potent nationalist message. Their tenor is evident from their opening lines. One began:

> How can you sleep soundly; get up from sleep [and] open the eyes at this time [when] the whole country is completely burnt. (Joshi *c.* 1930)

Another, The Drum of Swaraj, from a banned pamphlet of *pheri* songs (*Prabhat Pheri, Bhag* 2, *c.* 1930), likewise used the symbolism of awakening with the dawn and seeing a new day to make its political point.

1. The morning light is spreading and the night has hidden itself through fear of the sun. Awake, O sons, and awake O sisters of India.
2. Look, the auspicious moment has arrived, now do not shut your eyes.
3. The splendour of Swaraj is spreading. Look, the lustre of the Sun has risen.

There were many such songs sung by the groups as they traversed the city, sometimes accompanied by drums, cymbals and harmoniums. And there were many groups: an estimate in July 1930 put the total at around one hundred and twenty-five while the Police later claimed that every street and every *chawl* had its own *pheri*.[2] The groups varied in size and could range from ten to twenty-five people with some reaching as high as forty or sixty people on particular days. Since the groups were largely spontaneous in their formation there was initially no organization behind them, so that the size of groups varied dramatically from morning to morning. As the groups marched and sang their way through the localities, their paths might cross each other and at times they might join up before again separating.

As with the later salt volunteers, the *pheris* were creating through their paths a network, a web, which incorporated the localities they traversed. The *pheri* bands in theory were to finish their singing at sunrise—at about the same time the salt volunteers began their work and sallied forth on their salt making endeavors.

Both, as has been suggested, were creating through their paths an idea of an overall field in which everyone was linked, made part of a united field. But these *pheris*, unlike the salt-makers, had no specific objective, no destination. What was vital in their action was the journeying, the progression through city space, rather than towards any specific place or destination.

PROCESSION LINES

An evolution in the nature of organized Congress protest was concurrently occurring which had much the same affect as *pheri* activities in that it assigned primacy to journeying and traversal rather than the reaching of an objective or destination. Partly this was a response to the nature of police controls which were more frequently being imposed and were becoming more extreme in the methods the police deployed.

With the police *bundobast*, the procession became important as an assertion of the strength of the campaign, a signal of unwillingness to submit to foreign force. The act of marching and the traversal of city space became the point of opposition against an imperial and imperious *raj*. It counterposed the idea of a national regulated space over a British regulated space. Processions asserted the purposiveness of the *satyagrahis*, their nonviolent resistance and the national cause they espoused. Thus it was the presence of the demonstrators, their progress through the streets and their meetings that became the locus of opposition, as much as it was the specific breaking of laws and civil disobedience. Other events in the campaign later in the year provide excellent examples of such situations where the path, the journey as an assertion of space, and control of space, became more important than whatever was the ostensible objective.

Thus on Sunday, 8 June the Dadar Congress Committee organized a large three-hour procession from, and back to, Tilak bridge as the prelude to a mass rally in the nearby *maidan*. There were marchers of all kinds—volunteers, students, women, Seva Dal and Congress members—and there was a band and flag bearers with the national flag. A lorry bore an effigy dressed in European clothing labeled Mr Goonda Raj. All marched in an orderly procession, four abreast. People watched from the pavement and some joined in at the end of the procession. When the procession eventually returned to the *maidan* there were the usual proceedings—speeches, songs and slogans, but the meeting concluded with an enormous bonfire of the effigy and of five lakhs worth of foreign cloth (*Bombay Chronicle*, 9 June 1930). Here the spatial component was as crucial as the meeting itself: the tracing through the Dadar localities was important not as a means of getting directly to any specific destination but as a means of traversing space so as to cover the largest possible area and assert the primacy of the Congress cause—and to rally support for the meeting.

The track of resistance assumed a much more aggressive, more immediate character later in the year. In December after a volunteer, Babu Genu, had been killed by a truck while offering *satyagraha* against trucks carrying foreign cloth in Kalbadevi Road, his death procession the following day changed direction. Instead of taking the body to the cremation grounds, the large procession decided to go instead to Chowpatty, to the spot where Lokamanya Tilak had been cremated, and there cremate Babu Genu (see Map 1). The police stopped the procession and using bayonets dispersed a section that tried to break through and get to Chowpatty. The remainder of the procession sat down on the street and would not move. Around them in adjoining lanes and *wadis* the police made *lathi* charges on angry groups of demonstrators. Eventually what remained of the procession was permitted to take the body to the original destination, the cremation grounds. Like other funeral processions in less troubled times, Babu Genu's was an assertion of territorial imperatives and an assertion about the control of space, one that the procession was unable to establish in this particular case (*Bombay Chronicle*, 13, 16 and 22 December 1930; *Times of India*, 13, 15 and 16 December 1930; Masselos 1999b).

The territorial imperatives of processions during this period were most pronounced when Congress members and volunteers sought to move out from the predominantly Indian trading and residential areas stretching from Girgaum/Tardeo south to the Market/Dhobitalao localities. The objective was to move southwards into the business and European dominated areas of Bori Bunder, Fort, the Secretariat complexes and Apollo Bunder and to hold meetings at the Cooperage or on the *maidans* close to the location of British power in the city, near the Secretariat and Assembly buildings.[3]

On 6 May a procession responding to Gandhi's arrest the previous morning, went out from Congress House in Girgaum around 4 p.m. with about 3,000 volunteers and *satyagrahis.* It wended through Girgaum Back Road, along Sandhurst Road into Bhendy Bazaar, on to Pydhonie and into Kalbadevi Road and then to Cruickshank and Hornby Roads along Esplanade Road to Apollo Bunder and finally reached its objective, the Oval near Bandstand (see Map 2). By then having moved through Indian trading and residential localities, into the central business district and the European dominant sectors it had attracted some 50,000 people including four or five musical bands, numerous slogan bearers and numbers of prominent city identities as well as lots of ordinary inhabitants.[4]

Three days later a procession of cloth merchants followed a similar trajectory, though its numbers grew only to some 15,000.[5] Six days later a Youth League procession expressing sympathy with the Afghan Youth League and congratulating the latest batch of *satyagrahis* who had been arrested, managed to collect even fewer, about 5,000 people, though it had followed a similar path through the city, into the Indian and European sections concluding with a march past Apollo Bunder. It was not long thereafter that the inconvenience to Europeans in the Yacht Club at Apollo Bunder and their irritation with the processions was being forcibly expressed to government authorities, as also was the point that the constant sight of national flags and processions was having a deleterious effect on British troops.[6]

That other processions were less amenable to the discipline evident in these events was demonstrated later, when organizers lost control of processions and when popular elements less amenable to Congress organizational controls joined in.

A procession of merchants and traders representing some twenty-nine associations, set out from the Bullion Exchange around 4 p.m. on 23 May and was stopped at Bori Bunder shortly afterwards (See Map 2). This was expected. Earlier in the day, around noon the Commissioner of Police had asked a deputation

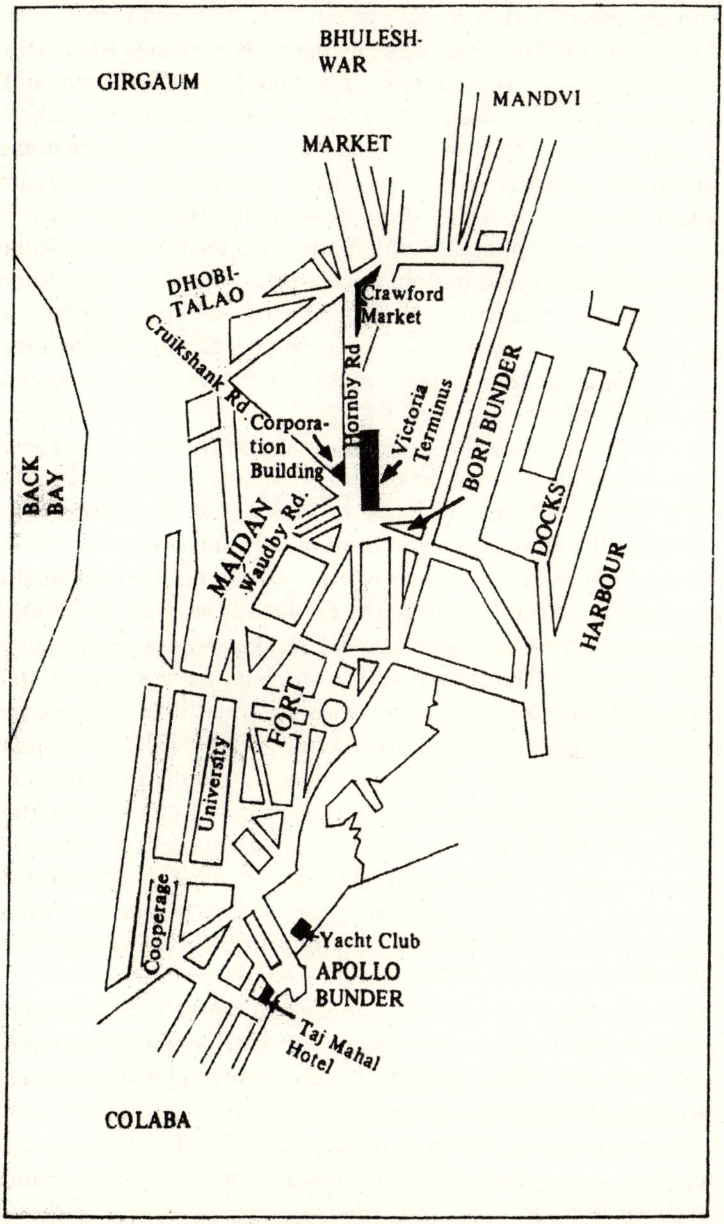

MAP 2: CITY AREA OF BOMBAY, *c.* 1930,
reprinted from Masselos 1991, p. 86.

of the organizers led by major city notable, Walchand Hirchand, not to go into the Fort area since on the three previous occasions traffic had been disrupted for over an hour in Hornby Road, and Europeans had been insulted by some of the crowd. Walchand Hirchand replied that a small matter like traffic dislocation shouldn't be considered when a nation was fighting for its freedom. In formulating his position he was underlining the significance of the path, of space and spatial access in the movement and how all related to national symbolism. The Commissioner responded by asserting he would stop the procession at Bori Bunder and that he was concerned with the provocative attitude some people in the procession might adopt towards Europeans.[7]

So, at Bori Bunder the procession sat on the road for about three hours while some of the city's wealthiest citizens negotiated further with the Commissioner of Police. Sir Purshottamdas Thakordas finally suggested a compromise: the procession would go from Victoria Terminus to Flora Fountain but there it would turn and go by a back route to the Esplanade *maidan*. The Commissioner agreed and went to the demonstration and spoke with G.D. Birla, Durgadutt and other leading magnates who accepted the compromise but with the modification they be permitted to go via the Share Bazaar. They and their fellow *satyagrahis* stood up as the procession was finally permitted to resume its way. But when it arrived at the Fountain, the leaders lost control and most of the processionists hived off, determined to go on to Apollo Bunder. This they did but once they got there, they turned around and headed to the *maidan* for the proposed meeting which finally began at 9 p.m. with Birla presiding.

It was becoming evident from these and other similar events that the meetings which were intended to be the culmination of the procession had become less important than the procession. What was important, judging by the determination of many marchers, was the act of traversing particular city space—they wanted to go into localities especially associated with the British government and distinctively different from those where most marchers lived and worked. The organizers seem equally to have been driven by similar imperatives as demonstrated by the interchange they had earlier had with the Police Commissioner before the procession began. But the wealthy asserted a further nicety: the Share Exchange was their space; it was Indian, not British.

Such an analysis thus makes the activity of the march more potent than its ostensible objective, the activity of the meeting at the end of the march. The decline of the meeting as climax may partly have been due to the way in which the movement was attracting wider popular support, people less willing to accept, or less familiar with, the controls the Congress wanted to apply to such events. But it was also about the underlying sense of the symbolism of city space, a sense of the control of that space. It may also relate to the way in which people in the city perceived their environment, and the mental maps they used in relating to it (for mental maps, see Masselos 1991: 33-63). Marching through localities that represented power, privilege and foreign domination was a different kind of experience from going around the familiar neighborhood territory that was traced by the salt-makers and the *prabhat pheris* in their morning rounds. This was another world and its occupation via the instrumentality of the procession rendered it part of the new nation in the becoming. The notion of British regulated space was here contested and replaced with a nationalist notion. Police opposition to the entry of processions if anything heightened the sense of achieving the new nation by polarizing the distinction.

While these developments were happening, the government and the police were re-thinking their policies about crowd handling and permitting demonstrations. By mid year they had decided they would ordinarily not ban processions unless they were rowdy or likely to cause "intolerable" interference with traffic—as would inevitably apply to any evening peak hour mass procession going into the Fort area and beyond.[8] So the decision not to interfere with processions in fact permitted the stopping of processions should they be large and assertive. Again, it would seem, the underlying core issue about the processions was contestation over space, a contestation over who was to control the space and what that space symbolized. It was finally the objective, the space of British Bombay, that became critical, rather than the culminating meeting.

One final dramatic example reinforces this line of interpretation. Every year since 1920 it had been the Congress custom to observe Tilak Day on 1 August, the day on which Tilak had died and the day on which the first non-cooperation campaign had been inaugurated. In 1930 the Bombay Satyagraha Committee decided to observe the day by organizing a procession through the city, along Hornby Road to a nearby *maidan* where a rally would be held. The police were happy for both the procession and the meeting to proceed but would not permit the procession to go through Hornby Road. The Committee in turn refused to accept the Police Commissioner's decision.[9]

In the event, on 1 August a Tilak Day procession said to be a mile long did proceed out from the Market/Kalbadevi area. It had started with only a hundred volunteers at Tilak's *samadhi* at Chowpatty in the mid afternoon. As was expected, when the procession reached Bori Bunder around 5.30 p.m. just at the beginning of the peak hour the police prohibited it from proceeding further (*Times of India*, 2 August 1930). The police asked the leaders to go directly to the meeting but they refused and insisted on taking the proposed original route. So there, at the junction of Cruickshank and Hornby Roads, opposite Victoria Terminus, five to seven thousand people immediately sat on the street, and began singing songs and chanting slogans. Traffic through what was probably Bombay's major intersection stopped. Enormous crowds gathered on the pavements to watch the *satyagrahis* and see what would happen. Initially the police did nothing for reasons explained in a secret telegram: "The procession numbered many thousands and could not have been dispersed without use of very considerable force."[10] After about five hours, around 10.30 p.m., the police decided to clear the crowds, not the *satyagrahis* sitting on roadway but those watching on the footpaths. There was a stampede as people rushed away but they returned—and in turn were dispersed six more times during the next two hours. It was not until around 7 o'clock the next morning that the police moved on those seated on the roadway. They arrested the leaders and forty-three women volunteers of whom all except four were later released. Some of the *satyagrahis* chose to move but a hundred and fifty remained seated and it was not until around 8:30 or 9 that the police dispersed them and Bori Bunder was quiet. In fact, much of the city that day was quiet since the volunteers called for a *hartal* in protest against police handling of the situation and the injuring, according to press reports, of over 275 people, reports government considered "ridiculous".[11] It put the number of casualties much lower, at around fifty. Privately, in a secret telegram to the Secretary of State in London, the Bombay Government justified its actions:

> Had they not been arrested the crowd would not have dispersed without use of great force which it was obviously preferable to avoid. Nor was it possible to allow procession to remain on the road any longer. Every minute numbers were increasing from daylight onwards.[12]

The incident brings together many of the elements that have featured in this examination of spatial elements in civil disobedience in Bombay during 1930. In particular it establishes the point about the traversal of space and its critical importance in the resistance offered. As the situation evolved during the year, the Congress leadership would seem to have become more concerned with the primacy of the procession and its progress through the Fort area of Bombay and increasingly less with the meeting which was the ostensible culmination of the march. Leaders during these months less frequently focused on the Indian spatial domain in the Girgaum to Dhobitalao area and more on that space southwards from Bori Bunder where the centers of power were understood to be or which were understood as signifying that power. Generally, leaders were unwilling to give up a march in order to hold a meeting: the march itself became the priority. The path was more important than the objective, and was assigned—and achieved—symbolic and actual potency. The struggle for national objectives was fought in Bombay within the parameters of the issue about who should have access to urban space and who should control that space. Much of the battle for *purna swaraj* was about access to the streets and about who could go through them.

Thus the physical track through the city and throughout the city became as important as the end action, whether it was the making of salt, the holding of meetings or otherwise offering civil disobedience. Perhaps here the journey had become as important as the arrival at the destination itself. Possibly it was even more important in terms of effectiveness in the struggle to win a nation and its support through non-violent resistance.

From a wider perspective the incidents discussed highlight differences in the ways that the track or the path functioned and in how they may be understood. As demonstrated in the Mahatma's initiating march and in the early salt making expeditions in Bombay, the track had a specific and clearly targeted objective and sought to culminate in that objective. Its progression was teleological: it aimed at making salt, opposing British rule and asserting the primacy of the subordinated nation. Over time the salt making excursions became less concerned with the teleological act itself, but in fanning out and criss-crossing residential localities so as to establish a field in which the national objective was unchallenged. When the *pheri* singing groups emerged and grew in numbers they reinforced the notion of the locality as part of the nation and its struggle. In such instances the path of such groups was diffuse, and did not have the specifically teleological endpoint of the salt march. Rather they used the traversal of space as a means of establishing a web, a net, a network. They created a field of common endeavor and defined that field. Yet another aspect of the path developed when processions themselves came to the forefront. With these events, what was important was not an end point, the meeting which usually provided the culmination of a march, but the route that the procession traversed. Here what was critical was that the march should enter space that was symbolically understood to be the location of power and privilege. The march thus acquired aggressiveness and force considerably different from the way Gandhi's salt march had worked. The intent here was to invade and occupy space, not define it nor use it as the path to something else. Just as space might function in different ways and have levels of different meanings, so too the path or the track through space equally had no single function, whether or not the actors involved in the traversal were fully aware of what was involved and what was represented on the ground, in the immediate minute to minute resistance of the time.

NOTES

1. See Hon. Sec., BPCC to President, AICC, 15 March 1930 in Nehru Memorial Museum & Library, New Delhi: AICC Papers, 1931, P-11, p. 207.
2. See the *Times of India* article, 11/12 August 1930 in Maharashtra State Archives: Home Dept. Special file 750 (40) A of 1930, p. 13 and Commissioner of Police Bombay to Sec. to Govt. of Bombay, Home Dept. (Political) no. 2193/H/3717 of 1 May 1931 in Maharashtra State Archives: Home Dept. Special file 750 (57) E of 1931, p. 11.
3. The accounts of what happened to these processions are based on reports in the *Bombay Chronicle* and the *Times of India* and reports in Maharashtra State Archives: Home Dept. Special file 750 (26).
4. Daily extract, Commissioner of Police, Bombay, 2066/H/3717 of 7 May 1930, in Maharashtra State Archives: Home Dept. Special file 750 (26), p. 3.
5. Daily extract, Commissioner of Police, Bombay, 2114/H/3717 of 10 May 1930, in Maharashtra State Archives: Home Dept. Special file 750 (26), p. 5.
6. See handwritten minute of conversation with Brigadier Charles, 16 May 1930 in Maharashtra State Archives: Home Dept. Special file 750 (26) of 1930, p. 9.
7. Extract, confidential letter, Commissioner of Police, Bombay, 2470/ H/3717 of 24 May 1930, in Maharashtra State Archives: Home Dept. Special file 750 (26), p. 15.
8. J.E.B. Hotson, Home Member, Govt. of Bombay to Healy, Officiating Police Commissioner, Bombay, 15 June 1930 in Maharashtra State Archives: Home Dept. Special file 750 (26) of 1930, p. 49.
9. Special Secret Telegram to Secretary of State, SD 3257 of 1 August 1930 in Maharashtra State Archives: Home Dept. Special file 750 (39)- III of 1930, p. 1.
10. Special Secret Telegram to Secretary of State, SD 3279 of 2 August 1930 in Maharashtra State Archives: Home Dept. Special file 750 (39)- III of 1930, p. 5.
11. Ibid.
12. Ibid. For another government version of the event see Maharashtra State Archives: Home Dept. Special file 750 (26), pp. 79-109.

REFERENCES

Bakshi, S.R., 1981: *Gandhi and Salt Satyagraha.* Malayattor: Vishwavidya Publishers.

Bachelard, Gaston, 1969: *The Poetics of Space.* Boston: Beacon Press.

Bombay Chronicle, 1930.

Brown, Judith M., 1977: *Gandhi and Civil Disobedience: The Mahatma in Indian Politics.* Cambridge: Cambridge University Press.

Dodgshon, Robert A., 1987: *The European Past: Social Evolution and Spatial Order.* Houndmills: Macmillan Education.

Joshi, D.S., *c.* 1930: *Swadeshi pracharak prabhat pherichin paden.* Girgaum: M.R. Shirodkar and G.T. Hublikar, New Manohar Printing Press. The pamphlet is kept with Maharashtra State Archives: Home Dept. Political file 534-I of 1930 at p. 113 and the translation is on p. 3.

Masselos, Jim, 1987: "Audiences, Actors and Congress Dramas: Crowd Events in Bombay City in 1930", in J. Masselos, ed., *Struggling and Ruling: The Indian National Congress, 1885-1985*, the Asian Studies Association of Australia South Asian Publications Series No. 2, and Delhi: Sterling, 1987, pp. 71-86.

——, 1991: "Appropriating Urban Space: Social Constructs of Bombay in the Time of the *Raj*", in S. Freitag, guest ed., "Aspects of 'the Public' in Colonial South Asia", Special Issue of *South Asia*, vol. 14, no. 1, pp. 33-63.

——, 1999a: "Controlling the Prabhat Pheris: Bombay 1930-1931", in A.R. Kulkarni and N.K. Wagle, eds., *Region, Nationality and Religion.* Mumbai: Popular Prakashan, pp. 94-114.

——, 1999b: "The Life of Dead Bodies: Corporality and Memory in Pre-independence Bombay", unpublished paper. Sydney: Eighth International Conference on Maharashtra: Culture and Society, the University of Sydney, 6-10 January.

——, 2007: *The City in Action: Bombay Struggles for Power*, Delhi: Oxford University Press.

Prabhat Pheri, Bhag 2, *c.* 1930: Girgaum, Bombay: P.B. Phatak, Stree Pandurang Vaibhav Press. The pamphlet is with Maharashtra State Archives: Home Dept. Political file 534-I of 1930 at p. 35 and the translation is on p. 37.

Times of India, 1930.

Weber, Thomas, 1997: *On the Salt March: The Historiography of Gandhi's March to Dandi.* New Delhi: Harper Collins.

13

Taking the Non-Violent Path: A Story of the Anti-Dam *Satyagraha*

RAJENDRA VORA

The Indian nationalist movement generated many controversial issues in Maharashtra. One of the issues around which controversies revolved was about the method to be employed by the movement. M.G. Ranade (1842-1901) and G.K. Gokhale (1866-1915) believed that change was to be achieved step-by-step by using constitutional means. They came to be known as moderate nationalists. For Lokmanya Tilak (1856-1920) the method was of secondary importance. It should be modified in accordance with the demands of the movement and the pattern of response from the colonial rule. He held that everything is fair in politics and believed in the principle of wickedness unto the wicked. Tilak's nationalism became known as extremist since he advocated actions such as boycott, non-payment of land-revenue and passive resistance. The means acquired prominence once again during Gandhian era. Mahatma Gandhi (1869-1948) replaced Tilak's doctrine of wickedness unto the wicked by the doctrine of "truth even unto the wicked".[1] By discovering new path of *Satyagraha*—of non-violent resistance—he took discourse of method of politics beyond moderate-extremist debate. The controversy which gathered importance after Gandhi's formulation of *Satyagraha* method was with respect to violence *vs.* non-violence. Terrorist nationalism of V.D. Savarkar (1883-1966) glorified violence and condemned Gandhian method of conquering hate by love or untruth by truth.

Post-colonial studies by basically directing their attention to Gandhi's critique of colonialism and Western civilization have generally speaking neglected the *Satyagraha* dimension of Gandhi's project and have not dealt with success and failure of his method. My paper seeks to understand the way Gandhi's method was applied in the anti-dam movement in Maharashtra and attempts to analyze the factors which led to its failure.

Satyagraha implies adherence to truth by non-violent means. It involves the pursuit of truth and in that pursuit you invite suffering on yourself and do not cause violence to anybody else. *Satyagraha* postulates the "conquest" of the "adversary" by suffering in one's own person. It seeks to effect change and operates within a conflict situation. A *Satyagrahi* (one who actively participates in *Satyagraha* actions) refuses to cooperate with those responsible for violation of truth. Mahatma Gandhi held that there is no way to find truth except the way of non-violence and believed that in the quest for truth it is not possible to inflict harm on others because in so behaving truth itself would lose its meaning.

Gandhi's method of *Satyagraha* emerged as the most commonly used technique of political resistance in Maharashtra since the 1920s. Mulshi *Satyagraha* was the first major instance where Gandhian non-violent method was tested by Maharashtrians. It was a protest movement against the dam the Tata Company proposed to construct on the confluence of Mula and Nila rivers in the Mulshi Peta (tract) of Pune District for the hydro-electric power generation. The electricity produced at this plant was to be supplied to textile mills and the railways in Mumbai city. However, it was estimated that nearly forty-eight villages would be submerged by the reservoir of the dam. The villagers organized by the leaders of the nationalist movement staged a protest against the scheme by employing non-violent method. This anti-dam struggle began in April 1921 and continued till December 1924. But despite the agitation of more than three years by the villagers and their supporters the Mulshi *Satyagraha* failed to achieve its aim. The Gandhian path could not take dam-affected people to their destination.

The Mulshi *Satyagraha* was a struggle between the poor farmers of the Mulshi tract and the Tata Company supported by the colonial government. The Tatas represented the rising class of businessmen and factory owners which had become stronger and confident after the First World War and was ready to make compromise with the government in order to seek concessions and benefits for the growth of industries. The Industrial Commission appointed by the government in 1916 had recommended a policy of encouraging Indian industry. No wonder the Mulshi project meant for providing electric power to the textile mills and factories in Mumbai city came to be supported by the government. Mulshi farmers thus fought a battle against a very powerful alliance and therefore faced a defeat. However, there were several other factors which pushed them towards the defeat.

GANDHI'S AMBIGUOUS STAND

One of the important reasons for the failure of the Mulshi *Satyagraha* Movement can be attributed to the ambiguity in Mahatma Gandhi's approach towards the movement. Gandhi was directly or indirectly connected with the movement from beginning to end. The leaders of the movement had consulted Gandhi before starting the *Satyagraha* in April 1921.[2] We do not have any record of the meeting. But Gandhi must have given advice in favor of starting the *Satyagraha* because this is what he said in his speech before the Maharashtra Provincial Conference held in Vasai on 7 May 1921:[3]

> Your love has drawn me here. I am sorry I cannot stay in your midst for long. With the president's permission, I shall say in brief what I want to. It is about Mulshi Peta (tract) that I must speak first. It grieves me that I have not been able to go there myself and acquaint myself at first hand with the grievances of our brethren there. My knowledge of the details of the struggle is scanty. I rarely get a chance to read a newspaper. I naturally hesitate to speak or write on any matter about which I do not know much. All the same, I have given my views on it in *Young India* without getting into details. I convey my sympathy to those who are attending this meeting as representatives of the *Satyagrahis* of Mulshi Peta. People fighting for their rights always have my sympathy. I understand that the people of Mulshi Peta are fighting to defend the ownership of their farms. I stand by them in their claim. I always support people who are ready to defend their possession at the sacrifice of their lives, but I can never join hands with those who are ready to kill

others, be it even for the cause of truth. These people can get my help only for deciding whether they are fighting for truth or untruth. When I was asked about the people of Mulshi Peta starting a *Satyagraha,* I had replied that, if the people had the necessary strength, the experiment was certainly worth trying. They have proved that they possess that strength. Whatever they have been able to achieve is good, so far as it goes. But they can have complete peace only when they are permanently assured of their rights. If a man does not want to relinquish his rights over a plot of land, it is not in keeping with the traditions of our country to obtain possession of it by recourse to law. I was once engaged in a small case, the man owned an ordinary piece of land but he was after me like a mad man to save it for him. As a father does not wish to sell his child, so also a man is naturally unwilling to part with his land. This has been our nature from ancient times. I hope our Tata company will take no steps against the *Satyagrahis* of Mulshi Peta. It is welcome to acquire land even without payment with people's goodwill, but I hope it will make no move to obtain it so long as even one owner is unwilling to part with his piece. It may be European civilisation to acquire land by recourse to a Land Acquisition Act, but I should have nothing to do with a civilisation which I believe to be Satanic. So long, therefore, as the people of Mulshi Peta carry on their fight on peaceful lines, the whole of India should back them. . . .[4]

Earlier Gandhi had publicly urged the Tatas to come forward for conciliatory talks through his letter published in the *Young India* on 27 April 1921:

My heart goes out to these poor people. I wish the great house of the Tatas, instead of standing on their legal rights, will reason with the people themselves, and do whatever they wish in consultation with them. I have some experience of Land Acquisition Act. I had nearly eighty cases to deal with. Here the reason for the acquisition was not industrial development but insanitation. I know that the people never got the exact equivalent. What is the value of all the boons that the Tata scheme claims to confer upon India, if it is to be at the unwilling expense of even one poor man? I dare say the problems of disease and poverty can be easily solved, and the survivors will live in luxury if the three crore half-starved men and women, and lakhs of decrepit humanity were shot and their bodies utilised for manure, or their bones utilised for making knife handles. And yet no one but a lunatic will put up such a suggestion. Is the case any weaker when men and women are not to be shot, but compulsorily dispossessed of their valued lands about which sentiment, romance, and all that makes life worth living, have grown up? I suggest to the custodians of the great name that they would more truly advance India's interest if they will defer to the wishes of their weak and helpless countrymen.[5]

PRO-COMPENSATION POSITION

In this letter Gandhi had not discussed *Satyagraha* as such. A careful reading of the letter reveals that he was, on the contrary, indirectly advocating negotiations and also the idea of accepting compensation. In the very next month, another article on Mulshi appeared in the *Young India.* On the one hand it criticized modernization and Westernization and on the other expressed views in favor of indigenous culture and social structure. The limitations of the Mulshi *Satyagraha* were spelt out at the end of the article. It is necessary to study this article closely because it reveals Gandhi's changing position. A gist of the arguments is given here: The Whole of Mulshi Peta was being acquired by the unethical use of the Land Acquisition Act. According to the Government the construction of dam was in the public interest as it would contribute towards industrialization. The Government showed no hesitation in using force for this purpose. Having said this, Gandhi went on to criticize the Western social system based on industrialization. He says that imperialism, capitalism and militarization are the hallmarks of modern culture. This Western culture would impose itself upon India. We would be forced to adopt an individualistic way of life in place of the traditional collective style of social life. Modernization carries individualism to its extreme. This would erode the very foundation of the institution of the family, too. The Mulshi Scheme was an example of an attempt to impose modern culture and unsettle the foundations of Indian social life. This would result in the alienation of man. Land acquisition was being justified on the basis of the theory of enhancement of material welfare of society through industrialization. Instead, we should have taken into consideration the highest criteria of the well-being of society. When it is a question of the moral and social welfare of the people living here since times immemorial, we should give greater importance to moral welfare and uphold the Indian way of life over and above material welfare. He was not against large industrial projects merely because they tended to destroy small and cottage industries. He believed that the material and industrial progress should not destroy our original social structure and our culture. Our social life should remain unchanged. Industrial progress of the capitalist kind should not erode the fundamental social values which are the foundation of our society. Imperialism, capitalism and militarization carry the seeds of the destruction of society. A society based on these three principles is bound to collapse. After this discussion, the author turns again to the Mulshi *Satyagraha*. Here he says only one question remains to be answered. No matter how brave, noble and praiseworthy the Mulshi *Satyagraha* was, no matter how exemplary a non-violent and patriotic struggle it was, it could not further the cause of *Swaraj* (home rule). And without *Swaraj*, India would not free herself from the clutches of imperialism, capitalism and militarization. No doubt the Mulshi *Satyagraha* was an example of the use of civil disobedience against the Government of Bombay and the Tata Company. But the type of civil disobedience that Mahatma Gandhi and Congress advocated was directly related to *Swaraj*. Its purpose was to fight one or more of the Government's branches whereas the Mulshi *Satyagraha* was mainly against the misuse of one act, the Land Acquisition Act.[6] The article thus exposed up the limitations of the Mulshi movement (putting the Mulshi *Satyagraha* in a poor light however, untenably). Many examples can be given of the movements led by Gandhi, that had a limited purpose. There had been movements against a single specific oppressive policy, tax or act and Gandhi had given those movements an all-India dimension. The question arises why the Mulshi movement was made an exception to this? On what basis was it decided that Champaran *Satyagraha* of indigo cultivators of north-west Bihar was directly linked to *Swaraj* while Mulshi *Satyagraha* was not?

DEMAND FOR ALTERNATIVE LAND

An article about making alternative land available had appeared in the *Young India* of 31 August 1922. Around that time a leaflet had been published which said that the search for suitable lands in other places had been stopped because nobody had asked for alternative land. *Young India,* commenting on this, says that the Mawalas (residents of Mawal region of which Mulshi tract was a part) had earlier been told by the Government that suitable land could not be found in Pune District. Hence, they must either accept lands in Nasik District or work as laborers on the dam. The editor asked whether the special officer of the Government had succeeded in getting land which would resettle the whole village in its original form. The Government must openly declare its compensation plan so that the Mawalas would not appear to be obstinate and unyielding. The Government must also keep in mind that no economically poor agricultural community could migrate a hundred miles from its original place.[7] It is evident from the above that the *Young India* avoided saying anything about the *Satyagraha* and that it was in favor of the resettlement of the Mawalas, in a place not far away from Mulshi.

In July 1923 Gandhi figured again in the picture of Mulshi *Satyagraha.* Shankarrao Deo, Annasaheb Dastane and others were sentenced to imprisonment in 1923, after being prosecuted for leading the *Satyagraha.* They had begun a fast as an act of protest against the unjust treatment they had received from the jail officials. Gandhi was also in Yerwada (Pune) jail at that time. On hearing of it he had intervened on their behalf and helped to end the fast.[8]

Dastane had consulted Gandhi when the Mawalas had begun to accept compensation and to slowly withdraw from the agitation. Gandhi had then advised him to stop the *Satyagraha* movement for three reasons, namely, that the Mawalas had accepted compensation, that the construction of the dam was already half completed and that the leader of the *Satyagraha* did not believe in non-violence.[9] The movement was then stopped. However, considering Gandhi's policy regarding Mulshi, it appears that had he been consulted at an earlier stage, he might even then have recommended its withdrawal.

THE EXPECTATION OF SACRIFICE

As early as 1922, M.R. Jaykar belonging to the group of moderate nationalists had sensed that Gandhi's support to the *Satyagraha* had decreased considerably. Tata, too, knew of it. As a result, representatives of the Tata Company were rigid in their approach when Jaykar met them to mediate a compromise. Shankarrao Deo, who became a staunch Gandhian in later years was one of the major leaders of the Mulshi movement. His observations on Gandhi's attitude towards the Mulshi struggle are worth noting. He says in his autobiography that the leaders tried their best to obtain Gandhi's support for the movement but Gandhi did not fulfil their expectations because in Gandhi's opinion the Mawalas were not prepared if necessary to dig into their trenches and make the ultimate sacrifice of their lives for the land of their birth. Although the Mulshi *Satyagraha* is witness to the fact that Gandhi was correct in his reading of the Mawalas, Deo says that even in hindsight he could never comprehend why Gandhi expected the ultimate sacrifice from the Mawalas and why he was reluctant to give priority to the question of their resettlement.[10] Thus we see that even a true Gandhian like Shankarrao Deo felt that Gandhi did not extend his wholehearted support to them in the *Satyagraha*. However, even if the Mawalas had decided to observe *Satyagraha* unto death, it would have been impossible to do so because the police arrested them and put them in jail as soon as they entered the area. Therefore, Deo's point about readiness to make the ultimate sacrifice does not appear to be valid. His other observation regarding resettlement is erroneous, too. As we have just seen, the *Young India* had made a strong case for proper resettlement. Gandhi was in support of the *Satyagraha* in May 1921 but later on he began to favor resettlement. It is possible that Gandhi supported the *Satyagraha* on the premise that the Government would be pressurized to consider the issue of compensation and alternative land. Once the Government started giving compensation, continuing the *Satyagraha* became, in his view, a pointless exercise.

But the contention that Gandhi did not attach much importance to Mulshi is justified to a large extent. Gandhi never visited Mulshi. Perhaps his involvement in the movement against the Rowlatt Act, in the Khilafat movement or the non-cooperation movement, did not have leave him with any time and energy to pay attention to a "local" or "regional" movement of "limited scope" like the Mulshi *Satyagraha*. But why did it remain "local" or "regional" in nature in the first place? Had he visited Mulshi and taken up the issue himself it could have greatly stepped up its importance. It was in his hands to make it a nationwide issue. Had the All India Congress taken it up, the movement would have become a national struggle and the Mawalas would have felt encouraged. It would also have boosted their leaders' confidence.

VERBAL SUPPORT

In this context, Jaykar's comment that Gandhi gave only verbal support is important. Jaykar has said that except for writing a letter in the *Young India* (27 April 1921) he did not do anything for the *Satyagraha.* He did not convert it into an all India movement, while he urged all Indians to support the Khilafat movement started by the Ali brothers.[11] He made the Khilafat movement a part of the Non-Cooperation movement of the Congress. But with Mulshi, Gandhi acted differently. Congress leaders at the national level too maintained a significant silence. This did not leave Maharashtrians unaffected. They realized that no matter how steadfast their commitment or how big the sacrifices they made, they would have to be content with the status of the Cinderella of the Gandhian movement.[12]

Just as he did not go to Mulshi to express support to the *Satyagrahi* volunteers and Mawalas he did not meet the Tatas on behalf of the Mawalas either (at least we find no record of it today). His acquaintance with the Tatas was, in fact, of long standing. Ratan Tata had at the request of Gopal Krishna Gokhale contributed Rs. 25,000 towards Gandhi's struggle in South Africa.[13] Had Gandhi intervened personally, the Mawalas might have got better compensation or perhaps land for resettlement as near as possible to their original location so that they could have all lived together again. He could have taken the initiative to stop the *Satyagraha* after the Mawalas started accepting compensation awards. But he refrained from doing so. In short it can be said that Gandhi did not take this struggle at all seriously. As a result, the movement neither met with success nor was called off after it had obtained the limited success it was to achieve.

A PARSEE COMPANY

If this movement had been only against the Government of Bombay it is possible that Gandhi, taking into account its importance in the nationalist movement would have extended active support to it. He might also have shown interest in it if the Tata Company had been a foreign concern like the estates of Champaran. But the Company involved in Mulshi was owned by the Parsees and Gujaratis. Purshottamdas Thakurdas, a Gujarati capitalist, was one of the directors of the Tata Company and it was he who represented the Company in the Legislative Council. The class of businessmen and capitalists in Bombay had consistently supported Gandhi's movement since 1919. Gandhi, himself a Gujarati, could not have politically afforded to distance himself from the Gujarati speaking people. The support that Gandhi's non-cooperation and *Swadeshi* movements got from Bombay Province came mainly from the city of Bombay.[14] The Parsees and Gujaratis dominated the city. Even the Congress party was controlled by the community. And Bombay was, in a sense, Gandhi's constituency. In this situation, it would have been suicidal for him to oppose a project that was profitable for the capitalist and business class of the city. This may be the reason why Gandhi did not give wholehearted support to the movement. Moreover the picture of the Maharashtra Congress had not become clear. The stand of the extremists—the supporters of Tilak—with respect to Gandhi and his policies had not yet become very clear. In a way, it may be said that Gandhi profited much from the Mulshi movement. It gave him a chance to gauge the inclinations of the leaders of Maharashtra and mainly of Pune after the death of Tilak. It enabled him to distinguish clearly between his supporters and opponents. Kelkar was an opponent. Now, if the continuation of the Mulshi movement was going to make Kelkar's leadership shaky why would Gandhi recommend calling off of the *Satyagraha*? Gandhi's point of view seems to have been to allow the *Satyagraha* to continue till the political picture revealed itself. If the Kelkar party was bringing about its own downfall he was not about to prevent it by advising them to stop the *Satyagraha*. The *Satyagraha* would also oblige the leaders of the Marathi speaking area of Central Provinces and of Karnataka to define their stand. In short, one can say that Gandhi had decided to wait and watch the progress of the *Satyagraha* movement. He was still sceptical about Maharashtra, and especially of Pune. Some proponents of terrorist nationalism like S.M. Paranjpe, Senapati Bapat and some of the extremists had joined the Gandhian *Satyagraha* movement. Gandhi tested them in the Mulshi *Satyagraha*. Thus we see that on the one hand, Gandhi did not actively support the *Satyagraha* because he did not wish to hurt the Parsees and Gujaratis while on the other he wanted the *Satyagraha* to continue because it would reveal to him the political alignments in Maharashtra.

Gandhi is thus seen to find himself not only in a political dilemma but in a dilemma of principles too. The Mulshi dam was to ruin the rural way of life so dear to him and to encourage industrialization which he opposed. The economic power in the hands of a single family would increase. The project would promote the advance of Western civilization destroying the indigenous way of community living. The very purposes for which he wanted *Swaraj* were to be defeated. The poor people for whose upliftment he had formulated the principles of *Sarvodaya* (welfare of all) would be forced to go to the cities and work as laborers. He had expressed this thought in the *Young India* of 25 May 1922. In spite of it all he could not support the *Satyagraha* actively because that would have worked against his immediate political objectives. He may be said to have given priority to politics over principles. His main aim at that time was to give an impetus to and maintain the momentum of the freedom movement. To that end, he felt constrained to compromise even his principles.

LUKEWARM SUPPORT

The Mulshi *Satyagraha* would have been successful even with this kind of equivocal support from Gandhi, had Maharashtra responded to it strongly. While the newspapers and periodicals were overflowing with discussions and editorials on the *Satyagraha*, the actual participation in the movement was gradually decreasing. According to an overview taken by Mulshi Satyagraha Sahayak Mandal (*Satyagraha* Support Organization) on 16 February 1923, 400 *Satyagrahis* had been to jail, out of which 96 were Mawalas and 304 were volunteers from all over Maharashtra. The total donations collected amounted to Rs. 50,000.[15] This figure was poor when compared to expectations expressed at the Mulshi Conference. It had been resolved at the Conference to collect a fund of Rs. 3 lakh, enlist three thousand volunteers who were prepared to go to jail and to continue the *Satyagraha* for a period of three years. Publicity to the effect had also been carried out throughout Maharashtra. Senapati (General—Bapat became known as Senapati (General) during this movement) Bapat and other leaders had toured the length and breadth of the province, to collect funds and volunteers and had used effective means like *Melas* (a form of folk theater), songs, procession, speeches, etc. to enthuse the people. Leaders like V.M. Bhuskute were in continuous contact with each and every village of Mulshi Peta to maintain the morale of the villagers and to keep them united. Public meetings with popular leaders to address them were organized. The leaders led from the front by example and were always the first to go to jail and face any atrocities in the hope that the Mawalas, their family members and volunteers would join the movement on a large scale and continue to participate and that the *Satyagrahis* would not fall prey to temptations and leave the movement. But the response in respect of money and manpower remained low in spite of all these efforts and precautions. The editor of the *Swarajya*, S.M. Paranjpe, who had himself participated in the *Satyagraha*, writing about the *Satyagraha* in 1925 has voiced the same feelings namely, that Maharashtra fell short of the leaders' expectations regarding collection of funds and manpower for this movement.[16] He has said that Senapati had to resort to *Shuddha* (Pure-violent) *Satyagraha* only because of the lack of sufficient response to the non-violent *Satyagraha*.[17] This observation was quite true. Senapati would not have had to consider violent means had there been a satisfactory response to the *Sama* (non-violent) *Satyagraha*.

In those days Maharashtra was torn apart on the issue of change and no-change, a fact which not unexpectedly affected the *Satyagraha* movement.[18] Those who were in favor of Nagpur

Congress (1920) resolution of non-cooperation became known as no-changers while those who insisted on modifying the resolution came to be known as pro-changers. Some supporters of Mulshi withdrew their support owing to this dispute. The non-changers like, Shankarrao Deo, who had once undergone imprisonment on account of the agitation, later completely dissociated themselves from the movement.[19] Once released from jail, activists like Deo did not wish to dedicate any time to the Mulshi struggle. The no-changers thought it more important to make efforts to acquire control over the Maharashtra Congress Committee. Building up the lobby of no-changers in Maharashtra was considered more important. Bhuskute expressed his regrets thus, "Mulshi was just a stepping stone for Shankarrao Deo to enter the provincial Congress Committee, and once there he gave himself up to its activities."[20] Thus, lack of wholehearted and consistent support by no-changers was also one of the reasons for the failure of the Mulshi movement. No-changers were in favor of continuing with the non-cooperation movement. These were the Gandhians who subscribed to the idea of *Satyagraha.* But if they were reluctant to support Mulshi, it is hardly surprising then that the pro-changers did not support the movement.

KELKAR'S APPROACH

N.C. Kelkar was the main leader of the pro-change group. He wielded influence over Maharashtra in those days. After the death of Lokmanya Tilak in 1920 he had stepped into the editorship of the *Kesari* and with that assumed also the leadership of Maharashtra. Therefore, Kelkar's approach towards Mulshi could be directly related to the outcome of the movement. As a result of Lokmanya Tilak's extraordinary leadership, the *Kesari* carried so much weight with the Maharashtrians that public opinion in Maharashtra was determined by the stand taken by the *Kesari. Kesari's* halo that he had inherited had definitely helped him. From the very beginning he had misgivings about Gandhi's politics. He disagreed with Gandhi's policies and did not find his methods suited to himself. Kelkar had also preferred to stay away from the politics of the masses, though Tilak, his mentor, was the first to employ this approach. After Tilak's death, Kelkar toned down the extremism of Tilak's politics and adopted moderate ways. In order to carry Tilak's politics into the next stage it was necessary to follow Gandhian way. But when Kelkar had reservations about Tilak's methods it was out of the question that he could take to the full-fledged mass politics of Gandhi.

This moderate leader, with an aversion for the politics of the masses and doubts about the efficacy of *Satyagraha* had been dragged into the Mulshi *Satyagraha* movement by the prevailing conditions. It was the *Kesari* which had brought the issue of the Mawalas of Mulshi into the open. Kelkar himself was the first to suggest that the Mawalas would make use of *Satyagraha* in the matter. But when *Satyagraha* seemed inevitable, he suggested suspension of the movement for a while in favor of attempts to arrive at a compromise. This suggestion was not accepted. In his article, written after the *Satyagraha* movement was withdrawn, S.M. Paranjpe says that to save the Mawalas land from being acquired, Kelkar had at first supported the *Satyagraha* movement and signed the declaration (12 April 1921) but he changed his views later on and then advocated the policy of compensation. The Mawalas had, therefore, put their faith in his pledge when they had themselves signed the declaration. The *Kesari* explained that Kelkar had supported the *Satyagraha* only because he thought it would induce amendments in the Land Acquisition Act and help the local people to avert any damage. But S.M. Paranjpe pointed out that Kelkar had not participated in the *Satyagraha* even for those objectives which he himself advocated. He accuses Kelkar and others not only of not participating in the *Satyagraha* but of creating unfruitful diversions in the movement. Kelkar expressed views concerning the acceptance of compensation which only the Government or the Tatas could be expected to hold. Paranjpe held that this attitude damaged the movement and was one of the factors leading to the failure of the *Satyagraha.*[21]

Vinayakrao Bhuskute had been an important leader of the movement from the very beginning. He too shared Paranjpe's views regarding Kelkar. Bhuskute says it was the *Kesari* which had first thought of protesting by means of a *Satygraha.* It stuck to this view till the first round of the *Satyagraha.* But it departed from its original position after an agreement was signed between the Company and the Government and the rates of compensation were declared. The *Kesari* confused the Mawalas by writing in favor of compensation awards. Bhuskute had not expected that such a policy would get support from Kelkar.[22]

PRO-COMPROMISE STAND

The accusations made by Paranjpe and Bhuskute about Kelkar were not fully justified. Kelkar had never been in favor of the extreme "*Jan or Jamin*" (life or land) stand. When the Mawalas and their leaders like Bhuskute, Deo and Paranjpe could not be convinced to suspend the *Satyagraha* and make efforts towards a compromise he was left with no choice but to sign the declaration to save the lands from submergence. He probably reasoned that the *Satyagraha* campaign would at least speed up the process of arriving at a compromise. Secondly, Kelkar's standing in the politics of the time was such that no political movement could be started in or around Pune without at least his nominal support. He was aware of this and that appears to be the reason why he signed the declaration. However, a careful reading of his editorials written during the first campaign of the *Satyagraha* shows that he was only reiterating his views expressed in the very first conference held at Baramati in March 1921.[23] He was strongly in favor of a compromise. At the same time the withdrawal of the hydro-electric scheme at Mulshi was not the kind of compromise he was looking for, even though the scheme did mean submergence of the lands, houses and temples of the Peta. In his presidential address at the Mulshi Conference (11 June 1922), B.S. Munje had suggested that the dam be constructed at some other site in the Sahyadri ranges, but a survey of suitable sites for hydro-electric schemes had already been made by experts. The Tata Company, too, had prepared an exhaustive plan of sites for the generation of hydro-electricity in the Bombay province. The Mulshi scheme was a part of this overall plan. It was inconceivable, therefore, that Tatas would give up that scheme. What then could be the nature of the compromise? An assurance could be extracted from the Company and the Government that alternative lands would be made available and liberal compensation would be given to peasants and other residents of the villages and the process of giving this compensation would begin without any delay. This was the kind of compromise that Kelkar expected. For this purpose he wished only to hold out the threat of a *Satyagraha* and keeping it in abeyance to force the Government and the Company to agree to the compromise. In his editorial in the *Kesari* on 25 October 1921, Kelkar had discussed the different prevailing opinions regarding the *Satyagraha* movement. One of the lines of thinking rejected the extreme position of "*Jan or Jamin*" and advocated a pragmatic view of looking for a just compromise between the Mawalas, the Government and the Company with the help of a third party. The *Satyagraha* could have been justified if it had been undertaken at the very beginning of the project. But the Tatas by mistake or due to lack of regard for justice had already spent lakhs of rupees. The Land Acquisition Act was also in force. Now the Company should be penalized by being made to pay for compensation, the amount of which should be fixed by an arbitrator. The Land Acquisition Act should be withdrawn and all transactions should be carried out amicably. The Act should be amended to prevent such incidents in the future. This school of thought was a conciliatory one. Those belonging to it wished to avoid *Satyagraha* as far as possible.[24] Kelkar was one of them. Hence, it is wrong to accuse him of being a turncoat or of taking on an anti-*Satyagraha* stand after the compensation awards were announced. A movement of the nature of a *Satyagraha* had absolutely no place in his political philosophy. He was consistently in favor of conciliation, from the very beginning till the end.

JAN OR JAMIN

Many of the leaders connected with the movement were of the opinion that the extreme position of "*Jan or Jamin*" adopted by the pro-*Satyagraha* group was the single significant factor for the failure of the movement. As we have just seen Kelkar was against such an extreme stand from the beginning. Senapati Bapat, analyzing the failure of the movement when he was sentenced to jail in 1925, observed that the *Satyagraha* was undertaken without leaving any scope for a compromise. The situation went out of hand when the conditions of a compromise, offered by the respondents in the cause on their own initiative were rejected by the *Satyagrahis.* In November 1921, after the first round of *Satyagraha* Lallubhai Samaldas had on behalf of the Company made a request to hold talks for a compromise. Accordingly, J.S. Karandikar, the President of the *Satyagraha Mandal* (*Satyagraha* Organization) made arrangements for talks with Ratan Tata and Lallubhai, the directors of the Company. But the leaders of the *Satyagraha* rejected this offer completely. The Company had been ready at that time to give land watered by the Nira right bank canal or to give an amount of money fixed by arbitrators. But the leaders declared that they had only one point on their agenda and that was *jan or jamin.* According to Kelkar these leaders of the *Satyagraha* ruined the Mawalas.[25]

Shankarrao Deo has himself admitted, in his autobiography, that this rigid stand was itself misconceived. The policy of *jan or jamin* was not the right approach from the point of view of the general well-being of the society. Resettlement was the real issue. If the movement had concentrated on that from the beginning, failure could have been avoided.[26]

THE POLICY OF COMPENSATION

Jaykar and N.V. Gadgil, too, shared this view. Jaykar intervened twice between the Tata Company and the *Satyagrahis* to bring about a compromise.[27] Gadgil did not join the *Satyagraha* because he was in favor of compromise. He witnessed the *Satyagraha* campaigns as a reporter of the *Bombay Chronicle.* The booklet entitled "*A Case for Mulshi Peta Satyagraha*" distributed among the shareholders of the Company in November 1921 was written by him. He was also a member of the advisory committee of the movement (formed at the time of the Baramati Conference). He has said in his autobiography that asking for alternative land or liberal cash compensation would have been appropriate from the point of view of the good of the nation but that view was not accepted.[28]

While commenting on the Mulshi *Satyagraha* after fifty years or so G.T. Madkholkar and Neelkanth Khadilkar in the *Tarun Bharat* and *Navshakti*, respectively, have criticized the extremist position taken by the *Satyagrahi* leaders. According to Madkholkar, short-sightedness and an impractical attitude were the reasons for the failure of the movement.[29] Khadilkar terms the movement itself as ill-conceived. In his opinion it would have been far better to follow the path (of compromise and accepting compensation) as shown by Kelkar after the *Satyagraha* had run for some time. But the leaders took the stand that peasants should not take any compensation at all. This naturally led to the failure of the movement.[30]

There is no doubt that if a conciliatory stand had been taken, the *Satyagraha* would have been successful. That is, the *Satyagraha* would not have lasted for so long, in the first place, if the *Satyagrahis* had started the movement with the limited purpose of obtaining the maximum possible compensation or alternative land. Certainly it would not have restarted in November 1921, because negotiations for a compromise could have been held at that time. The Mawalas would possibly have got the land which was watered by the Nira right bank canal. But that did not happen. The movement failed after three years of struggle because it demanded the closure of the Scheme. On the ground, both the movement and the project work went on simultaneously. And when the Mawalas started accepting compensation, the very purpose of the *Satyagraha* was defeated.

MORALE OF THE *SATYAGRAHIS*

The deteriorating morale of the Mawalas was one more reason for the failure of the *Satyagraha*. The leaders left the movement half way; and turned their attention to the wider movement of the Congress. Shankarrao Deo is a typical example of a leader who caused the Mawalas to lose their morale. When leaders like Bhuskute, Dastane and especially Senapati Bapat were arrested, the Mawalas were quite discouraged. While leaders and Mawalas were being arrested, not only could other Mawalas see that the moneylenders were accepting compensation all the while, but also that work on the dam was progressing unhindered.

At this time, there was not a single leader with the Mawalas who could have sustained their courage. If morale could have been maintained high enough to prevent the acceptance of compensation the *Satyagraha* could have continued retaining the support it already had. When this was not possible, working to obtain the maximum possible compensation would have been the pragmatic strategy. The policy of *Satyagraha* lacked conviction at this stage. After his release from jail, Senapati also realized, that the Mawalas who remained with the *Satyagraha* suffered the most damages. He, therefore, released the Mawalas from their pledge not to accept compensation. Other leaders of the *Satyagraha Mandal* did not show the moral courage to do the same.[31]

As a matter of fact, the Mawalas and the moneylenders had been accepting compensation ever since 1921. Government records show that nearly 15 to 17 per cent accepted in 1921 and 80 per cent in 1922 the remaining people accepted it in 1923 or in 1929-30. It is obvious from this statistics that the Mawalas and moneylenders were accepting compensation even as the *Satyagraha* campaign went on, because the fight was going out of them day by day.[32]

The non-Brahmans had opposed the *Satyagraha* from the start. A *Satyagraha* under the Brahman Congress leaders for the benefit of moneylenders was not acceptable to them. This opposition helped the Government and the Tata Company indirectly. The non-Brahmans tried their best to undermine the resolve of the non-Brahman Mawala peasants participating in the movement. The moderates also took an adverse stand with respect to the movement. The leaders and newspapers of the moderates adopted a position favoring economic growth and industrialization. By extending full support to the Scheme which benefited the Parsee-Gujarati capitalists of Bombay, they only ensured the failure of the movement. It must be remembered here that the moderates not only opposed the leadership of the extremists leaders of the Tilak school, but were also in opposition, on grounds of both principle and strategy, to the rising leadership of the Gandhi school.[33]

SUPPORT FROM OUTSIDE

The participation of the volunteers from outside Mulshi played a significant role in the outcome of the *Satyagraha.* In a way, the *Satyagraha* movement certainly benefited from the gathering of these volunteers. Because they came from the remotest corners of the whole of Maharashtra the entire province was swept by a wave of awareness of the *Satyagraha.* The number of *Satyagrahis* going to jail increased considerably. But there was another side to it, too. This was the Mawalas' fight. The proposed project would affect the Mawalas whose lands were to be submerged. It was perfectly understandable if outsiders joined the movement in sympathy with the Mawalas' cause and to register protest against the imperialistic and anti-people policy of the Government or the profiteering of the Tatas. But the outsiders' participation in the movement became questionable once the Mawalas began to leave the movement and accept compensation. The report of the *Mulshi Sahayak Mandal* (16 February 1923) records that 400 persons went to jail, only 96 of them being Mawalas. This means the remaining 304 persons were volunteers from outside Mulshi. If the struggle was indeed for and of the Mawalas, the number of outsiders going to jail was disproportionately large. Granting that their participation helped to spread the nationalist and Gandhian movement, their presence in the movement became open to criticism once the Mawalas began to withdraw from the agitation. The non-Brahmans and the moderates could make the accusation that the movement was organized to create an atmosphere of protest against the Government rather than to help the Mawalas. We see that this criticism too affected the movement adversely. In the later stages, the *Kesari* too took a neutral stand because Kelkar was strictly against outsiders conducting the *Satyagraha.*[34]

ANTI-DAM MOVEMENTS

Finally it must be reiterated that the Mulshi *Satyagraha* was a protest against the dam by the dam-affected people. The dam-affected population is always a minority as against the large population which benefits from the project. The anti-dam movements such as Mulshi basically involve tribals or farmers who lack social, political and economic resources. On the one hand they make very specific demand of stopping the construction of dam and on the other challenge the established model of economic development and also the entrenched interests. The failure to stop the construction of dam and to change the concept of development has remained the characteristic feature of all anti-dam movements since the Mulshi. The recent failure of the Save Narmada agitation to stop the huge dam on the Narmada river being constructed in Gujarat tells us the same story. The *Satyagraha* path has not taken the dam-affected people to their destination. It seems that a radical revision in the theory and practice of *Satyagraha* has become imperative so that the marginalized sections—displaced villagers do not take for an alternative path.

NOTES

1. Raghavan Iyer (ed.), *The Essential Writings of Mahatma Gandhi*, New Delhi, 1991.
2. S.N. Navare, *Senapati*, Mumbai, 1976, p. 93.
3. *Young India*, 27 April 1921.
4. *The Collected Works of Mahatma Gandhi*, vol. XX, April-August 1921, Delhi, 1966.
5. *Young India*, 27 April 1921.
6. Ibid., 25 April 1922.
7. Ibid., 31 August 1921.
8. Shankarrao Deo, *Dev Dete Pan Karm Nete*, Saswad, 1976.
9. Dattoba Dastane, *Eka Mook Sevakache Samarpit Jeevan*, Jalgaon, 1975, p. 36. Here Gandhi is referring to Senapati Bapat who joined the movement in April 1921 and became the sole leader from May 1922. In his early career Bapat was involved in terrorist nationalism. However when he joined the Mulshi agitation he took vow that he would abide by the rules of Gandhian method of non-violent *Satyagraha* which he called *Sama Satyagraha.* He had own idea of *Satyagraha*—the *Shuddha* (pure) *Satyagraha*—which he thought should be used when the non-violent methods have failed. The pure *Satyagraha* method of Bapat included destruction of the property and also the use of violence to achieve the truth. Bapat did employ this type of method with the help of five volunteers when the non-violent movement came to halt in November

1924. In a symbolic act the volunteers wounded the workers going to the site of the dam by train and Bapat fired a shot at the driver which hit his leg. He was sentenced to seven years of rigorous imprisonment and the volunteers also faced the punishment.
10. Deo, op. cit., pp. 82-3.
11. M.R. Jaykar, *The Story of My Life*, vol. I, Bombay, 1958, pp. 462-3. Khilafat movement was a pan-Islamic movement (1919-20) aimed at defending rights of Turkish Sultan—Khalifa after the defeat of Ottoman Empire. Indian Muslims participated in the movement.
12. Jaykar, op. cit., p. 463.
13. N.R. Phatak, *Adhunik Bharat Sevak*, Mumbai, 1967, pp. 80 and 195. See also, Sumit Sarkar, *Modern India 1885-1947*, Madras, 1986, p. 210.
14. Sumit Sarkar, op. cit., pp. 212-13.
15. *Loksangraha*, 20 February 1923.
16. *Swarajya*, 18 June 1925.
17. Ibid.
18. *Lokmanya*, 14 June 1925.
19. *Swarajya*, 18 June 1925.
20. V.M. Bhuskute, *Mulshi Satyagraha*, Pune, 1968, p. 170.
21. *Swarajya*, 2 August 1925.
22. Bhuskute, op. cit., p. 170.
23. *Kesari*, 26 April 1921.
24. Ibid., 25 October 1929.
25. Ibid., 23 June 1925.
26. Deo believed in *Jan or Jamin* position while he was in the movement. See Deo, op. cit., pp. 81-2.
27. Jaykar, op. cit., pp. 455-8 and 461-3.
28. N.V. Gadgil, *Pathik*, vol. I, Pune, 1964, p. 163.
29. *Tarun Bharat*, 1 December 1974.
30. *Navshakti*, 29 November 1967.
31. *Kesari*, 23 June 1925.
32. Conveyance of Land situated in the Mulshi Peta Dated 10th December 1936, the Secretary of State for India in Council to the Tata Power Co. Ltd., pp. 531-75.
33. Rajendra Vora, *Mulshi Satyagraha*, Pune, 1994, pp. 130-42.
34. *Kesari*, 23 June 1925.

REFERENCES

Bhuskute, V.M., 1968: *Mulshi Satyagraha*. Pune: Dastane Ramchandra Ani Company.

Dastane, Dattoba, 1975: *Eka Mook Sevakache Samarpit Jeevan*. Jalgaon: Devkinandan Narayan.

Deo, Shankarrao, 1976: *Dev Dete Pan Karm Nete.* Saswad: Saswad Ashram Vishwastha Mandal.

Gadgil, N.V., 1964: *Pathik,* vol. I. Pune: Venus Prakashan.

Iyer, Raghavan, ed., 1991: *The Essential Writings of Mahatma Gandhi.* New Delhi: Oxford University Press.

Jaykar, M.R., 1958: *The Story of My Life,* vol. I. Bombay: Asia Publishing House.

Navare, S.N., 1976: *Senapati.* Mumbai: Mauj.

Phatak, N.R., 1967: *Adhunik Bharat Sevak.* Mumbai: Mauj.

Sarkar, Sumit, 1986: *Modern India, 1885-1947.* Madras: Macmillan.

Vora, Rajendra, 1994: *Mulshi Satyagraha.* Pune: Pratima Prakashan.

14

Marg Shetkari Ladhyacha: The Agitational Means of a Peasant Movement

ARUNA PENDSE

The late 1970s and early 1980s saw an upsurge by farmers in many states of India. The farmers had certain common demands. The most important demand was for remunerative prices for agricultural produce. This demand was followed by other demands like reduction in the prices of agricultural inputs; an end to exorbitant increase in taxes and levies; and relief from indebtedness, etc. A demand for higher wages for agricultural laborers was also included in some of these agitations.

This peasant upsurge was unparalleled in the history of free India. Peasants in vast numbers came into action erecting road-blocks, organizing marches, *gheraos*, courting mass arrests, defying bullets and *lathis* of the police to defend their interests. These spontaneous peasant agitations later acquired such momentum and force that the governments in the respective states were forced to concede the demands of the farmers. The movements challenged the entire gamut of agrarian policies of governments and ruling classes. The most interesting feature of these movements was the unity of all the strata within the agrarian sector against the urban industrial sector represented by the state.

The present paper deals with the *marg* of a peasant movement in Maharashtra. There are various shades to the meaning of *marg* in Marathi. It means route, road, course, way or trajectory and means. Here it is used in its both connotations, i.e. as a course/trajectory and as a way or means. The aim is to trace the course of the movement—the way it has developed and changed over a period of time. The second interpretation, namely the "means" or the "ways" is to follow the means the Shetkari Sanghatana used to mobilize and organize the farmers and the agitations it launched. Different movements adopt different means in their agitations. The means depend upon the nature of the ideology and the goals of a movement. The course of a movement is determined by its nature, ideology and the external conditions in which it traverses its course. This paper discusses the movement of Shetkari Sanghatana in its historical context and attempts to analyze the means of organization, mobilization and agitation. Through this discussion, the course traversed by the movement, its evolution from a mass movement to a pressure group and subsequently to a political party also is traced.

THE CHANGED NATURE OF PEASANT MOVEMENT

The nature of peasant movement has changed over a period of time. The struggles during the early British period were basically of two types. One, there were anti-British, restorative movements which drew the peasants into them. Such revolts or rebellions were ruthlessly crushed by the British. There were also the peasant uprisings protesting against the unbearable burden of taxes or low wages at famine relief works. At times the peasant discontent was directed against the immediate oppressors like moneylenders. Some of these issues continued to concern the peasant struggles even later. But in the early twentieth century the causes for peasant discontent also included dispossession due to the acquisition of land by the government or private industries; increased amount of rent; insecurity of tenure and unjust forest laws. The introduction of the Gandhian means of agitation, namely, the *satyagraha*, also changed the nature of the peasant agitations in this period. The issues changed further after Independence. The struggles were now centered on the implementation of the new land-reform acts, redistribution of land, wages of the agricultural laborers and demand for work under the schemes like famine relief or the Employment Guarantee Scheme.

After Independence, the Left parties in Maharashtra tried to mobilize the poor peasants, the landless laborers, the tribals and tribal peasants. But barring the Peasants' and Workers' Party, none of them took up the issues of the interest of the middle peasants or of the peasantry as a whole. The Left parties had started voicing the demand of "remunerative prices" and mooting the idea of "united front of the peasantry". But they did not mobilize the farmers for these issues (Brahme and Upadhyaya 1979).

Though the Congress party ruled the state for over three decades and claimed to represent the farmers, the issues of peasantry were not seriously addressed by the Congress. Being dominated by the agrarian rich and upper caste Marathas who shared the power with the industrial bourgeoisie, the Congress leadership took the support of the middle and poor farmers for granted and ignored their problems.

EMERGENCE OF SHETKARI SANGHATANA

The movement of the Shetkari Sanghatana emerged in the context of the agricultural crisis of the mid to late 1970s. The increase in production and falling prices of the agricultural produce resulted in the discontent of the peasantry. The rich peasant class, which was the main beneficiary of the tax concessions, agricultural subsidies and the Green Revolution strategies, was disturbed by the decline in its profits due to the falling prices. Another cause of anxiety of this class was its declining position *vis-à-vis* the industrial bourgeoisie, which was its partner in the coalition of power. The rich peasant class needed to reassert its political strength and improve its position in the power bloc.

The uneven development in agriculture, the increasing indebtedness of the farmers, scarcity of water resources, and famines combined to increase the severity of the agricultural crisis in late 1970s. No political party took up the issues relating to the peasantry as a whole. The Shetkari Sanghatana emerged and dealt with the agrarian issues in this backdrop. A sophisticated leadership with fresh ideas and insights articulated the problems of peasants in a language that was, at once familiar and new to them. The movement concentrating on the issue of remunerative prices for farm produce started with the "onion agitation" in 1980. Its early success gave the movement a further boost and the new ideology spread in the countryside like wild fire.

THE IDEOLOGY

This "new" ideology was a populist ideology, which underplayed the agrarian class differentiation, asserting the basic unity of all peasants. It located the significant line of contradiction between the industrial and agricultural sector and insisted that the root cause of rural poverty was the exploitation of agriculture by industry by means of the unequal terms of trade between them. The terms of trade operated through the mechanism of determination of prices. Non-remunerative prices, which do not cover even the cost of production, were paid to the farmers leading to their impoverishment. Therefore, if the farmers were paid remunerative prices, the problem of rural poverty would be solved. The issue of better prices or minimum prices for agricultural produce had been raised earlier. The stand then was that prices should be raised to help the peasants to survive—almost as a favor. The unique stand of the Shetkari Sanghatana was that the prevailing prices were below the cost of production and thus consciously and artificially exploitative. With the help of economic arguments and costing data, the Shetkari Sanghatana demanded prices that would be remunerative and just—not as a favor but as a right of the agriculturists. Thus, the ideology was presented as an alternative strategy of development (Joshi 1985b: 78-81).

The demand for remunerative prices, however, was basically the demand of the rich, surplus producing farmers and the middle farmers who cultivated cash-crops. The agricultural operations and the produce of these farmers were essentially oriented towards the market. They were not subsistence or survival farmers but surplus and commodity producing farmers. Majority of poor/ small farmers did not benefit much through this demand. In fact, they could be adversely affected if the prices of food grains increased in the markets. The class of the agricultural laborers would be similarly adversely affected by the higher prices as the wages of the laborers do not increase in proportion to the increase in the prices of the agricultural goods. The real income of the laborers in such situations, in fact, declines, and their living conditions become even worse.

POPULIST IDEOLOGY

The Shetkari Sanghatana ideology, however, overlooked this problem and stressed the essential unity of all the farmers, irrespective of the classes to which they might belong. The ideology transformed the "price" demand into a "non-class" demand and successfully articulated the grievances of various classes of farmers excluding the landless laborers. An attempt to encompass their demand of wage increase was also made. A homogeneous and unified agrarian sector was constantly projected and emphasized. The slogan "*Shetkari Tituka Ek Ek*" embodied this point. The urban/rural or town/country juxtaposition was put in the formulation of "Bharat *vs.* India", Bharat being the rural, agricultural sector and India being the urban, industrial sector. The enemy was located in the state, though the overthrow of the state was not the aim of the movement. The movement only wanted to bring about some modifications in the system without effecting any structural changes. The ideology and the movement in that sense were non-radical or reformist.

It was a non-radical populist ideology because it was articulated, embraced and championed not by the dominated sections but by a fraction of the ruling class in its efforts to challenge the hegemony of the dominant fraction; i.e. the industrial bourgeoisie. The hegemony was challenged on ideological grounds and an alternative ideological framework was proposed to replace the dominant ideology. An attempt was made to comment on every possible socio-political phenomenon, interpretation of history, culture, etc. and to analyze various emerging issues. The ideology successfully made use of the idiom and symbols of the popular tradition of Maharashtra's peasantry, namely the Warkari sect. The leadership cleverly used the

Warkari idiom and discourse to its own ideological ends by altering the interpretation to carry the message of the movement to the masses.

The Shetkari Sanghatana scored a major point by the novelty of its agitational means. The rail and road blockades, the cattle march, the appeal to god Vithoba, *gaobandi*—that is prohibiting the entry of political leaders in villages, and later agitation for debt relief were all the examples of such techniques. The character of these mass agitations remained basically non-violent, modeled on the Gandhian *Satyagraha* (Joshi 1984b: 170). The success of the agitations increased the confidence of the peasants. The government's use of repression in cases of some agitations that resulted in the deaths of some *satyagrahis*, in fact, gave a moral edge to the Sanghatana *vis-à-vis* the government.

The Sanghatana projected the demand for "remunerative prices" as the demand of all peasant classes, as a non-class and popular demand. In this formulation, the state, government, or the ruling bloc (with its prevalent balance of power) were projected as antagonistic to the genuine interests of the peasantry. Hence, the movement was directed against it and made demands on it. To sharpen the antagonism, there was a persistent reference to a "conspiracy" to fleece the peasantry on the part of the government (acting at the behest of and for the industrial urban bourgeoisie). Shetkari Sanghatana repeatedly stressed that, no government would ever grant the demands of the farmers and if the farmers persist in their insistence, the state would use repression (Joshi 1984b: 105-8).

However, despite the acerbity of antagonism, the aim of the movement was not to radically restructure the state as a whole. By insisting on non-violent means of agitation and conducting the movement within the parliamentary democratic framework, the Sanghatana curbed and controlled the development of contradictions, not letting them acquire any revolutionary potential. Thus, antagonisms between the people and the power bloc were developed up to a point and then restrained. The existing socio-political framework was not disturbed. The methods used for agitation were ones as approved by the system. These were democratic mass agitations on the line of the Gandhian *Satyagraha, Rail and Rasta Roko,* hunger strike and so on. These means were strictly non-violent democratic that did not challenge the system. They only challenged the balance within the power bloc. The rationale of the existence of the state in its particular form was not questioned. That is why, the ideology was, and is non-radical, reformist and populist.

USE OF POPULAR TRADITIONS

Whereas the movement served the interests of the rich farmers and middle peasants, the concept of omnibus agrarian sectoral unity also necessitated the inclusion of the poor peasantry's interests or themes to bring them in the fold of the movement. To project a sectoral unity the Sanghatana ideology made use of the "popular traditions" to appeal to the emotions of the poor farmers and draw them into the "unified" agrarian bloc unity.

Popular traditions do not constitute consistent and organized discourses but are merely elements embedded in the articulation of class discourses (Laclau 1979: 167). In a way, popular traditions can transcend class identity, which they may have originally represented. That is precisely why the most divergent political movements can and do appeal to the same ideological symbols. Popular traditions represent the resilience of some unique historical experience and constitute a durable structure of meanings. There is in them dual reference to both the people and classes. That actually is the strength of the popular traditions.

Sharad Joshi, the main leader and exponent of Shetkari Sanghatana's ideology made use of such "popular traditions" in the discourse that he articulated. The popular traditions were used to evoke a sense of identity among the peasant classes, especially the poor peasants, towards such struggles against injustice as were waged by Shivaji or Jotirao Phule. The peasant was asked to join the struggle waged by Shetkari Sanghatana that claimed the lineage of those glorious struggles of yesteryears (Joshi 1984a).

Baliraja, Shivaji and Jotiba Phule were the symbols crystallized from these popular traditions, and were thus projected. Sharad Joshi also cast the entire idiom of his discourse in tune with this popular tradition. He used the symbols from the protest traditions in the religious field, such as the Warkari sect. The name of the first periodical publication of the Sanghatana was *Warkari* suggesting the above sect symbol of the religious pilgrim and at the same time implying a meaning, which suggests, "one who strikes". Another weekly publication of the Sanghatana was named *Gyanba,* again from the same tradition, implying a more familiar name of Saint Dnyaneshwar for the Warkaris. Sanghatana organized one rally at Pandharpur, the center of pilgrimage of the Warkari sect, on a day particularly auspicious to the sect. The program was called *Vithobala Sakade,* meaning persistent insistence with God Vithoba enough to embarrass and thereby to create a moral dilemma for him. *Sakade* thus puts the god in an awkward or difficult situation to pressurize him to grant the wish of the devotee. It has to be noted, however, that the use of Warkari sect idiom was not for the religious meaning attached to it, but to exploit the symbolic meanings associated with it in the popular (peasant) mind. The legend of mythical king Bali was interpreted in the same way as Phule had done. He was remembered to be the king whose reign was benevolent to the peasants. Sanghatana used the idiom *Ida Pida Talo, ani Baliche Raajya yevo* (Let the evil go and the reign of King Bali return) to convey the ushering of the peasant power as its major slogan. In the same way, Shivaji, the popular heroic figure in Maharashtra was projected as the king who represented the interests of peasants unlike previous or later kings who were basically plunderers or looters, of the peasantry (Joshi et al. 1988). Jotiba Phule had also represented Shivaji as *Kulwadi—Kul Bhooshan,* a peasant king. Sharad Joshi projected Jotiba Phule as the first thinker who voiced the woes of the farmers. Jotiba's attack on the caste system was interpreted as his attack on the exploiters of the peasantry (Joshi 1985a: 51-8).

Whether the interpretations of these popular traditions and symbols were correct or otherwise is not an issue here. The crucial point is the way "popular traditions" were exploited fruitfully and effectively by the Sanghatana's ideology, and thus used to muster the mass support. In the use of popular traditions, the Sanghatana evoked "peasant consciousness", the feelings of the oneness of the agrarian classes leading to sectoral unity. In the use of popular tradition, there was also a latent emotional appeal to the agricultural poor. While the rich and middle peasant classes had concrete benefit in the "remunerative price" demand, the poor farmers had an emotional appeal to hold on to in the movement. Peasant consciousness transcends peasant stratification and therefore reinforces the "populist" appeal of the ideology. The Sanghatana leaders also attempted to reinterpret history, culture, religion and literature. It was a conscious effort to exert the influence of the "peasant" "populist" formulation in all spheres of thinking and to capture ideological spaces within the general intellectual firmament.

Shetkari Sanghatana's concern with the women's question was also a part and parcel of the same logic. The increasing participation of women in rallies and agitations had made the potential of women's power in peasant movement clear to Sharad Joshi. In the wake of the emerging mobilization of women in urban as well as in rural areas, a formulation of women's question that would fit the overall populist ideology was seen as necessary to tap women's power and neutralize its possible antagonism and to assimilate it in the peasant struggle (Joshi, Gote and Basargekar, 1988).

The use of popular traditions, invoking the "peasant consciousness" and subsuming the ideological spaces in general by articulating ideas on history, culture and women's issues made Shetkari Sanghatana's agitations more forceful. They attracted large mass support and played an important role in the politics of the state and of India.

THE NATURE OF AGITATIONS

A social movement is a non-institutionalized collective political action, which strives for social and political change. The movements which strive for "political change", do not always struggle against the government alone. The collective actions of the people are at various levels against dominant caste class and ideology (Shah 1990: 19). Non-institutionalized collective action takes several forms, such as, protest, agitation, strike, *satyagraha, hartal, gherao*, riot. The various forms of protest can become part of a sustained political action, which develop into a movement. Interest in a social movement is many times centered on whether it brings about the political change it aims. Interest is also there to explore if the movement is reformist or revolutionary. The nature of a movement can be determined by its objectives and ideology as these represent certain class interests.

The attraction and significance of Shetkari Sanghatana's movement lay in its ideology and agitations. The ideology gave solid support to the well-planned mass actions. The Sanghatana resorted to various agitations demanding remunerative prices for different agricultural products at different times. A cursory look at the history of these agitations reveals that the important agitations centered around the issue of remunerative prices for cash crops like onions, sugar cane, tobacco and cotton. The issue of prices of food grains was not tackled by the Sanghatana through its agitations. The interesting aspects of an agitation are the methods of its planning, the manner of mass mobilization, the techniques and means of protest, the method of intensification and the mode of withdrawal of the agitation. Also interesting and significant is the role of the leadership and the cadre in an agitation. The language used for chalking out the plans of agitations was from the military parlance. The words like strategy (*rananeeti*) and tactics (*daavpench*) were commonly used by the leadership (Parulkar 1981: 63-8).

Shetkari Sanghatana launched major agitations from 1980 onwards. In 1980, it launched an agitation for the remunerative prices of onions and sugar cane. There was some element of spontaneity in onion agitation in some places. It ushered in the peasant issues with a bang. It also gave a boost to Shetkari Sanghatana's campaign. Onion agitation led to the sugar cane agitation. Both were to demand remunerative/higher prices for these agricultural produce. They also demanded support prices for these goods from the government.

In both these agitations, the striking feature was the spontaneous actions of roadblocks and rail-blocks by the peasant masses and use of repressive measures by the government against the agitating farmers resulting in some deaths. Many farmers and their leaders faced the cane charge and firing by the police. However, that did not dampen the movement. On the contrary, the movement got more support and momentum. In both these agitations, at the juncture of government's adamancy and use of coercion, Sharad Joshi declared his fast. His fast on the one hand gave moral strength to the agitating farmers and pressed them to continue their political action. On the other hand, it exerted pressure on the government to concede the demands of the farmers and desist from using the repressive measures. The Gandhian type of technique was resorted to by Sharad Joshi many times even in the later agitations with some success (*Shetkari Sanghatak*, Special Issue, March 1989; Parulkar 1981: 34-5).

In the case of the onion agitation, the main thrust was on actions like marches and roadblocks. In the sugar cane agitation, the emphasis was on blocking the movement of sugar cane from the farms to the factories. Sharad Joshi had told his farmers to "do nothing", "just sit on the edge of your field" and "don't allow anyone to take away the sugar cane". The main idea was to delay the cane-crushing operation of the sugar factories and thus, bring pressure upon them and the government to accede to the demand for the prices the farmers were asking (Parulkar 1981: 64-5). The agitation was basically peaceful. It was only when the police tried to break the roadblocks and rail-blocks forcibly that the situation changed. The movement received a lot of media attention due to these confrontations. The urban media till then had not taken note of the peasantry or its demands. Now there were discussions as to what the farmers—the "docile lot"—were up to. The issue of remunerative prices to farm products thus came to the center stage, which was one major objective of the movement. With an excellent organizational network and a team of dedicated activists, Sanghatana launched its subsequent agitations and programs. In February 1981, it started taking interest in tobacco growing farmers' problems and in March 1981 the agitation for remunerative prices for tobacco was started with 50,000 farmers squatting on the Pune-Bangalore highway. This blockade continued for 23 days. The farmers put up tents at the site and created almost a mini-town, which they named *Andolan Nagar* or agitation town. The government of Karnataka cracked down on the agitation and with tear-gas and cane-charges tried to disperse the farmers. When that became difficult, the police fired on the crowd and killed 13 people, injuring hundreds. However, despite this show of force, the government decided to compromise and gave in, accepting many demands of the farmers. This was perhaps the only agitation where Shetkari Sanghatana targeted the middle-men, along with the government as culprits (*Shetkari Sanghatak*, March 1989; *Sakal*, 7 April 1981 and 8 April 1981).

After tobacco, the Sanghatana decided to tackle milk prices. This agitation was launched in June 1982. The milk-producers were asked not to supply milk to any milk cooperative society or to private customers. The milk-carrying vehicles however were not forced to stop. The agitation was peaceful and non-violent. Farmers were asked either to process the milk at home or to distribute it free to neighbors and poor children. The government was adamant about the price and it was determined to break the agitation (*Sakal*, 26 June 1982, 1 July 1982).

This agitation failed. In the second phase of the agitation, Sanghatana decided to protest in a novel way. It organized a march of cattle to the district collector's office in Dhule city on 18 May 1983. The government banned this march. The government banned the entry of the leaders of the Sanghatana into the city and the police cordoned it off. Despite that, some 150 farmers entered the city with their bullock carts. The police cane-charged the farmers and beat up the cattle as well. However, the agitation attracted a lot of media and public attention (*Sakal*, 16 May 1983 and 19 May 1983).

The peasants resorted to roadblocks and rail-blocks time and again. One reason behind that could be the nature of the countryside. Geographically dispersed habitats and isolated villages and farms make the peasants gather at either market places or the nearby highway or a railway station where they can resort to such an action. Alternatively, this also becomes a very serious and significant action in an industrial country. The roads-highways and the rails are the arteries of transport and the blockades of any kind immediately bring the goods movement to a halt. The action thus becomes very significant and cannot go unnoticed.

Though the roadblock or *rail-roko* agitations create major stir, the agitators on their part consider these very passive actions. They are told, "You don't have to do anything. Just stay on the road or the tracks." The peasants/farmers do consider it a very simple action. Even women have participated in large numbers in such actions.

In the same year, 1983, Shetkari Sanghatana organized an interesting program—a rally of farmers to Pandharpur on 16 November 1983, on the auspicious day of *Kartiki Ekadashi.* The agitation was termed as *Vithobala Sakade* as has been mentioned earlier. The use of the Warkari tradition and devotion to focus upon the farmers' issues created quite a stir. The government was alarmed and thought that Sanghatana might disturb the Pandharpur *yatra* (pilgrimage). It banned the entry of the leaders of the Sanghatana in Pandharpur, which was later withdrawn. The *sakade* program actually became a rally of farmers in Pandharpur held on the outskirts of the town. It did not affect or disturb the devotees and pilgrims to Pandharpur. In this rally a major demand to scrap the Agricultural Prices Commission was made. The furore created by the term *Vithobala Sakade* helped to get a lot of media and government attention to farmers' demands (*Sakal,* 7 November 1983).

A major program that Sanghatana launched thereafter was *gaobandi*—prohibition to entry of the political leaders who take an adverse position against the demand for remunerative prices. Simultaneously, an agitation of *karz-mukti*—relief from indebtedness was also launched (Parbhani Convention Resolutions, a Handout, 1984).

The Shetkari Sanghatana took up the issue of cotton prices in 1985. This became a protracted agitation. By 1985, almost all parties had supported in principle, the demand for remunerative prices. The Sanghatana launched a different kind of agitation regarding cotton prices. It opposed Rajiv Gandhi's new textile policy of importing man-made fibre and cloth that it termed as *Rajivastra* and exhorted the cotton-growers and others to desist from using those. Programs of public bon-fires of the artificial cloth were organized (Joshi 1985b: 187-90). Memories of the independence struggle were renewed. *Swadeshi* concept of Tilak and Gandhi was in a way advocated. Babu Genu was now projected as a true martyr. Babu Genu was a young martyr from the *Swadeshi* movement of 1930, who had tried to stop the lorries filled with foreign made cloth from entering into market and was run over/mauled by a lorry.

In the context of the cotton agitation, Sharad Joshi tried to align with even urban trade unions that he had till then considered, part of "India"—the urban industrial sector as against "Bharat", the rural, agrarian sector. (A joint public rally was held at Shivaji Park in Mumbai with Kamgar Aaghadi, a trade union.) After 1985, Shetkari Sanghatana's agitations changed in character. The exuberance of the earlier agitations was no more there. The Sanghatana also started playing a role in party politics of the state. The momentum had gone.

The significant issue that the Sanghatana handled after 1986 was the women's question. Sanghatana held a huge rally of women in 1986 and made a demand for political power to women in local bodies. Later it took up the issue of grant of land rights to women. It advocated giving plots of land to women of the house by farmers. The women farmers were asked to go in for organic farming and become self-sufficient. The Sanghatana leader welcomed the process of globalization from the time the discussions on Dunkel Draft started. The liberal pro-globalization stand alienated many young activists who had joined the movement with expectations of radical changes in agriculture and rural areas.

The zest and spontaneity in the agitations had already gone. Most of the agitations of the Sanghatana culminated in dialogue with the government resulting in some agreement or understanding. The cotton agitation in 1986-7 ended without even reaching its peak. The leaders of political parties including the ruling party had already usurped the idiom of the Shetkari Sanghatana. After 1983, the Maharashtra Government hardly ever used repressive measures against Sanghatana agitations. This was an indication of the fractions of the ruling bloc finally coming to an understanding. A policy of appeasing the farmers by conceding to their demands was obviously adopted to keep the power base intact.

THE MEANS OF ORGANIZATION

It is believed that organizing the peasantry is a difficult task. Hobsbwam talks about the general passivity and subalternity of the peasants, the relative isolation of local communities, which makes their organization difficult (Hobsbawm 1973: 3). Hence, any study of a widespread peasant movement with a certain amount of continuity requires attention to the method of organization employed by the movement. The organizational aspects of a movement, viz., decision-making, program formulation, coordination in the action and mobilization are of vital importance to the success of a movement. As Ghanshyam Shah observes an impression is given by many studies of peasant struggles that peasant agitations were "spontaneous" and that they did not have any organized structure (Shah 1990: 63). But this is not true for a long sustained movement of peasants like the one by Shetkari Sanghatana. To launch effective and spatially widespread agitations it does require an efficient organizational structure.

For any movement, organizational structure becomes necessary to coordinate and regularize certain activities and programs. But at times, structure also proves to be an obstacle as the formality and rigidity which are part of a structure can mar the spontaneity of action which is of vital importance to any movement. Shetkari Sanghatana faced this dilemma in its initial years. The leadership, keen to preserve the vitality and vibrancy of the movement did not want to adopt a formal organizational structure, though it was essential to have some coordination and regularity of activities since the movement was spreading rapidly at that time (Joshi 1984b: 137-50).

So a very loose and informal organizational structure was evolved in the beginning and only in the later period, a formal structure was adopted due to the compulsions of the movement. This formal structure too was not of a permanent character and kept changing from time to time. Another reason for not adopting formal structure initially was the fear of the leadership that such a structure would be easily captured by the dominant political leaders in respective areas who would subvert the movement

(Joshi 1982: 14). This was especially true in a period when members of different political parties and groups were joining the movement. The movements' membership was open to the members of any political party or organization and the Shetkari Sanghatana was justified in having such a fear.

The leadership avoided formal structure, thus, to prevent any subversive takeover and to keep the movement free to adapt to new situations as they developed. But, in fact, the strength of any social movement lies in its agility and spontaneity. Frank and Fuentes observe that, "social movements generate and wield social power through the social mobilization of their participants. This social power is at once generated by and derived from the social movement itself, rather than from any institution, political or otherwise. Indeed, institutionalization weakens social movements and state political power negates them" (Frank and Fuentes 1987: 1504). They also believe that social movements require flexible, adaptive and non-authoritarian organizations as social goals cannot be pursued through random spontaneity.

This explains the dilemma before social movements regarding adopting any institutional or organizational/structural outfit. Without it, the movement has no direction, force and social power and with it there is a danger of it becoming staid, non-spontaneous and lacking what Frank and Fuentes call "social power", which is generated by and derived from "social movement" itself.

For the initial two-three years Sanghatana shunned formal structure. Then, with the increased strength and success of the movement, the danger of subversion of the movement by outsiders diminished and formal structures were gradually created as per the requirement and the demand of the participants. Structures were created to facilitate communication, propaganda, training of activists, fund collection and legal and medical help during agitations. Organizational units were first created at the village level in 1989. Villages having minimum fifty members of the organization became the primary units. But a full-fledged formal structure with constitution, etc. was still avoided.

Though membership drive was launched and village level units created, the Sanghatana did not have full time activists to carry out various functions. In 1984, at a Convention in Parbhani, decision was taken to appoint full-time activists of the Sanghatana who were to be paid workers. At the district level, "Agitation Committees" were formed that were to take responsibility of fund raising, training of activists, propaganda, organizing agitations and provision of legal aid to the activists if they were arrested by the police during agitations. The "Agitation Committee" was also expected to organize groups of agitators at the taluka level or at the market towns. A public trust with the name "Krishi Yogakshema Samshodhan Nyas" was instituted. The Sanghatana funds were to be deposited with the trust. Decision was also taken by the Sanghatana activists to wear the Sanghatana badge all the time whenever in public places (personally observed by the writer).

The Sanghatana at this juncture decided to contest elections of some sugar cooperative institutions. The control of the cooperatives was considered to be vital as it could give the Sanghatana financial and organizational strength. This was also considered to be a means to make inroads into the rural power base of the ruling party.

The organizational structure was more formalized in the same year by constituting an Executive body consisting of a Central Committee and district contact workers. This Committee was required to take responsibility of some specific work. A list of about thirty activities was prepared and these were divided among the Executive Committee members. A decision was also taken to emphasize organizational activities at the village and weekly marketplaces. Posts of President and Vice-President were also created. It may be mentioned here that, by this time, that is 1984, militant agitations of the Sanghatana were over. Hereafter, the only major agitation that was launched by the Sanghatana was on the issue of cotton prices and it was not like the earlier agitations, especially the sugar cane agitation. The earlier agitations involved a lot of mass participation, action on the road like road and rail block and some violence. Cotton agitation, however, used various other means, which could come under the non-violent *satyagraha* type, the boycott and bonfire of synthetic cloth.

Later on, the Sanghatana conducted reviews of the functioning of the structure as it had evolved. In 1986, it had taken up the issue of farmer women and women's political rights in general. For this purpose, changes were made in the organizational structure to facilitate women's participation. The element of internal democracy was introduced by adopting "election" of representatives to the Executive Committee as against the appointment till then.

By 1987-8, the organization had taken a more concrete shape. It was having a structure with Executive body headed by a High Command or High Powered Committee. The High Command consisted of eight members including Sharad Joshi. This committee was followed by a committee of regional chiefs representing chiefs from West Vidarbha, North, South and East Marathwada and North Maharashtra. Besides these committees, there was study committee and a body of District Chiefs. There was an inner organizational democracy as discussions had full scope in any meetings and the members and activists were free to express their opinions on various issues. However, in the entire organizational structure, Sharad Joshi was the undisputed "number one" leader. With this status and a near total devotion of the followers, Joshi invariably had final word in decision-making (personal observations on various occasions and interviews of some activists). Major decisions were always taken at the level of the High Command. Though women were given special representation in the Executive body, their participation in the decision-making was always peripheral.

LEADERSHIP

An important aspect of the Sanghatana's organization was its structure of leadership with three ranks. The first one consisted of only one leader that is Sharad Joshi. The second ranking leadership was the part of the High Command or the core group. The third rank consisted of the activists at the district and taluka levels. A large number of them hailed from non-Maratha, Other Backward Classes (OBC) and non-peasant background. Activists consisted of small town traders, teachers, doctors and lawyers also. There has been a total identification between Sharad Joshi and the Shetkari Sanghatana. He has been its supreme leader who effectively articulated the ideology, which mobilized the various strata of peasantry in Maharashtra. Joshi masterminded the agitations launched by the Sanghatana. He was the rallying point in the peasant movement in Maharashtra. He comes from a non-peasant background, Brahman by caste, with urban, middle class background, which makes him a non-organic leader of this peasant movement. His quitting a UN job and returning to India to organize a peasant movement lent him a glamorous image for both his peasant and non-peasant followers and his urban supporters and sympathizers.

The effectiveness of Sharad Joshi's leadership did not lie merely in his style of functioning. He possesses many extra-ordinary leadership traits like oratory; good organizational skills; accessibility and good political acumen. He made effective use of the rural idiom and symbols while addressing the rural masses. This enabled an instant rapport between him and them. His simple but non-ascetic lifestyle was also liked by the peasant masses. But the essence of his leadership lay in his effective articulation of the populist ideology. It placed Sharad Joshi in the enviable position of the leader of rural masses.

Though he was a charismatic leader, he was not a messianic leader as was considered by some (Bhole 1987: 25-30). His followers were organized on "economic" demands of which they were generally aware. The movement also did not operate in a pre-industrial pre-modern socio-economic or political stage but in a society at a certain higher degree of industrialization and modernization. As the movement also had a degree of institutionalization from within, its leadership was not a rule-free kind of leadership. It was a very modern and sophisticated one and the ideology it enunciated was also very sophisticated and modern in its contents. It was not revivalistic or magical.

The apparent sophistication of his arguments and leadership style earned for Sharad Joshi a sizeable support even among the urban middle classes. Joshi has a fine understanding of the modern media and he used them effectively for his ends. In his innovativeness regarding the techniques of agitations and sometimes the personal style of functioning, Joshi followed Gandhian steps quite consciously. Though Joshi had a tremendous hold over the masses he led, he did not have the moral authority of Gandhi. The movement of the Shetkari Sanghatana did not create spirituality or morality of the agitations as Gandhi did for his *Satyagraha*.

The third rank activists working at the district and taluka levels were the real strength of the Sanghatana. Most of them of younger age group (born between 1920s and 1940s) and barring a few from farmer families, most of them were non-farmers and well educated. There were traders, professionals like lawyers, doctors and teachers and activists from other political or social organizations such as Rashtra Seva Dal, Satyashodhak Communist Party, CPI(ML), Yuvak Kranti Dal, and Chhatra Yuva Sangharsha Vahini. The frustrated and demoralized activists from various organizations in the early 1980s looked at the Shetkari Sanghatana as the only organization scoring spectacular successes and gaining support of the rural masses. It was because of the dedicated activists of this rank that the Sanghatana had been able to create a strong organizational network and base in Maharashtra.

THE MEANS OF MOBILIZATION

An organization like Shetkari Sanghatana did not expect spontaneous mass-actions. It planned its agitations carefully. Such agitations required an assured mass base and mass support, which necessitated painstaking ground-work. Organizational work includes propaganda, fund collection, recruitment of new activists and members. It includes all such programs, which muster popular support and bring people in the organizational network and the movement (Joshi 1984b: 137-50).

The Sanghatana created various organizational fronts to reach to the various sections of society in order to strengthen the organizational network and mobilize the masses. There were fronts working with students, women, Dalits, Adivasis and landless laborers. Full time activists were associated with this work.

The activists and leaders would approach the people in smaller meetings at villages or at weekly marketplaces. The marketplaces were preferred because farmers from at least fifteen villages around the area could be contacted at a time. At such meetings, people would be told about the issues involved in the movement. The problems of the farmers would be discussed.

The ideology of the Sanghatana would be explained to them in speeches as well as through the circulation of published material. The more articulate men and women from the audience would be selected for further contact. They would be asked to join the Sanghatana and attend training camps. Membership fees would be collected and the members would be given Sanghatana badges. The Sanghatana slogans would be written on the walls in villages. This used to be the initial organizational work. However, to strengthen the base of the movement in an area the activists would work persistently (interviews with activists Tamaskar and Gunjal).

To muster popular support the activists would also undertake constructive programs such as drinking water facility, debt relief, recovery of compensation for government acquired lands, demands for work under the Employment Guarantee Scheme (EGS), drought relief, etc. The activists would also organize and mobilize the local people for some action to resolve local level problems mentioned above. These actions included *gherao* (encirclement) of officials like Mamledar or District Officer or EGS officials or marches to such offices at the local level. Success of such actions would create popular trust in the activities of the Sanghatana and bring the masses into its organizational network. Such programs being organized at marketplaces facilitated simultaneous contact with a number of villages. The other reasons for selecting markets for meetings and programs were the presence of important government functionaries like *talathi* (village land-record keeper), engineer, and revenue officers. They could become easy targets in the events of spontaneous actions. There are few police stations at marketplaces, which enable activists to move around more freely. In contrast, at district level, the police can easily thwart or foil a march or a *gherao* (interview with Tamaskar).

Resourceful activists would use various forms of communication to get through the message to the masses and attract them to the Sanghatana. Singing Sanghatana message songs in the style of *bhajans* (religious songs) or propagating ideology in the *kirtan* (religious story telling accompanied by songs) style were a few such means.

Apart from local level meetings, actions, rallies and conventions, Sanghatana also organized propaganda long marches (*prachar yatras*) covering a vast area at a stretch. Farmers had taken *dindis* (long marches) from Marathwada and had walked to Pandharpur to attend the *Sakade* programme in November 1983. There were also long marches in other areas. They were not on foot but in vehicles like jeeps, trucks and tractors. Such marches also served to show the strength of the movement and help further mobilization.

The reason behind such continuous organizational activity was that it fostered the unification of the support base. Otherwise, there would be fragmentation by the sheer inertia.

Shetkari Sanghatana's organization had certain definite lines of command, though the authority was concentrated in the hands of one person, Sharad Joshi, and legitimacy was derived from him. Though he never held the highest position of the organization officially, he had constantly been an extra-constitutional center of authority within the movement. The looseness of structure with its functional relevance helped the organization to launch spontaneous mass struggles and at the same time facilitate direct contact between the "supreme leader" and the masses, which was of vital importance.

The conscious efforts to encourage the emergence of non-Maratha, non-peasant leadership at the second and third rank might be precisely for this purpose. Such persons cannot rise and challenge the supreme leader by building up their own independent clientele among the peasants. Their importance to the peasant masses stems from the sanction they enjoy from the supreme leader.

An attractive ideological articulation with the use of popular parlance, borrowed from popular—religious as well as secular—traditions, coupled with the imaginative, simple looking yet very effective actions marked the means of agitation of the farmers' movement in Maharashtra. Shetkari Sanghatana, thus, through its agitations not only put forth the demands of the rich and middle farmers forcefully, but in the process also created for itself a role of political mediator in the politics of Maharashtra.

THE COURSE TRAVERSED: FROM MOVEMENT TO POLITICAL PARTY

As the organizational structure started becoming more and more formal, the movement had also started changing in nature. The spontaneity of action was not as expected, but flexibility of structure facilitated the movement's mass character. With institutionalization, the movement started turning into a pressure group. The leaders of the peasant movements were formally invited to join the Agricultural Costs and Prices Commission and later during NDA government, Sharad Joshi was appointed to a special Task Force on Agriculture.

The initial non-politicist stance was also a strategy rather than the genuine ideological position. To broaden the mass base the leadership welcomed people from all political hues to join the Sanghatana; but when it felt that Sanghatana had sufficient political power/strength, the electoral politics was also given a try, initially contesting elections as independent candidates, and later as a political party. Forming political party (Swatantra Bharat Paksha—on the lines of the Swatantra Party of the 1960s) has completed the evolution of Shetkari Sanghatana from a mass movement to a political party. In these stages, it had lost its momentum. The weakening of the movement also eroded its mass base which leadership had expected would have helped its electoral prospects. The Sanghatana could not improve its electoral tally after it turned into a political party.

While organizationally the Shetkari Sanghatana was evolving thus, ideologically also it had traversed a lot. At least outwardly, it seemed so. The anti-state position that Sharad Joshi had taken earlier has actually not changed. Though initially he was against the state's intervention to control agricultural imports or procurement of levy, he also favored state's intervention to give support prices to agricultural products of various kinds. He was drawing the significant line of contradiction between agriculture and industry and not between state and peasantry as such. He wanted free markets then too. But if that was not possible, he wanted the state to stop intervening on behalf of industrial and urban interests. His position has always been to favor the markets.

He targeted the state because its policies according to him were detrimental to the farmers. However, his asking for remunerative prices from the state confused many of his followers who had taken his ideology to be revolutionary. To them, his later position on globalization came as a shock.

GLOBALIZATION AND SHETKARI SANGHATANA

With the advent of globalization's current phase in the 1990s, Joshi took the stand of welcoming it. He wanted the market forces to rule rather than the state, and this stand created confusion and split among his ranks. A large number of activists who were looking at this organization and movement as revolutionary, in the sense that it would change the rural scene and abolish the poverty of the peasants got disillusioned and left it. The pro-globalization stand of Shetkari Sanghatana also isolated it from peasant organizations in other states like Rayat Sangh of Karnataka or Bharatiya Kisan Union of Mahendra Singh Tikait. Those organizations had joined the wider anti-globalization collective.

In this phase, Shetkari Sanghatana ceased to be a movement and became a pressure group. Its strength got further reduced after the establishment of the Swatantra Bharat Party. Leaders in movements can seldom transform their mass support into electoral victories. Sharad Joshi experienced the same. He was unable to get elected even from the area of his influence. As the movement subsided and became institutionalized, his charisma also waned.

Peasant movements of the 1980s were categorized as "new" social movements along with the environmental and feminist movements by some (Omvedt and Chetana 1988). The reasoning was the "non-class" character of all these movements. The issues of the women's movement and environmental movement were new and these movements offered an alternative world-view. But whether peasant movement can be categorized as new is debatable. As Frank and Fuentes observe, peasant movements cannot be considered as new as they have existed for centuries and even millennia in many parts of the world. Ironically, the working class movements, which have a comparatively recent origin, are considered as classical or traditional (Frank and Fuentes 1987).

The newness of the new social movements lies in their exploring new forms of organization and mobilization apart from being "single class" or "single stratum" movements. They also happen to be the movements of the middle classes who are disillusioned with the earlier forms of political organizations and the state. The peasant movement under consideration shares these features with other "new" social movements. Though it is not the movement of the middle class, it is the middle stratum of the peasantry, and the middle castes of the rural society, which was its mainstay. But contrary to the hopes and claims, the movement was not transformatory. It only re-oriented or reshaped the prevalent class balance. Basically representing the interests of the rich and the middle farmers, the movement was an "oppositional" one. Its main success was in bringing the agriculture on the main agenda of the nation.

Shetkari Sanghatana opposed the major environmental movement—the *Narmada Bachao Andolan*—which has been championing the cause of poor *Adivasi* peasants affected by the Sardar Sarovar dam. The Sanghatana does not share the concerns of the environmentalists or the project affected people. It tried to actively disrupt the *Narmada Bachao* agitations in their concern for the farmers who would be benefited by the dam water. The other reason could also be the opposition of the environmental movements to globalization and free market economy as against Shetkari Sanghatana's open welcome to it.

Gail Omvedt categorized Shetkari Sanghatana as a new social movement. While Shetkari Sanghatana was in its phase of a real mass movement during its sugar or tobacco agitations, Omvedt had termed it as rich farmers' movement (Omvedt 1980). It was only after 1986, when Sanghatana was more or less a spent force and had turned to its organizational activities, and focused on demanding political representation to women in local governmental institutions that she considered it having a "revolutionary" potential of a "new" social movement. As such, the anti-"class" stance was appealing to many. The continuously changing political stances and agitations of Shetkari Sanghatana also indicated its reaching dead end in a particular issue and so turning to a new direction or a new issue. The movement could be considered a failure as many of its agitations had failed. But the Sanghatana had achieved what it had aimed and that was putting agriculture on the nation's main agenda and reinstating the political balance between the industrial bourgeoisie and the rich farmers.

It had opposed the "state" and supported the market mechanism as a panacea for the problems of the peasantry. Though it wanted the state to intervene to operate support price mechanism, it considered the state as an instrument in the hands of the urban-industrial sector which it called "India" to exploit "Bharat". With its pro-globalization stand favoring market mechanism, the Sanghatana created an atmosphere conducive to globalization, and substantially reduced the chances of any major movement in the countryside to oppose it.

REFERENCES

Brahme, Sulabha and Ashok Upadhyaya, 1979: *A Critical Analysis of the Social Formation and Peasant Resistance in Maharashtra*, vols. I, II, III. Pune: Shankar Brahme Samaj Vidnyan Granthalay.

Bhole, Bhaskar Laxman, 1987: "Riddles of Ram and Krishna, Riddles of Sharad Joshi and Shetkari Sanghatna", *Paryaya*, November/December 1987, vol. I, no. 4, pp. 25-30.

Dhanagare, D.N., 1988: "An apoliticist populism", *Seminar*, December 1988, no. 352, pp. 24-31.

Frank, Andre Gunder and Marta Fuentes, 1987: "Nine Theses on Social Movements", *Economic and Political Weekly*, Mumbai, 29 August 1987, 22 (35), pp. 1503-10.

Hobsbawm, Eric J., 1973: "Peasants and Politics", *The Journal of Peasant Studies*, vol. I, no. I, October 1973, pp. 3-22.

Joshi, Sharad, 1982: *Prachalit Arthavyavasthevar Nava Prakash*. Alibag (Dist. Raigad): Shetkari Prakashan.

——, 1984a: *Shetkaryacha Asood: Shatakacha Mujra*. Alibag (Dist. Raigad): Shetkari Prakashan.

——, 1984b: *Shetkari Sanghatana: Vichar ani Karyapaddhati*. Alibag (Dist. Raigad): Shetkari Prakashan.

——, 1985a: *Prachalit Arthavyavasthevar Nava Prakash*, Part II. Alibag (Dist. Raigad): Shetkari Prakashan.

——, 1985b: *'Bharat' Speaks Out*. Mumbai: BUILD Documentation Centre.

Joshi, Sharad, Anil Gote and Rajeev Basargekar, 1988: *Shetkaryancha Raja Shivaji*. Alibag (Dist. Raigad): Shetkari Prakashan.

Laclau, Ernesto, 1979: *Politics and Ideology in Marxist Theory: Capitalism-Fascism-Populism.* London: Verso.

Lindbergh, Staffan, 2005: "Farmers' agitation, civil society and the state", in N. Jayaram (ed.), *On Civil Society: Issues and Perspectives.* New Delhi: Sage Publications.

Nadkarni, M.V., 1987: *Farmers' Movement in India.* New Delhi: Allied Publishers.

Omvedt, Gail, 1980: "Cane Farmers' Movement", *Economic and Political Weekly,* 6 December 1980.

——, 1986: "Peasants and Women: Challenge of Chandwad", *Economic and Political Weekly,* 29 November 1986.

——, 1988: "New Movements", *Seminar,* December 1988, no. 352, pp. 39-44.

——, 1993: *Reinventing Revolution: New Social Movements and the Socialist Tradition in India.* New York: East Gate Book.

Omvedt, Gail, and Gala Chetana 1988: "Peasant question is a class question", *Economic and Political Weekly,* 2 July 1988.

Parulkar, Vijay, 1981: *Yoddha Shetkari.* Pune: Rajhans Prakashan.

Shah, Ghanshyam, 1990: *Social Movements in India: A Review of the Literature.* New Delhi: Sage Publications.

Shetkari Sanghatak (Weekly Publication of Shetkari Sanghatana).

Sakal (Daily Newspaper, Pune).

Maharashtra Times (Daily Newspaper).

15

Mukati Kon Pathe: Emancipation, Which Way?*

GOPAL GURU

Let me at the outset argue that politics driven by the claims for superior truth tend to pose categories in a dichotomous way in either/or fashion. For example, primacy of political gets privileged over social or caste gets privileged over class. Thus, the nationalists in Maharashtra would insist for the primacy of political as against the social. In fact, they sought to oppose the primacy of social so vehemently even resorting to violently putting down such efforts.[1] To put differently, the extremist nationalist in Maharashtra insisted for the self-rule rather than self-respect.[2] On the other hand, the *Dalit-Bahujan* thinkers and leaders seem to have followed a more cautious route to mobilization and ultimate liberation of the oppressed masses. These leaders did assign primacy to social (self-respect) over the political (self-rule).[3] This paper argues that *Dalit-Bahujan* did not treat social as an essential condition but just an initial condition for emancipation. I am making a case for this perspective primarily because it can help us in undermining the dichotomous binaries that are always constraining rather than enabling. This particular methodological path seems to have been followed by the Dalits not out of whims and fancy but more as a logical necessity.

Let me argue that the socially oppressed in Maharashtra seem

* This title is originally from Bengali. It seems Ambedkar had used it in 1936 particularly after the conversion decision that he took in 1935.

to have adopted not just one but several and often cross-cutting paths for their emancipation. Some of them advocated the autonomous path for capturing political power for emancipation.[4] While others chose to rally round the mainstream political parties particularly the Congress for their emancipation.[5] Yet some of them chose to remain within the Hindu fold.[6] It would be outside the scope of this essay to cover all the routes that were chosen by different sections of Dalit in Maharashtra. Hence the present paper chooses to limit its scope only to conversion route that has been followed by Dalits who were led by Ambedkar in first half of the twentieth-century Maharashtra. It has to be noted that Ambedkar showed extraordinary patience with other routes while selecting conversion as one of the possible alternative. He formally announced to leave Hinduism in 1935. Like a good liberal in his early years of activism, he exerted morally evaluative pressure on the followers of Hinduism and made them realize how fundamentally they are at fault to treat Untouchables less than human being. Before 1935 he rather tactically suggested the caste Hindus to drastically amend their attitudes towards the Untouchables. Yet his decision was criticized by both the Dalits and the non-Dalits. Some of them suggested that the choice of this route was quite arbitrary.[7]

There are scholars and political observers both from within the Dalit community and also form outside who do not seem to have taken a hospitable approach to conversion decision that Ambedkar and his followers took in 1935. Dalit particularly the Mahars decided to leave Hinduism in 1935 and finally converted to Buddhism in 1956. For example, as mentioned above the Mahars from Nagpur did oppose the conversion move as suggested by Ambedkar in 1935.[8] The other two Dalit castes—Mangs and Chambhars also opposed this move. In the contemporary period, there have been several scholars and even Buddhist scholars who strongly criticized the conversion route followed by Mahars of Maharashtra. These include, Mangs,[9] some of the noted Buddhist organizations,[10] and even interestingly some of the Marxist scholars who treated conversion as the "reactionary step".[11] It is not, however, possible to offer full treatment to all these criticisms leveled against conversion route. I have decided to pick up two readings of Ambedkar's conversion movement by Gauri Vishwanathan, and Jayshree Gokhale-Turner. Gauri has provided interesting but problematic interpretation of Ambedkar's Buddhist conversion in Maharashtra. According to her, among other things, Ambedkar conversion was a definite route towards nationalism.[12] She further argues it was so because Ambedkar treated Christianity and Islam as the sources of denationalizing the Dalits.[13] Similarly, Jayshree Gokhale-Turner makes an interesting reading of Ambedkar's conversion decision. She argues that conversion decision taken by Ambedkar was influenced by his personal disdain for Hinduism. She further says that his decision of Buddhist conversion looked "mysterious" as it lacked pragmatism.[14] Keeping in view such an astounding reading of conversion, one feels it necessary to raise the following questions. Let me raise two sets of questions in response to the readings of Gauri and Gokhale-Turner.

First: Did Ambedkar visualize nationalist aspirations in the conversion? Did he ever use Islam and Christianity as the negative reference point in order to assigning nationalist orientation to Buddhist conversion? Can one relate Buddhist conversion to nationalism? Did Ambedkar's decision regarding conversion lack any democratic deliberation? To put differently, did he take the decision single-handedly without taking the masses into confidence? The question that needs to be asked is, was the route chosen by Ambedkar less self-reflective? Did it have an exclusionary consciousness that did not accommodate other routes suggested by other thinkers and leaders from Maharashtra? That is to say, did he ever try to impose his decision on the Dalit masses? Did he not respect their capacity to take decision on their own? How has he achieved social support for this tradition? Did he drag Dalit people behind him on this high way of emancipation? Did he ever coerce people into accepting his alternative path? Did he lay down the high way thus straightway starting from the universal? Or he also followed the Paulwat (by-lanes) ultimately leading to the express high way, for example, of Buddhism? Did he ever try to rush from the particular to the universal? What is the moral stamina that Ambedkar assigned to his alternative ways of definition?

Second: What has been the political and intellectual response of contemporary Dalits to this pathway? In what way, conversion to Buddhism accommodated individualism into its communitarians? Did Ambedkar treat conversion as the ultimate pathway or he treated it as the road connection to much larger alternatives? Did Dalits in the post-conversion period follow this route? If yes, in what way? To what extent? Does the contemporary Dalit imagination show any loss of grip over the intellectual/political legacy of Ambedkar's conversion? These are some of the questions that are addressed in the present paper.

This particular paper limits itself to the theoretical and political "road map" as laid out by some of the Maharashtrian social thinkers and leaders with the purpose to radicalize the masses in an organized manner. However, the paper will make occasional references to other ideological road maps drawn by other "cartographers" of the social movements in the state. To be more precise the major focus would remain on emancipatory movement led by Babasaheb Ambedkar during and after independent period. Obviously, the paper seeks to concentrate on the movement of the oppressed in Maharashtra.

LIBERALISM AS THE CONNECTING ROUTE TO CONVERSION

Let me argue that the arrival of liberalism in Maharashtra generated aspiration among various sections to seek self-definition. These included, women, Shudras and Ati-shudra groups in Maharashtra. This also opened up several possibilities for such group to explore different ways to give concrete meaning to this self-definition. The oppressed led by Babasaheb Ambedkar also imagined several pathways to embark upon. One of such pathways was conversion chosen by Ambedkar and largely followed by the Mahar, one of the dominant castes of the Dalit cluster from Maharashtra. The paper argues that liberalism can help in understanding the early response that the Mahar offered to conversion route suggested by Ambedkar. How does one understand this early response by the Mahar? Was it because Ambedkar was also a Mahar and hence the early response from the Mahar? I would like to argue that the Mahar did not follow this route on parochial grounds. In fact this early response has to be understood in terms of the arrival of liberalism enveloped with modernity in Maharashtra. The liberal element in the land relations together with the simultaneous inauguration of modernity in the urban centers of nineteenth and twentieth-century Maharashtra could supply the necessary context for the early response of Mahars to the entire project of Dalit emancipation of which conversion formed one path converging into the grand project of emancipation of everybody including Dalits. Liberalism itself arrived in Maharashtra due to the special conditions that prevailed in this presidency. The west coast and the cotton economy in Maharashtra provided necessary background for the early emergence of liberalism in this region. Let us discuss in brief how the arrival of liberalism in Maharashtra as the background condition prompted certain caste to embark on the road of conversion?

As we all know the Rayatwari system in Maharashtra led to the displacement of Dalits particularly Mahars from the village structures. They were displaced form the villages because they, like the other two castes, did not have skilled occupation. In the Rayatwari, an element of private property was introduced by the colonial state. This system made land a commodity that could be bought and sold by any person from any caste. Of course, Mahars were not the only beneficiaries of this land transfer. These changing land relations affected them only indirectly. They were pushed out of the land by the middle caste cultivating castes, which themselves were de-peasantized by the land transfer to the moneylender and merchant castes who had settled from outside Maharashtra. Secondly, Mahars found liberal public sphere in the urban cities as the relatively liberating promise as compared to the village ghetto. Displacement of Mahars from the traditional occupation proved to be a blessing in disguise for them. In the land transfer Mahars' services were not required on the land hence they migrated to the cities. Among these who were rendered jobless within the agricultural sector, Mahars constituted the majority. Compared to other two dominant Dalit castes, the Mang and the Chambhar, Mahars were displaced quite early.[15] This migration offered them an opportunity to set themselves free from the religious domination of the high caste Hindus. They also became free from the patron-client structures controlled by the Hindu village lords. This desirable displacement forces Mahars to take the road to the cities like Bombay, Manmad, Nagpur and Nasik. Liberalism involved both the push factor and the pull factor providing both intellectual and political conditions to chart out the journey on the road of conversions.

However, although liberalism created necessary social condition for Mahars to think of conversion as an alternate route for emancipation, it was not an easy task. As mentioned above, many Mahars took serious objection to such move made by Ambedkar. For example, the wealthy Mahars from Nagpur region criticized Ambedkar for taking the decision to leave Hinduism.[16] It could not have been easy for these Mahars to make hasty exit from Hinduism as the former were also tied to Hindus. Secondly, it is always difficult to escape the religious consciousness deeply rooted in the community. In other words, it is difficult to move from the particular to the universal. This is because the accumulation of Hinduism into the cultural consciousness takes time to be completely rooted out. The Mahar and not just the rich even the ordinary Mahars were in need of conversion. It seems it is the practical reason that drove them to walk out of Hinduism to either Christianity or Islam. They did not go for the theoretical reason to examine the pros and cons of conversion and make decision after due deliberation. It is because of the urgency to walk out from Hinduism many of Mahars particularly from the villages converted to Christianity and Islam even during Ambedkar's period.[17] Those who opposed conversion moves did so for two reasons. First, they were culturally still rooted into the traditions. Secondly, these rich Mahars particularly from Nagpur area identified more with the rich from among the Hindus. In fact, some of the Mahar were the *malguzaras* controlling several villages.[18] Some of them were not prepared to arrive at decision through deliberations. Those who migrated to the urban centers could make their mind for conversion through the comparative evaluation of different religions. In fact, it is the urban educated Mahars who took initiative in mobilizing the common Dalits about the need for conversion even. As compared to Mahars, the other two sub-castes of the Dalit cluster chose to stay out of the conversion decision. However, it was not voluntaristic on their part to stay out. This skepticism has to be understood in terms of the structural conditions. Mangs and Chambhars had the skilled traditional occupation like making rope, basket and leather bucket. This skilled occupation was needed for the pre-modern agricultural economy that was controlled by the cultivating castes that were dominantly Hindus. So the Mang and the Chambhar had stake in Hindus to the extent that they were tied to the agriculture. Mahars were relatively free from this economically rather constraining structure.

As it is clear from the literature, the common Mahars decided to walk with Ambedkar on the road of conversion not before they were completely convinced of this decision. They went for the deliberative mode for taking this decision. It is interesting to note that the Mahars used cultural medium to deliberate on the conversion issue. The Mahars used *Ambedkari Jalse* (as the folk theater) to advocate the importance of conversion.[19] Deliberative angle thus suggests that there was deep moral angle to Ambedkar's decision to conversion. He did not force people to accept his decision. That is to say, like a Pied Piper he did not mislead people into believing in things that could have proved detrimental to the larger interest of the latter. As mentioned above he chose a democratic approach to enlist the support of Dalits to his politics of emancipation. As a true practitioner of Buddhist principle '*Atta dipo Bhava*', he valued people as having equal moral capacity to take decision on their own. Secondly, he did not seek to coerce people by converting principles into rule and making the former follow it without any objection. It is in this respect he was different from Gandhi who did try to convert the principle of *ahimsa* (non-violence) into a rule, which by its very logic has to be compulsorily followed by the disciples. Finally, he did not reduce the complex social reality into the catchy slogans to be written on the wall as the sufficient condition for emancipation. On the contrary, he tried to lay out the theoretical road map of emancipation through his analytical ability. In short, he did not try to rush to conversion. The vehicle of utilitarianism that is aimed at quick success did not drive his path. On the contrary, he suggested a path which was quite bumpy, strenuous, full of challenges, setback, reversal and occasional defeats as well. Neither he was impatient with his own thinking nor politics. He was actually building up the movement with complete sensitivity to inter-subjectivity. That is to say, he never closed the social corridor between the Dalits and other emancipatory alternatives belonging to the same logical class. For example, he showed willingness and historical necessity to identify the Dalits with Bahujan in Maharashtra. Though he was quite critical of the non-Brahman movement for its less hospitable attitude towards the Dalit cause yet he understood the necessity to associate with the non-Brahman movement.

Ambedkar's announcement to leave Hinduism and convert to another religions in 1935 and the actual conversion that took place in 1956 only suggests that this was not the decision that was taken in great haste or out of personal frustration. Ambedkar and Mahars together chose conversion as the pathway very carefully. The very choice of Buddhism had enormous moral stamina and intellectual force. It was morally much stronger appeal in the sense that this religion did not have any national or international patronage. It had lost its material support right in the sixth century AD. In that sense, it literally remained less attractive to the people. It therefore demanded a greater moral and theoretical response from the people. It had its normative values and scientific tenants as the only rallying point. It did not hold out any material or spiritual promise to the people in question. It demanded greater commitment to its teaching which was its main attraction. Therefore one was required to make the choice of Buddhism as reinterpreted by Ambedkar completely out of conviction and not compulsion. This paper argues that he chose Buddhism as an alternative metaphysics of emancipation. He made Buddhist tradition critical by offering radical re-interpretation of Buddhism. He did not convert his alternative into Express Highway, which is a fast track that has a tendency to entice the drivers to speeding vehicles but only at their peril. He knew that in India the road is quite bumpy. Thus he did not suggest an ideological catharsis. His pathway has full of challenges with the possibility of successes and also an occasional setbacks. His model involved an element of cooperation and not adjudication. In the latter case, there is no scope for deliberation.

However, for Ambedkar it was a route to annihilate the sub-caste from within.[20] Ambedkar also outlines the material reasons for conversion. Within the material reasons, conversion to other religions so that one can promote individualism that according to Ambedkar is so necessary for selfhood. Ambedkar, at this point of time defends individualism or an unencumbered self partly because he wants to establish an equal relationship between two individuals and ultimately in the entire society. He is advocating conversion to eliminate inequality based on arbitrary distribution of resources. For him religion is not opium but cunning to keep people in intellectual slavery. He further makes an important point that it is not enough to say that the untouchability is the blot on Hinduism. In fact, he says, Hinduism itself is a big blot.[21] Ambedkar goes one step ahead and argues that conversion is beneficial not only for the Dalits but for the entire Hindu community itself. He argues that the real social contradiction between the Dalits and the Hindus is based on the notion of purity-pollution. If one wants to eliminate this contradiction he suggests that the Dalits should leave Hinduism. This according to him would make Dalits fight for temple entry. Logically, there will be no need for the Hindus also to oppose this temple entry. Ambedkar is suggesting that insulation from Hinduism is the best way to annihilate casteism. But how can one understand the conflict between Hindus and Muslim or the Christian and Hindus. It is because the source of conflict is not in religion itself but definitely outside it. Communal tension between the Hindus and the Muslim has to be understood in this way only. However, the conversion was not treated as the exit from Hinduism. Some of the interested parties tried to pull Buddhism into the fold first by treating Buddha as the ninth incarnation of Vishnu. This was done with the object to deny Buddhism revolutionary character. Conversion route was to achieve self-respect and not satisfy anybody. It was more the self. Conversion to Buddhism was more for seeking self-definition. That is to say: create identity for oneself that would be different from the natural entity like animals. Conversion was the route that mediated the natural into the cultural. It assigned dignified meaning to Dalits. They were no more identified with the defiling name that was given to them by the hierarchical system. For Ambedkar it is not simple religious conversion. In fact, he suggests that conversion would give the new and secular name, which will be completely different from the caste names that carry dirt with them.[22]

However, Ambedkar also considers conversion as the surest way to annihilate caste. He argues casteism is the basis of Hinduism. In order to get rid of casteism, Ambedkar suggests that leave Hinduism. In fact, he suggests that conversion is also beneficial for the Hindus. He argues that they would not have any reason to fight with the Dalits once the latter exit from the Hindu fold.[23] The conversion would eliminate the very source of social tension between Dalits and Hindus. For Ambedkar, temple entry, inter-caste marriage or right to community meals have been the source of tensions. Once Dalits exit from Hinduism, they would not have any need to fight for their right to temple entry or inter-caste marriage. Ambedkar thus treats conversion as a viable source of seeking conciliation between the two embattled social groups. Ultimately, in 1956, he chose Buddhism as the route for emancipation. The question that one has to address is why did he choose this religion and not other religions? Here I am not going to elaborate on the reasoning that Ambedkar offered in defense of his choice of Buddhism. He has discussed it in his seminal book *Buddha and His Dhamma.* It is in this context, it is necessary to examine Gauri's reading of Ambedkar's decision to convert to Buddhism.

Just to put the record straight, Gauri very rightly suggests that Buddhist conversion as a definite road to equality.[24] She is also right in rejecting the view that Ambedkar took the decision of conversion out of frustration or anger or to secure self-representation for the Untouchable.[25] She very rightly argues that it was more for creating new political identity. For her, conversion was the form of political and cultural criticism. It is also a form of dissent. However, Gauri Vishwanathan, somehow, enters the slightly problematic terrain and argues that Ambedkar went for Buddhism because his nationalism did not allow him to go for either Islam or Christianity. She is suggesting that Ambedkar treated Islam and Christianity as the "foreign" religions.[26] Gauri, I guess, is trying to infer from Ambedkar's writing what he does not suggest at all. For example he did not reject Christianity and Islam just because these religions were not Indians.[27] While it could be Gauri's reading but certainly not Ambedkar's. Of course, he was critical of Christianity and Islam but he always treated both these religions as better option to Hinduism.

The question that needs to be answered is: did Ambedkar choose Buddhism just to fit into the nationalist aspirations? Did he ever have such a narrow view of Buddhism or nationalism? The answer to this question is in the negative. He did not take such a narrow view of conversion. Ambedkar did say that he would convert the whole of India into Buddhism. However, his Buddhism conversion never had any territorial boundaries. He always interpreted Buddhism as the normative world order to be followed by people all over the world. Thus, conversion as the articulation of the normative community based on the Buddhist moral principles cannot be confined within the nationalist boundaries. It was much larger than the nation inviting people at large to join its mission. Secondly, his notion of nationalism was not based on the indigenous view of religion. His nationalism was based on the universal principle of democracy, autonomy and freedom. This is amply clear from his seminal work *Pakistan and Partition.* His critique of Hindu nationalism emanates from this normative concern and not because Hinduism as religion *per se.* He continuously argues that Hinduism cannot be the basis of nationalism primarily because it denies these normative principles. If at all one wants to relate Buddhism to nationalism it has to be done only on the normative promise that Buddhism offers.

Ambedkar is interested in building road not between God and human being but between person and person. It is in this sense that the conversion is material and not spiritual. Ambedkar rejected Islam and Christianity because the known history of conversion did not bring any respite to Untouchables. Ambedkar could see in his own time both these religions in India reproduced the caste system with its obnoxious nature. Hence, these religions were not the choice before him. Of course, he went a little closer to Sikhism. But he found this religion less attractive in terms of the total promise that Dalits wanted from the philosophy. The present paper is aware of two difficulties that it suffers from. First, it acknowledges the need to answer the question: did Ambedkar ever suggests conversion as the ultimate route to emancipation? Ambedkar does not see conversion as the final route in emancipation. He suggests the social revolution to annihilate the caste system.[28] And secondly, how does his

Buddhist conversion accommodate the question of individualism within the framework of neo-Buddhism? This question becomes significant in the context of the Buddhist thrust to create moral community based on the *Tri-saran* and *Panchsheel*. However, this is not an adequate answer to this huge question. Though both these questions are absolutely important and require serious treatment, however, I am unable to take them here just for my convenience. I have chosen to focus more on the background conditions within which the decision of conversion has taken shape.

In the last section, let me explore to what extent, this route helped the Dalit get recognition to their self-respect? To what extent has it been able to elevate Dalits from the identity of "walking carcass" to dignified Buddhist self? Could they become the reference group for other Untouchable caste within the cluster of Scheduled Castes? Who among the Dalits followed this route out of conviction? These are questions that warrant attention.

DALIT RESPONSE TO BUDDHIST CONVERSION

As the practice of last 50 years shows, Buddhist conversion never had an easy trajectory and it was full of challenges posed by its main adversaries the Hindutva leaders. For example, certain sections of the Hindu society, tried to stall the conversion by denying the Untouchables the advantage to choose Buddhist conversion without any compulsion. As we all know, the Dalits were going to loose the Reservation benefits if they were to convert to any religion other than Hinduism and to some extent Sikhism. The argument that these leaders made was since Buddhism does not believe in caste those converting into this religion would automatically forfeit the benefits accruing form caste. This put a lot of moral pressure on Dalits. Some of the smarter one decided to deviate from the path as laid down by Ambedkar. They for theoretical purposes chose to remain within the fold of Hinduism for the sake of getting Reservation benefits. Only in practice some of them followed Buddhism at the cultural and ritual levels. Very few of them have chosen to offer response to conversion at the intellectual or hermeneutic level. Even today, in the post-

Ambedkar period, there are some attempts to take the Buddhist conversion route. This is happening particularly in the north Indian situation. While in the south the Dalits are taking the conversion to Islam and Christianity. However, one does not know whether the conversion route that is taken by these Dalits is complete and transparent or partial and discursive? The indications are such moves are less driven by the need to achieve moral and intellectual power to transcend oneself and also the other. It is in fact motivated more by the need to acquire an instant recognition and visibility. It does not give complete guarantee to stand up against the Hindutva forces, as is the case of Mahars in Maharashtra. However, one should not romanticize the case of Mahars from Maharashtra. The Buddhist practice among the ex-Mahars of this region shows that they lack complete and thorough commitment to Buddhism. The more educated seem to have very calculated commitment to Buddhism. As mentioned above, such elite have developed a Janus-faced cultural identity. On the contrary, it is the common Dalits who have developed and sustained the total commitment to conversion. Theirs is the unconditional investment in Buddhist conversion influenced not by any other things except to redefine oneself for further cultural/ spiritual elevation. In Maharashtra, what one finds is that political implication of conversion have sustained secular consciousness among at least Mahars. This consciousness is so active and socially vigilant that it does not tolerate even a simple shake hand of Dalits with the BJP or Sena leaders from the state. It deploys the same mechanism of social ostracism against those Dalits who deviated from the conversion and crossed over to the socially regressive side. Common Buddhist has shown a tremendous moral courage to also become Buddhist on paper. They knew that their sons and daughters were going to loose the Reservation benefits and yet they converted. Compared to this, the educated Dalits did not follow the route completely. They did not become Buddhist on paper. Doing so would have been risky for the later generation of these educated elite. As far as Maharashtra is concerned, these educated Buddhists avoided conversion route that was useless for achieving positional good. Ironically they tried to follow it to gain primary good like dignity and self-respect. Unfortunately, their efforts have not achieved any spectacular success. They are still reduced to their Mahar identity.[29]

However, it is very interesting to note that Buddhism has been a very potent cultural resource for the Dalit women. It has helped them to gain social respect within the Dalit community. In fact, they have taken over the cultural landscape of Buddhist community in Maharashtra. Some of them have taken over as the Buddhist monk. They have established their cultural power to solemnize Buddhist marriages in many villages in Akola District.[30] This is not a mean achievement of conversion. At the subaltern level, however, one could find people accessing Ambedkar through cultural symbols and writing on the wall. However, it is more a rhetorical reception of Ambedkar rather than the reasoned internalization of the former.

NOTES

1. Eleanor Zelliot, 'The Mahar Movement in Maharashtra', unpublished thesis submitted to Pennsylvania University, Minnesota, 1967.
2. This is the famous statement that was made by Bal Gangadhar Tilak.
3. *Muk Nayak,* 1921. Government of Maharashtra, 1989, p. 16(76).
4. Ibid.
5. The Matangs from Ahmadnagar, Akola, Sangali and Solapur districts seem to have supported the Congress. For more details please refer to Khairmode's biographies of Ambedkar, vols. 5 & 6, Pune: Sugawa Publications, 1989.
6. D.D. Kosare, *Dalit Movement in Vidarbha,* Nagpur: Buddhist Publication, 1980, p. 23.
7. Khairmode, op. cit., vol. 5, p. 123.
8. Ibid.
9. Vitthal Sathe, *Zala Buddha Mahar,* Pune: Pune Publication, 1983.
10. This has been widely recorded by several scholars about the Mahabodhi society, Calcutta. The society said, it is not Buddha and his Dhamma, but Ambedkar and his Dhamma. They indicate that Ambedkar almost deviated from original Buddhism.
11. W.N. Kuber, *Dr. Ambedkar: A Critical Study,* New Delhi: People's Publishing House, 1973, p. 96.
12. Gauri Vishwanathan, *Outside the Fold,* New Delhi: Oxford University Press, 1998.
13. Ibid.
14. Jayshree Gokhale-Turner, *From Confrontation to Concession: Dalit Movement in Maharashtra,* Mumbai: Popular Prakashan, 1993, pp. 172–3.

15. Zelliot, op. cit.
16. Vasant Moon, *Madhya-Prant ani Vaharadatil Ambedkarrpura Asprunchi Chalval* (Marathi), Pune: Sugawa Publications, 1987, p. 107.
17. *Bahiskrut Bharat*, Dept. of Education, Government of Maharashtra.
18. Moon, op. cit.
19. Krishna Kirwale, *Ambedkari Shahiri: Ek Shodh*, Pune: Nalanda Publication (Marathi), 1992, p. 107.
20. *Janata*, 13 June 1936.
21. Arun Kamble, ed., *Babasahebanche Janatatil Agralekh*, Mumbai: Granthali, 1986, p. 63.
22. Ibid., p. 70.
23. Ibid., p. 74.
24. Gauri, op. cit.
25. Ibid., p. 212.
26. Ibid., p. 234.
27. B.R. Ambedkar, *What Congress and Gandhi have done to the Untouchable*, Bombay: Thacker and Company, 1949.
28. *Writings and Speeches of Ambedkar*, vol. 5, p. 471.
29. Vitthal Sathe, op. cit.
30. These are Buddhist women who have organized them in a Buddhist organization called Panchsheel Mahila Mandal in the Panchgaon village in Tellhara Block of Akola district in Maharashtra.

16

Lavani, Tamasha, Loknatya and the Vicissitudes of Patronage

VEENA NAREGAL

INTRODUCTION

This paper looks at the divergent patterns underlying the careers of two major practitioners of the *lavani/tamasha* traditions in the first half of the twentieth century. These two instances provide two contrasting models through which the popular *tamasha* form entered the Marathi cultural sphere emerging around the working class culture of Bombay in the years just before the onset of the First World War to approximately the decade after Independence. This period arguably was the most assertive phase of the history of the Bombay working class. The *lavani* and *tamasha* have had an important presence in the cultural life of the Deccan, with a long and evolving history of at least three centuries, and despite the inroads of film and electronic media, have been attracting renewed patronage in the past decade or so from at least one important political family in Maharashtra, the Mohite-Patils of Akluj. The *lavani* and *tamasha* are particularly interesting as they make for a significant field through which to analyze avenues of patronage available towards the making of a regional modern popular culture to vernacular forms bereft of national recognition in the 1950s and early 1960s—the period when the cultural policies of the Indian nation-state were enunciated. In large measure, the momentum and logic to these processes whereby the regional/national were mapped onto earlier boundaries of *marga/desi* was provided by cultural hierarchies and political alliances that were put in place through the negotiation of interests between the colonial state and native groups through the nineteenth century. Performative forms such as the *lavani* and *tamasha* that are integrally associated with lower-caste groups stood only a delayed chance of—if at all—making their mark in the arena of colonial print culture. And yet despite being marginalized by print and forced to adapt to these circumstances, these forms continued to survive because they remained pertinent to the cultural experience of large numbers who remained excluded from the provisions of colonial literacy programs.

Given the long history of the *lavani* and the *tamasha*, as a cultural historian, I find it important to ask both (a) when and how shifts in the form and its status have occurred, and equally, (b) to understand the perceptions of various segments within the Marathi cultural world *vis-à-vis* the significance and potential of the *lavani* and *tamasha.* My aim within this paper is far more limited; however, a little later I will flag the wider implications of an inquiry along these lines. Mainly performed by low-caste communities such as the Mang-Matang, Mahar and Kolhatti communities, the repertoire and status of the *lavani* grew during the Peshwa period as it attracted elite patronage first as performances meant to entertain the Maratha armies during their long military campaigns. The forms then gradually entered aristocratic households and court arenas. With the colonial period, came not only loss of this patronage from elite circles but also a revaluation of these forms within official colonial and upper-caste native discourse as "low", "vulgar" and "obscene", all of which severely affected their reception but did not erase their popular following. There are *lavanis* in several regional languages including Hindi, Kannada, Gujarati and Telugu about which I know nothing —but mention this to point to the spatial spread of the form, which combined with the fact of its elite patronage, can potentially rupture any easy grading of the *lavani* and *tamasha* on the scale of high low culture or even against the *marga/desi* distinction.

I will not go into much detail here about the forms except to point towards the two main contextual variations within which the *lavani* is practiced.[1] Firstly, there are the *sangeet bari* "parties" which comprise of four or five women and their accompanists.

These "parties" are mostly managed by women and perform *lavanis* and other music and dance numbers over a 45 minute slot every night against one-year contracts at *sangeet bari* theaters, where they live during that period. Incidentally the numbers of such theaters have increased significantly in the last decade or so, a story that will have to be told separately. It doesn't require a great deal of insight to make the connection between the *sangeet baris* and *kotha* culture. Besides, *dholki phads* are the other type of groups that perform the *lavani.* The latter are much larger, presently often numbering over a 150 people in the case of the well-known troupes, and involve large budgets. *Dholki phads* are basically touring companies that hire artistes and labor on monthly salaries and travel to perform as many shows as they can find contracts for over a nine-month period between Dussehra to the summer month of *Chaitra* in the Hindu calendar. The *dholki phads* perform the full-length *tamasha,* which comprises of several discrete capsules within a single show that typically starts after 10 p.m. and lasts till about 3 a.m. This format of the *tamasha,* particularly, with the inclusion of the *vag*—basically a full-length prose drama that can extend over a few hours—has been evolving over the last 150 years or so.[2] More or less contemporaneous, then, with the *sangeet natak,* it is interesting to speculate about the formal and aesthetic differentiation that occurred between the two generic formats, one that came to be seen as a befitting expression of a reformed culturally distinctive, modern Marathi theatrical practice, and the other as epitomizing a "low" and licentious taste whose popularity could—if at all—be conceded, when viewed through a censorious gaze. The most popular parts of the *tamasha* in the recent past have been the *rang bazi* which today is made up of mainly traditional and Marathi filmi *lavanis* and Hindi film songs and the *vag,* whose importance is now said to be declining; yet, there still are troupes that offer the *vag* as their special attraction.

One of the objectives of this paper is also to open up a discussion about the space for caste-specific *desi* traditions to recast themselves as the basis for re-making regional cultures along modern/democratic/popular lines. To focus on the careers of two very differently-remembered *lavanikaars,* Patthe Bapurao and Annabhau Sathe, as I wish to do here, is important because it allows us to raise questions about the ways in which (i) the work of these men and their legacy has been embodied within different strands of political and scholarly discourse and (ii) these caste-based forms have been inscribed into a nominally inclusive public sphere that officially disclaims the logic of *jati.* These processes need to be ultimately viewed against the dual contexts of the articulation of upper and low-caste agendas within the regional political formation and, simultaneously, of official cultural agendas befitting the post-colonial nation state in the decades after Independence. We know something about the ways regional traditions have entered the national arenas of high culture instituted through the setting up of the patronage system that included the Sangeet Natak Akademi, National School of Drama and cultural programming on AIR, DD (Cherian 2005). On the other hand, we also know generally about forms that have rapidly languished because they could not stake a claim to these avenues of official patronage, a decline that has been part of the story of rapid depletion of regional cultural repertoires that post-colonial intellectuals writing in the vernaculars have been acutely aware.[3] There are of course important exceptions—for now—to the story of this decline sans official patronage, of which Habib Tanvir's work is a towering example (Deshpande 2004). The case of the *lavani* and *tamasha* sits somewhere in between these two main scenarios outlined above. Despite the avenues afforded by its enduring popularity, the exposure of many creative people involved with the Indian People's Theatre Association (IPTA) in the late 1940s and 1950s to the *lavani* and *tamasha,* these forms neither found their Habib Tanvir nor found it amenable to assert their claims as a "classical" form in the post-Independence period. That this was the case in the state of Maharashtra with its history of early lower-caste assertion reflects at once upon the regional structures of dominance, the cultural orientation of the Dalit leadership, as well as the effective marginalization of the Dalit movement at least until the recent past from all major Marathi cultural arenas, of which theater enjoyed a unique and central importance. Various progressive Marathi writers, critics and theater personalities have either dismissed the *lavani* and *tamasha* as devoid of political and contemporary potential, or when they have used it, it has been mostly by way of appropriating some of its elements at an experimental level for technical embellishment or to provide cultural authenticity, basically, without necessarily caring to engage with their history or with the few exceptional attempts that have been made to radicalize the *tamasha.* For a host of as yet unexplored reasons, the *lavani* and *tamasha* proved recalcitrant to the kind of comprehensive reformist initiatives that other equally "degraded" performative traditions such as *kathak* and *bharat natyam* lent themselves to. Had that happened, we may have well seen *lavani* included in the canon of classical dance forms alongside *bharat natyam, kathak, oddissi,* etc.—and suffering the consequences of being authorized for national-level patronage. But things never came to that, and the *lavani* and *tamasha* have had to survive on a string of symbolic gestures from successive governments and ambitious political aspirants in the state.

As these questions amply suggest, neither patronage nor the survival of reputations within public memory are simple matters. Elite patronage or participation in subaltern forms can never be equated with approval or easily as affording a resolution of social cleavages. In fact, often patronage foreshadows attempts to appropriate or regulate that which causes simultaneous fascination and distaste, and therefore, anxiety. If anything, this is particularly true of the *tamasha* and *lavani.* Within the *tamasha* tradition today, the Brahman poet-performer, Patthe Bapurao enjoys a pre-eminent iconic status whereas the subaltern legacy of Annabhau's poetry and performance is all but forgotten, even as his renaming of the *tamasha* as *loknatya* [people's theater] has since been widely accepted by *tamasha* artistes as a more dignified label, but who are otherwise totally unmindful of his contribution. How do we read the ironies of this situation?

One way to address the challenging questions raised by the immense popularity, chronological proximity along with the disparity in their posthumous reputations of the two *lavanikaars* I want to discuss would be to usefully look at the nature of support or approval that they received from political elites and leadership from different quarters. In our times, as potential governments-in-the-making, political parties are as important as states as sources of patronage. The record of support for these forms from various political leaderships demonstrates the same uneasy mix of elite fascination and distaste that I spoke about earlier. Aware of their popular appeal, various parties including Satyashodak/non-Brahman and Ambedkarite groups, the Socialist Rashtra Seva Dal (RSD) and the Communist *kalapathaks* have used these popular genres for effective mobilization. Instances could be multiplied, but key examples would include the campaigns of the 1942 Satara Rebellion, Dalit assertion in Vidarbha and Marathwada areas in the pre-1947 years or subsequent decades and the critical 1952 and 1957 elections in the Samyukta Maharashtra movement (Omvedt 1976; Guru 2001; Rege 2001). However, it appears that much of this attention was grudgingly given, only ephemeral or simply opportunistic. Gopal Guru's important essay points out the disillusionment of many Dalit perfomers and composers who toiled as cultural activists in the Ambedkarite *jalsa* troupes and *kalapathaks.* We can speak of a remarkable and almost continuous tradition of work by low-caste writers/performers such as Kisan Phaguji Bansode in the 1920s, Kerubuwa Gaikwad in the 1940s and later, Annabhau Sathe from early 1940s until his death in 1960 and his younger contemporary, Nilu Phule. And yet, there appears a strong resistance to theorize, debate or even acknowledge their contribution within the movements that they saw themselves as part of. Thus in writing about the RSD *kalapathaks* in his autobiography, *Mee S.M.*, S.M. Joshi does not once mention the *lavani* and *tamasha,* or the Mahars and Mangs, leave alone admitting the possibility of using these forms for broad-based empowerment of these marginalized communities (Joshi, S.M. 1975). Similarly, in writing what he admits was a solicited piece to Annabhau's collection of *shahiri,* S.A. Dange's highly abstract and largely prescriptive introduction—to anticipate the discussion in section on Annabhau Sathe below—seems engaged in writing-out Annabhau's own vision of his work as located as much in the subalternity of caste as class; rather he hopes the introduction will prove useful in helping Annabhau's poetry to become truly revolutionary by overcoming his "inadequate" sense of history (Dangle 1998: 1139-46). This marginalization of lower-caste performers, even as some forms are appropriated for political, commercial or creative ends, is indeed part of a larger story of how the "backward-looking" discourse of caste has been, at once, variously subordinated within the "higher" discourses of nationalism, development, modernization and citizenship, even as it has been exploited in non-transformative ways by parties/ leaders across the political spectrum since at least the 1940s. For my purposes here, it is important to stress the extent to which upper-caste elite attitudes have proved hegemonic in containing initiatives that could have emerged into alternate modes of engagement with these popular lower-caste forms.

I will conclude the opening section by briefly introducing the two major protagonists of the account I am trying to lay out here. Born in a Brahman family, Patthe Bapurao (b. Sridhar Kulkarni, 1866-1945) and Annabhau Sathe (1921-69) from an illiterate Matang family, both men came from the Satara-Sangli region to make their careers as successful and extremely popular *lavanikaars* and *tamasha* artistes in early and mid-twentieth-century Bombay respectively. Sridhar Kulkarni already saw himself as a *lavanikaar*, and came to Bombay almost expressly to make a career in the *tamasha* theaters, where his success made him into Patthe Bapurao. On the other hand proud and talented, Tukaram later Annbahau Sathe had played with a *tamasha* troupes belonging to his extended family on his mother's side, but clearly, had little idea of any future as a writer or a performing artist when drought forced the family to make the long journey to Bombay on foot, probably in the early 1930s (Sathe 1980).[4] Coming from very different backgrounds, Bombay played a very important role in shaping their careers and reputations, though, in different ways, in each case. Having made a name in Bombay helped both men acquire an enthusiastic following throughout the state. Further, the city is thematized in important but different ways in their work, for as I will show, Patthe Bapurao's relationship with the city never had the politically engaged qualities that characterized Annabhau's understanding of Bombay. All this is important because for all effective purposes, the *tamasha* story is invisible within scholarly accounts of the Bombay working class as well as within the way the history of theater in Bombay, both in Hindi and Marathi, has been imagined.[5]

Patthe Bapurao's career, which roughly spanned the years 1905-36 visibly pointed to the existence of a "low-brow" performance circuit that spanned city and country by this time. This echoes an important pattern I have traced elsewhere, where I have argued that an important reason for the success of the touring upper-caste *natak-mandalis* that emerged from the 1840s onwards was because they performed a crucial function in forging cultural links between provincial elites and the new circles of colonial-educated, urban intellectuals in Bombay and Pune, in the process, also combining traditional forms such as the *pauranik khel* and the emerging "high" genre of the "bookish" or printed *natak* (Naregal 2001). *Tamasha* groups had been visiting the city since at least the 1890s, though there is almost no mention of them in newspaper or other printed records of the time. Patthe Bapurao's career demonstrated that there was by the early years of the twentieth century an alternative performance circuit, extending across rural areas, particularly western Maharashtra, to the working class areas in Girangaon and other Marathi-speaking areas in Bombay. Further, the Grant Road Theatre or the Play House had been an important and prestigious venue of the Bombay stage since its opening in 1846. However, by this time, it had become better known as "Pila House", and was now an important *tamasha* venue. How this came about remains unclear as the relation between the performance circuits frequented by upper-caste *mandalis* and touring *tamasha* groups respectively is entirely unexplored. Besides the Pila House, a chain of about 19 theaters, mostly owned by the Bangdiwaleseth family—about whom again not much seems readily known apart from the fact that they were Muslim traders—stretched northwards from Crawford Market, along the docks, across the mill district to the edges of Girgaum. Interestingly, it seems that the Kamathi community, which had provided construction labor for Crawford market, and with whom Jyotiba Phule had developed some political links, may have thrown up some of the early contractors on the *tamasha* circuit. There is also evidence that the Bombay *tamasha* theaters were frequented by many Maratha political aspirants during their visits to the city, as indeed is true for the rash of *sangeet bari* theaters that have mushroomed since the 1990s in various parts of Maharashtra, particularly, Pune, Sholapur, Satara and Nasik districts.

In contrast to Patthe Bapurao, Annabhau was still illiterate when the family reached Bombay after a long and tortuous journey in the early 1930s. Earning his way in Bombay through a wide variety of jobs on the city's casual labor market, Annabhau showed his mettle by emerging as an early radical Dalit writer and a leading figure on the cultural and political scene in Bombay from the early 1940s to the mid-1960s. A founding member of the Lalbawta Kalpathak of the Communist Party, and an important mobilizer in the Samyukta Maharashtra campaign, Annabhau went on to produce some 14 *loknatyas* or *tamashas*, 10 *povadas*, one play, a travelogue to Russia, 22 short- story collections, some 30 novels, including the best-selling *Fakira* [currently in its 19th edition], and 12 screenplays. He courageously defied the hostile ban on *tamasha* shows during Morarji Desai's tenure as Home Minister in the Bombay government in the late 1940s by boldly renaming his popular performances as *loknatya*. As a leading activist and constant, presence during the campaign for Samyukta Maharashtra, he invested personally in the city's future, and could never consider leaving the city even after he was disillusioned with the Communist Party and with the shape of politics after 1960. In contrast, from all accounts, Patthe Bapurao made little attempt to come back to Bombay once his performing career had declined. Annabhau's audiences came from similar working-class and Marathi speaking loçations as Patthe Bapurao's. And yet, since he performed mostly in the contexts of public meetings, election campaigns and workers' rallies, one may speculate that the appeal of his work was wider than that of Patthe Bapurao's, although ironically, today it is the latter who is remembered and recognized within the performing traditions, even by artistes. Patthe Bapurao spent the last decade or so of his life in poverty in Pune, but nevertheless, saw his work published and hailed by the Pune literati before he died in 1945. Recognition for Annabhau's work has been belated and mostly nominal, and these efforts have been mostly part of the gestures in the 1990s to appease the OBC constituency in Maharashtra.[6]

The next two sections will successively focus on relevant

highlights from the careers of Patthe Bapurao and Annabhau Sathe. In doing this, I will implicitly argue that their careers demonstrate two contrasting strategies that attempt to reinscribe/efface the category of caste in presenting the *tamasha* within the public domain. The brief concluding section will then offer some preliminary explanations as to why the less progressive legacy of Patthe Bapurao has outlived Annabhau's far more engaged exertions as a *lavanikaar.*

A BRAHMAN AESTHETE TURNS MAHAR?: THE CASE OF PATTHE BAPURAO

Patthe Bapurao was apparently born in 1866 into a poor *purohit* household in the village of Harnaksh Rethare in what is currently Sangli district. As a boy, Sridhar developed a great fondness for singing the *ovi,* generally identified as women's verse form, and also showed a remarkable ability in composing his own verses at an early age. A gifted student at school, however, his musical and poetic inclinations soon attracted him to the sounds of the *tamasha* emanating from the village Maharwada. Not surprisingly, his family was not happy when he began composing for his new lower-caste friends. The family was first able to secure support from the Aundh court for Sridhar to continue his education there, and then it seems his talents won him the favor of the Baroda court and a monthly stipend at the Kalabhavan. However, this happy situation ended prematurely when his frequent association with visiting *tamasha* artistes incurred his patron's displeasure. Sridhar decided not to heed these warnings, instead he chose to give up his position and returned to his village.

This is interesting because it also suggests that court patronage for forms such as the *lavani* now designated as "low" may have been shrinking in keeping with the cultural hierarchies being put in place at the time. This, of course, was not the first instance of a Brahman poet taking to the *lavani* form. We are aware of at least two well-known Brahman *lavanikaars* from the Peshwa period, Ramjoshi (1758-1813), who came from a learned family and Anant Phandi, who belonged to a Yajurvedi Brahman family. It would be useful here to extend a point made in the previous section: patronage for the *lavani* and *tamasha* during the Peshwai seems to have been a complex affair. Evidently available patronage would attract upper-caste composers, yet it is open to question in what ways this necessarily benefited the status of the genres or the communities who practiced them. Elite patronage or participation did not generally redeem these forms as a socially acceptable profession for upper-caste literati, particularly in a culture where writing skills remained scarce and were zealously guarded. In other words, if at all, patronage was only obliquely meant to acknowledge the strength of these performing traditions, their enjoyment in elite arenas simply recast them as part of elite consumption. Patronage for these lower-caste forms may have helped build political legitimacy, their incorporation into the regime of privileged consumption kept them within the normative frameworks of brahmanical sanction that the Peshwa ruling elite seemed concerned with advancing. Although Patthe Bapurao belonged to a time long after the Peshwai had ended, I would argue that significant episodes from Patthe Bapurao's career seem to exemplify these propensities within traditional patronage. Both the emerging public arena and Patthe Bapurao's reputation are characterized by a high degree of ambivalence that needs to be recognized. The emergence of a working class popular cultural arena thus also saw the reiteration of caste boundaries and a renewal of an earlier cultural dispensation that was displaced—but not—obliterated by the new norms introduced via colonialism. All this meant that the adoption of a subaltern genre by a Brahman performer, then, did not inevitably demonstrate a democratic mind-set, but could remain largely a basis for the display of upper-caste virtuosity and reinforcing a parochial agenda. A reference a little later on to the very different emphases and tone of the *lavanis* on Mumbai that he and Annabhau composed will highlight my point about the inherent conservatism of Patthe Bapurao's legacy (Nalge 2003: 36-40; Dangle 1998: 64-5).

Soon after his return from Baroda, Sridhar decided to seek his future as a *tamasha* artiste, and probably had few options other than to come to Bombay. It is not clear when he made the move, but it could have been some time in the 1890s, when he would have been in his twenties. Existing accounts of his life make no mention of his early years in Bombay but it was probably not long before Patthe Bapurao had established himself as a performing artiste at the *tamasha* venues in Bombay with a reputation for a lifestyle of luxury and flair. Soon he also met Pavla (1870-1939), a Mahar woman dancer supposedly of great beauty and talent from Sangamner, who had apparently come to Bombay with another troupe. At this time, it was still apparently not at all common for women to perform on the *tamasha* stage. Pavla and Patthe Bapurao began performing together, and also began to openly live together in flamboyant style. This created quite a stir, something that Patthe Bapurao didn't seem particularly averse to. He seemed to instinctively know that such an act of transgression would only enhance their appeal on stage. Initially, the couple encountered antagonism that, quite interestingly, was most marked from their fellow-artistes from Maratha and other Mahar troupes, who refused to perform with them, because of which the shows had to be temporarily halted (Jintikar 1954: 13). But the hunch proved right in the long term as there were few signs of the audience demand to see them abating. Not knowing how to end this impasse, apparently Patthe Bapurao called a meeting with his theater bosses, where he is said to have proposed that shows be held in the open to accommodate larger numbers against inexpensive tickets so that they could put up money to support him and Pavla on a substantial monthly remuneration. Considered an outrageous demand within the *tamasha* circuit of the time, it showed that Patthe Bapurao was quite uncannily aware of his star-like appeal. And to prove him right, the crowds to watch him and Pavla only seemed to grow.

All this however also gave rise to a chaotic and unruly situation, in the midst of which, rumors escalated in Bombay that Patthe Bapurao—through his association with Pavla—had "converted" to a Mahar. The resulting situation seems to have led a paranoid police force, possibly at the behest of others, to file a case against Patthe Bapurao for inciting public disorder.[7] The court hearing for this case apparently created a sensation: when questioned if indeed he had become a Mahar, reveling in all the attention in the courtroom, Patthe Bapurao is said to have invited the judge to visit the theater to hear his answer on the question. Finally, addressing a full house on the set date, Patthe Bapurao is said to have declared that true artistes had no caste, but added that on account of his love for Pavla and her art, he had indeed become Mahar as there was no way she could become a Brahman.

Though widely recounted the story could still well be apocryphal. The facticity of this litigation is no doubt important, and yet even if the court case didn't actually occur, the story still remains important as most possibly having been invented by Patthe Bapurao as part his self-narrative. It then was clearly part of the myth underlying the resurrection of his reputation at the hands of the Pune literati in the early 1940s, several years after his career had ended, in the years leading up to his death in 1945, and thus may contain indispensable clues about how the poet's self-projection fed into the valorized and accepted common sense about Patthe Bapurao's significance within the *lavani/tamasha* tradition. In either case what we have to grapple with is how to read this self-proclamation by a Brahman poet at the height of his popularity of having turned Mahar, and thus of seemingly having voluntarily relinquished his high-caste status? In itself it would seem like a startling, if not, a most radical forfeiture of privileged upper-caste status. Yet, as I have been suggesting, this seemingly sensationally democratic gesture needs to be contextualized against the tenor of autobiographical references available within Patthe Bapurao's *lavanis* that also bear clues as to how he may have perceived himself within the larger cultural milieu. Consider the opening verses of his autobiographical *lavani*, composed towards the end of his life:

shrestha varna mee brahman asuni sovale
thevle ghaluni ghadi
mashaal dharli hati tamashachi
laaz lavli deshoghadi

(Nalge 2003: 11)[8]

Meant as a grand opening, their effect is reinforced as we move into the text as, increasingly, Patthe Bapurao comes across as egocentric, even proud of his own recklessness and with a definite fondness for hyperbole. Eventually we come to verse 10, where we find the lines:

ek vikali, baajaari tatadi
ryn devuni Maharin anali[9]

—a disconcerting reference to his life with Pavla, for it seems to clearly invoke the not uncommon upper-caste view of low-caste women as an acquirable commodity—a point that was to be echoed in an episode we come to below, viz., Ambedkar's seemingly dogmatic refusal to accept Patthe Bapurao's symbolic gesture of political support. Whatever the politics of Ambedkar's own position, surely the conservative tone of these sentiments warn us against any happy exaggeration of Patthe Bapurao's claims to have "truly become" a Mahar. A summary reading which is as much as can be afforded for the argument here of Patthe Bapurao's *Mumbaichi lavani*, only accentuates the need for such caution.[10] Meant to re-create the successive scenes of an imaginary carriage-ride through Bombay, the *lavani* is in the voice of the male lover promising to gift his beloved with every joy that Mumbai can offer. It is full of bold and picturesque detail and captures the exhilarating variety and momentum of life in Bombay. For a large part, it is a catalogue of the beautiful women and other pleasures and indulgences that the city holds out. He describes many landmarks, places and other luxuries that he playfully offers to buy up as gifts in a great rush of love, including the docks, the playhouse, the bungalows on Walkeshwar, fine gold ornaments and so on. In short, the city is celebrated for offering itself as the scene of multiple pleasures, limitless desire and indiscriminate enjoyment. All this seems to resonate with and extend my previous point about the privileged limits upon which hinged the upper-caste enjoyment of and participation in the *lavani*. Further examples show that Patthe Bapurao viewed his lower caste fellow-*tamasgirs* with evident disdain, and was wont to alluding to them in his verse in distinctly contemptuous terms, thus bolstering the impression of the inherent conservatism of Patthe Bapurao's world-view. The next section sets these sentiments against Annabhau Sathe's perceptions of the city in his *Mumbaichi lavani*, the underlying assumptions of which also inform much of his writing and verse: the contrast will be only too evident.

That brings me to the final episode I want to recount with respect to Patthe Bapurao's life. We fast-forward to late 1927, the time of Ambedkar's *satyagraha* at Mahad. Realizing that the campaign would require funds, Ambedkar had called for donations and contributions from well-wishers of the cause, including Dalits and caste Hindus. Besides individuals who responded, several *sangeet natak mandalis* [which tended to be homogeneously upper-caste] offered to donate proceeds of sponsored shows to the Mahad fund. Hearing of these donations from proscenium theater groups, Patthe Bapurao apparently contacted Ambedkar saying he too wished to make a contribution. A meeting took place on 10 September 1927, where Patthe Bapurao is said to have arrived, magnificently attired, escorting two attractive Mahar women, one on either side (Khairmode 1968: 141-2).[11] When asked to accept the proceeds from eight of their shows, an angry Ambedkar refused. He returned the money, much to the bewilderment of Patthe Bapurao and even some of his own followers. The reason Ambedkar apparently gave was that it was utterly insulting and degrading for him to accept money made through a systematic exploitation of Mahar women. Interpreting Ambedkar's position here is not easy. Growing up in a Mahar household, Ambedkar would have been well acquainted with the *lavani* tradition, and equally familiar with the stigma attached to it. Further, it seems pertinent also to allude here to Ambedkar's well-known exhortations to Mahar women activists that they adopt the demure middle-class style of draping the sari, which—as we know—was a fashion that evolved in relation to strong anxieties latent within upper-caste reformist discourse about the need to clothe female bodies in "respectable" and culturally distinctive ways before they could be admitted to public spaces or accepted as political subjects.

Yet, despite all this there remains some evidence that Ambedkar did not merely see the *lavani* as synonymous with the appropriation of lower-caste female sexuality. Also it must be pointed out that Ambedkar was an avid and sophisticated reader, who enjoyed literature and theater, even the work of Gadkari

(Kamble 2001: 38-42).[12] Nevertheless, unlike Annabhau—who was formally uneducated—despite the work of the *jalsa* troupes in propagating Ambedkarite ideas, and not by mere accident, Ambedkar himself seems to have persistently refused the possibility of investing these vibrant performative traditions with a subaltern cultural pride. That they could have potentially contributed to the emancipation process, particularly to the important possibility of forging an alliance among the various backward castes such as the Mahars, Mangs, Kolhattis and Chambhars is not a prospect that Ambedkar seems to have ever entertained. No doubt taking their cue from Ambedkar, later Dalit leaders of the different factions of the Republican Party of India (RPI) too, have shown little interest in engaging with such matters, even as the Dalit movement has been plagued by persistent factionalism. Moreover its inability to mount an effective theoretical or political critique of the exclusive and hierarchical basis of caste consciousness have remained serious challenges the movement has faced at least from Ambedkar's time. The next sections will implicitly raise the question of the consequences of the attenuation of lower-caste cultural tradition, also actively and consistently abetted by the Dalit leadership and how this may have proved corrosive for the prospect of a progressive popular culture in the vernacular and contributed to the above political scenario. In the light of this discussion, the next section will consider Annabhau Sathe's career as *lavanikaar* and *loknatya* writer, and examine the nature of support available to his work from various political quarters.

THE CASE OF ANNABHAU SATHE: A "PEOPLE'S" POET?

Annabhau's work too belongs to the urban milieu of Bombay. However, it bears the mark of a radically different historical moment and a sensibility intent on challenging social hierarchies in ways that far exceeded the thrust of Patthe Bapurao's seemingly radical postures. The post-Depression years were political tumultous times in Bombay, as in the rest of the country. They brought another wave of migrants from the famine-stricken hinterland to the city. Arriving in Bombay at this juncture,

Annabhau would have been aware of a rising scale of political confrontations on several fronts: the ongoing struggle of the Bombay workers, the persistent state repression aimed at curbing the significant degree of Communist influence among them, the growing momentum of the civil disobedience movement, the temple entry campaigns launched by Ambedkar and the escalating dissonance between him and the Congress on that account. Athough as a child Annabhau had played with *tamasha* troupes before coming to Bombay, evidence suggests he embarked on his career as composer and writer from the early 1940s as a result of his radicalization through his experiences in Bombay and contact with the significant Communist presence in Girangaon. Raj Chandavarkar's work has tellingly documented how the Communist Party trade unions earned a significant following among the Bombay textile mill workforce during this period by being responsive to everyday struggles and local issues that the workers had to confront both at their workplace and in their neighborhoods (Chandavarkar 1998). Annabhau's work and involvement in establishing the Communist Lalbawta Kalapathak is eloquent testimony to that influence and its inherent limitations.

Against this context then, Annabhau's first composition was a *povada* on Nanking, apparently composed in 1942 but currently unavailable, followed by the ones on Stalingrad and Berlin, which are said to date to 1942 and 1946 respectively. *Povadas* memorializing current events on the national scene came next and these included *Bengalchi haak* (1944), *Punjab dilliche dange* (1947), *Telanganacha sangram* (1947), *Maharashtrachi parampara* (1947), *Mumbaiche Kaamgar* (1949). In the context of the discussion here, however, I will dwell on two of his major *lavani* compositions thematizing Bombay, namely, *Mumbaichi lavani* and *Majhi maina gavavar rahili.* The opening lines of Annabhau's *Mumbaichi lavani*

mumbait unchavari malabar hill indrapuri
kuberanchi vasti tithe sukh bhogati
parelaat rahanaare raat divas raabnaare
milel te khavuni ghaam galati

(Dangle 1998: 64-65)[13]

set up a stark contrast between the lifestyle afforded to the affluent on the idyllic heights of Malabar hill as against the lives of the toiling poor in Parel, who survive literally by the sweat of their brow. (This depiction may be easily consistent with the representations of the city in IPTA-influenced Bombay cinema of the time, but would count as more unusual within the world of contemporaneous Marathi writing.) Here too, Mumbai is the scene of a flurry of activities, but our attention is repeatedly drawn to the deprivation that characterizes the lives of many of its residents, particularly those living in *chawls*—within walls unadorned by fresh paint, while their children play in the dirt outside. The abiding images in the description converge around the extreme contradictions of an environment where men prey on each other, either exploiting or getting exploited [*manasala manus khata lutata ani lutali jaata*], making Mumbai a city seething with energy, prone to periodic eruptions, simply waiting to explode:

teen lakh lok eka jagi rahati
bhadkun uthati maadhiadhi dangekhor hovun kadhi
aapsamadhe karun gardi mudade padati[14]

In a very different vein from Patthe Bapurao's *lavani* discussed above, *Majhi maina gavavar rahili* describes the bustle of the city in the voice of the lover who has recently arrived there in search of work after leaving his beloved behind in his village home—like so many before him:

ya mumbait gardi bekaaranchi tyaat bharti jhali majhi . . .
hee mumbai yantranchi, tantranchi, jagnaraanchi, maranaaranchi, shendichi, daadhichi hudsongaadichi, nylonchya ani georgettechya talam saadichi
(Dangle 1998: 61-2)[15]

Written in the midst of the campaign for Samyukta Maharashtra, the love theme in the *lavani* is thus also an allegory for the political anguish felt by the Marathi working class over the possibility that they would have to accept the separation of Bombay from the new state of Maharashtra.

Besides his *lavanis* and *povadas*, Annabhau also used the *vag* of the *tamasha* form in extremely powerful and successful ways as part of his tireless work for the Samyukta Maharashtra campaign. Written in 1945, Annabhau's first *tamasha*, '*Aklechi*

Gosht' [A Matter of Intelligence] was built around the story of how a hardworking and politically aware farmer is able to outwit the corrupt duo of the village trader and moneylender, it proved immensely popular with audiences across the state. As has been well-documented, the Congress revised its stance *vis-à-vis* the demand for a unified Maharashtra state with Bombay as its capital only after the debacle it faced in the 1957 elections (Phadke 1975). Until that point, Congress governments in the state had responded with hostile and repressive measures, aimed particularly towards efforts to mobilize the Bombay working class. The huge following that performances of the Lalbawta Kalapathak elicited provoked the Bombay government into imposing a ban on Annabhau's work on more than one occasion in the late 1940s and 1950s. *Majhi Mumbai* (1948) dramatizes the conflicting claims over Bombay city made by Munimji, a Gujarati *bania* and an articulate mill-worker named Vishnu. Known for his strong views against Maharastrian claims over Bombay, Home Minister, Morarji Desai, decided to overrule the license issued by the police department, and banned its performance. However, accounts suggest that helped by covert support from a sympathetic police-force, neither Annabhau's troupe nor the huge audiences gathering to watch the play were deterred by the ban. In 1952, as Chief Minister, Morarji Desai once again imposed ban orders on '*Lokmantrayacha Daura*' [The (People's) Minister's Tour], Annabhau's satirical expose of the duplicity and inefficacy of the first Congress cabinet in the state ; yet again, performances continued despite arrest orders being issued against Annabhau (Gurav 1999: 147-60; Sathe 1980: 97-103).[16]

At one level, the demographic profile of Girangaon may have allowed the Communist and the larger leadership to project the Samyukta Maharashtra campaign as a class struggle between the Maharashtrian working class and the Gujarati *bania*-capitalists, one which seemingly succeeded in briefly overcoming ideological and caste differences to win unanimous support among the Marathi public. Still, the role of the Bombay Communists in this campaign clearly represented a gradual shift in the party's ideological approach towards its constituency, and this awaits careful analysis. Scholars have speculated that this tilt towards the politics of vernacular/regional nationalism was dictated by the desire to recover some of the ground lost in the early 1940s when the Party refused to oppose Britain's determination to involve Indian troops in its war efforts or to extend its support to the Congress led Quit India movement (Chandavarkar 2005). Even if definitive views on the subject need to be backed by further work, it is clear that Annabhau's work and involvement with the Communist Party seems to have overlapped squarely with the time-frames of this transition and the underlying issues at its crux. Provisionally, it might be useful to extend Raj Chandavarkar's point about Communist strategy in the 1930s being moulded by the militancy and expectations of the mill-workers to this later period when the Party possibly sensed in the mood of the Bombay working class a ripe opening to broaden their influence to rest of the state via the campaign for Samyukta Maharashtra.

And yet, it seemed, such a plan suffered from major drawbacks as there seemed serious limits upon how far the Communist leadership would go in conceding the significance of political parameters that did not fit into schemes of Marxist orthodoxy, most important of these being the issue of caste. Testimonies of several erstwhile activists—some of them from low-caste backgrounds—who spent many committed years with Leftist trade unions in Bombay have amply endorsed this failing.[17] Caste represented something of an anomaly to the Left leadership, as exemplified by a statement carried in *Kranti*, a newsletter brought out during the 1928 textile strike. Entitled *herapasun savadh raha* [beware of mischief], the statement intended to warn workers about "enemy trouble-makers", who were expected to raise issues of Brahman/non-Brahman difference. Describing anyone who would be susceptible to such "rumours" as "unmanly", the notice asserted that while all Brahmans, Marathas, Mahars and Ghatis were equal [*ek*], still, workers ought to remain unsympathetic to such "secret" and "unseemly whispering".[18] Further it would be apt to elaborate here on Dange's Introduction to the anthology of Annabhau Sathe's work issued in 1952, noting the reasons and manner in which Annabhau's work is commended (Dangle 1998: 1139-46). As a counterpoint, I would also alongside allude to an address that Annabhau made to the Dalit Sahitya Sammelan held in Mumbai in 1958 (Dangle 1998: 1175-8). It is interesting to note while both texts share an understanding about the economic basis of dominance, exploitation and marginality, the term "dalit" figures only once in Dange's essay, and that too to reiterate what he terms the "internationalist" dimension of contemporary Dalit consciousness by which Dange means the ability of the working class to seek out international allies, and which he also commends as the hallmark of the Communist poet. A large section of the short essay is given to recounting the hostility and bias that left-oriented writers and the Communist *kalapathak* have encountered at the hands of the state and the elite Marathi literary establishment respectively. Evidently within this scheme, evidence of persecution counted as superior political capital, and was the most effective proof that Dange could offer of the efficacy and merit of Communist mobilization and as a corollary, of Annabhau's work. Citing the *Dnyaneshwari* and the Mahanubhava literature as outstanding examples, Dange claims the distinction made out between "good" and "ideological" literature to be a false one, for historically true art and dissent have gone hand in hand. He goes on to commend Annabhau's evocative description of the city in *Mumbaichi lavani* as a powerful example of how class politics can inform poetry. Further, Annabhau's *povada, Maharashtrachi parampara* celebrating the cultural and political ethos of the Maharashtrian people is singled out for praise. And yet, oddly, each laudatory remark is immediately checked with qualifying comments about the need for further improvement, and Annabhau is even peremptorily taken to task for not delving beyond conventional interpretations of Marathi history. Despite their most dedicated efforts it seemed that even in the leftist trade union movement, low-caste subaltern activists like Annabhau could not hope to be regarded as providing more than mere, albeit important, cultural labor that was expected to fit pre-given moulds determined by a theoretical elite—thus noting recent deliberations within the Party on the importance of establishing vital links between regional literatures and mass democratic struggles, Dange concludes on the unabashedly patronizing hope that Annabhau and his colleagues will be guided by the Introduction in their future work. While not deviating from the underlying assumptions of the Party position, it is interesting to note Annabhau's forceful foregrounding of caste as class in his opening remarks to an early Dalit Sahitya Sammelan. He points out that a separate literary meeting of this kind was necessitated precisely on account of the widespread tendency to disavow caste as a category of marginality and the implicit refusal to recognize Dalits as comprising a large and distinct class whose cumulative experience and labor effectively constitute the social and cultural foundations of the national fabric who, yet, remain marginalized and invisible within mainstream regional literatures.

As a Dalit intellectual, Annabhau clearly acknowledges his debt to Ambedkar, yet his work seems to strike a perceptibly distinct note from the dominant rhetorical strategies of later Marathi Dalit writers that emphasize Dalit "victimhood" resulting from Brahman treachery and exploitation.[19] If the above discussion explains why Annabhau would have felt marginalized within IPTA (Sathe 1980: 94-5), particularly on account of the highly superior privileges and funding available to the Hindi troupe, in conclusion, it would be useful to speculate on possible reasons that such an artiste remained unacknowledged by the Ambedkar's SCF and the later RPI. That both political parties were dominated by Mahars particularly those who embraced neo-Buddhism under Ambedkar's guidance is well known. As a Dalit leader, it would stand to reason then that Ambedkar would be interested in optimizing the number of Dalit conversions to Buddhism. And yet the evidence suggests that aware as Ambedkar acutely was about the difficulties of creating an inclusive culture proceeding from a caste-based ethos, his own efforts at persuading other Dalit groups as well as the Mahar community to sink their caste rivalries were less than successful. There are several examples now available of Ambedkar's addresses to Chambhar and Mang-Matang assemblies: one of these will have to suffice here (Kamble 2001: 51-4) to suggest why, apart from his alliances with the Communist Party, Annabhau may not have felt welcome in the SCF. Addressing a 1936 Matang *parishad* meeting called to bridge the growing differences among Dalit groups, Ambedkar begins by insisting that he will not exhort

Matangs to convert, as that decision must voluntarily come from the community. However, he does not hesitate to add that it would only be in the Matang self-interest to do so because as a numerically dominant segment, the Mahars needed the Matangs to a lesser degree than vice versa. The rest of the speech elaborates on the political gains Matangs have reaped thanks to the forward-looking and truly generous political leadership of the Mahars, and emphasizes how Matang leaders needed to realize that they had few options other than to accept the liberality of Mahar leadership in seeking to make common cause with minority Dalit groups. The pointed and somewhat unaccommodating tone of the speech is matched by other examples, which at least indicate that the relationship between the Dalit leadership and Matangs was less than receptive and equal. Further, despite the work of the Ambedkari *jalsa* troupes, as Gopal Guru has shown, lower-caste composers in the oral tradition have remained severely marginalized within the turn taken by the Dalit literary movement since the late 1960s and early 1970s (Guru 2001: 160-94), ensuring really that the *lavani* and *tamasha* traditions would remain primarily susceptible to conditions of patronage amenable to a combination of market forces and elite cultural and political considerations.

CONCLUSION

This paper has looked at two distinct configurations within which the popular performance traditions of the caste-based *lavani/ tamasha* forms have made their mark in the modern Marathi public sphere, emphasizing the lack/avenues of patronage the artistes involved in each of these instances had to contend with. Each of these examples represents a different strategy through which that supposedly inadmissible anomaly, the category of caste, was actively disavowed by patrons as a condition of acknowledging the widespread appeal of these forms. Effectively this has resulted in dissociating their popularity from any considerations of marginality of their communities. As a result, aspirations of *lavani* and *tamasha* artistes—both creative as well as material remain totally subordinated to the cultural and political interests of dominant groups. Seen in this light, it is not difficult to understand why the more conservative legacy of Patthe Bapurao may have been preferable to that of Annabhau, and was indeed actively valorized by cultural and political elites in Maharashtra in the 1940s and 1950s, a critical period of cultural and political transition. It is important to remember that Annabhau was already active and known to audiences in the state when the process of recuperating Patthe Bapurao's reputation got underway in the early 1940s. Interestingly, the newly-rebuilt Aryabhushan Theatre, restarted in 1943 as the most prominent *tamasha/sangit bari* venue in Pune, became an important location in this as well as a series of efforts mooted by the state in conjunction with Brahman and Maratha elites to "revive" and reform these forms in the late 1940s and 1950s (Nalge 2003: 92-5; Joshi 1984: 162-5).[20] More work delving into the careers of other popularly followed performers and *tamasha* troupes is needed to further explore the links between shifts in the *lavani/ tamasha* tradition and nature of available patronage. However, sadly but not surprisingly, it seems we can be certain of one fact that namely, at least since the late 1950s, almost every initiative to represent the community of *lavani/ tamasha* performers in cultural and political arenas has come from a range of self-appointed external agents and mediators, surely the reason why upper-caste elite attitudes have proved hegemonic in containing alternate modes of engagement with these popular lower-caste forms.

NOTES

* This paper owes much to Prof. Ram Bapat's unstinting intellectual generosity. I am grateful to Prof. Naito and Prof. Kotani for the invitation to present this paper and for comments from Vidyut Bhagwat, Suhas Palshikar, Umesh Bagade, Gopal Guru and Rajendra Vora; the responsibility for any errors remains mine.

1. These variations need to be historicized, which I shall not be attempting here. For an excellent introduction to the *lavani* and *tamasha,* see Sharmila Rege, "Conceptualising Popular Culture: '*Lavani*' and 'Powada' in Maharashtra", *Economic and Political Weekly,* 16 March 2002, pp. 1038-47.

2. Excluding the political *vags* of the Ambedkari troupes and the Lal Bawta Kalapathak, the three main categories of *vags* are the *pauranik, aitihasik,* and *samajik;* interestingly these anticipate and parallel the narrative genres that figure in early Indian cinema: an area that begs further inquiry.
3. The loss of caste-based cultural repertoires is registered in the Indian English sphere only occasionally. Even if the articulation of caste occurs more frequent in regional literatures, the theme of cultural loss and depletion of vernacular repertoires tends to be mostly posed as a problem *vis-à-vis* the dominance of English and the mass/electronic media. Rarely has the erasure of lower-caste expressive traditions been seen as central to, or even contributing to the depletion of regional language repertoires. For a set of related but not identical reasons, then, a major analysis of the implications of a loss of cultural resources that were previously linked with caste groups is yet to be written either in English or other Indian languages.
4. A biography by Annabhau's brother recounts that the family worked in the labor camps at the site of the Kalyan tunnel when it was being constructed, and that later, Annabhau practiced reading while watching subtitle and credit cards for the silent movies he loved to watch in Mumbai. See Shankarbhau Sathe, *Majhe Bhau Annabhau,* pp. 50-73.
5. Again, there are reasons for this, nevertheless, I'd like to strike an optimistic note by adding that Prithvi Theatre, which in some ways has inherited the IPTA mantle, has been working to explore linkages between the worlds and personages working in Hindi and Marathi theater and that herein may lie hope for at least the prospect of a better understanding of this important slice of cultural history that the *lavani* and *tamasha* represent.
6. Besides the many awards and cultural organizations that have now been floated in Annabhau's name, two major examples of this would be a special commemorative issue of 1 November 1993 of *Lokrajya* a state government fortnightly, published from Bombay, and the collected edition of his works, *Lokshahir Annabhau Sathe Nivdak Sahitya,* issued under state auspices in 1998. After spending 22 years in a Ghatkopar slum, he moved to a modest house in Goregaon, provided by the government in 1968, only a year before he died. Despite a state government award for *Fakira* in 1961, Annabhau died politically isolated, broken and utterly poor, after enduring the humiliation of trying to secure a regular modest pension, and also the ignominy of finding his family name missing from electoral lists in the 1960s on more than one occasion.
7. A word on sources: most of this material is drawn from Jintikar's biographical introduction based on his close friendship with Patthe

Bapurao, which appears as a preface to the collections of his compositions compiled and published in the late 1940s. A first round of systematic efforts to trace these events in native press summaries, newspaper files and government records have yielded no references; I plan to persist with further investigations since dates mentioned in the Jintikar article could be misleading.

8. Translation [mine]: Born a high Brahman/ Yet I put away my sacred thread/ And held the torchlight of the *tamasha*/ (For which I) was put to shame everywhere.
9. Translation [mine]: [having sold] one at a loss/ [I] incurred a debt and b[r]ought a Maharin.
10. See n. 5.
11. I am indebted to Prof. Ram Bapat for this reference.
12. He even occasionally mentioned the *lavani* as an important part of the Marathi literary heritage. See also his review of Prabodhankar Thakre's play, Arun Kamble and Sarojini Vaidya, 'Prastavana', in Arun Kamble, ed., *Janata Patrateel Lekh.*
13. On the heights of Malabar Hill in Bombay [is] Indrapuri
    Here live the gods of wealth in utter comfort
    [while those who] live in Parel toil night and day
    eat what they can find and sweat it out [translation mine].
14. Three lakh inhabitants live in a single place
    they erupt in anger from time to time, [and are] sometimes prone to violence
    [then] in the midst of jostling crowds, some even die [translation mine].
15. I joined the hordes of unemployed in this city of Mumbai. . . .
    [In] this Mumbai [filled with] machines, constant ruses, the living and the dying, those with [upper caste] hair tufts, [and others with] beards, Hudson cars, nylon and georgette saris [translation mine].
16. See Baburao Gurav, *Annabhau Sathe: Samajvichar ani Sahityavivechan,* pp. 144-60 and Shankarbhau Sathe, *Majhe Bhau Annabhau,* pp. 97-103.
17. See testimonies of Narayan Surve [pp. 210-11], Vasant Bhor [p. 136] and Kesarbai [p. 142] in *One Hundred Years, One Hundred Voices: The Millworkers of Girangaon.*
18. See *Kranti,* 25 November 1928, Bombay, accessed at Teen Murti Library, Delhi.
19. Annabhau's best-known novel *Fakira,* first published in 1960, is an account of Mang valor, depicted through the principled resistance offered by its young hero, Fakira, who dies fighting against unjust colonial laws seeking to criminalize his community. The novel is dedicated to Ambedkar with the lines: *jag badal ghaluni ghav/sangun gele mala Bhimrao* [Rupture and change the world/ Was Bhimrao's message to me].

20. Patthe Bapurao was living in isolation in Yerwada but seems to have gravitated to the vicinity of the Aryabhushan Theatre at this time, relying on the little money that came his way from performing troupes. Jintikar—a *tamasha* enthusiast, Gurav by caste and postman by profession, a rental dealer in costumes and other properties, and a self-confessed participant in litigation to claim Brahman status for Guravs—befriended Patthe Bapurao in the early 1940s, transcribed and collected his compositions, and had them published between the late 1940s and 1950s. Leading Pune intellectuals and leaders such as Datta Vaman Potdar, Abasaheb Mazumdar, N.C. Kelkar, Kakasaheb Gadgil, Balasaheb Gore and Keshavrao Jedhe contributed prefaces many of whom were also present in a series of events held in Pune in 1942-3 to honor Patthe Bapurao. Although he died in poverty, clearly Patthe Bapurao was gratified enough by the turn of events to acknowledge them in his autobiographical *lavani* mentioned earlier.

    A Tamasha Sudhar Samiti was appointed in 1948, presided over by Datta Vaman Potdar: its recommendations touched upon suggestions to remove "obscene" elements and humor, the need to ensure that no physical contact occurred between female artistes and spectators during performance, particularly in the practice of *daulatzada.* Further efforts in this direction led to the first Tamasha Parishad being convened at the Aryabhushan Theatre on 25-6 June 1956, thanks to the initiative of owner-contractor, Ahmedseth Tambe. The sessions were presided over by Keshavrao Jedhe, and attended by several Maratha leaders and prominent Marathi intellectuals.

REFERENCES

Chandavarkar, Raj, 1998: *Imperial Power and Popular Politics: Class, Resistance and the State in India, c. 1850-1950.* Cambridge: Cambridge University Press.

——, 2005: "Introduction", in Meera Menon and Neera Adarkar, eds., 2005: *One Hundred Years, One Hundred Voices: The Millworkers of Girangaon: An Oral History.* Calcutta: Seagull Books.

Cherian, Anita, 2005: "Fashioning a National Theatre: Institutions and Cultural Policy in Post-Independence India", Ph.D. thesis submitted to NYU.

Dangle, Arjun, ed., 1998: *Lokshahir Annabhau Sathe Nivdak Sahitya.* Mumbai: Maharashtra Sahitya ani Sanskriti Mandal.

Deshpande, Sudhanva, 2004: "Upside-Down Midas: Habib Tanvir at 80", *TDR: The Drama Review,* vol. 48, no. 4, Winter 2004, pp. 71-80.

Gurav, Baburao, 1999: *Annabhau Sathe: Samajvichar ani Sahityavivechan.* Bombay: Lokwangmayagruha.

Guru, Gopal, 2001: "The Interface between Ambedkar and the Dalit Cultural Movement in Maharashtra", in Ghanshyam Shah, ed., *Dalit Identity and Politics.* New Delhi: Sage Publications, pp. 160-94.

Jintikar, B.M., 1954: *Patthe Bapurao Kulkarnikrut Dholkivareel Rangbazi Lavanya.* Pune: Self-published.

Joshi, Laxmanshastri, ed., 1984: *Marathi Vishwakosh,* vol. 7, Bombay: Maharashtra Rajya Sahitya Samiti.

Joshi, S.M. 2003: *Mee SM,* [1975], 3rd edn. Pune: Continental Prakashan.

Kamble, Arun, ed. 2001: *Janata Patrateel Lekh.* Mumbai: Popular Prakashan & University of Bombay.

Khairmode, C.B., 1968: *Dr. Bhimrao Ramji Ambedkaryanche Charitra,* vol. 3. Pune: Sugawa Publications.

Menon, Meera and Neera Adarkar, eds., 2005: *One Hundred Years, One Hundred Voices: The Millworkers of Girangaon: An Oral History.* Calcutta: Seagull Books.

Nalge, Chandrakumar, 2003: *Maharashtrache Shilpkar Patthe Bapurao.* Mumbai: Maharashtra Sahitya ani Sanskriti Mandal.

Naregal, Veena, 2001: "Provincial Elites, Urban Intellectuals and a New Marathi Theatre (1840-1875)", in special issue, Hanne De Bruin, ed., *Seagull Theatre Quarterly.* Calcutta.

Omvedt, Gail, 1976: *Cultural Revolt in a Colonial Society: the Non-Brahman Movement in Western India, 1873 to 1930.* Bombay: Popular Prakashan.

Phadke, Y.D., 1975: *Language and Politics.* Bombay: Himalaya Publishing House.

Rege, Sharmila, 2001: "Dalit Public Culture in Maharashtra". Delhi: Draft report prepared for Sarai.

——, 2002: "Conceptualising Popular Culture: 'Lavani' and 'Powada', in Maharashtra", *Economic and Political Weekly,* 16 March 2002, pp. 1038-47.

Sathe, Shankarbhau, 1980: *Majhe Bhau Annabhau.* Pune: Sugawa Publications.

17

An Enterprise Called Faith? Tale of a *Devasthan* in Maharashtra

SUHAS PALSHIKAR
AND
RAJESHWARI DESHPANDE

This is a story about the rise of a *devasthan* in western Maharashtra. In many ways it is a familiar narrative about the many surprising transformations of religious centers that one witnesses across the regions of Maharashtra[1] and of India in the recent period. The narrative raises some questions about the role of religiosity, faith (*shraddha*) and devotion (*bhakti*) in the context of modern social settings and their interface with politics. Religion and religiosity, as modes of public expressions of faith, seem to have multiple significances in contemporary India. They undeniably have significance as normative regimes governing the choices to be made by the individuals. Secondly, they have a collective significance as the underlying thread that binds communities. Thirdly, religion and religiosity are employed as markers of collective assertion and distinction and levers of power. The nature of religion as it shapes at the present moment, is complex and opens up various *margas* leading to various destinations. Our attempt here is to explore the role of *shraddha* and/or *bhakti* as the *marg* that leads to a pathway to local power. At the same time this *marg* leads to a peculiar politics that lacks legitimation and does not require a popular democratic basis.

The argument in the paper develops at three levels. We trace how a new kind of religiosity emerges in the locality in the context of changing nature of political economy in India and in the region. Then the paper discusses how this religiosity is available for commodification and consumption at various levels. And finally we narrate how the new religiosity gets subsumed under, and tries to subsume under it, politics of power.

NEW RELIGIOSITY?

The use of religion as a *marg* of local power traverses through a long route in the present context of India's political economy and of political economy the world over. Contrary to the early sociological imaginations of modern world as a space of shrinking religiosity, religion has become perhaps more consequential than ever in today's global politics (Appadurai 1996; Davis 2004; Rao 2004). The "sacred" in religion is always invoked for the purposes of the "secular". There is nothing new or contemporary to the process. However the present moment of capitalist development has led to such articulations and distortions of the "secular" that a new kind of religiosity is emerging on the scene. Religion is always seen as a means to bestow legitimacy on social life and to help in resisting the onslaught of chaos (Berger quoted in Madan 1991: 10). Both these roles of religion get combined in its contemporary expressions. Invasion of consumerism, cyber-culture, expanding media networks and social fads have led to "transmogrification" of religion under globalization (Radhakrishnan 2004). Religion is fast becoming a commodity in the global market. At the same time, economic shocks since the 1980s, growing inequalities and the resultant anomie have also forced individuals to regroup around pooled cultural resources like religion. Interestingly, this religion does not merely symbolize an escape but is also a staging ground for action. Religious identities are being rapidly transformed and are acquiring new political roles at the national and international levels.

Contemporary global capitalism entails a common civilizing mission and flattening of life experiences. At the same time, globalization also becomes a deeply historical, uneven and even localizing process. Different societies appropriate its materials differently. It was in the 1980s that the Indian society experienced first pangs of globalization, liberalization and a new phase of its capitalist development was in the offing. During the same period a new female deity emerged on the Indian religious scene—Santoshi Mata. The rise of Santoshi Mata symbolized many aspects of the new religiosity that we want to discuss here. It was not a traditional deity. It did not have links with the high or the little traditions of religion. Santoshi Mata was invented in the context of certain material needs that people wished to get fulfilled through the deity (most of the times it was desire to bear a male child). Popularity of Santoshi Mata grew rapidly across regions and across different sections. Many factors contributed to it. One, the relationship with the deity was simple—of a "give and take" variety. Two, a full-length feature film was made in praise of the deity that took the goddess to every small town of the country. Three, the emergence of the deity coincided with the period in which the rising middle class of the country was exposed to various anxieties—both in the material realm and the cultural realm. This class, joined by the aspiring middle class from among the lower middle sections, popularized and celebrated Santoshi Mata throughout late 1970s and early 1980s.

Many such deities and god-men/women arrived on the scene in the later decades. Simultaneously, the more traditional religious centers—centers of pilgrimage underwent a rapid transformation. The number of devotees visiting these places grew considerably, adding to the resources that these centers possessed. This was followed by institutionalization of religion in terms of establishment of trusts that initiated many secular activities under their control (Ahmed 1997). On the other hand many commercial agencies invested their surplus in religious activities.[2] On the whole; places of worship became remarkably visible in urban and rural settings. Religion was made visible in the public realm; was made available to the public for consumption. Capitalist development contributed to these changes in two direct ways. One, by facilitating modes of transport and communication to different religious places and secondly, through interventions of mass media. Easy transportation facilities (mostly illegal) became—quite literally!—the main vehicles of the rise of *bhakti*-tourism among middle-class families. State tourism departments actively supported these initiatives.

But the role of the media proved to be more crucial in making religion available for consumption and for its commodification. The "cassette revolution" in the 1980s and the entry of cable television in early 1990s marked the rise of a "pirate" electronic culture in India (Sundaram 2004). It was that kind of a culture where experience was essentially commodified and informationalized and populations were increasingly drawn to the commodified forms of experiences. The T-series cassette company, a leading firm from the pirate world, brought out series of devotional songs and movies about different centers of worship in the country. The T-series phenomenon remarkably contributed to the popularity of religious centers. But more than that it linked the religious experience to consumption in the form of entertainment, to material anxieties and aspirations and to the search for easy solace. The collective experience of mass media created a shared and flattened version of religion available to all. One study of a Marathi calendar notes how the print media of the 1990s absorbed many scattered places of religious and spiritual significance into a new spatiality of the region (Sanjay Palshikar 2006). The activity of the media linked the hitherto local, unselfconscious and (at least overtly) non-political religious events to the larger regional cultural and political context during the 1990s. As a complex outcome of these processes religion was firmly integrated with the larger political economy of India in the last two decades of the twentieth century.

RELIGIOSITY AS BASIS OF COMMUNITY

Detailed empirical assessments of the exact extent and dimensions of new religiosity in India are yet to come. However, the existing information base supports our submissions regarding its emergence. In at least one national level cross-section survey, over one-third of the respondents reported increased involvement of their family members in religious activities over the past ten years (Palshikar 2004: 5428). This study further noted that extent of religiosity is higher among upper caste, upper class, educated persons. In that sense the expanding Indian middle class emerges as the proponent and carrier of new religiosity. The middle class used religious resources to fulfil its growing worldly (consumerist) aspirations and also as an escape from agonies of consumerist capitalism. Deities that could fulfil material aspirations of devotees became most suitable for new religious practices. On the other hand, abstract power of religion to move beyond materiality was invoked to seek token solace. The logic of capitalism penetrates and dismantles the existing communities but it also necessitates formation of new communities. Contemporary forms of religion create such communities that are capable of moving from shared imagination to collective action.

Appadurai refers to them as communities in themselves that are always, potentially, communities for themselves (1996: 17). The Indian context saw this aspect of religiosity unfolding in the politics of Hindutva. Substantive empirical evidence to suggest a direct link between rising religiosity and communal politics is lacking. However, survey data referred to above supports such a conjecture (Palshikar 2004). The contextual nature of Indian democracy (Frankel 2000), a legitimate space that it offers to mobilizational politics and the historical processes of shaping of religious identities have all contributed to the making of politics of Hindutva. A spectacular, visible religiosity arriving in the recesses of new capitalism consolidates these political claims in a nuanced manner. The new religiosity transforms devotion and belief into identity. Identity becomes a mobilizational commodity in the established democratic framework. The process of shaping of religious identities reinforces commodification of religion. At all these levels the sacred in religion becomes available for, and amenable to, secular usages that are entangled in the play of power, domination, hatred and realignment of social forces. Our narrative of Shani Shingnapur is an attempt to trace some of these links as they unfold at the micro level.

THE RISE OF SHANIDEV DEVASTHAN

Situated 5 km off the Aurangabad-Ahmednagar State highway, Shani Shingnapur is a small village near village Sonai in Newasa taluka of Ahmednagar district. It is 75 km from the famous

Shirdi *devasthan.* The myth of Shani Shingnapur dates back to about three hundred and fifty years according to the belief of the local villagers. On a rainy day long ago, as the story goes, a stone idol was discovered in the small stream near the village (Panas nala). When the shepherd boys tried to move it with a stick, the stone started bleeding. The same night, Shanidev visited a devotee (name unknown) in his dream and ordered him to install the stone idol in the village without building a roof over the place. So, the stone turned out to be the *murti* of Shanidev.

As part of the local folklore, Shanidev also wished that the village houses should have neither doors nor locks and anyone who stole or robbed would be penalized by Shanidev himself. Thus emerged the core of the fame of this village: a village where there are no thefts, no doors and no locks; something unknown to the modern mind. This *devasthan* however, was not known much outside the village and its vicinity for a long time. In 1963, a local *sannyasi,* Udasi baba encouraged the villagers to formally establish a trust and run the *devasthan* through that trust (Shri Shanaishwar Devasthan Trust). This was done and the *devasthan* started becoming famous slowly. The trickle of the devotees also increased as the *devasthan* facilities improved and approach to the *devasthan* village also improved. Incidentally, canal water from the Mula River reached the Shingnapur village and the Sonai village and converted dry land farming into irrigated agriculture. Sugar cane became the main crop and the village and localities around it became "developed".

POLITICAL ECONOMY OF MAHARASHTRA

It is noteworthy that these developments in the village and around it were not taking place in isolation. As noted above, this village is situated in the Ahmednagar district, which was in the forefront of the establishment of cooperative sugar factories in the State. The decade of the 1960s was a period of much beneficence and hope in the context of the political economy of Maharashtra. A new linguistic State was created, the regionally dominant caste of Marathas was enjoying political power, the Maratha leadership was seen as hegemonic (Lele 1990), politics of the State was characterized by "elite pluralism" (Lele 1982) and it was widely believed that the State of Maharashtra would be a model of combining agrarian and industrial interests. The formation of the State on linguistic basis, in a sense, blurs the in-built contradictions in the society of Maharashtra. There are three intersecting contradictions that have implications for the kind of political economy that developed in the State in the post-1960 period: one is the Brahman *vs.* Maratha conflict which has a long tradition and many twists and turns (Vora 1994; 1999; Vora-Palshikar 1990); the other is rural vs. urban disparity and the third is the tension between agriculture and industry (Kamat 1983; Palshikar 2002). Politics in Maharashtra has developed in the context of these three contradictions. The latter two are not very specific to Maharashtra alone and are in fact part of the trajectory of capitalist development in the country as a whole. The onward march of industrial capitalism required that democratic energies from the rural sector be accommodated in the formal democratic structures and that the material aspirations of the rural-agrarian elites should be attended to. The political economy of Maharashtra aimed at these objectives within the framework of welfare democracy and elite domination.

More specifically, the creation of elective local governments at district, taluka and village level and the expansion of the rural cooperative network marked both democratization and institutionalization of social and political life at the grassroots level. If one were to use the more contemporary and colorful description, capitalist development was accompanied by the generation of "social capital" in the form of cooperatives, trusts, elective local bodies, and an overall potential for redefinition of rural social relations. As noted already, Ahmednagar was in the forefront of this phase of institution building and formation of a new political economy. Apart from the contextual effect that this atmosphere of development and institutionalization may have on the village Shani Shingnapur, developments in the vicinity directly affected the trajectory of the Devasthan Trust and its rise to fame.

The formation and progress of the Mula cooperative sugar factory in the vicinity of Shingnapur contributed to the publicity of the *devasthan*. Most sugar cooperatives in Maharashtra have been much more than mere sugar factories. They have also been nodal agencies of development around the village (Baviskar 1980: 209), they take charge of social, cultural activities and "progress" in and around the village where they are situated. They run educational institutions, they organize cultural programs, they patronize traditional folk forms of art, in short; they are the entrepreneurs of regional culture and contractors of cultural development of the locality. Mula factory was not an exception to this. During the late 1970s and 1980s, a number of cultural and social functions came to be organized by the sugar factory and this brought a number of celebrities to this area. Whenever these urban celebrities would visit the sugar factory, they were told about this weird village where there were no doors and no locks and they used to be suitably impressed and would then take a guided tour of Shingnapur village. This would further add to the glory and fame of the village and the fame of the Shanidev and his *devasthan.* The village and the *devasthan* boast to have been hosts to literary figures, public personalities, artists, film persons and so on. The famous film producer-director Basu Bhattacharya was so impressed with the idea of a village without doors that he wanted to make a film on this. The film was never made, but the *devasthan* got publicity. The small time *devasthan* now became conscious of its distinction and attracted more attention. Late 1980s and the 1990s saw the transformation of the famous *devasthan* into a star attraction and busy enterprise of faith. In early 1990s, singer Anuradha Paudwal and cassette-king Gulshan Kumar visited the *devasthan* and were so impressed that Anuradha Paudwal prepared a cassette containing devotional songs dedicated to Shanidev. The cassette became a "hit" and was followed by the film produced by Gulshan Kumar, "Suryaputra Shanidev" (Son of Sun—Shanidev, released in 1994). The T-series company of Gulshan Kumar introduced Shanidev as a new deity to the "pirate" world that we have discussed earlier.

SHANI MAHATMYA AS FAITH AND FEAR

Instantly, Shani Shingnapur became the center of attraction for anybody and everybody. For the Marathi and the non-Marathi, for the resident Indian and the NRI, for the rich and the poor, this became a "must visit" place, if you were a believer. And even if you were not a believer, the sheer wonder of houses without doors would always have a social-cultural value. To be sure, this attraction was not merely the urban white-collar search for authentic forms of our tradition or simplicity of the rural folk. The myth surrounding Shani Shingnapur probably has wider relevance. The entire myth and its vast attraction are potent with many possibilities. Most importantly, the myth serves as a counterpoint to our actual existences of suspicions, insecurities and self-aggrandisement. Immersed in the capitalist logic of self and self-interest, people keep subconsciously searching for symbolic negations of the very logic that governs their lives. Myths such as this provide this negation, notionally though. The absence of a community is compensated by the examples like Shani Shingnapur where the people trust each other through their faith in the myth and thus produce an image of community based on religion and culture. The fragmented and individuated existence in a life of severe competition and marketization finds momentary relief in the "simplicity" of the possible community hidden behind the myth of Shanidev.

If the myth of Shanidev symbolized a negation of the existing capitalist relations, the profile of Shanidev, as it appears in *Shani Mahatmya* (an account of grandeur of Shanidev), legitimizes the logic of capitalism and endorses it. It is for fulfilment of their worldly wishes, of their material aspirations that people worship Shanidev. The traditional image of God, particularly among the Marathi speaking, is that of a compassionate and helping lord, *Kripalu-Karuna Sagar*, one who is satisfied with whatever is offered to him by saint-devotees like Namdeo or Chokhamela. This image is changed in the case of Shanidev. As *Shani Mahatmya* develops the story, Shanidev is a god who believes in a give and take relationship with his devotees. He needs offerings to pacify him and to get the wishes fulfilled. In the entire narrative of *Shani Mahatmya*, Shanidev is constantly angry over small issues, demands that things should always be the way he wants them, himself has material desires and severely punishes those who do not follow his commands (Tapas 1992). The image of Shanidev and the myth about Shingnapur create a perfect combination of faith and fear, of anxieties and solace suitable for the contemporary moment of religiosity.

Obviously, Shingnapur became one more of the long list of places of spiritual-cultural tourism during the 1990s. Innumerable cassettes and books in different languages feed the public curiosity about the myth and the deeds of Shanidev. The insistence of the village and the *devasthan* to retain the tradition of not having doors and locks has also helped in fanning the myth. Modern gadgets like the close circuit television sets add to the pomp of the deity and accentuate the myths surrounding it. In the last ten years, all the four Shankaracharyas have visited the village apart from film personalities, politicians and other persons of fame. This has added to the glory surrounding the myth.

Ironically, though, there are no banks in the village and the offices of the village panchayat and the credit cooperative societies from the village are situated in the nearby village. All the same, the two-some police force posted in the village is resistant to register cases of theft because the village is not supposed to have thefts! One instance of the way in which the myth survives should be interesting: a story makes the rounds that once a petty thief attempted to snatch the golden chain from a woman. However, he managed only to get hold of the *Tulsi mala* that the woman was wearing. The believers, spurred by some trustees started saying that because of the protection of Shanidev, the golden chain transformed into the *Tulsi mala*! Even Trust officials acknowledge that many devotees too, do not want to risk loss of their belongings and avoid staying in the lodges in the village. Now, the Trust is planning to construct a *Bhakt Niwas* in the adjoining village where the lodgings would have proper locks! Thus, it is in the midst of these and many other ironies that the myth of Shanidev lives.

The foregoing discussion has tried to make two points implicitly. Firstly, we have attempted to draw attention to the possibilities existing within the overall context of political economy for shaping certain kind of religiosity. Taking off from deep-rooted faith and religious sentiments, this religiosity focuses attention on symbols, on escape routes from material insecurities, on rediscovery of age-old myths. Such a religiosity shifts focus from the principles of love and piety to the factors of threat and danger. Religion is seen more as amelioration of worldly worries than the search for the spiritual and the moral. We have already suggested that religion keeps traversing the two universes of the secular and the sacred. The religiosity that evolves from the contemporary political economy firmly situates religion in the realm of the secular. Following from this, the second point that the foregoing discussion makes is about faith and religiosity being available for commodification. In fact, religion itself becomes a commodity in the political economy of capitalism. But more specifically, faith and devotion are transformed into commodities at the intersection of the universal (national level context of economic development) and the particular (local manifestations of commercial power). In the following section, we elaborate on the local context further to demonstrate how the Devasthan Trust is instrumental in manipulating the contemporary moment of religiosity.

THE ECONOMICS OF "TRUST"

The *devasthan* is run and managed by a board of trustees with eleven members. As the prestige of the *devasthan* increased, so also the turnover of the devotees and the resources of the *devasthan* increased.

The Shani temple has to be a place that is without a roof. It is said that many tried to construct a formal temple with a roof for Shanidev, but they were warned against it by Shanidev himself (appearing in their dreams). So, the famous Shanidev is there on a small stone platform—a *chouthara*—without a roof. Instead, the Trust has constructed a lavish temple just in front of the old platform where stone idol of Shanidev exists. In this temple, all kinds of deities and saints are idolized—Udasi Baba, Gajanan Maharaj, Vithoba-Rakhumai, Dattatreya, Krishna, Saint Dnyaneshwar, Namdev, etc. There are small but lavish temples separately constructed for other gods. Besides these temples, the Trust has developed this area to a great extent. There is a separate hall for various activities, a meditation center, library, a huge dining hall (that can accommodate five hundred devotees at a time), all with opulently attractive architecture. All this construction testifies to the plush financial condition of the *devasthan.*

The most important source of income for the *devasthan* is donations by the devotees. Stories of huge donations abound. Some devotees donate in kind; say by constructing parts of the buildings, or a *dharmashala.* Some others donate gold ornaments and other kinds of valuables. Most choose to offer cash. The *devasthan* now has a facility of instantly giving the necessary certificate for income tax rebate to those donors who donate cash or cheques! At the same time there is a box to facilitate *gupta daan* (undisclosed donations). The other source of income is the charges for various rituals: special *poojas, abhisheks, satyanarayans,* and so on. The collection through these two sources is certainly not inconsiderable. But more than the donations of the devotees, the resources of the *devasthan* owe much to the enterprising skills of the *devasthan* trustees. As one approaches the temple complex, an area of about hundred square meters adjoining the parking lot is owned by the Trust. In this area, more than one hundred shops selling all material required for a traditional *pooja* are put up for sale. Most devotees who come here want to offer the *pooja* and the rates of the material vary depending upon the shopkeeper's assessment of the client's financial ability. So, the business is brisk and lucrative. The Trust gives away these stalls—or rather the place for the stall—to shopkeepers for financial consideration. The practice is to announce an auction and distribute the stalls among the highest bidders on a contract of eleven months. The Trust provides electricity free of charge to the stall-owners. Depending upon how strategically a stall is located, the stalls fetch huge auction money. For instance, shop keepers say that a number of stalls at prime locations are rented at the rates of one hundred thousand rupees to hundred and fifty thousand rupees (one lakh to one and a half lakh) while other stalls are rented at modest rates of fifty to twenty-five thousand. Considering the fact that this is the annual income per stall for about hundred stalls at least, one can imagine the corpus collected by the Trust every year from rent. Then, there are other minor sources of income for the Trust. One really ridiculous source is the coconuts offered by the devotees and other packed *pooja* material. Most of these are sold back by the Trust to the shop owners at a reduced price, thus making small money! But some sources of this resale and recycling are not so immaterial. For example, Shanidev is traditionally offered edible oil. Most of this oil used to go waste till the 1990s. As the number of devotees increased and as rich devotees started offering oil in large quantities (there are stories of devotees offering not just cans of oil, but small tanks of oil!), the Trust arranged a large storing place where the oil is poured and then this oil is sold to soap making factories at competitive rates. It is in this sense that we have argued above that religion is now available as a commodity for material consumption.

One can perhaps estimate the resources at the disposal of the Trust if one looks at the ongoing projects and constructions: the Trust is constructing facilities worth thirty million (three crores) rupees for devotees plus school complex worth another ten million. Apart from the plush temples and rich offices, the Trust also owns an ambulance and intends to construct a hospital with a cost of fifty million. A project of creating a dumping ground and compost plant is also in the offing. Besides, the Trust hopes to purchase a large tract of land outside the village (over six hectares). The Trust has an office staff of one hundred and fifty employees. As the Sarpanch of the village rues, the village panchayat has an annual income of fifty thousand while the daily income of the Trust (on an ordinary day) is possibly to the tune of one hundred thousand! The Trust has an official annual turnover of about sixty million rupees.

BUSINESS OF FAITH

But apart from the resources of the Trust, the *devasthan* has a very definite impact on the economic activity in and around the village. In a sense, this is not surprising because, whenever any place of worship becomes popular, it attracts a range of economic activities. Material activities merrily follow the spiritual and flourish with the blessing of the spiritual. Shingnapur is no exception to this experience. Broadly speaking, three kinds of related economic activities have flourished in the shadow of Shani Shingnapur. One set of activities is related to the material required for the *pooja.* As noted above, the Trust rents over a hundred stalls on the space owned by it. Besides this, in the vicinity of the temple complex many more stalls are situated though not at very advantageous locations. All these stalls are engaged in the sale of material that the devotees require for the *pooja.* The rate of the material for the *pooja* can be anything between hundred and fifty rupees to fifteen hundred rupees. Then, the other set of economic activity is related to lodging and boarding. The huge number of devotees visiting Shingnapur need food provision and they also need a room for a brief rest. Very seldom anyone actually stays overnight. Yet, a large number of hotels, lodges and eateries of various kinds exist in and around the village. The third economic activity involves transport facility and petty commissions. Shingnapur is situated on the State highway linking Pune and Aurangabad. But, for a tourist-devotee, the best way to approach Shingnapur is via Shirdi, itself a renowned place of attraction for the tourist-devotee. A continuous stream of vehicles of all sorts keeps plying between Shirdi and Shingnapur. Public transport facility is not very efficient and convenient. The visiting devotee goes to Shirdi and then hires a vehicle to reach Shingnapur. Alternatively, vehicles also transport devotees from nearby towns with railway stations, like Rahuri and Ahmednagar. Apart from transport business, a petty business of commissions also takes place. A horde of youngsters keep loitering around the *devasthan* and as the vehicles approach, take the tourists to certain shops selling goods for the *pooja* and/ or certain lodges. In most cases, the drivers (and in most cases, they are also the owners of the vehicles) do this business themselves. Once the vehicle takes the devotees to a particular shop or lodge, the devotee is very unlikely to turn away and go to some other place. Therefore, the drivers of the vehicles earn extra incomes by working as agents for the shop owners and lodge owners.

On an ordinary day, the number of devotees visiting the *devasthan* may not be more than a thousand. However, more devotees visit on Saturdays (the day of Shanidev) and on every Shani Amavasya and Gudi Padva and Shani *jayanti,* the devotees throng the place in huge numbers. Gudi Padva is almost like a *jatra* (fair) when about a hundred thousand devotees visit the temple complex. Thus, it is difficult to estimate the exact number of devotees visiting the *devasthan*, but a conservative guess would be that during any year, almost ten hundred thousand devotees visit the *devasthan*. Therefore, all the economic activities mentioned above, become reasonably lucrative with considerable returns to those engaged in the activities.

POLITICS IN THE *DEVASTHAN* VILLAGE

Shingnapur is a small village. It used to be part of the Sonai village. Both Sonai and Shingnapur are villages with Maratha majority. The Bankar, Shete, Darandale and Borude families are numerous in the village. Shingnapur has a population of around six thousand. (As per the 1991 District Census Handbook, Shingnapur had 1,237 households and a population of 5,635. Dalits accounted for only 5 per cent of the population. The village had 35 per cent literacy and half of its population was classified as main workers. Among them, 15 per cent were cultivators-landowners and 70 per cent were agricultural laborers. The village has a cultivable land of 240 hectares and 225 hectares of this are under irrigation.) As mentioned at the beginning, Sonai and Shingnapur have seen better days after canal water reached them and the sugar cooperative factory became the hub of the economic activity of this area.

Shirdi and Shingnapur have, however, changed the nature of economic activity in this area altogether. Spirituality and faith have become the main enterprises for a large number of people here. While Shirdi has become a more famous and lucrative place of business, local people from the vicinity dominate economic activity in Shingnapur. Ironically, while there is no proverbial "outsider" element here in the sense of non-Marathi people dominating businesses, there are some complaints that very few people from Shingnapur itself are in the business. Thus, a major source of disappointment about the Trust is that it does not help the local villagers and have an eye only on the income angle exclusively.

Curiously enough, the Trust does not involve itself in the politics of the village panchayat. (In fact, the latest election to the post of Sarpanch—June 2005—was a unanimous affair. The post was reserved for OBCs and one member from the Shete clan managed to claim Kunbi-OBC status and was elected unopposed.) The village factions are not according to the clans since all these Maratha families intermarry and as such they are in-laws. In Shingnapur village the main division is between the Trust and the rest. The might of the Trust has rendered the village panchayat irrelevant and therefore, the Trust is the center of power and of material domination in and around the village. The eleven trustees constitute this center of power.

The faction opposed to the Trust has many complaints. Hidden in these, the main complaint seems to be that of exclusion. The Trust is not very accommodative of the aspiring persons from the village. Work of the Trust involves lot of influence and monetary comforts and the Trust is not willing to share it with many people. Besides this, the opponents complain that the Trust does not do much for the development of the village. Though the money of the Trust does bring some improvement in the facilities around the village, it is a fact that barring the area of the *devasthan*, most of the village bears no signs of much improvement in terms of infrastructure. This is mainly because Shingnapur *devasthan* is situated at such a place that the visiting devotee has no intention of staying there. This puts a limitation on the development of the village. But the villagers expect that the Trust, with its funds should take a less commercial approach and improve the condition of the village. Another grouse of the villagers is that in the commercial activities spurred by the *devasthan*, villagers are given no consideration at all. The Trust mostly goes by the strict commercial approach in this regard too, and gives away contracts to the highest bidders so as to ensure financial prosperity of the Trust. As a result, most of the stall-owners in the area are from outside the village. Shop-owners from the village have to be satisfied with the small and less strategically located shops on the private plot adjacent to the *devasthan*. In short, the *devasthan* has not brought much prosperity to the village or to the businessmen from the village.

In political terms, what the Trust has done is to push back normal village politics and has itself become the center of power. The distributive capacity and patronage potential of the panchayat and the ordinary politician has no meaning in Shingnapur. So, on the one hand, the village aspirant has no share in the influence and resources of the Trust and on the other hand, the normal power of patronage of the aspiring politician has become unimportant due to the might of the Trust. To say that the Trust does not interfere in the village politics is not a very correct assessment. It would be more accurate to say that the Trust has replaced more routine and formal avenues of power and politics.

POLITICS WITHOUT THE "PUBLIC"

What are the characteristics of this new politics that the Trust represents? The power of the Devasthan Trust is without any popular legitimation. It is based on two factors; one is of course the resources the Trust controls. The other is people's reverence for religion and religious activity. But the trustees do not owe their power to either the local people or the devotees in general. Secondly, the Trust is undemocratic in the sense that it is not accountable to or answerable to anyone. In this sense, the Trust is an instance of the modern phenomenon of unaccountable "private power". Capitalism breeds and shelters many such organizations with private power. They are based on resources and organization. Through the Trust, the phenomenon of private power spreads to the rural areas like Shingnapur. In this respect, the Devasthan Trust is not really an exception. On the contrary, it represents the emergence of centers of private power that exist and operate outside the formal democratic constraints and norms.

On the one hand, villagers are not involved in the running of the Trust and thus, are not part of the politics of the Trust. On the other hand, the devotees are momentary citizens of this empire of religion-based power. As such, they have no interest and no inclination to make the Trust accountable. In fact, the real strength of the Trust lies in this peculiar situation: its real "clientele" is floating and non-resident, perhaps not even regular. As we mentioned earlier, places like Shingnapur thrive on the basis of *bhakti*-tourism. The pilgrims-cum-devotees have no interest in the management of the Trust or the relationship of the Trust with the local villagers. This development can perhaps be captured by the idea of disappearance of the "public". The alienation of the village locals, the steady stream of touristy pilgrims and the access to resources without accountability constitute this disappearance of the public. As if it were, the public is drowned by the din of the crowd of devotees. When there is absence of the "public", depoliticization of politics occurs. At the root of the grouse entertained by local panchayat of Shingnapur, there lies this malady of depoliticization.

Thus, two different power games are unfolding simultaneously and parallel to each other in the Shingnapur village. One is the power game within the village—its panchayat, its routine party factions, and so on. This unfolds in the public sphere, is relatively open to many more members of the public, is and has to be sensitive to the popular sentiment. The other is the power game that obtains in the Devasthan Trust. This is restrictive, internal to a small clique, inaccessible to most of the villagers and also the devotees. The former unfolds in the public sphere, but lacks in resources and substance. So, it becomes very formal and ephemeral. On the other hand, the latter game of power has substance, it has the capacity to overpower the former or to take over the former; but it is exclusive and non-public in its character and location. Religion and the sanction generated by religiosity (combined with resources) sustain this non-public nature of the politics of the organizations like the Devasthan Trust. In this sense, for the handful of trustees the *devasthan* is a source of material-political strength—*shakti*—while for the hundreds of thousands of devotees the *devasthan* continues to be a center of faith—*shraddha.*

CONCLUSION

We would like to argue that the case of Shingnapur is in no sense exceptional. In fact, the narrative of Shingnapur is representative of the many similar places where *shraddha* and *bhakti* are the driving forces in shaping *satta* and *shakti* (power and domination).[3] While this fact poses a challenge for the student of politics, it also produces a riddle for the student of religion. Cases like Shingnapur alert us to the many shades of meanings and implications that religiosity and faith have.

In its secular incarnations, religiosity takes many forms. We have already noted how religiosity is transformed into a commodity: as a driver of *bhakti*-tourism; but also as a driver of the accumulation and utilization of vast resources (of the *devasthan*). In a sense, this secular role of religiosity is not very new. *Devasthans* are known for their control over resources and their keen search for accumulation of resources. The stories of Tirupati or Balaji or Guruvayur are legendary. This aspect only reinforces our claim that religiosity keeps traversing the two universes of the sacred and the secular. Success in one accentuates its salience in the other universe. Resources ensure more respect in spiritual realm and higher status in the spiritual realm brings more resources to organizations that are administrators of this religiosity.

The story of Shingnapur, however, helps us go beyond this scenario. Shingnapur helps us understand the process of evolution of a "place of worship", its growth and graduation into a big organization. This process begins with the rise and acceptance of new objects of worship, devotion and faith. As already noted, Santoshi Mata or Shanidev signify the constant search for "modern" deities, gods, gurus, spiritual figures, etc. Search for community, lack of deep-rooted linkages with tradition and culture, a sentimental understanding of religion and tradition, all contribute to this search. The search is also exacerbated by the forces of publicity, commodification and entertainment. So, the story of Shanidev throws up the question about new religiosity or redefinition of religiosity.

Apart from the obvious context of capitalism and our contemporary materiality, this question is also related to the more specific turn that contemporary political process has given to the meaning of religiosity. This refers to the politics of Hindutva. One important dimension of the politics of Hindutva has been to redefine religiosity. Our narrative of Shingnapur does not directly touch upon this issue. And yet, the story of Shanidev may have some bearing on this issue. Both the politics of Hindutva and the rise of Shanidev have one thing in common: both are engaged in redefining religiosity. Through both, new symbols and new deities are projected; through both, religiosity is employed as lever of power; through both, the public is redefined. Although the narrative itself does not show any direct links between the two, can the two projects of converting *shraddha* (faith) into *satta* (power) be separated conceptually?

We submit that the two projects articulate two different aspects of the existing power relations and thus share invariable connections that remain masked in the present narrative of Shanidev. The new religiosity as it emerges in Shingnapur delegitimizes the secular political realm and survives on the basis of a floating clientele of devotees. The politics of Hindutva brings back the new religiosity in the realm of secular democratic politics in its appropriations of the available mobilizational space. The mobilizational politics of Hindutva has every possibility to render a more permanent, more political character to the floating identities of the devotees. The commodified, pirate and uniformly shared religion contributes to the process in a definite manner. The sacred in religion sanctifies the secular in Hindutva and consolidates its mobilizational aspect. The politics of Hindutva on the other hand encourages action based on expression of and distinction among religion-based groups. If the diffuse crowd of devotees of Shanidev, which lacks an identity and a face, is a community in itself, the politics of Hindutva helps the transformation of such communities into "communities for themselves".

In both these projects religiosity is appropriated and reconstructed in the recesses of modern material life conditions. From the point of view of the religious persons, this newly invented religiosity and sources of faith continue to be pathways to consolation in the difficulties of life. For both, the commercial as well as political entrepreneurs of this new religiosity, faith and religiosity are good business and useful politics—pathway to power in competitive politics.

NOTES

1. We try to understand this transformation in an ongoing collaborative research project titled "Contemporary Expressions of Religiosity". This project seeks to study the political economy of religious practices in contemporary Maharashtra with an aim to understand the hidden

linkages between the religiosity that we are discussing in this essay and the political articulations of religiosity as they are expressed through the politics of Hindutva. The Department of Politics, University of Pune and Unique Features, a media initiative from Pune are jointly conducting the project. The project involves in-depth case studies of traditional and newly emerged religious centers across the regions of Maharashtra. Ten major religious centers have been selected for the initial fieldwork of the project. The present paper is an initial reporting of issues emerging from our investigations at these centers. The other scholars who are part of the consulting team include: Professor Vora, Dr. Suhas Kulkarni and Dr. Nitin Birmal.

2. Venkateshwara Hatcheries, a leading company from the poultry industry, has constructed its own Balaji Temple in Ketkavale, a small village near Pune. The temple Trust, managed by the company, offers excellent infrastructure and services to devotees free of cost. Thousands of devotees visit the temple as it is en-route to another newly emerged center for pilgrimage—Narayanpur. Local groups from Ketkavale village, who had initially opposed the construction of the temple, are in all praise for the company since the temple has geared up many petty business opportunities for the local people.
3. Two of our case studies reveal complex patterns of such interaction. Akkalkot in south Maharashtra, a newly emerged religious center in the name of a godman turned deity, witnessed a straightforward equation between political and religious power relations. The town saw intense contestations between two rival factions of the dominant Maratha caste for control over religious resources. This has led to formation of two parallel trusts for managing the affairs of the *devasthan* (Unique Features 2005a). Tryambakeshwar in north Maharashtra tells a different story. As a place of Shiva this center is traditionally famous for the last rites of ancestors. Since the 1980s it became popular across the country for *Narayan nagbali*—a ritual for fulfilment of the wish to bear a male child. Growing popularity of Tryambakeshwar has resulted in gradual consolidation of the traditional dominance of Brahmans in local society (Unique Features 2005b).

REFERENCES

Ahmed, Imtiaz, 1997: "The Political Economy of Places of Worship", in Ghanshyam Shah, ed., *Social Transformation in India*, vol. 2. Jaipur: Rawat Publications, pp. 651-5.

Appadurai, Arjun, 1996: "Modernity at Large: Cultural Dimensions of Globalisation", *Public Worlds*, vol. 1. Minneapolis: University of Minnesota Press.

Baviskar, B.S., 1980: *The Politics of Development: Sugar Co-operatives in Rural Maharashtra.* Bombay: Oxford University Press.

Davis, Mike, 2004: "Planet of Slums: Urban Involution and the Informal Proletariat", *New Left Review,* vol. 26, March-April, pp. 5-34.

Frankel, Francine, 2000: "Contextual Democracy: Intersections of Society, Culture and Politics in India", Introduction to Francine Frankel, Zoya Hasan, Rajeev Bhargava and Balveer Arora, eds., *Transforming India.* New Delhi: Oxford University Press, pp. 1-26.

Kamat, A.R., 1983: *Essays on Social Change in India.* Mumbai: Sommaiya Publications.

Lele, Jayant, 1982: *Elite Pluralism and Class Rule: Political Development in Maharashtra.* Bombay: Popular Prakashan.

——, 1990: "Caste, Class and Dominance: Political Mobilisation in Maharashtra", in Francine R. Frankel and M.S.A. Rao, eds., *Dominance and State Power in Modern India,* vol. II. New Delhi: Oxford University Press, pp. 115-211.

Madan, T.N., ed., 1991: *Religion in India.* Delhi: Oxford University Press.

Palshikar, Sanjay, 2006: "Inhabiting Times and Producing Spaces", in Rajendra Vora and Anne Feldhaus, eds., *Region, Culture and Politics in India.* New Delhi: Manohar, pp. 253-70.

Palshikar, Suhas, 2002: "Political Economy of Maharashtra: some Posers for Civil Society Initiatives", unpublished paper presented at the seminar on Civil Society and States in India, Mumbai: organized by the Dept. of Civics and Politics, University of Mumbai.

——, 2004: "Majoritarian Middle Ground?", *Economic and Political Weekly,* vol. 34, no. 51, 18 December, pp. 5426-30.

Radhakrishnan, P., 2004: "Religion Under Globalisation", *Economic and Political Weekly,* vol. 34, no. 13, 27 March, pp. 1403-12.

Rao, M.S.A., 2004: "Religion and Economic Development", in Rowena Robinson, ed., *Sociology of Religion in India.* New Delhi: Sage Publications, pp. 68-83.

Sundaram, Ravi, 2004: "Uncanny Networks: Pirate, Urban and New Globalisation", *Economic and Political Weekly,* vol. 34, no. 1, 3 January, pp. 64-71.

Tapas, Vijay, 1992: "Mahabhayacha Ugra Tanatkar: Shani Mahatmya" (Marathi), *Aajacha Charvak,* Annual Issue, pp. 56-65.

Unique Features, 2005a: "Gaon Swamy Samarthancha" (Marathi), *Vegala Anubhav,* Annual Issue, pp. 28-41 & 154-6.

——, 2005b: "Brahmanancha Gaon" (Marathi), *Deepawali,* Annual Issue, pp. 92-9 & 130-2.

Vora, Rajendra, 1994: "An Agenda for the Study of Political Economy of Maharashtra", Occasional Paper no. 1, Pune: Dept. of Politics and Public Administration, University of Pune.

——, 1999: "Maharashtra Dharma and Nationalist Movement in Maharashtra", in N.K. Wagle, ed., *Writers, Editors and Reformers: Social and Political Transformations of Maharashtra: 1830-1930.* New Delhi: Manohar, pp. 23-30.

Vora, Rajendra and Suhas Palshikar, 1990: "Neo-Hinduism: A Case of Distorted Consciousness", in Jayant Lele and Rajendra Vora, eds., *State and Society: Changing Social Bases of Indian Politics.* Delhi: Chanakya Publications, pp. 213-43.

PART IV

PILGRIMAGE AND FOLK RELIGIOUS PRACTICES

18

Mārg(a)kramaṇ of Maharashtrian Princely Families: A Search for Self within the Boundaries Made for Others[1]

IRINA GLUSHKOVA

Marathi accounts of pilgrimages, i.e. *tīrtha-yātrās*, actually performed during the span of the eighteenth to early twentieth centuries, constitute a unique source of information on this subject due to a specific historical configuration which provided pilgrims of the Marathi speaking region with much better opportunities than those of people from other parts of India. In addition to its convenient geographical location in the middle part of the peninsula, a steady flow of Maharashtrian Brahmans to various sacred spots, especially north off Maharashtra, and a political connections net established when the Peshwa-led Maratha confederacy was at its prime, helped in transforming the idea of *tīrtha-yātrā par excellence* into a real achievement.

As I have argued in my previous studies, going on pilgrimage by the lay public was an exception rather than an established practice, pilgrimage goals were multifaceted and the whole enterprise required a solid financial base. I shall here extend my study by examining a few *mārg(a)kramaṇs*, one performed in 1783 by Saraswatibai of the Miraj Patwardhan family, and the other in 1909 and 1911 by Raghunathrav Shankarrav[2] Pandit of the Bhor Pantsachiv family. The former demonstrates the thoroughly planned character of the pilgrimage and the scope of women's adjustment to it. The latter not only adds new facets to the practice of princely families "moving between sacred places" but also substantiates the growing link between the *tīrtha-yātrā* of olden days and modern tourism. Both examples also contribute to understanding the reasons leading a person to undertake a pilgrimage and the limitations of his/her quest. Strengthening and/or legitimizing one's status are among those reasons which are not normally pronounced.

My recent research has shown the historical transformation of a *tīrtha-yātrā* and the essentials which distinguish it from other types of religious activities. Drawing from the *Mahābhārata* Pandavas' pilgrimage and its impact on Serfoji II, the Maratha prince of Thanjavur,[3] who had gone on a couple of pilgrimages in the beginning of the nineteenth century, I suggested defining a *tīrtha-yātrā* as a combination of distinctive features, each of which by itself or in smaller clusters might be found as structural components of different religious performances (Glushkova 2004: 275). I have also scrutinized financial aspect ("money") of a movement and introduced a concept of "wonder" as an equivalent of a contemporary idea of "drive". Both notions resulted from my analysis of a pilgrimage practice of Raghunathrav Vincurkar, a prince of the Vincur,[4] who had undertaken a few journeys to holy places in the second part of the nineteenth century (Glushkova 2006). The present paper is based on correspondence of Saraswatibai Patwardhan of the Miraj principality during her pilgrimage of 1783 (Khare 1912) and on memoirs of journeys made at the beginning of the twentieth century by Raghunathrav Pantsachiv of the Bhor princely state (Pantsachiv 1936, 1939). I will focus on the performance of a *tīrtha-yātrā* as a part of *rāja-dharma,* which, as J.D.M. Derret notes, "has always been an aspiration, seldom a reality" (Derret 1976: 608). While journeying, members of princely families used to keep engaged in political and social issues and through these engagements strengthened their authority and status both within and beyond their own states.

MIRAJ

The small principality of Miraj[5] on the bank of the Krishna River in south-western Maharashtra was founded in 1750 by a Peshwa general Govindrav Patwardhan, a Chitpavan Brahman. His son

Gopal Govind Patwardhan, the most famous of Miraj *sardārs*, lost his first wife and on compulsion from his parents had to remarry against his choice around 1764[6] (Khare 1898-1899: 474-5). There was no issue from this marriage, and it is difficult to argue whether the marriage had been consummated at all, as Gopal Govind fell in battle in 1770 when his wife Saraswatibai was still about fifteen. After his death his widow moved to the town of Haripur at the sacred confluence of the Krishna and the Varna, and in 1783, at the age of aproximately 28, expressed the intention (*saṅkalpa*)[7] to start on a *kāśī-yātrā*, synonymous with *tristhaḷī*, i.e. a pilgrimage to the three most revered Hindu *tīrthas* of Kashi, Prayag and Gaya. Her intention matured under the impact of practices well established by that time at the court of the Peshwas, the actual rulers of the Maratha state, and their subordinates. Historical documents provide information about several other characters who had previously performed pre-planned (and not a spontaneous, by-the-way kind of) travel to the *tristhaḷī* places and back. At least three of them were widows of the Peshwas' clan. Radhabai, a widow of the first Peshwa Balaji Vishvanath, went on pilgrimage in 1735;[8] Kashibai, a widow of Bajirao moved northwards in 1746, and her daughter-in-law Sagunabai, a widow of Janardan Bajirao, traversed the same route in 1757. Long before each of these pilgrimages, special envoys (*pratinidhi, mutsadī, vakīl*) supplied with the Peshwas' letters to the emperor of Delhi and the nawab of Awadh, to the Holkar and Scindia rulers and to local nobility and fiscal agents (*rājerājvāḍe, jamīdār, kamāvīsdār*) were sent along the itinerary. The envoys were responsible for solving practical problems of the royal pilgrims and their retinues and dealt with food supplies, night stays, and waiving the tax (*jakāt, kar*) both *en route* and in the *tīrthas*. The Peshwas' patronage was decisive in cutting down financial expenditures as no ruler dared to neglect the requests of the Peshwas, still in their prime before the battle of Panipat in 1761. Each of the pilgrim widows was accompanied by kin and servants, and crowds of indigenous people, drawn both by religious motives and for perspectives of safe travel under the protection of armed guards.[9] One Tryambak Hari Patwardhan, another Miraj *sardār*, went on *kāśī-yātrā* in 1769.[10]

Saraswatibai was certainly aware of these facts. For example, there is a direct reference to Shivaji Vitthal Vincurkar in the

Miraj correspondence (Khare 1912: 3699-3700). A son of the founder of the Vincur princely state, Shivaji Vitthal had visited the *tristhalī* towns accompanied by fifty horsemen, a British platoon (*phalṭan*) and a British agent (*kārkūn*) shortly before Saraswatibai's *yātrā* started and succeeded in getting a preferential treatment there. Saraswatibai described the details of her own pilgrimage in her letters sent to Miraj to her brother-in-law Gangadharrav Patwardhan, alias Balasaheb,[11] then the raja of Miraj. V.V. Khare, a Miraj historian and Sanskrit school teacher, edited, commented and published the letters in the seventh volume of "A collection of historical documents" (Khare 1912).

Saraswatibai's journey followed a solid preparatory work. Many letters were sent to the north both from the prince of Miraj and the Pune minister Nana Phadnavis who acted in the name of Madhavrao II, still a minor. Later Ahilyabai Holkar, who then ruled from Maheshvar, and Mahadji Scindia of Gwalior, who was a chief mediator between Saraswatibai and a British governor-general in Calcutta,[12] were in constant touch with the caravan moving northwards. Simultaneously, the news of a forthcoming *tīrtha-yātrā* by a woman famous for her piety and charity, excited places around Miraj. By the time it began, besides many aspirants from Miraj proper, people from other princely states and local settlements such as Sangli, Kurundvad, Ganeshvadi, Haripur, Tasgav, Ichalkaranji, Jamkhindi, Terdal, as well as Manoli, Nargund, Ramdurg, etc., located at a greater distance, joined the caravan. At the time of the departure from Miraj in October 1783 the procession consisted of four to five hundred pilgrims, but many more participants joined the *yātrā* at each halt on the way. The impressive caravan and retinue (*lavājamā*) reflected the high standing of Saraswatibai. Balasaheb saw that there were camels loaded with luggage, horses, palanquins, horsemen, infantry, and various attendants (*śāgird-peśā*). V.V. Khare later declared: "This gathering could be named a *yātrā* as much as it could have been named an army (*yā samudāyās yātrā he nāv jitke yogya hote titkec svārī he nāv suddhā yogya hote*!)" (Khare 1912: 3758). His statement is more than appropriate as the whole procession was even built according to military tactics:

renowned warriors placed in the vanguard, the middle part and the rear-guard of the caravan looked after those who were exhausted or fell ill and brought them onto hired carts (Khare 1912: 3776). Night watch guarded the pilgrims' camp throughout the whole journey, while local nobles, too, recognized the safety of the pilgrims as their responsibility. Each one according to his resources provided either twenty-five horsemen or two hundred soldiers to accompany the procession to the borders of their territories (Khare 1912: 3761, 3789). Those were unstable times, and danger arouse from both unfriendly neighbors and Bhils' riots, professional thieves or famine-stricken people from the north who would not hesitate to snatch a half-eaten bread out of the pilgrims' hands (Khare 1912: 3784).

At the stopover in Toke where, according to tradition (*asā pūrvīpāsūn praghāt hotā*), the caravan stayed till the month of *kārttik*, which was a time for beginning military campaigns, the number of pilgrims was estimated as four thousand, and by the time of arrival at Maheshvar, Ahilyabai Holkar's capital, the number reached ten thousand. With the exception of renouncers (*bairāgī, sannyāsī*) and those bound by the vow of celibacy (*brahmacārī*) who moved on their own, everyone else traveled in groups, and for each pilgrim under the guardianship of Saraswatibai it was a unique opportunity to visit *tristhaḷī*-towns with a chance to come back (Bhave 1976: 326). Therefore, various Brahmans (*śāstrī, paṇḍit, bhikṣuk, haridās, purāṇīk, agnihotrī*), warriors, royal widows (a widow of Nilkanthrav Patwardhan of Kurundvad was one of them), rich citizens with their families and poor servants in transition joined to compose a panoramic view of the Maharashtrian society preserved in the idiom of "eighteen turbans" (*aṭhrāpagaḍ jāt*), various types of turbans standing for different castes.[13]

A process of actual movement from Miraj to Rahimatpur—Baramati—Gardaund—Toke—(crossing over Kasarabarghat)—Jalgav—Bhadgav—Varangav—Barhanpur—Ashirgad—Maheshvar— Sagar—Bhelse—Prayag—Kashi—Gaya—Kashi and back was slow because of the difficult terrain on the way. In addition, every stage was preceded by dispatching mediators with a guard and then waiting for their return with favorable news about safety of the next passage (Khare 1912: 3762). Another complication resulted from the fact that Prayag, Kashi and Gaya were already under the British rule, and no advancement was possible without permission (Khare 1912: 3763). The British, however, were ready to cooperate with the Marathas. In view of a few defeats in battles with the still powerful Marathas and anticipating a lasting confrontation with Mysore, they could not turn down the Peshwas' requests and provided the leader of the caravan with transit passes (*rahadārīce dastak*) and tax exemption documents (*mahsulīcā caktī*). As a result, throughout visits to all the *tristhaḷī* towns, Saraswatibai succeeded in getting the whole caravan excused from taxes; besides, the British authorities issued a special order for ritual agents (*prayāgvaḷs, gaṅgāputras,* and *gayāvaḷs*) in each sacred place to perform their religious duties without extorting extra payment from pilgrims and thus put the whole procedure under their strict control.

Throughout the pilgrimage, Saraswatibai proved herself to be a skillful negotiator, talented financier and experienced manager. By the time of the arrival at Prayag, three other pilgrim caravans led by other Maharashtrians, two of whom were also women, happened to have reached there.[14] As suggested by Saraswatibai, all caravan leaders made a common agreement with *prayāgvaḷs* to escape from extortion on behalf of local priests (Khare 1912: 3764). When it became evident that in Gaya only pilgrims from Miraj were released from a pilgrimage tax, Saraswatibai sent her representatives with gifts to Warren Hastings, the governor-general of Bengal on a short visit to Lucknow, and begged him to treat all members of the ten thousand strong procession equally and have all of them exempted from taxation. Hastings did not accept the garments and jewellery worth two thousand rupees and informed Saraswatibai that a positive answer had already been forwarded to Scindia. More than a month, till the return of Saraswatibai's representatives, the caravan had been in suspense (Khare 1912: 3765). The noble woman from Miraj spent ten thousand rupees of her own to get the people under her guardianship exempted from taxation (Bhave 1976: 337). Both on the way to *tristhaḷī* and back Saraswatibai kept a finger on quantity of food required for the needs of her caravan, and hired two hundred mobile shops from bazaars of various towns (Khare 1912: 3766).

A few months stay in each of the *tristhaḷī*-towns naturally prolonged the actual period of the pilgrimage. The performance of *śrāddha* rituals in Gaya, for example, took three months at the speed of three to four hundred rituals a day. Saraswatibai got the rituals for her family members performed only at the end of the stay in Gaya. Along with performing rituals characteristic of each place, Saraswatibai and her closest courtiers kept paying official visits to British administration officers and local nobilities. For example, after a meeting with an English *subedār* (governor) of Kashi, Saraswatibai wrote in her letter, "politics and other things were discussed (*rājkī vagaire bolṇe jhāle*)" (Khare 1912: 3782). After returning from Gaya back to Kashi, the caravan had to wait till the end of the rainy season (*cāturmāsya*), and Saraswatibai took advantage of the stay to make acquaintances with other noble pilgrims (Khare 1912: 3767).

According to historian V.K. Bhave, a steady movement from Pune to Prayag with night stops only took around forty to forty-five days; a way from Prayag to Gaya via Kashi took twenty to twenty-five days more, from Kashi to Gaya—fourteen days at the speed of 8-10 *kos* a day, i.e. 25 to 32 km (Bhave 1976: 326, 338). According to Khare, the caravan covered from 4 to 12 *kos* per day (12 to 38 km), depending on a distance between halts and settlements. He evaluated a distance between Pune and Kashi as about 461-72 *kos*, i.e. 1475-1510 km (Khare 1912: 3797). In fact a movement to sacred places lasted much longer as the caravan stopped at every *tīrtha* on the way. For example, it stopped in Kaygav famous for its Maratha Brahman residents, and in Toke, and stayed a week in Pravarasangam, at the confluence of the Pravara and the Godavari etc. (Bhave 1976: 335).

The slow advancement to the sacred goal was determined by other factors as well: Saraswatibai could halt the movement by waiting for messengers (*jasūd, ajūrdār*) from Miraj and Pune and anticipating a delivery of a regular *huṇḍi*,[15] a kind of a travel cheque, as a financial provision for the *tīrtha-yātrā*[16] (Khare 1912: 3788-9). Saraswatibai's maladies (*āmce śarīrī samādhān navhte*) also made the caravan stop for a while (Khare 1912: 3784);

the movement was also affected by various epidemics and, consequently, deaths, which sometimes prompted relatives of those deceased choose to turn back to Gaya for performance of *gayāvarjan* ritual. Bhave also mentioned several cases of *satī* performed on the way (Bhave 1976: 338). Childbirths *en route* were also a routine event of a pilgrimage—arithmetic testifies that those born were conceived after the pilgrimage had started. If a woman was a person in attendance, Saraswatibai stopped the caravan for a twelve-day period of pollution (Khare 1912: 3803). As Bhave put it, "With the exception of marriages every other ritual, including initiation (*muñj*), used to be performed as prescribed" (Bhave 1976: 334).

A detailed description of day-to-day trivia of the caravan life in the correspondence of Saraswatibai indicates that a *yātrā* was perceived as an extraordinary and ordinary phenomenon simultaneously. As the latter it was a replica of the world left behind, a kind of a polity on march, a mobile polity, managed in accordance with statecraft regulations. Saraswatibai acted as the highest authority within this establishment combining responsibilities of a ruler, manager and financier[17] she had never been in her mundane life. By leading a procession to the religious goal and protecting subjects under her patronage, by solving both political and everyday problems with resolution and persistence, and, finally, by being officially received and honored here and there, Saraswatibai was legitimated as a religious and political leader and found a place in the history of Maharashtra. Her example inspired new flocks of visitors to the *tristhaḷī*-places. Three years later, for example, "[i]n the year 1786, as many as 170,000 Maratha pilgrims elected to increase their merit by travelling to Allahabad in an opulent armed convoy" (Bayly 1983: 127).

Thus, the documents of the second half of the eighteenth century present *tīrtha-yātrā* as a journey to the *tristhaḷī*, i.e. Prayag, Kashi, and Gaya, perceived to be an appropriate practice of the Maratha elite, and especially of its women. Whereas men found themselves at the *tīrthas* outside Maharashtra mostly as a result of pursuing a military campaign, i.e. by chance, an intentional movement to those *tīrthas* was desired by Maratha widows of high standing. As it happened, going on *tīrtha-yātrā* was the only device to overcome limitations put by widowhood and womanhood. When *en route*, high-ranking Maratha widows acquired freedom unthinkable for married women and demonstrated the qualities pertinent of a ruler. Their late husbands were either rulers or generals, and the widows took on their husbands' *rāja-dharma* as a standard behavior which could be achieved only at the time of *mārg(a)kramaṇ*.

BHOR

The small princely state of Bhor (910 sq. miles) with the capital of the same name on the Nira River was situated at the border of modern Pune and Satara districts. Over three-fourths of its area was covered by the Sahyadri mountains, and one-fourth located on a plain. The princes of Bhor were known as the Pantsachivs, a surname derived from the title of *saciv*[18] of the *aṣṭapradhān* (the eight ministers of state), which was granted in 1698 to their ancestor Shankar Narayan Gandekar by Rajaram, Shivaji's son. A scribe at the court of Shivaji at the beginning of his carrier, this Deshastha Brahman later proved himself an outstanding warrior and governor. He was rewarded with a land grant and founded a principality.

Raja Raghunathrav Shankarrav Pandit Pantsachiv, alias Babasaheb (1878-1952), was the eleventh descendant of the dynasty and a nominal ruler of Bhor at the time of the British Raj. He was enthroned in 1922, after the demise of his father Shankarrav (Raosaheb) who had been known for his religiosity.[19] Having lost six of his eight children Shankarrav used to be continuously pilgrimizing hoping by these means to keep the remaining son and daughter alive. V.P. Joshi, a biographer of the Bhor family, explained: "A despair (*udvigta*) dwelled in Raosaheb and his wife Jijisaheb's hearts, and they constantly thought about going on *tīrtha-yātrā* (*koṭhe tarī yātres jāve*)" (Joshi 1939: 55). In 1888 Shankarrav with his wife, their son and a retinue becoming to his status visited *tīrthas* of the Indian south;[20] in 1890 the family moved to north-west,[21] and in 1891 they again started for the southern *tīrthas*.[22] Joshi states that while traveling not only did Shankarrav, unlike his companions, not get tired, but he "was still obsessed [with pilgrimages] (*nādac lāglā hotā*)" (Joshi 1939: 58). While on his journeys he meticulously performed each and every ritual prescription even as he simulteneously looked upon a *tīrtha-yātrā* as a relatively ordinary event too. For example, teachers of Marathi and English accompanied a pilgrimage party to continue his son's education. Normally, any family ritual, such as performance of *veṇidān* at the triple confluence (*triveṇī*) in Prayag by the second wife of Raghunath Pantsachiv, would become a motivation to start for a *tīrtha-yātrā* (Joshi 1939: 211-12). The whole family would leave Bhor and stay away for a few months, taking an opportunity of seeing as many novelties as possible. Some of the members also found it proper to visit such places as Jabalpur or Calcutta with no particular religious aims in mind.

Some time after Shankarrav and his wife turned sixty, which is considered an old age in India, Jijisaheb expressed a wish to go on pilgrimage to sacred places of the Himalayan mountains. Conveniently enough, local *śāstrīs* dug out a clarification: a married woman, too, with the consent of her husband would be allowed to perform a *tīrtha-yātrā*, so Shankarrav gave his permission to his wife and stayed behind. Jijisaheb was accompanied by her own brother and his wife along with other relatives and attendants. Over fifty dwellers of Bhor used the rare opportunity and joined the *yātrā* too (Joshi 1939: 214-15).

These preliminaries are narrated to illustrate that Raghunath Pantsachiv whose travels are scrutinized in this part of the paper, had been nourished in the atmosphere of frequent journeys, and still when a child had had access to almost all the famous *tīrthas*, visiting them within compound *tīrtha-yātrās* undertaken by his parents. Later in his life he never missed a chance, too, and he used to begin a new trip at whatever pretext was at hand—be it an acquisition of personal experience as in 1909, his participation in the Delhi darbar as in 1911, or an urge to lessen the pain of his own child's death as in 1919 ("He decided to start for south India [Rameshvaram] to alleviate his emotional state (*manaḥ-svāsthya miḷavṇyākaritā*)"[23] (Joshi 1939: 217). What is remarkable is that many years after Raghunath had become the legitimate ruler of Bhor, he, drawing from his diary and additional reference sources, transformed his travel experience into a literary activity. Almost 28 years after the actual journeys he authored two books published under a common title of "Our travels to various places in India" (Pantsachiv 1936, 1939).

Pantsachiv's personal authorship and his use of *saphar*, an Arabic term related to visits to Hindu *tīrthas* by no means, in the title rather than *tīrtha-yātrā*, suggest changes in motivation of his personal movement while still an heir apparent or in his presentation of that movement to public. Each of his travels had lasted from two to three months, and though they did not begin in the month of Kārttik immediately after the festival of Daserā as per tradition of Maratha *tīrtha-yātrās*, they were preceded, in accordance with the tradition, by an articulation of *saṅkalpa* (Pantsachiv 1936: 2). During the first one in 1909, Raghunath was escorted by a dozen men, spent 9,992 rupees out of ten thousand given to him by his father, and traveled from (Bhor) Pune to Bombay—Baroda—Ahmadabad—Abu—Ajmer—Pushkar—Jaypur—Amber—Galta—Bharatpur—Agra—Mathura—Vrindavan—Simla—Kashi—Ayodhya—Manmad and back to Pune (Bhor) (Pantsachiv 1936: 2, 119). His second trip, timed to the Delhi darbar of 1911, was in the company of 25 men; he spent 11,300 rupees, three thousand of which were given to him by his father and 8,300 were his own, and he traveled from (Bhor) Pune to Bombay—Delhi—Hardwar—Dehradun—Masuri—Lucknow—Kanpur—Allahabad (Prayag)—Benares (Kashi)—Sarnath—Mogalsarai—Bhopal—Sanchi—Manmad—Vinçur—Bombay and back to Pune (Bhor) (Pantsachiv 1939: 1). A cliché "many things are worth seeing here (*pāhṇyāsārkhyā baryāc goṣṭī*)" comes repeatedly throughout both "Travels", along with many figures related to expenditures and the monetary evaluation of things around. Insatiable curiosity towards the world "seen with one's own eyes" and thorough calculations were characteristic of earlier pilgrimages by both Serfoji II, a Maratha prince of Thanjavur, and Raghunatrav Vincurkar, a ruler of Vincur. During his travel south in 1919 the Raghunath Pantsachiv stayed at the descendants of the fisrt in Thanjavur[24] (Joshi 1939: 218); he was related by bonds of blood and personal friendship to the descendants of the latter. It seems likely that the Bhor princes knew well the poetical narrations of pilgrimages of Serfoji II (*Tristallī* 1951) and a rather popular account of *tīrtha-yātrās* of the prince of Vincur (Tryambakkar 1964). One of the poems on Serfoji II's pilgrimages (*Tristhallī Yātrechyā Lāvanya*) was attributed to the Thanjavurian prince himself while the narration of Vincurkar's *tīrtha-yātrās,* first published in 1885, was based on correspondence and financial accounts of the participants of those pilgrimages. These compositions might have even served as an inspiration and model, leading Raghunath Pantsachiv, a Deccan College alumnus, to continue the tradition of princely travelogues.

While commenting on the first independent journey of Pantsachiv in 1909, Joshi, his biographer, explains, that Raghunath's father, Shankarrav, considered "visits to sacred places and performance of religious duties to be the general goal, and that was the main predisposition at the time of preparation of itineraries. He was not guided by a modern outlook regarding travels. That is why, while accompanying his father to holy places Babasaheb was treated to the accounts of local mahatmyas and consequently did not benefit as he might have benefited had he traveled on his own" (Joshi 1939: 120). Pantsachiv himself makes it clear that his main goal was "broadening of his mental outlook and knowledge increment (*dñyānārjan*)" (Pantsachiv, 1936: 2): "travels and nothing else are a means to overcome the mentality of a frog living in a well (*kūpmaṇḍūkvṛtti jāṇyās pravās hāc ek mārg āhe*)" (Pantsachiv 1936: 1). Whatever the travels of the heir apparent looked like in reality, as a ruler of Bhor Raghunath presents their retrospective version, selecting, interpreting and supplementing his old impressions.

It is well known that throughout the nineteenth century the British administration pursued politics of isolating Indian princes. The latter needed official approval for travels, and they had to apply through a British resident or political agent in their own principality. Residents and agents acted in collaboration with a provincial governor, and sometimes resorted to the highest authorities in Calcutta, playing the key role in determining the itineraries, which were later controlled by residents of principalities and British collectors *en route.* The British mainly encouraged princes' departures from their domains because their absence did not have any practical political implications. On the contrary, it could even strengthen the position of the colonizers. Simultaneously the British minimized undesirable contacts among Indian princes which might have resulted in particular ties and coalitions.[25] As the princes of Bhor as early as the beginning of the nineteenth century made themselves known as loyal supporters of the British, complying with their requests by entrapping their compatriots and giving them up, both Shankarrav and Raghunath could expect full cooperation from colonial officials. As for the officials, in accordance with a recognized ranking, they felt responsible for maintaining the status of a ruler beyond the borders of his principality as manifested in the number of those greeting and seeing him off and in etiquette meetings and official dinners. The publisher of the first book of "Travels" reminds in his Introduction that "A ruler's travel should be arranged in a dignified manner as per his status, pompous receptions are expected everywhere (*svāgat sammān sajj*), nothing should lack" (Pantsachiv 1936: 8). The author himself never fails to mention a first class carriage booked for his personal passage, his retinue traveling by second class, and a train stopping at a station and breaking a railway schedule for his own comfort (Pantsachiv 1939: 3). He remarks, "We are compelled to be in keeping with our status. Even if our attachment to comfort is apprehended critically, it does not become a person of our standing to travel in a different way" (Pantsachiv 1936: 3). In accordance with the obligations of his standing he also could not but take care of his escort, providing them with warm clothes, etc. and informing his readers about it 28 years later. As he explains, "All the time we dutifully cared about our family" (Pantsachiv 1939: 82).

Both statements should be taken into account while coming across multiple references to officialdom—from British officers to Indian princes and nobility of Maharashtrian descent holding various positions outside Bhor. Along with names of British residents who authorized Raghunath's movements and gave permission for visits to particular sites at each place, there are many mentions of the Vincurkar royal family related to the Pantsachivs and references to Sayaji Gaekvad of Baroda and other ex- or incumbent maharajas, rajas and sultans met at the time of travels. There are numerous references to *divāṇs* of other princely states, revenue members and other position holders who received and saw off the Bhor company at various places. On insistent requests of some of them Raghunath even prolonged his stay in some place, and by moving to special guest quarters acquired a rank of a "state guest". Everywhere hosts and their guest adhered to a ritual greeting ceremony called by metonyms *pānsupārya* and *cahāparṭī*.

The travel program depicted in both books of the "Travels" comprised absolutely everything: from city/town-sightseeing to inspecting new factories and performing religious rituals. For example, in Bombay, Raghunath Pantsachiv paid a visit to the "Old Bombay" exhibition scheduled for the arrival of George V. Pantsachiv did not like the layout of the exhibits but enjoyed a Bombay map of 1672 (Pantsachiv 1939: 5). In Benares he attended a lecture on theosophy by Annie Besant (Pantsachiv 1939: 128). Still, even in the chaotic enumeration of events characteristic of the style of the "Travels", particular subjects unfailingly draw the interest of Raghunath Pantsachiv. They are: (1) sanitary characteristics of places and peoples in terms of "clean" and "dirty"; (2) peculiarities of town-planning with top priority given to the quality of roads in terms of "straight" and "curved" or "broad" and "narrow"; (3) architectually unusual buildings; (4) man-made ponds; (5) public parks[26] and (6) local industry.

"Straight and well seen from afar" streets were distinguished by Pantsachiv as a specific feature of Baroda (Pantsachiv 1936: 11). He also praised the Baroda's public park: "By laying out a public park the prince has contributed a lot to the common weal. Concentrated not on pure entertainment but on increasing knowledge he got a beautiful spacious building erected to house a museum and an art gallery" (Pantsachiv 1936: 14). Contrary to the Baroda experience, he found the streets of Ahmadabad "too narrow and curved. Though Ahmadabad is known throughout the Bombay province, we have nowhere seen an untidier city. Dirt and dust are reigning in four directions" (Pantsachiv 1936: 24). That he still, many years later spoke with passion about these kinds of things reveals how deeply he had been under the influence of the Enlightenment ideas of betterment and progress which he believed he would be able to bring to his own domain.

In the first book of "Travels" the author does not pay much attention to religious matters and sometimes even speaks a bit ironically about these: "wherever you go you are unable to find a path that would not bring you to a temple" (Pantsachiv 1936: 23). He provides the most trivial information on traditional *tīrthas* like Pushkar ("it is here that Brahma had performed his sacrifices" [Pantsachiv 1936: 47]) or Mathura ("it is here that Krishna had been born" [Pantsachiv 1936: 96-7]). Still he followed strictly whatever rituals prescribed in each place, seeking services of the family ritual agents (or their descendants) and checking signatures (*lekh*) of his ancestors. Thus, in Mathura he was shown signatures of Shankarrav Raghunath, the sixth prince of the Bhor family, made in 1795; of Radhabai Sachiv, made in 1849; and his own father's, made in 1891 (Pantsachiv 1936: 99). So, even performing his first independent travel—*saphar,* and not *yātrā*—Pantsachiv clung to the more familiar itinerary. But while preparing a written account for publication he does not hesitate to include purely mundane reminiscences as well, such, for example, as a picture of a funny monkey reposing on a tortoise's back (Pantsachiv 1936: 111). He also seems to have enjoyed sharpening his expressive ability by describing natural phenomena and architectural details.

When in Kashi during his 1909 travel, Pantsachiv planned a five-day stay in Bhorkar-*mandir,* which was a family property, in order to perform all rituals prescribed. His ablutions at various *ghāṭs* took turns with a tight program of profane activity like a visit to a local park or a meeting with a collector who honored him by providing him a constable as an escort (Pantsachiv 1936: 111). Pantsachiv also paid a one-day visit to Ayodhya for *darśan* of Rama, the Pantsachivs' *kuldevatā,* where he was attended by the same priests who had attended to his father in 1879 (Pantsachiv 1936: 114). When back in Kashi, he arranged a traditional feeding of 111 Brahmans with a 10 anna distribution to each. This was followed by a meeting with one hundred *paṇḍits* and a one rupee *dakṣiṇā* gift to each. Simultaneously his wife, who joined him most probably in Kashi, arranged a *haḷadkuṃkuṃ* ceremony with five-six hundred married women invited.

28 years later recalling his first independent travel Pantsachiv

concludes in the final part of the first book of "Travels": "As we anticipated while planning this travel, by observing various people, their traditions and rituals of various localities, our previous ideas underwent some changes, we drove away boredom and improved our health" (Pantsachiv 1936: 120).

The second book of "Travels" deals with another journey which happened less than two years later under the pretext of participation in the Delhi darbar of 1911. Though many of the places visited were the same, Pantsachiv felt an urge to write an additional volume. He explains: "The previous book was our first attempt in creation of a sample of literature, and the subject has not been exhausted. The new one will include besides trivia, historical data as well, and religious explanations to substantiate our own ideas. In this way we hope to achieve a narration more intelligible, didactic and captivating" (Pantsachiv 1939: 4).

Frankly speaking, there is not much difference between the two books other than differences in the respective itineraries. Wherever the author went, his attention was invariably drawn to a city/town arrangement, roads, ponds, parks and the like. Some additional historical information is included on Delhi and Bhopal in particular, which are described in more detail, with additional data drawn from guide-books and travelogues. Mythological data is attached to holy places like Hardwar and Prayag, where he performed rituals, fed Brahmans and counted his expenditures. There are occasional passages of ethical concerns and landscape descriptions.

Still there is a distinct interest that helps to justify the new publication. From the very beginning of his 1911 travels Pantsachiv keeps encountering Indian princes, those who already lost their domains (like Vincurkar or Bhosle of Mudhol) and some still incumbent. Most were invited to the darbar, and the Bhor camp was set up in the area allotted to princes from the Bombay province (Pantsachiv 1939: 8). The disposition of princes at the ceremonial event was in accordance with their ranks recognized by the British. There were both sitting and standing facilities in the area. "Our father was standing in the second row to the left, and we were standing immediately behind him in the third row" (Pantsachiv 1939: 73). After the darbar formalities were over Pantsachiv began his new independent travel.

This time he visited both Prayag and Kashi. When in Prayag he stayed at the palace belonging to the Holkars of Indore (Pantsachiv 1939: 120). In Kashi, notwithstanding the availability of the Bhorkar-*mandir*, he chose to stay at the palace of the Gaekvads of Baroda (Pantsachiv 1939: 128). In the Muslim state of Bhopal he enjoyed full-scale hospitality provided by the Bhopal ruler-begum (Navab-sultan Jahan-begum), who acted on a request of a Bhopal resident. It was here that Pantsachiv was finally granted permission to visit a gun-powder factory (Pantsachiv 1939: 135-40). On his railway journey back he was glad to meet the ex-raja of Mudhol and to have a good companion for chatting; he made a stop in Manmad to drop in Vincur for a game of tennis, and then proceeded to Bombay where he paid official visits to the police chief and the Pune collector, alias Bhor political agent, who came to Bombay on purpose to greet Pantsachiv (Pantsachiv 1939: 143-4). The latter also arranged a ceremonial party to celebrate an eleven-gun salute—a privilege raising a prince's status as per a table of ranking which was granted to his father Shankarrav, the incumbent ruler of Bhor, after the Delhi darbar.

Three supplements attached are an absolute innovation in the second "Travels". At the first sight, they are related to the goals stated by the author neither in theme nor in chronology. The first supplement deals with the Delhi darbar as a state event and with the announcement there about the transfer of the capital of British India from Calcutta to Delhi. The description of Delhi is repeated on the basis of Pantsachiv's later visits and is reiterated with a primary attention to the grandeur of imperial buildings and comparison to other government buildings in Canada, Australia, New Zealand, and South Africa (Pantsachiv 1939: 146-82).

The second supplement is entitled "Formation of the Chamber of Princes and our activity as its member". The section, unrelated to the theme of the "Travels", tells about the political activity of Shankarrav outside Bhor, including his participation in the Conference of Princes of 1917,[27] to which he was accompanied by the author, and about the formation of the Chamber of Princes in 1921 and Raghunath Pantsachiv's personal contribution to its work. Though all princes with a permanent salute of eleven guns or higher were recognized eligible for membership (Ramusack

1978: 88), Shankarrav was not among them because his "salute privilege" was "personal" and not "hereditary".[28] Enthroned in 1922 after the death of Shankarrav, Raghunath Pantsachiv could enter the Chamber only if elected a representative from one of twelve groups of 128 minor principalities. Initially the group to which Bhor belonged had been represented by an ex-ruler of Akalkot who suddenly passed away in 1923. Taking this opportunity and not hiding his political ambitions, Pantsachiv, after separate talks with princes of his group, nominated himself and was thrice (1923, 1924, 1927) elected as a member of the Chamber. During his membership he eighteen times addressed a meeting with various proposals, comments and concerns which he details in the supplement (Pantsachiv 1939: 183-7).

The third supplement contains information on the Museum of Asian antiquities in Delhi, Mohenjo-Daro excavations and marble temples built by Birla in Delhi (Pantsachiv 1939: 183-7).

On the whole, both books of the "Travels" are an eclectic narration, void of consistency and literary merits. The author defines their genre as "notes on travels (*pravāsvṛttipar likhāṇ*)" (Pantsachiv 1939: 118). It is hard to believe that published 28 years after his travels they could serve as an authentic travel-guide: most of the information had become outdated, including transportation fares or service fees. In any case, not many people could afford traveling in a way becoming to an heir apparent of a small but still formally independent state. Many details occurring throughout both books are highly insignificant, such as references to timings of the day, hygiene trivialities or post-lunch respites. Some physiological accounts along with medical bulletin and information on the author's weight (one *maṇ* 23 *śer* [Pantsachiv 1936: 9]) add nothing to the travel report.

Still a firm conviction about the special duty of a ruler, i.e. *rāja-dharma*, is expressed in several places. Though not explicitly called as such and understood in the context of changing times, the *rāja-dharma* priority recognized as caring attitudes towards one's subjects, is invoked in Introductions to both books. It is *rāja-dharma* that makes a ruler leave his domain and search for a new experience and knowledge. It is his duty to observe other rulers and their relations with their subjects, their rituals and laws and to introduce the best of them for the benefit of his own state. It is his duty to take interest in roads and ponds, parks and new technologies. A good ruler is obliged to travel for his state's sake as travels "provide a new intellectual and spiritual upgrowth . . ., and in the world of developed societies they are a main means of acquiring new knowledge" (Pantsachiv 1939: 5). Despite the hardships on the movement, a ruler should learn to overcome them and be careful not "to see things through the eyes of those who are responsible for a show" (Pantsachiv 1939: 8).

Finally, the second book cites a famous *ślok*: "By traveling one makes friends with pandits and paves his way into a higher circle (*deśātaṇ kelyāne 'paṇḍit maitrī sabhet sañcār' vagaire phāyde hotāt he sāṅgnārā ślok prasiddhac āhe*)" (Pantasachiv 1939: 3). Thus comes a legitimation of a ruler irrespective of the fact whether he rules or not. A ruler of a small and politically insignificant principality must have felt a need for ritual and political affirmation of his royal status, and hence he moved in search of contacts with his peers and more prominent princes (like, for example, the linguistically and spatially close prince of Baroda). As Barbara Ramusack puts it: "The energetic rulers of middle-sized states attempted to dominate by their personal contacts and accomplishments, since they lacked the resources of the largest populations and revenues" (Ramusack 1978: 186). Staying far away from a decision making Delhi, there was no other way for "dominating" as to be a part of the Chamber of Princes, a useless but still prestigious body. Ramusack adds: "The princes had seen the Chamber as an institution that would give them direct access to the viceroy and the political secretary, and as a forum for evolving policies through mutual agreement" (Ramusack 1978: 187). Therefore, it is no wonder that the supplements on the capital's grandeur and Pantsachiv's involvement with imperial politics found their way into the "notes on travels".

Since the rulers of even the largest princely states could hardly affect the course of the last decade of the British Raj, little other than reminiscences remained in the 1930s as an expression of one's own royal status. Both of Pantsachiv's books were not meant for sale but as gift editions and were distributed primarily among fellow Maratha princes, whether incumbent or lapsed.

MĀRG(A)KRAMAṆ

This paper juxtaposes pilgrimages and travels of two historical figures divided by a 150-year gap, gender, age, status, etc. but united by their religious, linguistic, and social background. The juxtaposition aims at a further reconstruction of the cultural dimensions of *mārg(a)kramaṇ*, especially as a movement towards Hindu holy places, within a *tīrtha-yātrā* model proposed by me earlier.

A marked difference between the movements of Saraswatibai Patwardhan and of Raghunath Pantsachiv is found in their namings: while Saraswatibai went on pilgrimage (*tīrtha-yātrā*), Pantsachiv kept traveling (*saphar*). The first was motivated by a religious goal, the latter was driven by a search for knowledge, though based on a *tīrtha-yātrā* pattern. In earlier centuries pilgrims certrainly enriched their knowledge immensely by traversing unknown regions and meeting strange people and rituals. They might have been even more exposed than later travelers who used modern transportation facilities with fewer immediate local contacts. According to Bhave: "A *yātrā*'s itinerary was arranged so as not to miss anything of interest" (Bhave 1976: 336). While also not missing anything of interest, Pantsachiv did not overlook a religious component of his wanderings, and he calculated the duration of his stay in sacred places by giving priority to ritual activity. Besides his personal faith, for Pantsachiv a ruler's status, following the kingly ideal, also was dependent on accumulation of religious merits.

Notwithstanding the different names, there are more structural traits in common between the movements of these two royal characters which imply a special function, besides the religious one, of *mārg(a)kramaṇ* within the Indian context. For Saraswatibai and Pantsachiv *tīrtha-yātrā* or *saphar* was not a private affair but an event of public importance which required a lot of preliminary preparation and significant monetary expenses. There were diverse political players relevant to the times—from Peshwas, princes and landlords to British authorities—directly and indirectly involved in the arrangements. It was not by chance that the dissemination of news regarding Saraswatibai's pilgrimage resulted in alerting public attention and consequent growth of the number of pilgrims. It was not an idiosyncratic act when on his return to Bhor Pantsachiv lectured on his travels, published articles, and later worked to promulgate his experiences for contemporaries and to be remembered in the future. A transit from place to place could not but broaden social and political contacts, thus revealing a function of social integration pertinent of both *tīrtha-yātrā* and *saphar*. This integration included various princely clans and landlords whose domains were traversed; noblemen of many regions met at the *tīrthas* or at the Delhi darbar and other places, along with the lower strata representatives termed as "eighteen turbans" who constituted a considerable part of a pilgrimage caravan (as in case of Saraswatibai's).

At the same time, the mere possibility of such movements and their entourage—both in providing maximum escort and facilities appropriate to the rank of a person in transit and to securing various privileges and ensuring etiquette *en route*—testifies to a general recognition of the high status of a pilgrim or traveler, whether a widow from a noble family famous for its military deeds and related to many prince families of Maharashtra or an heir apparent educating himself to become a ruler. To rephrase Hermann Kulke, social integration can be interpreted as strengthening of vertical (inner) legitimation, and demonstration of a recognition of a person's status—especially important in the case of Pantsachiv against the background of his complete loss of real power—as strengthening of horizontal (outside) legitimation (Kulke 2001: 161). It is *mārg(a)kramaṇ* that was utilized to get both goals achieved.

As per *tīrtha-yātrā per se*, though it is habitually percived as an extraordinary practice, its valorization by the Maharashtrian princely families turned it into an ordinary practice as well, which did not presume staying aloof from everyday routine but maintaining it on the way. Moreover, an explicit objective of a pilgrimage or a journey becomes less significant in view of an implicit objective of proving one's princely status. Be it in a traditional or colonial society, movement was potent to ensure an individual's search of his/her royal self within a frame of traditions and political expedience and boundaries made for others.

NOTES

1. I am thankful to Drs Elena Karachkova and Lee Schlesinger for brushing up the English language of my paper.
2. I prefer to spell a honorific affixation as -rav in accordance with its actual spelling and pronunciation in Marathi. More habitual names of the Maratha Peshwas (like Bajirao etc.) are written in their historical form.
3. Venkoji, a step-brother of the Maratha king Shivaji, captured Thanjavur from the Nayak rulers in 1676.
4. Vincur with adjoining villages was granted to Vitthal Shivdev, an ancestor of Raghunathrav, by the Peshwa as a special land assignment (*sarañjām*) to support government troops and maintain forts. Vitthal Shivdev had distinguished himself at the seizure of Ahmadabad by Marathas in 1755.
5. Miraj was partitioned in 1820. The combined area of Miraj Senior and Miraj Junior equals to 550 sq. miles or 1,494 km^2.
6. Satyabhamabai, Govind's mother, was from the beginning indignant by her son's straightforward comment that "the bride [was] bad" (*navrī vāīṭ*). Her son's reluctance to remarry intensified after the bride was taken ill with small pox but his mother remained adamant being aware of a possible protest from Brahman folk (*brahmaṇdveś*), and a renowned warrior submitted to his parents' will (Khare 1898-9: 474-5).
7. "Solemn and formal enunciation of purpose as preparatory to entrance upon any important religious rite or work (e.g. ablution at a *tīrtha, śrāddha, gopradān, pṛthvīdān, dīpdān,* or other *dān-dharma*). This utterance is made by the subject himself or by a Brahman for him" (Molesworth 1975: 807).
8. Radhabai had been *en route* for almost a year and a half (from February 1735 to June 1736). Her itinerary was as follows: Pune—Burhanpur—Badhvai—Udaypur—Nathdvara—Jaypur—Mathura—Vrindavan—Kurukshetra—Prayag—Kashi—Gaya—Sagar—Badhvai—Pune (Ok 1991: 76).
9. A caravan led by Kashibai consisted of about 30-40 thousand at the time of its arrival at Kashi (Bhave 1976: 330-1).
10. On his caravan's way back to Miraj, while crossing Pune, around two thousand abandoned the caravan and stayed in Pune (Bhave 1976: 333). The figure of "two thousand" might give an idea about the whole number of pilgrims in the caravan.
11. There are other letters, too, written to other people as well, but a constant resort to house names based on kin terms makes it difficult to understand who writes to whom.
12. In one of her letters Saraswatibai left a detailed explanation why it was nobody else but Mahadji Scindia who should be approached for

his established contacts with Englishmen, and how he should be approached (Khare 1912: 3699). Scindia is known to have stopped his struggle against the English by 1780s hoping to be recognized by them as a ruler independent of Pune.

13. Compare, for example: "The aspect foregrounded for the pilgrimage was that of the ruler responsible for all those in his state, irrespective of caste or creed" (Balzani 2003: 146).
14. One was led by a mother of a *divāṇ* of Mahadji Scindia; the other was led by Balubai, a daughter of Mudhoji Bhosle from Nagpur; the third was led by one Ganpatrav Dikshit from Nasik (Khare 1912: 3764).
15. A mail was delivered within a period of a month to two months.
16. As per Bayly, "In 1815, Rs. 150,000, or between 5 and 10 per cent of Benares transactions with its best trading partners, the Maratha dominions to the south, was accounted for by the provision of cash for pilgrims" (Bayly 1983: 128).
17. Every letter contains some lines on the pilgrimage's finances and calculations. At the same time Saraswatibai was taking a keen interest in prices—from gold to rice—observing them on the way and comparing to those in Miraj.
18. J. Sarkar explains *saciv* as a superintendant: "He had to see that all royal letters were drafted in the proper style, to revise them, and to write at the head of charter the words Shuru shud, or 'Here begins'. He had also to check the accounts of the *mahals* and *parganas.*" (Sarkar 1952: 361). S. Gordon states, that *saciv's* "position was advisory, their duties vague and overlapping" (Gordon 1993: 107).
19. Compare, for example: "During the reign of Shrimant Raosaheb, . . . a considerable large portion of the State revenue was allotted to temples and other religious institutions, including a grant of 28 villages to the Shri Rama Sonthan [*sic*!] . . . . Under attack at home for his conservative politics, Raosaheb spent the best part of his latter years visiting Hindu holy places, and virtually his last public act was to endow a temple in Banaras" (Copland 1982: 38).
20. Their itenarary was as follows: (Bhor) Pune—Kulbarga—Tarpanna—Madras—Chidambaram—Navpan—Rameshvaram—Ramnathpur—Dharmashayan—Madura—Trichinapalli—Tinvelli—Shrirangam—Thanjavur—Kumbhakoynam—Chingalpattam—Kanchi—Tirupati—Raychur—Pune (Bhor) (Joshi 1939: 55).
21. Their itenerary was as follows: (Bhor) Pune—Bombay—Dakur—Ahmadabad—Porbandar—Dwarka—Somnath—Sidhpur—Ajmer—Pushkar—Jaypur—Agra—Prayag—Kashi—Ayodhya—Haridvar—Ambala—Kurukshetra—Deli—Mathura—etc.—Itarsi—Nasik—Pune (Bhor) (Joshi 1939: 57).
22. Their main goal was a visit to Gokarna (Joshi 1939: 58).

23. This travel is not described by Raghunath Pantsachiv and hence is not analyzed in the paper.
24. He was greeted there by Shivaji III, a grand-grand-son of Serfoji II. No more an incumbent ruler, but still a holder of a "raja" title, Shivaji III, in accordance with kshatriy etiquette of hospitality, at the time of parting gifted to Raghunath Pantsachiv rich clothes (Joshi 1939: 218).
25. "There are also links between pilgrimage and politics in both colonial and post-colonial India. In colonial times princes were forbidden to contact other rulers for all but personal matters and any political matter had to go through the British. A devout prince could, none the less, go on a pilgrimage (clearly non-political) and in passing through another ruler's state might pay a visit to the prince of the state and in this manner conduct forbidden discussions of political nature" (Balzani 2003: 126).
26. Horticulture also happened to be one of the strongest hobbies of Serfoji II, who used to take an opportunity of his *mārg(a)kramaṇ* for collecting new plants and seeds for his palace gardens and public space in Thanjavur. A beautiful albeit decaying park with broken statues and fountains borders the royal palace which is used both as a museum and a marriage pavilion in Bhor today.
27. "At their informal meeting on 3-4 November 1917, the princes expressed great concern over the issue of precedence at social functions and ranking of princes by salutes" (Ramusack 1978: 74-5).
28. A different explanation is found by Ian Copland: "Most of the Southern Maratha and Satara states were exluded from the Chamber in 1921 on the grounds that they were 'not sovereign princes but Jagirdars". Some, along with Limbdi in Kathiawar, were later admitted to membership by special dispensation of the government, but this only added to the sense of injury felt by the others, like Bhor and Aundh (which were both relatively progressive and well-administered principalities)" (Copland 1982: 246).

REFERENCES

Balzani, Marzia, 2003: *Modern Indian Kingship: Tradition, Legitimacy & Power in Rajasthan.* World Anthropology Series, ed. Wendy James & N.J. Allen. Oxford/Santa Fe: James Currey/School of American Research Press.

Bayly, C.A., 1983: *Rulers, Townsmen and Bazaars: North Indian Society in the Age of British Expansion, 1770-1870.* Cambridge: Cambridge University Press.

Bhave, Vasudev Krishna, 1976: *Peśvekālīn Mahārāṣṭra.* Navi Dilli: Bharatiy Itihas Anusandhan Parishad.

Copland, Ian, 1982: *The British Raj and the Indian Princes: Paramountcy in Western India 1857-1930.* Bombay: Orient Longman.

Derret, J.D.M., 1976: "Rājadharma", *Journal of Asian Studies*, no. 35.

Glushkova, Irina, 2004: "Moving God(s)ward: The Idea of *Tīrtha-Yātrā*", *Bulletin of the Deccan College Post-Graduate and Research Institute*, vols. 62-3 (2002 and 2003). Professor Ashok R. Kelkar Felicitation Volume. Pune: Deccan College.

——, 2006: "Moving God(s)ward, Calculating Money: Wonders and Wealth as Essentials of a *Tīrtha-Yātrā*", *South Asia*, vol. XXIX, no. 2.

Gordon, Stewart, 1993: *The Marathas 1600-1818: The New Cambridge History of India.* New Delhi: Foundation Books.

Joshi, Vasudev Narayan, 1939: *Rājā śrīmant raghunāthrāv paṇḍit pantsaciv rājesāheb saṃsthān bhor yāñce caritra.* Khand pahila. Bhor: Vinayak Bapurav Deshpande.

Khare, Vasudev Vaman Shastri, 1898-9: *Aitihāsik lekh saṅgrah. Mādhavrāv Ballāḷ ūrf Īrāvsāheb Ī peśva yāñcī kārkīrd.* Bhag dusra. Kurundwad: Miraj High School Samskrut Shikshak.

——, 1912: *Aitihāsik lekh saṅgrah: Sevāī rāvsāheb peśve yāncī kārkīrd (epril 1778 te epril 1784).* Bhag satva. Pune: Aryabhushan.

Kulke, Hermann, 2001: "Royal Temple Policy and the Structure of Medieval Hindu Kingdoms", *Kings and Cults: State Formation and Legitimation in India and Southeast Asia.* New Delhi: Manohar (rpt.) .

Molesworth, J.T., 1975: Molesworth's *Marathi-English Dictionary.* Corrected reprint. Poona: Shubhada-Saraswat.

Ok, Pramod, 1991: *Peśve gharāṇyācā itihās.* Pune: Continental Prakashan, (dusri avrutti).

Pantsachiv, Raja Raghunathrav Shankar Pandit, 1936: *Hindustānātīl āmcyā ṭhikṭhikāṇcyā sapharī.* Pune: Samartha Bharat Press.

——, 1939: *Hindustānātīl āmcyā ṭhikṭhikāṇcyā sapharī: Saphar dusrī.* Pune: Samartha Bharat Press.

Ramusack, Barbara N., 1978: *The Princes of India in the Twilight of Empire: Dissolution of a Patron-Client System, 1914-1939.* Columbus: Ohio State University Press.

Sarkar, Jadunath, 1952: *Shivaji and his Time.* Calcutta: M.C. Sarkar (5th edn.).

Tristalī, 1951: *Yātrechyā Lāvanya (by King Serfoji) and Sarabēndra Thēērthavalli (by Siva)*, critically edited with Introduction and Synopsis in English by Sri A. Krishnaswami Mahadick Rao Sahib. Tanjore: T.V.S.S.V. Library.

Tryambakkar, Lele G.S., 1964: *Tīrthayātrāprabandh.* Pune: Deshmukh Ani Kampani (dusri avrutti).

19

Pilgrimage to Pandharpur: Pathway (*Mārg*) to Better Social Life

V. L. MANJUL

Pilgrimages are characteristic of most of the higher religions. According to E.B., pilgrimage means "a journey to a saint's shrine or other sacred place, undertaken for a variety of motives, with the object of gaining supernatural help". The Jewish Encyclopedia defines pilgrimage as "a journey, which is made to a shrine or sacred place in performance of a vow or for the sake of obtaining some form of divine blessing". The word pilgrimage originally came from the Latin word "peregrimus" meaning "foreign". This is also interesting. In short, "this is an act of thanksgiving or of penance for the sake of devotion".

Pilgrimages to holy places are both accepted/recommended and also rejected by great Indian saints. The very act of going on a pilgrimage is its own praise, and the rejection comes from no lesser a person than Shri Kabir, who is the doyen of Indian sainthood. For him pilgrimage, litanies and vows are all empty beliefs.[1] Even Shri Nanakaji, the founder *guru* of Sikhism, when asked by a Muslim: "Why you did not turn to the direction of Mecca to pray?", replied saying "there is no place where there is no God". Similarly the great Gujarati saint Shri Narasi Mehta also suggested the same philosophy. He said "he (the Vaishnava?) himself is the center of all pilgrimage" (*Sakala tirath tena tana mare*). It seems that some of the north Indian saints have not strongly recommended the act of pilgrimage and even not accepted as obligatory to Indian devotees. It may be possible because of *saguna* and *nirguna bhakti* system. Most north Indian saints follow *nirguna bhakti* in which image worship and pilgrimage may not be accepted, that is why these saints avoid this ritual.[2]

On the contrary Maharashtrian saints (from the thirteenth to twentieth century) by starting from the great saint Dnyaneshvar-Namadev founders of the Varkari (Bhāgavat) cult, upto Tukadoji Buvā and Gādagebābā, Social workers-cum-modern saints who followed *saguna bhakti* strongly recommended pilgrimage to common man. In the case of the Pandharpur pilgrimage Maharashtrian (Marathi) saints made it obligatory to the Varkari cult; there are several *abhangas* (poems) which describe the holiness of the Lord Vitthal, river Chandrabhāgā and the city Pandharpur; they insist devotees to attend *vāri* regularly. Dnyaneshvar (thirteenth century): "My lifetime wish is to visit Pandharpur" (*majha jivici avadi | pandharpura nein gudhi*); Namadeva (same century): "This Pandharpur is the only holy place famous in the three worlds" (*pandhariksetra pavana-pavitra | mahima vicitra tribhuvani*); Tukaram (seventeeth century): "You can attend all the religious places, if you visit Pandharpur only" (*sakala hi tirthe ghadati ek velā candrabhāgā dolā*); and Eknath (sixteenth-century): "Attending Pandharpur *vāri*, says there is no need of doing anything else" (*sādhan te sār pandharici vāri | an na tu kari sayasace*). All these great *gurus* of Varkari cult often suggested their followers to undertake *vāri* (*jay jay tu pandhari | hoy hoy vārkari*).[3]

Marathi society is devotional by nature. Since the medieval period, there is an unbroken tradition of devotion comprising of a number of sects and cults. Devotion for god Vitthala (Vithoba) is not only predominant but has a continuous tradition in Maharashtra, year after year. The Varkari pilgrims following medieval socio-cultural rituals, continue to visit Pandharpur (in Solapur district) to pay the obeisance to god Vithoba standing on the banks of Bhima River popularly known as Chandrabhāgā.

The tradition of *vāri* is an integral element of Maharashtrian culture. The *vārkari* sets out from his home in some sense as an individual, leaving behind his societal roles and social status, joins the procession which carries the *pādukā* (silver sandals) of saints from their native places (birth or *samadhi* place) to Pandharpur. This spiritual journey (of more than 250 km in three weeks' time) is not bereft of social contact "on the road". There is an interaction between great tradition which manifests through several "*bhakti*" texts in Sanskrit and this small tradition through which the same philosophy is depicted; both the traditions are manifested in their totality as far as *bhakti* (devotion) is concerned.[4]

In a caste ridden and caste dominated society, caste as a factor does not figure in any way in this religious ritual at the pilgrimage, the *vāri*. This becomes more of a dialogue (*loka-samvada*) of the people and with the people, where communicative interaction takes place through the medium of the *vāri*. The key to the success of *vāri* lies in this dialogue and therefore it is flourishing even in the present technologically advanced society.

Normally people in Maharashtra go on a small pilgrimage from town to town; which are held in honour of folk-deities, and known as *jatrā*. The ritual for these *jatrās* are sometimes the same. For Vitthal of Pandharpur devotees are attending pilgrimage four times in a year, Ashadhi (July), Kartiki (November), Maghi (February) and Chaitri (April) but in these four pilgrimages, Ashadhi is the biggest one which is celebrated by the procession and congregation of all saints at Pandharpur.

The *vāri* to Pandharpur is quite famous and popular in Maharashtra and regions around it. Participants are coming from Karnataka, Andhra, Tamil Nadu and Madhya Pradesh. The pilgrim is called *vārkarī*. This word is composed of two words: *vāri* meaning a regular practice of going on a pilgrimage to Pandharpur, and *karī* meaning one who undertakes it, and his cult is called the Varakari or Bhāgavata cult (Map 1).

Such is the *vārkarī*, a pilgrim; all set to tread the path, 250 km long leading to Pandharpur, the center of the cult of *bhakti* in south India. But he does not tread it alone and silently; he moves with a crowd of thousands all singing devotional songs to the rhythm of the cymbals (*tāl*), occasionally doing *kīrtan*, *pravachan*,

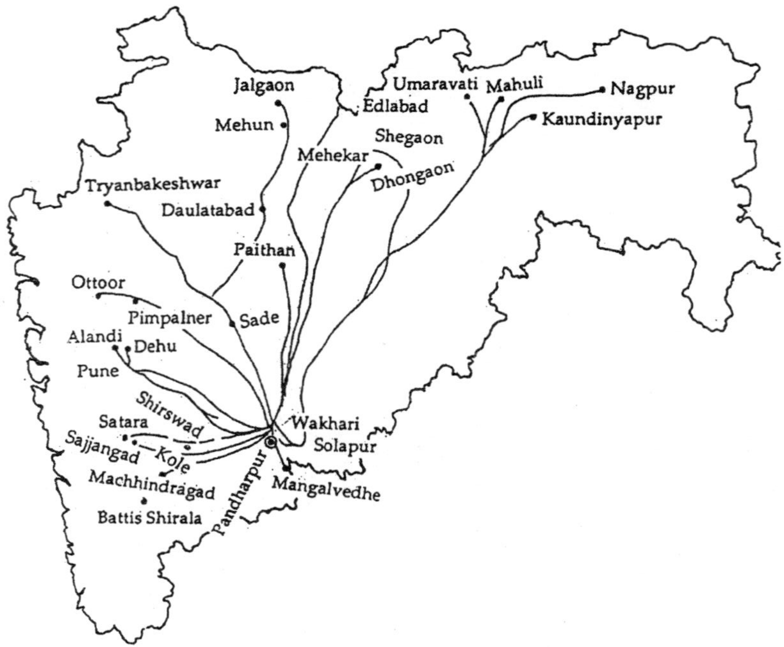

MAP 1: MAP OF MAHARASHTRA SHOWING ROUTES OF PALKHIS OF VARIOUS SANTS (CATCHMENT AREA OF THE *VĀRI*).

bhajan, bhārūd, etc. The concept behind this pilgrimage which takes place every year in the month of June-July is very novel. The pilgrims carry with them in a palanquine the symbolic holy feet (*pādukās*) of two great saints of Maharashtra, Dnyanadev (thirteenth century) and Tukaram (seventeenth century). The first lived at Alandi and the second at Dehu, both the places being situated in the vicinity of Pune. It was saint Dnyanadev who laid the foundation of the cult of *bhakti* (Bhāgavata) or devotion of which Tukaram became the pinnacle. Both were devotees of the god Vitthala of Pandharpur and their followers take their symbolic feet every year to meet the god of Pandharpur. It is the meeting of the god and his devotees that the whole pilgrimage aims at. The pilgrims wearing a rosary of *tulasī* beads round their necks and carrying ochre coloured banners, cover the distance in 18 days, walking on an average about 16 km every day. They are divided into different groups which are called *dindis* and each *dindi* has its own leader who is called "Vinekari Buva". The pilgrims along with the palanquin carrying the saints' symbolic feet halt for the night at prearranged places where religious discourses like *bhajan-kīrtan-bhārūd*, etc., take place. As they approach Pandharpur the number of participants goes on swelling and it crosses a hundred thousand on the outskirt of the town named Wakhri, where palanquines of other saints join the main stream. It is a self-disciplined mass pilgrimage born not out of any religious code but out of the enthusiastic devotion of the *vārkarīs*, the most devoted devotees of Lord Vitthala; they love the road, the tread, because it leads to their heart's desire which is Pandharpur.[5]

Though this pilgrimage is strictly for Hindus, there is an exceptional example of "Muslim" *dindi* led by Muslim woman saint Jaitunbee from Poona district. From Mumbai there is a separate women's *dindi* named "Santabai Dindi". Both *dindis* are observing the same ritual as others do. In Harale Vaishnava *dindi*, while *kīrtan* is going on, women became *tālkarī* in Palakhi-Sohalā this is only exceptional case.

The procession of *vārkarī* with palanquins is called "Palkhi Sohala". This was started in 1832 by Shri Haibatbaba Arphalkar and then Sardar Shitole of Ankali joined him. This procession has a definite structure. In the midst of procession there is a chariot (*ratha*) carrying the saints' *pādukā*. The *ratha* is driven by bullocks. Traditionally twenty-six *dindis* walk in front of the *ratha* and about one hundred and fifty behind it. These *dindis* are registered ones, and behind them several un-registered *dindis* wait for registration. All *dindis* are numbered and governed by the Temple Committee. The procession is led by *sanaī-choughaḍā* (sort of band) and two horses. According to *vārkarī* faith saint Dnyaneshvara is believed to ride one of the horses, and this horse is called "shri's horse". The other horse with a rider escorts shri's horse. This structure has been followed for the last century and more. Change in the structure if any can be effected by the "Dindi Pramukha Sabha" which is a mandatory body. Most of the *dindis* belong to different castes. There are mixed caste groups also. Inspite of untouchability removal, three untouchable castes' *dindis* that are Rohidasa (cobbler), Ajamela (Matanga) and Chokhamela (Mahar) constitute units 24, 25 and 26 respectively in front of the palanquin. However any untouchable can mix freely with any other *dindi* (Figure I).

The *dindis* are not a haphazard group of *vārkarīs*; the above is just an external structure they follow but they also have an internal structure. The number of *vārkarī* in *dindis* varies from 60 to 600. At the beginning of the *dindi* there is a line of *zendekarī* (the *vārkarīs* holding the saffron flags, a symbol of Varkari cult). Here the *dindis* never put a banner but only their number. After the *zendekarīs* follows a group of women carrying *tulasī* plants on their head and *handāvāli* (drinking water container). Then come the *tālakarīs*. They are traditional *vārkarīs*, playing on the cymbal *bhajan*, with singing and dancing. In between *tālakarīs* "*pakhavāji*" (drum player) and "*veeṇekarī*" (the string instrument *veena* player) walk. The *veeṇekarī* is normally a spiritual teacher (*guru*) and also chief of *dindi*[6] (Figure II).

These *dindikarīs* follow the procedure of whole procession. For instance, *ringan, dhāvā, jāgar,* etc. Besides every *dindi* has its own program, like *pravachan, kīrtan, bhajan, bhārud,* etc. The individuals also can follow his own *ānhika* (worship, *pārāyana, japa,* etc). Every *vārkarī* is expected to do *ānhikas*. This refutes Prof. Deleury's notion that individual worship and meditation plays no part in *dindi* (Deleury 1960: 105).[7]

Usually the pilgrims on arrival at their destination where they

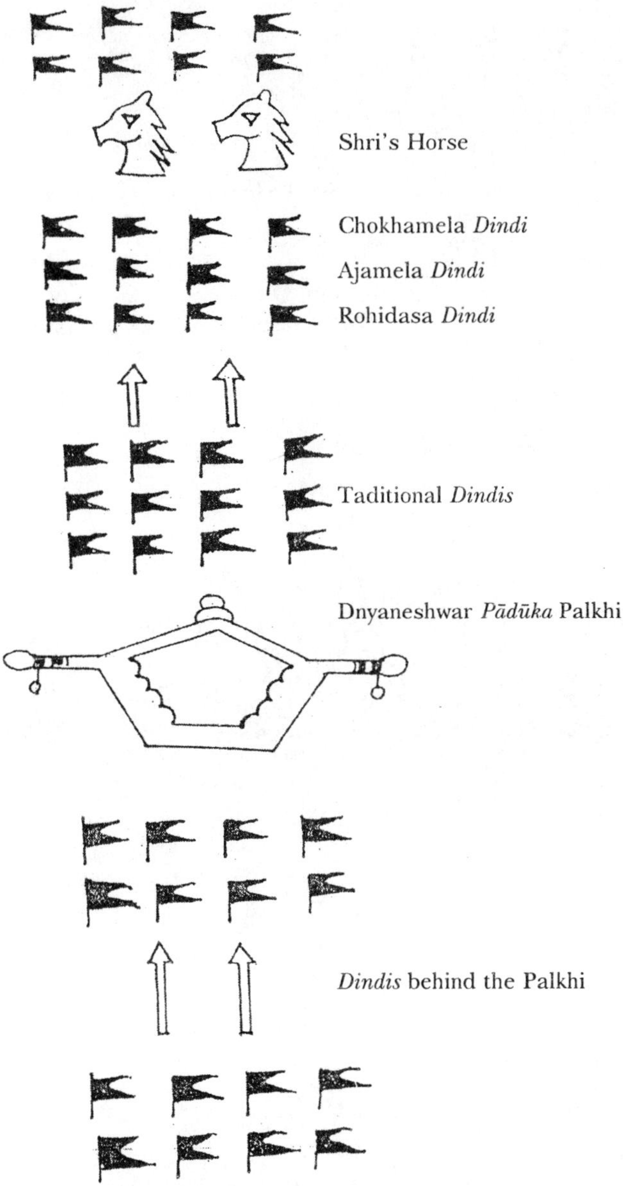

FIGURE I: ORGANIZATIONAL PATTERN OF THE *VĀRI*.

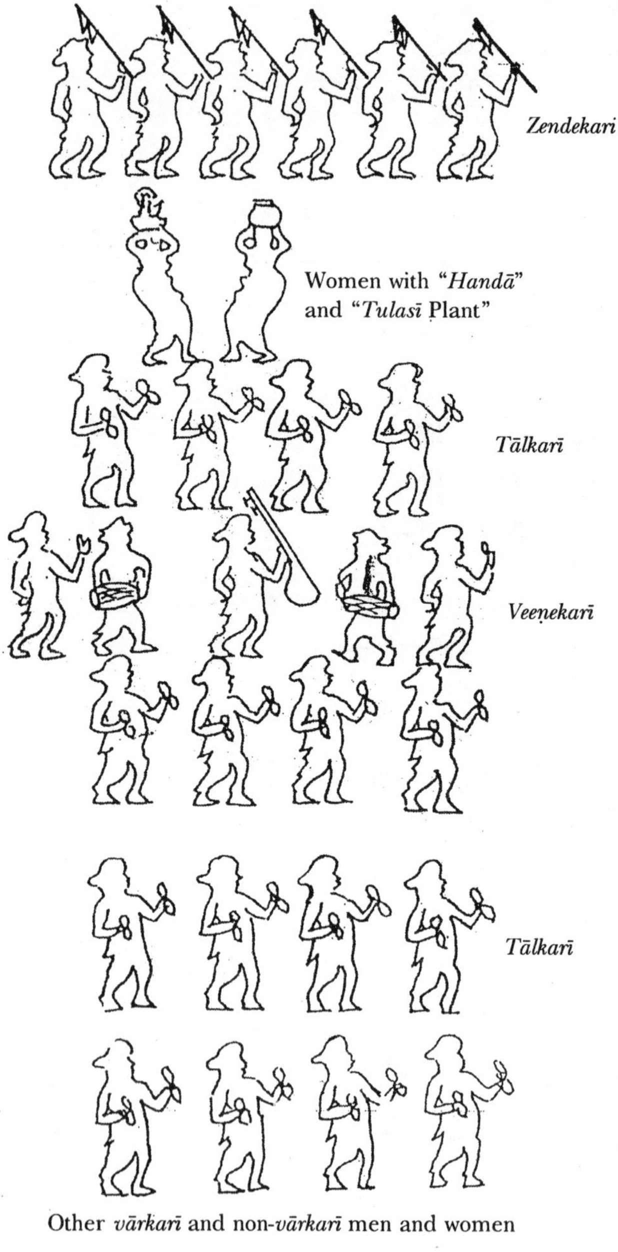

FIGURE II: INTERNAL STRUCTURE OF *DINDI.*

halt for at least three days, bathe, visit the temple, arrange *naivedya* (food), flowers and *dakshiṇā* (money) to be offered in the temple. They give some coins to the priests, tell their wish, read sacred books and join other pilgrims in attending recital, religious music or exposition by a *pandit* (scholar). But in Pandharpur pilgrimage, there is no specific ritual to do, except taking sacred bath at Chandrabhāgā River, circumambulating the city (*nagarapradakshiṇā*) and attending the religious discourses (*kīrtan*) and, if possible, taking *darshan*, touching the feet of god Vitthala or seeing at least the pinnacle of the temple and returning back with *prasād* (sweets).

The basic philosophy of *vārkarī* is *bhakti* and the *vāri* is its manifestation; saints Dnyanadev and Namdev spread the message of *bhakti* in society. The *bhakta* is so engrossed that when he sings *bhajan* and dances to it with his fellow devotees, he forgets himself and this mundane world. In fact *bhakti* through *bhajans* is a dialogue between the god and devotee. The *vārkarī* "on the road" is also engrossed in dancing and singing to the accompaniment of *bhajans*. This community feeling of happiness is a festival which gives the *vārkarī* very happy experience. One who joins the *vāri* alone, prefers to walk to the soft tunes of *veeṇā*, rhythm of *tāl* (cymbal) and the sound of *murdang* (drum) and when the *vārkarīs* dance in a trance it makes them forget his everyday worries. This feeling of happiness and joy through *bhajans* is contagious and the whole Vaishnavite community gets engrossed in it. Sant Tukaram describes this experience in a couplet "as dancing joyous ripples in the deep lake of joy" (*anandāce dohi anand tarang*).[8]

It was mostly uneducated people who were the participants of "Palakhi Sohala", but nowadays the educated also take keen interest in this ritual. More and more people are interested in *vārkarī sampradāya* (cult), its ritual and philosophy attracting them towards its cultural and social tradition and brotherhood, though they belong to different castes.[9]

In daily life women are always kept away from social activities in the village, but that gender problem is not seen in this *vāri*. Women who do not even step out of their houses in the village, who cover their heads with saris and speak to men with downcast eyes, change completely when they become *vārkarnīs*. They play *phugaḍī, hamāmā,* sing *bhārud* and dance. They walk shoulder to shoulder with male *vārkarīs.* While playing *phugaḍī* they do not even look to see whether the partner is an acquaintance or from the outside village. Even the food preparation during the *vāri* is shared by both genders; filling tanks of water lifting and making large pots of food (*bhājī-bhāt,* etc.) and distributing it, these tasks usually done by servants, are done by men of classes. Women focus on preparing *bhākarīes* or *chapatis* (the main food).

The procession passes through three districts, Pune, Satara and Solapur. In each district, government officers welcome the procession and provide help with problems. In other pilgrimages and *jatrās,* hundreds of people are hurt or killed due to the lack of discipline and other factors recently. This does not happen in the Pandharpur *vāri.* If any individual or group of *vārkarīs* has a complaint against another person, group or system, he simply sounds his cymbals to get the attention of the Trustees and complaint. They then take the guilty party to the offended for a formal apology. This is a sort of court justice system which took place in "Samaj Arati" at evening of every hault. There is no punishment except that the guilty person or party apologize for his action.[10]

Thus, some observations on Pandharpur pilgrimage go as follows: (1) While traveling in *dindi vārkarīs* observe self-restraint which they strictly follow: They avoid non-veg food and alcoholic drinks. Even smoking while being in *dindi* is strictly prohibited. Eating tobacco is common in Maharashtrian village. But in *dindi* it is also prohibited. *Tulasīmālā* is supposed to be the control symbol of self restraint. (2) Whatever food the *dindi* people are preparing at the halt, is first offered as a *naivedya* to Dnyaneshvar and Tukaram and that is why no uncommon or special food is prepared at *dindi.* (3) In such a huge crowd missing persons always cause a problem to the organizer (here the police department is not responsible for this task). These missing persons only known by their *dindi* number, and not by name of *dindi*; missing persons, loss of valuable things were announced at "Samaj Arati". (4) Thousands of *vārkarīs* traveling from village to village, every village becomes host for them and offer hospitality, good shelter and food, as their social duty.

There are no written rules for a *vārkarī* as to how he should behave while on pilgrimage to Pandharpur. The *Dindipramukha* guide them. But traditionally some rules and regulations are there which *vārkarī* should follow strictly for the whole life. (1) Wear *tulasīmālā* all the time and *gopichandan-bukkā* as a *tilak* after bath. (2) Observe fast on each Ekadashi (eleventh day of month). (3) No non-veg food, no liquor, no smoking, respect for women, no theft, etc. (4) Strictly follow daily ritual of devotee "*pujan*, watering *tulasi* plant, reading Bhāgawat-Dnyāneshvari-Haripath *bhajan* at least five *abhangas* (*panchapadi*)". (5) Pilgrimage to Pandharpur and Alandi without fail every year. (6) Acceptance of truth (*satya*), non-violence (*ahimsa*), mercy for every being (*bhutdayā*), non-acceptance (*aparigraha*), etc.: ideal habits be cultivated. Most of *vārkarīs* are observe these rules, which enrich their social life. According to modern technology changes are coming in this procession.

For the last 50 years a few Western scholars have been taking keen interest in this ritual to study it in detail. Some of them have published their views. The scholars include the following:[11]

(1) Prof. Iwao Shima (Kanazawa University, Japan)
(2) Dr. Chihiro Koiso (Tokyo, Japan)
(3) Dr. Eric Sand (Copenhagen, Denmark)
(4) Prof. I.M.P. Reside (London, U.K.)
(5) Prof. Günther Sontheimer (Heidelberg, Germany)
(6) Prof. Ch. Vaudeville (France)
(7) Dr. Remond Crow (U.S.A.)
(8) Dr. Anne Feldhaus (Arizona, U.S.A.)
(9) Dr. Charles Pain (U.S.A.)
(10) Dr. Skyhauk (Germany)
(11) Prof. Winand Callewaert (Belgium)
(12) Dr. G.A. Deleury (France)
(13) Dr. Irina Glushkova (Russia)

CONCLUSION

Pilgrimage (*vārī*) is usually supposed to be a religious activity; a ritual between God and devotees but it has something more than that: (1) It is a sort of socio-cultural effort which regularly takes place nourishing good relations among various castes, (2) It endures physical exercise and fitness, healthy life for participants, (3) It leads to an exchange of views, among people speaking different languages, (4) It opens the door to fraternity. It helps in economic development of Pandharpur region and people around. This type of pilgrimage has served to unite people throughout India in a common cultural and religious consciousness as well as to help growth of commerce and Industry.

NOTES

1. Ch. Vaudeville, *Kabir*, London: Oxford University Press, 1974, p. 286.
2. S.G. Tulpule, "Pilgrimage to Pandharpur" (unpublished article, Indian Institute of Advanced Study, July 1987).
3. R.C. Dhere, *Sakalasantagāthā*, Pune: Varada Books Publications.
4. Vasudha Thakur, "Vari to Pandharpur", in *Pilgrimage: Concept, Themes, Issues and Methodology*, ed. Makhan Jha, New Delhi: Inter India Publications, 1995.
5. S.K. Neurgaoker, *Palakhi Sohalā: Alandi Devāsthan*, Pune: Alandi Devsthan Prakashan, 2001.
6. Vasudha Thakur, op. cit.
7. G.A. Deleury, *Cult of Vithoba*, Pune: Deccan College, 1960.
8. Vasudha Thakur, op. cit.
9. R.B. Mancharkar, *Bapa Rakhuma Devivaru*, Pune: Wamanraj Prakashan, July 2005.
10. V.L. Manjul, "Palakhi Sohalā Samajik Shistichā Pāth", *Bapa Rakhuma Devivaru, Vari Special Issue*, 2005.
11. V.L. Manjul, *Maze Maher Pandhari*, Mumbai: Aswad Prakashan, 2003.

BIBLIOGRAPHY ON *VARI*

Bhagwat, Durga, 1970: "Pandharicha Vithoba", *Paisa.* Bombay: Mauj Prakashan, pp. 32-43.

Jadhav, N.B., 2003: *Payi Vari Pandharichi.* Pune: Vaishnav Prakashan.

Jevane, Dipak (ed.), 2003: *Maze Maher Pandhari.* Bombay: Aswad Prakashan.

Joshi, A.S., 1994: *Palakhi Sohala.* Pune: Indrayani Sahitya Prakashan.

Karve, Iravati, 1974: "Watchal", in *Paripurti.* Pune: Deshmukh Prakashan.

Kavade, Shirish (ed.), 2002: *Bapa Rakhuma Devivaru, Vari Special Issue*, vol. 3, nos. 9-10. Pune: Wamanraj Prakashan.

——(ed.), 2002: *Bapa Rakhuma Devivaru, Vari Special Issue*, vol. 3, nos. 10-11. Pune: Wamanraj Prakashan.

——(ed.), 2004: *Bapa Rakhuma Devivaru, Vari Special Issue*, vol. 4, nos. 9-10. Pune: Wamanraj Prakashan.

——(ed.), 2005: *Bapa Rakhuma Devivaru, Vari Special Issue*, vol. 5, nos. 10-11, Pune: Wamanraj Prakashan.

Marane, Rajendra, 2004: *Payi Vari Pandharichi*. Pune: Utkarsh Prakashan.

Menjoge, Sitaram, 1998: *Ek Vari Nanapari*. Vasai and Thane: Dimple Publication.

Mokashi, D.B., 1964: *Palkhi*. Bombay: Mauj Prakashan.

Naik, M.B., 1995: *Dindi Chalali Dnyanobachi*. Solapur: Sant Sahitya Seva Sangh.

Neurgaokar, S.K., 2001: *Palakhi Sohala*. Pune: Alandi Devsthan Prakashan.

ENGLISH WORKS

Deleury, G.A., 1960: *The Cult of Vithoba*. Pune: Deccan College.

Engblom, Philip. C., 1987: *Palkhi: An Indian Pilgrimage* (tr. of D.B. Mokashi, *Palkhi*, Bombay: Mauj Prakashan, 1964); Albany: State University of New York Press, 1987.

Jha, Makhan (ed.), 1985: *Dimension of Pilgrimage*. New Delhi: Inter India Publications.

Kane, P.V., 1953: *History of Dharmaśāstra*, vol. IV. Pune: Bhandarkar Oriental Research Institute.

Stanley, John, 1981: 'Pandharpur Pilgrimage' Ritual and Process, unpublished paper, Pittsberg Conference.

Turner, Victor, 1973: "The Centre Out There: Pilgrim Goal", *Journal of History of Religion*, vol. II, no. 3.

20

Two Maharashtrian Ways of Performing Devotion: The *Nāradiya* and *Vārkarī Kīrtan*[1]

ERIC FERRIÉ

This contribution is about the different ways of doing *kīrtan*: an oral performance in Maharashtrian Vaiṣṇav devotion.[2] The comparative way of analyzing this topic has not only been suggested by this methodological concern that has so far proved its pertinence, but it is also the way the concerned people spoke to me about this topic during fieldwork. Indeed, when I first enquired about the *kīrtan*, I was told that there were two types of *kīrtan*, the *nāradiya* and the *vārkarī* ones. Moreover, this comparative approach is not only a way of showing once again the cultural dimension of the expression of feeling underlying the apparent outpouring of devotion, but it is also a dimension very much taken for granted by the people themselves who, when asked about the difference between the *kīrtan*, used to reply: "They are only two different ways of reaching God." After having briefly situated the *kīrtan* in Hindu religiosity and put both types of *kīrtan* back in their respective settings, I shall then compare them in order to understand the multiplicity of ways of expressing devotion in that context.

A WAY OF SALVATION

Kīrtan is first of all a "way of salvation" (*bhakti mārga*). *Bhakti* is then a way in the sense that the devotion to a particular divinity or the initiation into a particular devotional movement is not bestowed upon an individual according to his social or familial belonging even if it is a family tradition as it is often the case. Besides, it can on the opposite be a way of protest against caste determinism. One cannot choose his family deity but the "favorite" deity (*ārādhya*), as the word speaks for itself, is very much personal: so much that most of the times, it is decided according to the individual's horoscope when it is not the fruit of a mystical experience of some divine signs revealed to the individual.

Among the other deities of the pantheon that are worshiped in the devotee's altar, this deity has often a central place and can be represented under several forms and images (*mūrti*, chromos, etc.). The deity can also be alone in the case in which the devotee has a separate house with his nuclear family and the familial, that is the (patri-)lineage deity, is then in the eldest brother's house. But in any case, the religion of *bhakti* is not a monotheism. This deity's position, as I was told, is analogous to a presidential one for the devotee concerned. One can visit his family deities, above all goddesses, at some steps in the course of life, or to repair some infortune but the favorite deity is the one to whom the devotee entrusts himself. He then expects some guidance and the protection necessary for a good life in this world and after. This universal aspect explains why this deity is also called *dev* (in the absolute) or *bhagvān*, the Lord.

The devotee is generally so attached to this deity that he considers it as his family deity *kuḷadaivat* on a more affective ground than the family deity toward which he has some obligations. As such, the devotee consecrates himself to a more regular and intensive worship, that is why his deity is also called the *upāsya* one, on account of the fast and prayers undergone by the devotee. This *bhakti* religiosity is more sustained on emotional ground. So much that devotion (*bhakti*) and emotion (*bhāv*) have almost become synonymous in colloquial language as it is stressed by the expression *bhakti-bhāv*.

NINE WAYS OF DEVOTION

The *kīrtan* is only one type of "nine ways of worshiping" god (*navavidha bhakti*) (referred to as "nine-ways" in the following). This classification which *kīrtankār* regularly refers to is a

Bhāgavata Purāṇa's Prahlād's retort to his father when this one asks him about what he learned from his master. But like the *Bhagavad Gītā,* it has become a piece of theology in itself. It is a distich juxtaposing all the different types of worship in a serial and laconic manner, as following: "*śravaṇa kīrtana viṣṇoha smaraṇa pādasevana / arcana vandana dāsya sakhyamātmānivedan*". All these terms refer to an attitude towards Viṣṇu and a particular relationship to him: "to listen, to praise Viṣṇu, to remember (him), to serve his feet, to worship, to honor, (to be his) servant, friendship-and-soul offering".

These "nine-ways" are an attitude that involves all the senses. The devotee is present to god in speech, action and thinking. The simple fact of listening is here truly an action. All the body and the human faculties are consecrated to god.

Besides the attitude of piety, the different modes of relationship with god are also characterized. They include relationships as opposite as the asymmetrical service and humility in front of the all-pervading god and the equality of friendship that ends up in identification or even a fusion with god.

These nine-ways then focus on the two main aspects of Hindu piety: a personal, intimate relationship, with an anthropomorphic deity. As such, it is the most comprehensive exponent of the *bhakti* religiosity's conception of devotee's body which becomes the center of religious experience and the medium of divine interiorization. To put it in saint Tukārām's words: "Glory to the Kirtan (by which) one is (consubstantially) one with god" (*kīrtan cāng kīrtan cāng/hoy ang hari rūpa*) and "the body is god's temple" (*deha devāce mandir*). The body then becomes a cosmic body that transcends the social determinism of a particular individual at a universal level: "ridiculously small, Tukā (rām) is as big as ether" (*aṇureṇuyā thokḍā / tukā ākāśāevaḍhā*).

Surprisingly enough, *darśan,* to see the deity, minimal act of piety and major concept of Hinduism is nevertheless conspicuous by his absence. It is true that if in day-to-day religiosity, *darśan* is a devotional practice, in mythology and hagiography, it is more of a goal towards which tends the devotee and a favor granted by god who reveals himself by showing a vision of his true divine nature. Moreover, against Brahman priests' monopoly on the access to temple and to self-realization, the low caste's saint's hagiography insists on a pervading presence of god (the man-lion god Narsiṃhā, didn't he emanate from a pillar to prove to Prahlād's demon and demoniac father who was testing his devoted son that god was also in that pillar as this latter maintained against his father?). May be this can explain why *ātmānivedan*, which is more of the accomplishment of consecrating oneself to god than a way of devotion, concludes the "nine ways"?

DIVERSITY AND CREATIVITY IN HINDU INDIVIDUAL AND COLLECTIVE PIETY

Concretely, the Hindu piety, enumerated in the "nine-ways" is as much a matter of individual practice as it is a collective and congregational performance. Indeed, the devotee is present to god in the depth of his consciousness while saying the rosary (*jap*), chanting the praise of god (*bhajan*) or reading sacred texts (*pārāyaṇ*), preferably in sacred spaces like temples, not for silence and quietness but for more proximity to god, and during the liminal time of a pilgrimage. Some rituals like bathing and fasting consecrate the individual to his religious activity but they are also devotional acts in themselves: bathing in the Ganges can be the goal of the pilgrimage to Kashi. As a consecration, they are steps in the progressive involvement and identification to god of the devotee whose body, painted or even marked by the name and signs of a god undergoes a sacred transformation (*pavitra*). This transformation is strengthened by the participation to collective meetings, to listen to sermon (*pravacan, kīrtan*), to sing devotional songs (*bhajan*), etc. There the devotee gets the benefit of religious congregation, the *satsang* and god's blessing through *prasād* (which refers to the sign of identification to the divinity on the forehead as well as the sweet and even the full meal offered to the god).

Both individual and collective practices can intermingle and one can for example see a devotee writing down the names of god in the middle of a *kīrtan* which then constitute a more appropriate place and time inside the temple frame. Of course, personal adjustments don't undermine the normative aspect of devotional practice underlined by religious principles and representations of Hinduism but the flexibility and the personal initiative and freedom in that field is such that pre-eminence is given to personal feeling, *bhāv*, and that makes it so creative (and to some extent allows deviation if not deviance, as for example during the "home-made" *pūjās*' short cuts or liturgical innovations in one's "style" of performance) that it is sometimes difficult to relativize things and to find one's own way into it!

TWO WAYS OF PERFORMING *KĪRTAN*

In this regard, it is then interesting to study the *kīrtan* because there are two ways (*paddhat*) of performing it: the *nāradiya* way and the *vārkarī* one. Moreover, *kīrtan* is a collective practice and has a sectarian dimension (in the sense of the transmission of spiritual knowledge from *guru* to disciple). *Kīrtan* in Maharashtra can't be reduced to a song of praise only, it is also and above all an oral performance of devotion[3] and an oral ritual (Mauss 1968). As such the *kīrtan* is efficient in the sense that it is a complete act in itself, whose efficacy is intrinsic, *sui generis*[4] and may be this is why performers refer to it as one of the "nine-ways". Indeed, to praise is not only an act of enunciation (to a deity) but also and above all a way of enunciating and a goal in itself. As for any act of piety, the performer or *kīrtankār*, and the audience, get some religious merits in this world and beyond that justify a good life. And the only fact to go to the *kīrtan* is considered as a divine favor in itself: at the end of the performance, god is indeed requested to grant the devotee the favor of eternal service of devotion through such practices. This is their liberation, here below and from life to life.

Through the *kīrtan*, the audience is also taught about spiritual knowledge and devotion as it is revealed by the saints' poetry and in the pedagogic wise mythological narratives. The *nāradiya* way of performing *kīrtan* is called after the sage Nārad. Nārad is a story-teller of puranic narrative lore. He tells the stories as much as he is involved in them, most of the time curving the course of events. But he belongs as much to the stories as there is no story of Nārad. In accordance with its emblematic figure, the narration is the main characteristic of this *kīrtan.* This tradition includes all stories of gods and devotees from mythology and hagiography (and even history with the nationalist or *rāṣṭrīya kīrtan*). They have been composed by Brahman poets in a "scholarly poetic" style (*pant kavī*) in which performers, Brahmans, are acquainted if not poet themselves. Most of the time they perform in front of the image and the audience in the temples where they have been invited.

The *vārkarī kīrtan* belongs to the *vārkarī's* vast set of performances. It's not only a collective practice, in which any listener can participate in singing, but a community one, as all the participants follow the *vārkarī* way of salvation. The *vārkarī* are devotees of Viṭhobā and of his saints whose most famous figure on account of his lyrical poetry is Tukārām. Tukārām and the other poet-saints are not only the poets whom *vārkarī* refer to, they are above all the *vārkarī* way of worship itself as to sing the saint's poems during the pilgrimage (*vārī*) between Āḷandī (Saint Jñandev's sacred place) and Paṇḍharpur (Viṭhobā's one) is the very point by which *vārkarī* define themselves, *vārkarī* meaning those who do the *vārī.* The *vārkarī* "community" is formed by local independent groups (that can extend to bigger ones under the influence of a religious leader). But the community is here more in the religious practice than a sectarian monastic organization in the orthodox Hindu sense. Unlike the *nāradiya kīrtan* in which the performer tells a story to his audience, in the *vārkarī* one, all the *vārkarī* join the *kīrtankār* to sing the poems he quotes during his sermon in which he explains saint's knowledge. The *kīrtankār* has still a central place in the *kīrtan,* but the distinction between speaker and audience is blurred and the "participants" are also to some extent performers. The *vārkarī kīrtan* usualy takes place in Viṭhobā's and saint' temples but it is on the way to Paṇḍharpur that *kīrtankārs* get out all their authority and fame, above all if they perform in front of saints' palanquins and on a special occasion as Viṭhobā's and saints' days of *ekādaśī* (11th lunar day).

The two *kīrtans* "are only two different ways of reaching god", as it is commonly repeated on fieldwork, but out of the broad description just sketched, it seems that the differences between the place of performer (and audience) and his performance, the way of performing and the context in which they take place are not minor ones. We shall then concentrate on these structural elements of comparison. But while studying the relations between these elements inside each type of performance, we won't go into the details specific to each type of *kīrtan*, as for example the strategic and pedagogic methods of *kīrtankār*, their narrative and rhetoric skills, the accommodation of their particular style (*śailī*) to the normative framework of the *kīrtan*.

THE *NĀRADIYA KĪRTAN*

The *nāradiya kīrtankārs* often distinguish their performance as a "one-man-show" (*ekpātrīprayog*), an expression that clearly marks the distinction with *vārkarī kīrtan* but also betray their liking for theater. Very much aware of standing up on a carpet called "Nārad's see", wearing Pune's Brahman headdress, the *pagḍī*, or a turban (*śemlā*), and a stole (*uparṇa*), he is the only master in the performance. The audience can sing and repeat but only if it is invited to do so by the *kīrtankār* and nobody can interrupt the flow of his sermon on his own. This doesn't mean that the audience is passive. As we have seen, listening is an act of piety in itself.

This *kīrtan* is a narrative type of performance. In fact, it can be described as a series of narratives windows each embedded in the other in the puranic mythology's style of story-telling. And all the *kīrtankār's* skill consists of landing on his feet, *mūḷa padāvar* as they call it, which is to come full circle on the main topic at the end of the *kīrtan*. Of course this is not that chaotic and all that is linked to a main topic drawn out of a main tale or *ākhyān*.

While performing, the *kīrtankār* plays all the figures of the story. To enhance all the characters' qualities, he has at his disposal a huge toolbox made of a literary corpus of different meters, narrative as well as lyrical, including saints' poetry, to be fitted to a proper *rāga* in order to express the depth of feelings and to arouse emotion in the audience. For his performance, he plays cymbals and is accompanied by a *tablā* and a harmonium. The performer can also support his knowledge and know-how with scenographic gestures and enliven his speech with commentaries and analogies overall enhanced by a hint of humor or irony. Alone, the *kīrtankār* incarnates all the characters in order to show their qualities according to the pedagogic topic of the *kīrtan.*

Indeed, these stories do not only have an entertaining intention. They are fit to each other with a poem taken as the subject matter at the beginning of the *kīrtan.*[5] This theme has a didactic importance and a normative relevance: it deals with the proper way of life for the devotee to follow according to the narrated models in order to get god's favor and may be to hope to get his vision. This more metaphysical part is dealt with in the first part of the *kīrtan* where the principals of spiritual knowledge and salvation are elaborated. However, the narrative part can't be reduced to only an illustration of the first one, and from the audience's point of view, which is keener on stories, it is on the opposite the performance's pick itself. *Kīrtankār* doesn't appreciate to see people skipping the first part to come on time for the story and keep telling them that the first part prepares to the second one.[6]

Even more significant than this logical link is the ritual one articulating both the parts of the performance. Indeed, during the interval (*madhyāntar,* as it is called), the *kīrtankār* is garlanded and his forehead endowed with black-coloured basil tree ashes called *bukkā,* symbol of identification with Viṭhobā, by the temple manager after this latter has presented it to the deity. In his turn, the *kīrtankār* then spreads the powder and then handles the plate containing it round among the audience for the devotees to endow themselves with *bukkā.* They most of the time let some coins in the plate as a gift. As for the *kīrtankār,* he finally takes out his stole from his shoulders and ties it around his waist before starting the second part. So the first part does not only prepare for the second one, it also opens the way to a consecration.

The *kīrtan* is concluded by an *āratī,* a ritual of honor to the deities. Usually it is addressed to the temple deity, but it is not always the case and the *kīrtankār* can sing the *āratī* of his favorite deity, or he can include also other deities depending on the occasion. While singing, camphor is burned on a plate and the priest circumambulates it around the deity in the clockwise direction. Then the devotees hold their hand over the flame and impregnate themselves of this divine presence before it vanishes, camphor being completely burned, without ashes. However, in the *kīrtan*, the temple manager or priest stands besides the *kīrtankār* without circumambulating the flame during the *ārati* conclusion. Before leaving, the devotees impregnate themselves with the camphor and let some gift in the plate for the *kīrtankār* in front of whom they then bow down to touch his feet. Finally, the *kīrtankār* will also prostrate himself in front of the deity before leaving. So the *kīrtankār* provides knowledge and benediction that the devotees pay with the *guru* honorary fee (*dakṣiṇā*).

The fame of the *kīrtankār* can go beyond the *kīrtan* and he can be invited at the devotees' place for a meal. The *kīrtankār's* fame depends of course on the success of his *kīrtan*, and he can be rewarded for that by prestigious titles like *kīrtan-ratna* or *kīrtan-būṣan*, but he is also established on account of a family tradition that he keeps going on and the *kīrtankār* relys a lot on it. Actually, the transmission is double: there is the transmission of *kīrtan's* knowledge and know-how with a *kīrtankār*, one's father or another *kīrtankār*, and there is the initiation that can be done by the same person but in very few cases and that have a different significance. Indeed, initiation is a spiritual transformation that habilitates the *kīrtankār* to this teaching. It is a necessary condition, a step, even if it is only a *mantra* whispered into disciple's ear. This transmission, that is not necessarily a sectarian initiation and a monastic engagement as such, establishes an intimate relationship between the *guru* and his disciple. From this initiation, the *kīrtankār* holds all the legitimacy that contributes a lot to his authority.

It's at the *kīrtan's* beginning that one comes to know about the *kīrtankār's* sectarian tradition when, after having propitiated Gaṇesh, Saraswatī and the Guru entity, the *kīrtankār* verbally bows to his tradition's deity. There are three traditions of *kīrtan* in Maharashtra: the *Nāth*, worshipping Dattatreya, the *Rāmdāsī*, called after the Brahman saint Rāmdās, devotee of Hanuman and Rāma and the *Nāradiya*, which sing the glory of Kṛṣṇa.[7] On a comparison ground, we will take the case of the *nāradiya* tradition on account of its similarity with *vārkarī* tradition: indeed, the *nāradiya* salutation is based on the famous *vaiṣṇav* formula: *Jay Jay Rām Kṛṣṇa Hāri.* This song designates *Bhāgavata-Purāṇa's* Kṛṣṇa *avatār* and recalls his deeds and qualities as follows:

"Jay Jay Rām Kṛṣṇa Hāri (refr.)
[Similar to] a new cloud which brings water, butter love, mischievous
Hāri [the one who] carry Govardhan (hill)/ the dancing cowherd, [the one] who removes obstacles in Gokuḷ
Hāri [the one who] discards misfortune, defeat enemy, [the one who] brings to his feet those who have surrendered, with compassion"[8]

Although this introductory part of the *kīrtan* called salutation (*naman*) is just a necessary liturgical formality from the audience's point of view, the *kīrtankār* considers it as one of the most essential part of the performance: a successful *kīrtan* depends on a right *naman* and this one can last for twenty minutes for a *kīrtan*'s total duration of around two hours. In *kīrtan* schools, the proper performance of the *naman* constitutes almost the first year of *kīrtan* teaching. The *naman* allows the *kīrtankār* to concentrate on his *kīrtan* but it is above all the moment of the privileged relation with his favorite deity in the depth of spiritual intimacy, eyes closed in the presence to god. The *kīrtankār* H.Bh. P. Kolhatkarbuvā[9] explained in this regard that the *naman* must be sung on the sweet and slow *dhumāli* rhythm in order to bring out a serene feeling of plenitude, called the *sthāyī-bhāv* in art classification, which contrasts with the other feelings by its neutrality, or more exactly its absolute state, focusing on god.

A brahmanic tradition, the *nāradiya kīrtan* then extols the position of *guru* and his pedagogic mission for which it refers above all to the puranic lore through the emblematic figure of Nārad. The *kīrtan* is independent of the temple image routine except when *kīrtankārs* come to celebrate the birthday of a god for example and in which case the narration of god's birth is harmoniously set on the temple ritual timing of *pūjā.* But while performing in front of the temple image, he nevertheless incarnates a multiplicity of divine figures through the narration of their deeds and qualities in such a way that some *kīrtankārs* call their performance a mental *pūjā* (*manas pūjā*) (which has nothing to do with shaivaite ritual as such). This is why, from the point of view of some *kīrtankārs, āratī* is not performed directly in front of the temple image.

THE *VĀRKARĪ KĪRTAN*

This *kīrtan* is embedded in *vārkarī* Viṭhobā and saints' cult. As such it is one of the many *vārkarī* performances. The *kīrtan* doesn't always take place inside a temple. The *kīrtankār* can even perform in front of one's personal picture of the deities but one of the most appropriate places is on the pilgrimage's road, in front of saint's sandals (*pādukā*), and on the Bhīmā River's bank of Panḍharpur.

The *kīrtankār* is of course the main initiated performer. Standing on a carpet, he wears a white turban on the head, and a white stole. But his position is to some extent relativized by his attendance (more than his "audience"). Each and everybody is not bound to participate in the *kīrtan.* Let alone the women who usually don't participate in the *kīrtan,* some *vārkarī* would rather sit down and listen to the *kīrtankār* than stand up with cymbal to accompany him in singing. Others are cymbal players, or *tāḷkarī,* and they stand up laterally on both sides of the *kīrtankār* in a semicircle. There can be few people standing up in a *kīrtan* as well as hundred of them depending on the size of the group and the occasion. In the middle of the *kīrtan* stands also the drum player (*pakhavāj*) and at the extreme of the left range from the *kīrtankār* is the *vīṇā* (lute) holder or *vīṇekarī.* Even if the *vīṇā* is tuned and the *vīṇekarī* plucks its strings from time to time, this instrument is more a symbol of ineffable divine sound and an attribute of the devotee as we shall see.

The *kīrtankār* exclusively sings the saints' poems famous for their lyrical depth expressing the longing of the devotee for god. The most famous of these poets-saints are Jñāndev, who composed a Marathi commentary of the *Bhagavad Gītā* at the end of thirteenth century, Nāmdev, Viṭhobā's devotee, hagiographer and contemporary of Jñāndev, Eknāth, who corrected Jñāndev's work four-centuries later but is also known for his sweet songs on the infant Kṛṣṇa called *gauḷaṇī* and his satirical *bhārūḍ,* and Tukārām, the seventeenth century's "dome" of the "*vārkarī* temple" as says the metaphor on account of his thousands of lyrical poems sung all the way of pilgrimage by the *vārkarī*.

Out of this "temple" of *vārkarī* tradition, the iconography distinguishes two types of saints. Jñāndev and Eknath are shown sitting down writing their work. By contrast, Nāmdev or Tukārām hold a *vīṇā*, singing song and even dancing as in Nāmdev's usual representation. These figures then draw a distinction between the erudite and the devotee, that is to say between the establishment of the path of salvation and the model to its achievement. This distinction is operated in the ritual through the *kīrtankār's* status and the *vīṇekarī's* role.

The *kīrtankār* starts his sermon with the main poem like in the *nāradiya kīrtan*, but he then sticks to it distich by distich. Loyal to these saints, the *kīrtankār* expounds their spiritual teaching quoting many other poems in the process in such a way that the *kīrtankār* seems to thread a garland of poem all along his performance. Actually, all the art of this *kīrtan* is to fill in the poem in a coherent and appropriate manner. For the cymbal players, it means an occasion to sing the poems. Sometimes as well versed in saint's poetry as the *kīrtankār*, they can't help themselves introducing a poem in the *kīrtankār's* discourse. It is then left to the *kīrtankār* to judge the relevance of this tentative and to go on singing this poem or to interrupt it to proceed with his discourse.

Besides, the *kīrtankār* is not the only one to stand on his place. At the end of the *kīrtan*, he can invite some *vārkarī* from the assembly to sing poems. More significant, it's not the *kīrtankār* who starts the *kīrtan* and he does leave it before it ends. Unlike the *nāradiya kīrtankār*, it is a total eclipse! The liturgical "formalities" are almost handled by the *vīṇā* holder. Indeed, the *vīṇekarī* starts the *kīrtan* singing the following formula: *Jay Jay Rām Kṛṣṇa Hāri*. He doesn't sing it on an ornamental melody as in the *nāradiya kīrtan* but in crescendo and echoed by cymbal players. Then instead of a description of Kṛṣṇa's attributes and deeds follows a contemplative description of Viṭhobā's form attributed to saint Tukārām:

"*how beautiful is the [mental] image (dhyān) standing on the brick/*
his hands on his lips || (refr.)

a garland of Tuḷsī-beads round its neck and a silk garment around its loins /
I shall always love this [mental] image (dhyān) ||
The crocodile-earrings adorn him/
the kaustubh jewel looks beautiful at the throat ||
Tukā says: all my joy is in this [image]/
I shall [always] contemplate god's face with lot of admiration ||" [10]

It's only after the *vīṇekarī* has finished this song that the *kīrtankār* comes into the *kīrtan.* They proceed to a transfer of the *vīṇā* from the *vīṇekarī* to the *kīrtankār* framed by each other's prostration. Then the *kīrtankār* sings the *Jay Jay Rām Kṛṣṇa Hāri* formula in his turn, still in crescendo and still echoed by the cymbal players, after which he sings the following poem, attributed to saint Jñāndev, still contemplating the image of Viṭhobā:

"*looking at [that] form in the eyes*[11] */ happiness overcomes me ||* (*refr.*)
So beautiful is this Viṭṭhaḷ/ so beautiful is this Mādhav ||
lot of merit accumulated/ that's why my pleasure is in Viṭṭhaḷ ||
recipient of all happiness/ the father, husband of goddess Rakhumāī || "[12]

Then the *kīrtankār* sings the main poem he has chosen to explain in his *kīrtan.* Then only can he give back the *vīṇā* to the *vīṇekarī,* transfer always framed by prostrations to each other. But before starting the *kīrtan,* he ties his stole around his waist.

The *vārkarī kīrtan* is not as codified as the *nāradiya* one obsessed by classifications. There is no so-called *naman* as such. The *kīrtankār's* status is also correlatively more relative and his performance merged into the community liturgical framework.

The *Jay Jay Rām Kṛṣṇa Hāri* formula is more an invocation of Viṭhobā than it is evocative of the god qualities like in the *nāradiya kīrtan* that describes God Kṛṣṇa's deeds. Viṭhobā is then invocated as a form and a name, much more anthropomorphic than the attributes declined in the *nāradiya kīrtan.* The *vārkarī kīrtan* indeed insists more on the proximity to the god as a person (Tukārām, doesn't he draw his inspiration from the painful separation (*viraha*) that separates him from Viṭhobā when he is not in Paṇḍharpur?) than on the didactic character of divine attributes. At the same time, this particular form is not considered as one of the manifestation of Viṣṇu but as its very original essence (*svarūp*). Besides, all references to Gaṇpati or Saraswatī are omitted.

Much importance is then given to the lyrical effusion as showed by the *vīṇekarī's* position and the *kīrtankār* must handle the *vīṇā* and invocate god before starting the performance: without devotion, no knowledge, is *vārkarī's* leitmotiv. As an attribute of the devotee that ensures permanent presence of god, the *vīṇā* is supposed to be played permanently by its holder. The distinction between the *kīrtankār* and the *vīṇā* holder is actually more of a division of labor to stress the complementarities of both erudite and devotional figures. Indeed, in the ritual, anybody among the *vārkarī* group can hold the *vīṇā*. More significantly, when, in the middle of the *kīrtan*, the *kīrtankār* is honored with garland (and *bukkā*), so is the *vīṇā*, while the *vīṇā's* holder must contend himself with the *kīrtankār's* garland that the latter will remove to hand it over to him through one of the cymbal player without further ado.

At the end, the *vīṇā* holder will come back on *kīrtankār's* place, from which the latter left or stepped back, to perform *āratī* program. Actually, not only the *vīṇekarī* but also all *vārkarī* present there sing and recite this liturgical part together. This program is not peculiar to the *kīrtan* but to *vārkarī* liturgical framework in general. We won't be able to see it in detail despite its crucial interest for *vārkarī* representations, but to sum up, Tukārām's poem of supplication to the saints to remind Pāṇḍuraṅga (Viṭhobā) of his pleading is sung in *bhairavī rāga*, the sweetest one for a lyrical and humble request. Still more humble is the recited poem supplicating saint Jñāndev to forgive him for his "distorted child's language" (*bolile lekure veḍīvākuḍī uttare*) and to keep him as his servant in spite of that, after what Viṭhobā, Jñāndev and Tukārām's respective *āratī* are sung. It is to be underlined that the singing of *āratī* is not always performed with the waving of the flame, depending on the place and occasion. It can be orally self-sufficient. Moreover, the singing of *āratī* is preceded by Tukārām's description of this ritual: "let's do *āratī* [and] wave the flame around Cakrapani . . ." (*karūnī ārtī cakrapāṇī ovāḷitī*). *Āratī*, among others rituals, is then, in the *vārkarī* tradition, more than anywhere else a performative oral one.

Seen from another scale, the *kīrtan's* frame, being actually the *vārkarī's* one, is then common to all *vārkarī* performances and as such, almost similar to the *bhajan* performance (Kiehnle 1983) (except the fact that the *vīṇekarī* begins the *bhajan* with Jñāndev's poem of contemplation only). Yet, in the *bhajan*, the *vīṇekarī* is clearly the leader and tends to be always the same appointed person. This is even more stressed in the *vārkarī* pilgrimage itself where the *vīṇā's* holder is the only member of his group (and its ritual leader) to be kept to complete all the pilgrimage, going to Panḍharpur and coming back to Āḷandī.

The *kīrtankār* and *vīṇekarī's* status varies according to the ritual context (and also to the historical tribulations of the sectarization, in the sense of "sampradayization" of *vārkarī* tradition, which tends to "freeze" ritual functions) but the liturgical formalism of devotional practices is structured by saint's figures of erudition and devotion.

To conclude this brief comparison of *nāradiya* and *vārkarī* ways of worship, we can say that if *bhakti* religiosity opened the way to all categories of people without consideration of caste and creed, this way is not uniform. On the contrary, the diversity of devotional practices shows the creativity, not to say the competitiveness, in that field. As we have seen through the different ways of performing *kīrtan*, this is one example of the appropriation of divine presence, at the same time complementary to the image temple cult but also trying to underline its independence and its own peculiarity.

Moreover, if *bhakti* has opened his way to those who didn't have direct access to ritual monopolized by the sacerdotal class of Brahmans, this doesn't mean that Brahmans didn't find their proper place in that religious reformism. In the *nāradiya kīrtan*, brahmanical in the way of performing and in the repertoire, the *kīrtankār*, Brahmans, extol their authority through the *guru's* concept and aura, that includes *guru*-fee.

Not less legitimized in his community, the position of the *vārkarī kīrtankār* is yet merged into the liturgical formalism of the *vārkarī* type of performance structured by saints model of piety, humility and their intercession.

Finally, the contrast between *vārkarī* collective and congregational aspects on one hand and *nāradiya* priesthood on the other seems correlative with the distinctions between the devotional immediate relationship between god and the devotee and the sacrificial relationships in which the ritual relation is established on the trust (*śraddhā*) between devotee and priest, linked by the fee (*dakṣiṇā*) (Malamoud 1976).

NOTES

1. For a more pleasant reading, I shall omit the "a" of the syllabic writing (and above all the final one) in the recurrent words in accordance with the pronunciation. Thus *kīrtan* instead of *kīrtana; kīrtankār* (the one who performs the *kīrtan*) instead of *kīrtanakāra; vārkarī* instead of *vārakarī*. However the final "a" of *nāradiya* is pronounced.
2. I am indebted to the *kīrtankār* C. Aphle who "opened me the way" to the *kīrtan* and explained me in details, and with all the pedagogic talent for which he is renowned, the intricacies of the *nāradiya* type of *kīrtan*. I am also very thankful to V.L. Manjul who has always been available to speak about this field in which he is himself involved. My thanks also to the *kīrtankār* Balasaheb Udaphe, to Mr. Kunjir and to the Aryaneshwar Bhajan Mandal of Pune who helped me to understand *vārkarī* performances. Two years fieldwork, 1998 to 2000 have been made possible thanks to the support of a Franco-Indian (ICCR) scholarship.
3. The practice of *kīrtan* varies from region to region: in north India, *kīrtan* refers to a collective singing without sermon (Slawek 1986) much like a *bhajan* in the maharashtrian sense. It can also be a song of praise filled in a sermon like a *kathā* (Lutgendorf 1991).
4. Not on account of some prescription like in politeness customs for instance (Mauss 1968: 403).
5. For instance, *kīrtankārs* often quote Tukārām's poem "difficult is to find the (right) way without the true-guru . . ." (*satgurūvāconī sāpaḍena soy*) along portraits of saints depicting (true) *guru's* qualities (the emphasis on his knowledge and/or his humility depending on each *kīrtankār*). In his book on *kīrtan* tradition in Maharashtra, Y. Pathak gives a list of no less than 181 cases of such associations between the main poem and the story from many *kīrtankār's* personal notebook (Pathak 1980).
6. In fact, *kīrtankārs* themselves show some more affinity for the story which is their *kīrtan*'s peculiarity compared to the *vārkarī* one. It's not by chance if Pathak, who himself belongs to the tradition, chose to insert his list (cf. note 5) in the *ākhyān* chapter instead of putting it in an appendix. *Kīrtankār's* older notebooks even mention only the story in the summary (I am very thankful to Mr. Manjul for providing me with these documents).
7. This tradition is called after this type of *kīrtan* due to a tentative of

renewal and homogenization of *kīrtan* by Govindbuva Hoshing in the beginning of nineteenth century (Pathak 1986).

8. *Jay jay Rām Kṛṣṇa Hāri/navanīradasama navanītapriya, navalavinodavihārī/ govardhandhara gopālanarata, gokuḷasaṅkata hārī / rāvaṇamadahara dīnajanoddhara, suravaramocanakārī.*
9. H.Bh.P. is *kīrtankār's* title. It means "follower of Hāri's devotion" (Hāri Bhakta Pārāyaṇ). "Buvā" is a suffix of respect for pious person and *kīrtankār* by excellence.
10. *Sundara te dhyāna ubhe viṭevarī/kara katāvarī ṭhevoniya/tuḷsīdhāra gaḷā kāse pīṭāmbara/āvaḍe nirantara heci dhyāna/makarakunḍale taḷapatī śravaṇī/kanṭhī kaustubhamaṇī virājita/tukā mhaṇe mājhe heci sarva sukha/ pahīna śrīmukha āvaḍine.*
11. Old Marathi is sometimes very tricky. I am very thankful to D. Citre who cleared my doubts about the translation of *locanī* as "in the eyes" instead of "by the eyes" (in which case it would have been "*locanānnī*").
12. *Rūpa pāhatā locanī/sukha jāle vo sājaṇī/ to hā viṭṭhaḷa baravā/to hā mādhava baravā/bahuta sukrutācī joḍī/mhaṇunī viṭṭhaḷī avaḍī/sarva sukhāce āgara/ bāpa rakhumādevivara.*

REFERENCES

Deleury, G., 1994 (1960): *The Cult of Viṭhobā.* Pune: Deccan College.

Eck, D., 1998: *Darshan: Seeing the Divine Image in India.* New York: Columbia University Press.

Kiehnle, C., 1983: "A *Vārkarī Bhajan* Programme: Elements and Structure, Text and Translation", in Thiel-Horstmann, ed., *Bhakti in Current Research, 1979-1982.* Berlin: Dietrich Reimer, pp. 195-212.

Lutgendorf, Ph. 1991: *The Life of a Text: Performing the Ramcaritmanas of Tulsidas.* Berkeley: University of California Press.

Malamoud, Ch., 1976: "Terminer le sacrifice", in M. Biardeau and Ch. Malamoud, eds., *Le sacrifice dans l'Inde ancienne.* Paris: Presse Universitaire de France.

Mauss, M., 1968: "La prière et les rites oraux", in *Oeuvres,* vol. 1: *Les fonctions sociales du sacré.* Les éditions de minuit.

Pangarkar, L.R., ed., 2000: *Navavidha Bhakti.* Mumbai: Keshav Bhikaji Dhavale.

Pathak, Y., 1986: "Govindbuvāncyā shodāt", *Mauj* Magazine (Divalī Issue), Mumbai: Mauj Prakashan.

——1980: *Nācu kīrtanāce raṅgī. Marāthī kīrtanasansthecā cikītsak abhyās.* Pune: Continental Prakashan.

Slawek, S.M., 1986: 'Kīrtan: A Study of the Sonic Manifestations of the Divine in the Popular Hindu Culture of Banaras'. Ph.D. Urbana University Microfilms Inc.

21

Walking and Thinking[1]

ANNE FELDHAUS

Human bodies are an important tool for making spaces into regions. People in Maharashtra, as elsewhere in India, conceptualize not only landscapes but also regions in human bodily terms. In addition, people use their own bodies as a means of traversing areas that thereby become enacted as regions. This paper will present some examples of each of these two kinds of phenomena, and will suggest that there is a link between them.[2]

THINKING ABOUT THE LANDSCAPE

McKean's work on Bharat Mata (McKean 1996) and Ramaswamy's on Tamiltay (Ramaswamy 1997), personifications of India and the Tamil language, respectively, illustrate the power of the female body as a means of representing entities to which people have affective relationships, whether on the national or the regional level. In Maharashtra, as elsewhere in India, rivers too are generally conceived of as feminine, and they are treated as women in ritual terms. In a recent book (Feldhaus 1995), I have discussed rivers' femininity—as well as the masculinity of the mountains from which the rivers originate and of the oceans toward which they flow. However, while gender is clearly an important aspect of the bodily metaphors that people in Maharashtra use to think about the landscape, non-gendered bodily imagery is also to be found.

One kind of device that texts sometimes use to pick out and link a number of different places along a river, and thereby also to express quite vividly the unity of the river valley as a whole, is to designate various places along the river its body parts, thereby implicitly viewing the river as a (human) body. The *Payoṣṇī Māhātmya* (Ballāḷ 1913: 30.16), for example, calls Kṛṣṇakrīdan *tīrtha* the "heart" of the Payoṣṇī, or Pūrṇā river, and the *Narmadā Māhātmya* (Buḷe n.d.: 22.7) calls Siddheśvar at Nemāvar the navel of the Narmadā. But the most elaborate example of such imagery that I have found is in the Marathi *Godāvarī Māhātmya* by Dāsagaṇū (1921: 31.83-85). This text identifies eight organs or limbs (*aṣṭāṅga*) of the Godāvarī: Brahmagiri (at Tryambakeśvar) is the Godāvarī's head (*śir*); Puṇatāmbe is its mouth or face (*mukh*); and Purī, "near the *kṣetra* of Paiṭhaṇ", is the river's neck (*kaṇṭh*). The heart (*hṛday*) of the Godāvarī is Mañjarath; the navel (*nābhi*), Śaṅkha *tīrtha* (at Nānded̩); Manthan (Manthanī) is the hips (*kaṭī*) and Dharmapurī the knees (*jānu*); while Rājamahendrī is the eighth limb, the feet (*caraṇ*). A Brahman resident of Paiṭhaṇ who was aware of this image of Dāsagaṇū's pointed out its similarity to the Puruṣasūkta of the *Ṛgveda*, the hymn that portrays the strata of society and of the natural world as deriving from the parts of the sacrificed cosmic giant, Puruṣa. In Doniger's translation (O'Flaherty 1981: 31), this hymn reads in part as follows:

10.90.11. When they divided the Man, into how many parts did they apportion him? What do they call his mouth, his two arms and thighs and feet?
10.90.12. His mouth became the Brahmin; his arms were made into the Warrior, his thighs the People, and from his feet the Servants were born.
10.90.13. The moon was born from his mind; from his eye the sun was born. Indra and Agni came from his mouth, and from his vital breath the Wind was born.
10.90.14. From his navel the middle realm of space arose; from his head the sky evolved. From his two feet came the earth, and the quarters of the sky from his ear. Thus they set the worlds in order.

T. Nīlakaṇṭh Kavīśvar Śāstrī gives a strikingly similar interpretation of an analogous image of the Kṛṣṇā. The image is found in a verse of a poem by Ṭembe Svāmī entitled "Kṛṣṇālaharī":

Your mouth is at the base of the Sahyādris;
You have Narahari's compassionate heart;
Your navel is in a town in Andhra;
Your two feet are in the east.

Although the verse does not name specific *tīrthas* or *kṣetras*, it is generally taken to portray Wāī as the Kṛṣṇā's mouth or face (*mukh*), Narsobācī Vāḍī as its heart, and Kurugaḍḍī or Kuravapūr in Andhra Pradesh as its navel, while the two feet are taken to be the two mouths by which the Kṛṣṇā reaches the ocean. In interpreting the verse, T.N.K. Śāstrī explains the reason for calling Wāī the mouth of the Kṛṣṇā: many Brahmans live in Wāī, and Brahmans are the mouth of Viṣṇu; Śāstrī identifies Viṣṇu with the Vedic Puruṣa, whose mouth, according to the Puruṣasūkta, "became the Brahmin"; "the scriptures" (possibly the *Kṛṣṇā Māhātmya*), according to Śāstrī, identify Viṣṇu with the Kṛṣṇā river (Śāstrī 1982: 122).

To identify a river as a human body is to use a powerful cosmological image, one that implies that the river is organic and that it is human. Moreover, to identify the river with the body of the Vedic Puruṣa implies in addition that the river valley is a microcosm of the whole world. At the very least, this imagery of a human or human-like embodied being serves to bring disparate places into a conceptual unity. It serves to make them a region.

WALKING THROUGH THE COUNTRYSIDE

The relationship between the human body and the conceptualization of regions can also be viewed from a different standpoint. Besides imagining the landscape or some of its features as a body, people use their *own* bodies not only to walk with, but also to think with, as they move around creating regions within Maharashtra.

Here I will describe some of the exceptional kinds of walking that some people in Maharashtra perform. I will focus on three different pilgrimage traditions that I have learned about in the course of recent field work. Each of them involves a pilgrimage that people undertake as a group at a particular time of year. In each case, the pilgrims transport some special object or objects from one place to another. Each group of pilgrims traces its tradition to an original devotee whose journey they re-enact. And each group of pilgrims is led by a descendant of the devotee they imitate. I will describe, first, a pilgrimage in which people carry the goddess Jāṇāī's palanquin from Jejurī to Navkhaṇ; secondly, one in which people carry water pots slung from poles (*kāvaḍs*) from Sāsvaḍ and other places to Śiṅgṇāpūr; and, thirdly, a pilgrimage in which people carry an empty palanquin and an empty bedstead from Ghoḍegāv and Rāhurī to Tuljāpūr.

JĀṆĀĪ: JEJURĪ TO NAVKHAṆ

The goddess Jāṇāī is sometimes called the sister of Khaṇḍobā of Jejurī, but she is his sister primarily in the sense that she lives near him but is not his wife. Her temple in Jejurī is located in the town, not within or adjacent to Khaṇḍobā's temple on the hill above the town. Jāṇāī's original—and still most important—temple is located about 100 km to the south of Jejurī, in Navkhaṇ, a small place in Pāṭaṇ Taluka, Satara District. She is said to have been brought from there to Jejurī by Nāgo Māḷī, a man of the gardener caste whose descendants, the Jhagaḍes, still live in Jejurī.

The story of Nāgo Māḷī is typical of many stories of the way in which a god or goddess came to be settled in a place that his or her devotees now visit. For many years, Nāgo Māḷī paid regular visits to Jāṇāī's temple at Navkhaṇ. After a long time, he became old and weak, and could no longer make the trip. The goddess then followed him home to Jejurī. The pilgrims who travel from Jejurī to Navkhaṇ imitate Nāgo Māḷī's pilgrimage by following his route. However, instead of simply traveling to Jāṇāī's temple or bringing her back with them, as he did, they carry the goddess home to visit her original place.

Jāṇāī's pilgrimage involves a series of events spread over several weeks preceding and following the festival of Hoḷī. On the first day, a palanquin holding several brass masks of the goddess processes around the town, preceded by two tall poles (*kāṭhīs*) and accompanied by a variety of drums and an ever-larger number of people dancing in possession. Three days later, the palanquin sets out for Navkhaṇ. Nāgo Māḷī's descendant Mahādū Jhagaḍe and his wife accompany it on foot, along with a small group of other citizens of Jejurī. These people travel by a direct route, overland; others make the trip in jeeps, meeting the palanquin a few days later, when it arrives in Navkhaṇ. For the next two days, a series of palanquin processions and food offerings takes place, climaxing in the simultaneous decapitation of two male sheep and the collective offering of huge gunny-sack parcels of unbroken coconuts, accompanied by loud drumming, unrestrained dancing, and the shouts of men and women possessed by the goddess.

On the afternoon of Hoḷī, the palanquin returns to Jejurī. People from Jejurī wait at an intersection at the southern end of the town; they greet Mr. Jhagaḍe by pouring water over his feet and putting colored powder on his toes. People also make food offerings to the goddess in the palanquin, they touch their babies' heads to it, and they line up their children on the ground like railroad ties for the palanquin to be carried over them. Again there is drumming, and again people become possessed. Only after the palanquin has reached Jejurī, it is said, may Hoḷī fires be lit in the town.

Five days later, on Raṅgapañcamī, there is another sheep sacrifice, a meal of mutton for hundreds of townspeople, and a Gondhaḷ, a kind of song-and-dance performance in honor of goddesses (Ḍhere 1988). The final event of the pilgrimage takes place a few nights after that. It is held in the Jhagaḍes' fields. This event is called "Nāgo Māḷī's Boḷavaṇ", the "send-off" for Nāgo Māḷī. This time the group of participants is smaller and more intimate. Once again there is a meal, once again Gondhaḷīs perform, and once again people become possessed. The meal, the Gondhaḷ, and the possession take place in front of a row of small shrines in the field. The most important of the shrines on this evening is that of Nāgo Māḷī and his wife. Mrs. Jhagaḍe becomes possessed by Jāṇāī and a number of other goddesses, and at one point by Nāgo Māḷī. Thus, Mahādū Jhagaḍe embodies Nāgo Māḷī in a triple sense: he imitates him, he is descended from him, and his wife becomes possessed by him.

SĀSVAḌ TO ŚIṄGṆĀPŪR

The second pilgrimage I will describe here is the one to Śiṅgṇāpūr in the month of Caitra (March-April). Pilgrims to Śiṅgṇāpūr carry water there in small, medium-sized, or quite amazingly large *kāvaḍs* (water pots slung from poles). The pilgrims pour the water over the *piṇḍ* (the Śivaliṅga) in a Śiva temple that crowns the huge, almost free-standing mountain at Śiṅgṇāpūr. This is the mountain that appears in Dhangar oral epics (*ovīs*), for example, in the role that Śiva's heavenly mountain plays in Sanskrit Purāṇas: it is the place where Śiva lives with his wife, where he plays parcheesi and argues with her, the place from which he issues his orders and rules the world.

The pilgrimage festival at Śiṅgṇāpūr is Maharashtra's most elaborate example of the kind of pilgrimage in which people carry water from home to pour on a distant god. People travel from villages and towns on all sides of the mountain, bringing the water of numerous rivers and wells to pour on the god in the temple. In my book on rivers (Feldhaus 1995), I discuss the way this pilgrimage parallels the story of the descent of the Gaṅgā, a story in which the river flows from heaven *first* onto the top of the cosmic mountain, and *then* onto the head of Śiva. I point out that the pilgrims recreate the image of Śiva with Gaṅgā on his head and invert the image of the cosmic mountain—making the water travel *up* the mountain instead of flowing *down* it. Further field work on this festival has revealed that the most knowledgeable pilgrims see as its central rite the wedding of Śiva and Pārvatī. In this context, the *kāvaḍs* that come to Śiṅgṇāpūr, sloshing water on the god and the mountain, come there to celebrate the wedding.

The most important of the *kāvaḍs* comes from Sāsvaḍ, far to the north-west of Śiṅgṇāpūr. It has the honorary right (the *mān*) of proceeding *last* up the cliff on the mountain's north-west face. The group that carries this *kāvaḍ* is led by a Telī, a member of the oil-presser caste. He is a descendant of Bhutojī Telī, a devotee who used to carry water to Śiṅgṇāpūr to pour on the god. Not only the group that travels with *this kāvaḍ*, but also those that travel with the large *kāvaḍs* that precede it, understand themselves to be following the example and maintaining the tradition of this man's devoted service.

Men attached to the Sāsvaḍ *kāvaḍ* and to its rival from a neighboring group of five villages identify themselves in terms of, and see their ritual as expressing, a kind of fierce Śaiva devotion (*bhakti*). Their trip, which they make on foot, cross-country, in the hot month of Caitra, has a distinct ascetic element. This is especially true for the leaders, who must make the trip in their bare feet and without eating meals. The theme of renunciation is also present, to be seen most clearly when the second-most-important, rival *kāvaḍ* circumambulates the site of the original Bhutojī Telī's house before leaving on the pilgrimage. This place is called Jalate Ghar, "Burning House", in memory of Bhutojī's practice of burning his house down behind him, and not looking back, as he set off for Śiṅgṇāpūr.

The element of physical difficulty and even danger reaches its climax in the final ascent of the mountain, up an extremely tall, sheer cliff. To get the heavier *kāvaḍs* up this cliff, the men carrying them—all young, strong wrestlers—must struggle and strain, slipping and scrabbling all the way. Most of the large *kāvaḍs* are pulled up from above by ropes, as well as being pushed from below by the young men, but the last *kāvaḍ* reaches the top without the help of ropes, each of the men pushing up with his head on the buttocks of the man before him. A piece of cloth attached to the vertical pole of each large *kāvaḍ* serves as a kind of sail, the men explain, and Mahādev provides the wind that fills the sail and helps propel the *kāvaḍ* to the top.

Nowadays the *kāvaḍs* are carried empty up the cliff, but even so the big ones are extremely heavy. In former days, the men say, there used to be water in the *kāvaḍs*, and Bhutojī Telī is said to have carried his up loaded with sand. Some say he got his name "Bhutojī"—from "*bhūt*", "ghost"—for his ghost-like power to get the heavy contraption up the precipice. Nowadays even empty *kāvaḍs* sometimes fall back down from partway up, and occasionally men get hurt. At the foot of the cliff is a shrine to a young man who died there, trying to get one of the large *kāvaḍs* up to the top of the hill.

PALANQUIN AND BEDSTEAD TO TUḶJĀPŪR

If the Śiṅgṇāpūr pilgrimage is characterized by a rather fierce, athletic, Śaiva devotion, my final example, although directed to a goddess rather than to Śiva, is also not without its elements of athleticism. The goddess is Bhavānī of Tuḷjāpūr, and the pilgrimage consists in two rival, related groups carrying an empty palanquin and an empty bedstead (*palaṅg*) to Tuḷjāpūr for the festival of Navarātra and Dasarā. For both the palanquin and the bedstead, the journey lasts more than a month, and in each case the route and the halting places are fixed. The bedstead starts from Ghoḍegāv, in north-west Pune District, and the palanquin from Rāhurī, in northern Ahmadnagar District.

While the bedstead is carried relatively sedately, at first by four men and eventually, I'm told, by as many as fifty, the empty palanquin gets passed along more wildly from village to village along its route. To the sound of large *ḍhoḷ* drums and accompanied by groups of young men dancing in the energetic, rhythmic manner called *lejhīm*, the extremely heavy wooden palanquin proceeds sporadically from one village to the next, twisting around in circles, jumping up and down, at times running far off in the opposite direction from its goal. Sometimes the strong young men hold it atop their upraised arms, sometimes it rests on their shoulders, and once, as it was being tossed around by twenty young men at a time, I saw it fall to the ground. At the border of two villages, I saw two huge wrestlers, one on each end of the palanquin, fighting for control of it. In each village where the palanquin or the bedstead stops, people come to have the sight (*darśan*) of it and to perform *pūjā* to it, and in some of the places a small festival is held.

The palanquin and the bedstead meet in Bhiṅgār, a village on the eastern outskirts of Ahmadnagar. The bedstead proceeds on foot toward Tuḷjāpūr, making no more overnight stops, while the palanquin waits in Burhāṇnagar, also near Ahmadnagar, and then goes on to Tuḷjāpūr by train. Both arrive in time for the last night of Navarātra. On that night—or, rather, very early on the morning of Dasarā—the palanquin serves to carry the main image of the goddess (not any smaller, festival image, but the main one from the inner shrine) around the courtyard of her temple in a boundary-crossing (*sīmollaṅghan*) procession. The goddess is then put to rest on the bedstead, where she sleeps until the full-moon day, while the crowd in the temple courtyard hacks to pieces all but the long, curved bar of the palanquin, the people ripping the palanquin's cradle apart with their hands and dashing it repeatedly against the ground.

The leaders of the groups that accompany the bedstead and the palanquin are both Telīs. They claim to be 27th-generation descendants of Jānkojī Devkar, the devotee who started the pilgrimage; five generations ago, the family split into the bedstead-carriers (whose surname, appropriately, is Palaṅge) and the palanquin-carriers (with the surname Bhagat), the one group descended from a sister and the other from a brother.

According to Arjun Kisan Bhagat, Jānkojī was a Telī who lived in Burhāṇnagar. One day a little girl with a skin disease showed up at his house. Jānkojī and his wife adopted her. They named her Ambikā. After the girl had joined the household, Jānkojī began to prosper. Magically a moneylender gave him a loan that enabled him to get his oil mill going. He began to sell large amounts of oil, and he was able to build seven houses. But when Jānkojī and his wife tried to arrange their daughter's marriage, she hid from any prospective in-laws who would come to see her. Finally she disappeared altogether. Mad with grief, Jānkojī wandered around, searching for his daughter. Finally he came to Tuḷjāpūr. There he went to the monastery where the goddess plays parcheesi (*sāripāṭ*) with Bhāratībuva. As soon as her game was over, Jānkojī resolved, he would kill himself by jumping into the well in the courtyard of the monastery. The goddess continued playing parcheesi; she played more and more slowly, and kept delaying the end of the game. Finally Jānkojī recognized her: the goddess of Tuḷjāpūr was his own daughter.

Jānkojī's descendants understand themselves to be carrying on the father-daughter relationship between Jānkojī and the goddess of Tuḷjāpūr. Arjun Bhagat goes to Tuḷjāpūr to meet his daughter, the goddess, just as Jānkojī did. At the climax of the festival, on the last night of Navarātra in Tuḷjāpūr, Bhagat carries a food offering in to the goddess; he explained to me that he carries it over his stomach, in a cloth tied around his waist, because that is how one carries food for a child. I'm not quite sure what he meant by this (certainly it is too far-fetched to say that he makes himself look pregnant), but his wife's parental gesture was unambiguous, when she explained the tender way her husband puts his hand under the goddess's head as he places her in the palanquin—another thing he gets to do during the last night of Navarātra. "Like a daughter", I said, interpreting the movements of Mrs. Bhagat's hands. "Yes", she said, and smiled.

On the morning of Dasarā, after the palanquin procession and the literally riotous tearing up of the palanquin, at 7 o'clock or so the Bhagat family and those who have journeyed with them gather at Jānkojī's *samādhi*, which is in Tuljāpūr. They sit on the platform where the palanquin rested before being carried to the temple, and they eat as *prasād* a sweet, thick liquid they have brought from the temple, as well as the food offering that Arjun Bhagat had wrapped around his waist to carry in to the goddess. The food consists of chapatis and a vegetable typical of Telīs: a cooked mixture of *methī* leaves and the husks of sesame seeds from which the oil has been removed. Like the more dramatic possession episodes after Nāgo Mālī's descendants' return from their pilgrimage to Jāṇāī's temple, Jānkojī's descendants' ritual meal reinforces their identity with their founding ancestor and model devotee.

WALKING AS THINKING

The pilgrimages I have described are but three examples of many that take place in the Maharashtrian countryside every year. These pilgrimages involve the human body in several ways. First, they involve a good deal of physical effort for those involved. This is especially true for the leaders, who must generally travel on foot, walking barefoot on rough and often hot ground, and who in most cases must fast for long periods of time. For the other participants, too, the pilgrimages involve energetic physical activity—most obviously in the rough cross-country journey from Jejurī to Navkhaṇ, the struggle to hoist the heavy *kāvaḍs* up the cliff at Śiṅgṇāpūr, and the riotous tearing apart of the palanquin at Tuljāpūr, but to some extent in all the pilgrimages—for travel is never easy, and travel that involves transporting heavy, complicated ritual objects great distances is all the less so.

In the three pilgrimages I have described here, bodies also become focal points of interest through the notion of ancestry. Each of these pilgrimages is led by a man or men understood to be descended from an original devotee whose journey the modern-day pilgrims imitate. In the case of the Tuljāpūr pilgrimage, the leader even understands his ancestor to have been related—albeit by adoption—to the goddess whose temple forms the goal of the pilgrimage. In the case of Jāṇāī's pilgrimage, the physical link between the original devotee and his modern descendant extends even to the devotee's entering the body of his descendant's wife in possession.

Most basically, though, and most importantly for understanding the relationship between pilgrimage and regional consciousness, these pilgrimages require that their participants move *bodily* from one place to another, across the area in between. By doing this, the pilgrims connect the places—the place they leave from, the place they go to, and all the places in between, as well as the places that other pilgrims come from and pass through. The pilgrims connect these places by means of their own bodies. They thereby make these places real for themselves, and they make possible the conceptualization of the places as connected to one another—as forming, that is, a region.

The American (but Continental) philosopher Edward Casey (1993: 72) sees the living human body as the basis for a sense of place—as opposed to mere space:

> it is around and in terms of my live and moving body that right and left, above and below, before and behind come into concrete play and interplay. In each instance, my body is at once differentiating (as continually bifurcating) and organizing (as connecting the variously portioned parts of place in accordance with the disposition of my bodily members). The precipitate of this differentiation-cum-organization is the very place, indeed the many places, my body assumes and inhabits.

The body is also central, for Casey, to the notion of region:

> When the range of the here includes not just the place through which I am now moving (and which therefore reflects my immediate bodily movement) but all of the places to which I can effectively move, I

> experience a properly regional here. . . . I take myself to be *here* in this house or block or neighborhood, in this state or nation, whenever I am convinced that (a) I can in principle move (in person or by proxy) to any part of this region, however far-flung this part might be; (b) some other more or less comparably extensive region stands opposed to my current here-region: *another* neighborhood, *another* state, over there and in relation to which I am now truly here, on *this* side (*diesseits*) of whatever boundary or difference demarcates the two regions in question. A region, therefore, is a concatenation of places that, taken together, constitutes a common and continuous here for the person who lives in or traverses them.

In the pilgrimages I have described here, as well as in most other pilgrimages in South Asia, the pilgrims enact their conviction that they *can* move through a region by in fact *doing* so. At the same time, they reinforce the same conviction for those who, though they remain at home, are aware of the pilgrims' journeys. This does not, I realize, mean that the pilgrims have met Casey's second criterion of a region—that it be conceived as opposed to some other, more-or-less commensurate one. But it does meet, and exceed, his first criterion, that the region be conceived as a set of places through which one can in principle move. This step in the process of conceptualization of a region is not necessarily—and certainly, in the case of most pilgrims I have spoken with, not very—articulate in a verbal sense. And yet it is the basis for the possibility of such highly developed verbal imagery as that with which I began: the view of a river valley as a human body, its parts the different places along the river's banks. Movement through an area with one's own body, or a clear realization of the possibility of such movement, is a condition for being able to imagine the area not only as a body, but as a region in *any* coherent sense.

NOTES

1. I am grateful to the organizers of the Tokyo Maharashtra Conference for inviting me to submit this paper even though I was unable to attend the conference. The paper was originally presented at the Maharashtra Conference in Sydney in January 1999. I am grateful to Jim Masselos for permission to publish it in the present volume.
2. For further discussion of the rituals and imagery described here, see Feldhaus 2003.

REFERENCES

Ballāḷ, Tryambak, 1913: *Payoṣṇī Māhātmya.* Bombay: Śaṅkar Printing Press.

Buḷe, Śakuntalābāī Nārāyaṇrāv, n.d.: Śrīnarmadāmāhātmya. Dādar: Narendra Book Depot.

Casey, Edward S., 1993: *Getting Back into Place: Toward a Renewed Understanding of the Place-World.* Bloomington: Indiana University Press.

Dāsagaṇū, 1921 (Śake 1843): *Śrī Gautamī Māhātmya.* Nāndeḍ: Dāmodhar Vāman Āṭhavale.

Feldhaus, Anne, 1995: *Water and Womanhood: Religious Meanings of Rivers in Maharashtra.* New York: Oxford University Press.

——, 2003: *Connected Places: Region, Pilgrimage, and Geographical Imagination in Maharashtra.* New York: Palgrave.

McKean, Lise, 1996: *Divine Enterprise: Gurus and the Hindu Nationalist Movement.* Chicago: University of Chicago Press.

O'Flaherty, Wendy Doniger, translator, 1981: *The Rig Veda: An Anthology.* Harmondsworth: Penguin Books Ltd.

Ramaswamy, Sumathi, 1997: *Passions of the Tongue: Language Devotion in Tamil India, 1891-1970.* Berkeley: University of California Press.

Śāstrī, Tryambak Nīlakaṇṭh Kavīśvar, 1982: "Śrīkṣetra Kuruvapur va Kṛṣṇece Vaiśiṣṭhya". *Śrīkṛṣṇamāīce Nābhisthān Śrī Kṣetra Kuruvapūr.* Haiderābād: Hindu Vijay Prakāśan.

22

Mariai Cult in Pune

MUSASHI TACHIKAWA

MARIAI FESTIVAL

A woman was on her knees on the ground, stretching both arms back and twisting her body from side to side. She was wearing a red and lapis lazuli colored sari. Pronounced by the movement was the prominence of her breasts and hips, recognizable through the folds of her garment. Grimacing and swaying her long dark hair in rhythm, she entered a state of trance.

Some women were lying on the ground, rolling about frantically. Others were sitting and wailing loudly. There was one woman jumping up and down incessantly, who collapsed suddenly to the ground, remaining motionless on the spot, looking like a lump of meat. There were more than ten-odd women in total, who I suspected to be in a trance.

Some were sitting on a riverside, yelling and shedding tears. There were people taking care of the entranced women. Many men were walking and moving about, shouting aloud. Some were playing the drums or pipes, which added to the uproar and agitation at the *ghāṭ* (a level place on the edge of a river for ritual proceedings). Two or three women in a trance were issuing oracles orally in reply to people's questions. They were wearing red saris, and were supported on both sides by others. It was not clear whether their eyes were open. It was evident, however, that they were not focusing their eyes on those in front of them. Although they could hardly support themselves and looked likely to fall at any minute, they kept talking in shrill high pitched voices. When people walked closer to face these women, they stooped down to show their respect, extending both hands to touch their feet. After listening to the oracle respectfully for one or two minutes, they left the spot.

I was standing at a *saṅgam ghāṭ* in the city of Pune (Poona), about 180 km east of Mumbai (Bombay), India. It was on 25 July 1997 that I had the opportunity to witness the ritual proceedings of the "Mariai" festival at this particular *saṅgam ghāṭ*. "Mariai" is one of the native religious cults, which have been thriving for a thousand years in Maharashtra and other states in south India. The festival was to be carried out on the fourth Friday of the month of Āṣāḍha in the Hindu calendar (virtually corresponding to July or August in the Gregorian calendar). The ritual signified "worship of and devotion to the awesome Hindu Goddess Lakṣmī".

"Mariai" is the name of a goddess worshipped by local people in Maharashtra and Karnataka areas. At the same time, she is also called "the awesome Goddess Lakṣmī" of Hinduism, the goddess of fortune, luck, wealth of the earth and prosperity. Lakṣmī has long been well known in the tradition of orthodox Brahmanism. In Buddhism, this same goddess is called "Śrī-mahādevī". As I explain later, however, the indigenous deity Mariai worshipped by local people in Maharashtra is not exactly the same as the one officially recognized by orthodox Brahmins. In fact, it is only those who observe their indigenous religious practices, worshipping the deity "Mariai", who have unilaterally adopted the name "Lakṣmī" to refer to their goddess. For this reason, even today, there exists strong antagonism between the religious practice of Mariai and the order of "orthodox Hinduism". The latter is centered on caste, in which Brahmins have the highest authority.

In the Mariai cult, the phenomenon of being possessed by the supernatural plays a pivotal role. It would be right to say that this particular fact is one major reason for this order being at odds with orthodox Hinduism. As far as I have observed, those female followers of the faith of Mariai entered the state of possession quite naturally and comfortably as if they were enjoying a sport.

As a matter of fact, it is not uncommon that, when major festivals of Hinduism are in progress, many people work themselves into a trancelike state. This phenomenon could take place in various orders, which are not necessarily on bad terms with orthodox Brahmins. For example, situated in the old town of Pune is a Hindu temple enshrining the Goddess Jogeśvarī. This goddess has been worshiped by the local people of Pune for hundreds of years as "Grāma Devatā" (village deity). She is a rather important goddess for the upper castes in Pune such as Brahmin, Kṣatriya and Vaiśya. Perplexingly enough, when the Navaratri (Festival of 'nine nights') is held during the month of Āśvina, which is around September and October in the Gregorian calendar, a large number of women appear near this temple, who dance about and issue oracles in a trance. This fact itself does not mean that Hinduism, in which orthodox Brahmins are placed at the center of the community and have the highest authority, has tolerated and acquiesced in unorthodox religious practices such as possession by the supernatural or being in a trance as a legitimate way of exercising religious faith. It would be more accurate to say that, during the festive season of Navaratri, orthodox Brahmins become more lenient towards outsiders who approach the shrine of Jogeśvarī, the indigenous guardian goddess of the local Hindu community. It is said that those who enter a trance in the neighborhood of the temple of Jogeśvarī "are simply ordinary and normal citizens". Presumably, even among those in higher castes, there are some who are predisposed to possession by extraordinary emotions. Once they are in a trance, these people are physically attracted to the proximity of the temple, which is "prestigious" in the local religious tradition. Therefore, it is not the case that the higher castes are immune to being possessed by such extreme emotions. There should be some who enter trances. Probably, put more precisely, the point is how much weight is given to such modalities of worship as trances or possession by different orders and communities in the entire spectrum of Indian religion.

Certainly, as far as those who worship Mariai are concerned, immense gravity and weight is given to such ritual proceedings as possession by extraordinary emotions and trances, much more than in the rest of Hindu religious practice, in which a pivotal role is played by orthodox Brahmins.

I have described how important the phenomenon of possession by the supernatural is in the Mariai cult. I believe that this religious order contains elements of shamanism as well. People in India and Nepal call these ritual modalities including elements of shamanism or supernatural possession, "Tantrism-like" or "Tantric". Often, the term "Tantrism" is used with negative implications.

PRIESTS IN THE GUISE OF WOMEN

In the course of Mariai worship, priests disguise themselves as women when presiding over ritual proceedings. During the specific ceremony I witnessed at the *saṅgam ghāṭ*, there were about two priests in the guise of women in each group, guiding the participants. People were following the instructions given by these priests. Furthermore, two days before that particular ceremony, one of the three groups of people had been engaged in a rain prayer ritual at the same spot. On that occasion, priests in the guise of women led the participants, with a leather cane called *cabuka* in their hand.

These men, the priests, also entered a state of trance, although in a slightly different manner from that of women.

I saw a young man wearing a vividly colorful skirt for young girls standing on the spot, bowing his head down slightly, and closing his eyes. Surrounding him were about one hundred spectators, dancing and shouting loudly. At one point, an old man with a wooden pipe looking like a Portuguese flute called *charamela* in his hand approached the young man. The old man started to play the pipe very close to the left ear of the young man. The sound was so loud that I found it astonishing, even though I was more than 20 meters away from the place. Despite the noise, however, the young man remained completely still for the next two or three minutes.

Then there came another young man, also in girl's costume, approaching the first. He walked up very close, and whispered something into the right ear of the first. Finally, he shouted aloud, "Glory to the Goddess Lakṣmī" (Lakṣmī Jaya). Upon the second man's exclamation, the first, a young priest, fell forward onto the ground. Two or three men around the spot raised him in their arms, and rubbed red powder (*kuṅkum*) onto his forehead. More accurately, they sprinkled plenty of red powder all over the young man's face. The next moment, the young priest suddenly jerked up and started to move like a zombie called back to life. He joined other priests in women's dresses, guiding the festival proceedings.

These priests in colorful skirts wore long dark hair hanging down their backs. Although they were also in a sort of trance, their movements were somewhat different from those of entranced women. The young priests sometimes lost control over themselves and collapsed. Unlike some women, however, they did not stay motionless on the spot for a long time. Instead they stood up again soon. While dancing and using the cane skilfully, some of them performed a brief drama, that is, a skit. Upon hearing the sound of wooden pipe, which evoked them into a trance, some young priests suddenly began running. They dashed through the walls of spectators and tried to run into a nearby forest. When that happened, several other men immediately chased after them, and brought them back. At one point, a young priest was caught just before vanishing into the forest, and brought back to the place where the rituals were in progress.

It would be impossible to explain clearly what mental and physiological states these priests were in at that time. Obviously they were extremely excited. However, they do not seem to have been in so-called possession by a supernatural power. Probably, upon hearing that loud awakening sound of the wood pipe played right into their ear, they became semi-possessed. It was evident, however, that they had not lost consciousness. They were aware of themselves. It would be fair to say that dashing into the forest or the river was also a kind of performance, while they remained conscious of the spectators around as well as of themselves all the time.

At one point, two priests ran underneath a big piece of cloth, hiding themselves below it for a few minutes. Then suddenly they jumped out of the cloth and started to run. When reaching the riverside, they caught a chicken and bit its head off with their teeth. They threw the head of the chicken into the water. This act was performed by one of the three groups involved with the ceremony on that day. In fact, such a tradition of animal sacrifice is one of the main causes of the long standing feud between those who worship the deity Mariai and orthodox Hindu Brahmins.

As far as the ritual of animal sacrifice is concerned, however, it should be understood that the hostility between the two sects has something to do with the idiosyncrasies of the city of Pune and the region of Maharashtra. Unlike other places in India, there remains a more deeply rooted conservative Hindu practice in this region, centered round respect for the authority of orthodox Brahmins. By contrast, in places such as Bengal and Nepal, animal sacrifice has long been a relatively common practice. Therefore, people's reaction to animal sacrifice varies from region to region.

By the way, why do those priests opt for "disguise as women"? Is it because Mariai is a goddess and that those men were possessed by the supernatural power of this goddess? Certainly, the young priests were attempting by way of disguise to gain the power and resources that were unique to women. At least we could say that they believe that essential female power and resources would be indispensable for them to preside over the ritual successfully. It seems that they choose a female disguise because the essentially submissive nature and qualities of women would be more conducive to elicit godly, spiritual or superhuman powers into their bodies and souls.

MARIAI WORSHIP AND ORTHODOX BRAHMINS

I imagine that none of the participants in the Mariai festival which I saw that day were members of higher castes such as Brahmin or Kṣatriya. When foreign tourists visit these Indian festivals, witnessing the rituals, the proceedings naturally look as if they constituted part of Hinduism. This is because foreigners observe them from an outsider's point of view. According to the local people's perspective, their faith in Mariai or another religious faith in Maharashtra, the worship of an indigenous deity, a devilishly figured buffalo called Mhasobā, has nothing incongruous as part of authentic Hinduism. Some Brahmins in India, however, dismiss such an idea blatantly, contending that the worship of Mariai or Mhasobā falls outside the boundary of authentic Hinduism. One of the reasons for them to deny the legitimacy of these local faiths is that the worship of Mariai is not endorsed by any *sūtra* or established religious doctrine.

India has an astonishing number of so-called indigenous religious practices and forms of worship. The distance between indigenous forms of worship on the one hand and "Hinduism" on the other varies from case to case. Some indigenous religious faiths have been integrated into the tradition of Hinduism and are well tolerated by orthodox Brahmins. On the other hand, there are other religious traditions intensively denied by them. One example is the faith in Mariai. Although effort has been made by local followers of Mariai to get along with orthodox Brahmins, as shown by the fact that they call their deity "Lakṣmī", one of the established goddesses in Hinduism, their tradition is still rejected by orthodox Brahmins, failing to gain an official acknowledgement from them.

Should we encompass such indigenous worships in the spectrum of Hinduism as well? Some marginal regions of the Indian Subcontinent such as parts of Assam and north India can be excluded from the debate, because Hinduism hardly exists in these places. As to this question, understandably enough, the answer varies depending on how we define Hinduism. More accurately put, it depends on how we define religion itself. Should we think that orthodox Brahmanism and the worship of Mariai are completely alien to each other? Or should we consider that they represent two different aspects of the same religious complex sharing a uniform structure? At the end of the day, the answer is determined by whether or not we think that Brahmins and those in "lower castes" share the same religious sentiment or empathy, by which they are bound together in the religious dimension of life.

Some people would launch an outcry immediately, registering their opposition to such a notion. From their perspective, what is important is not "whether the followers of 'Hinduism' and those of other faiths share the same or similar religious sentiment". Instead, what matters is what sort of cultural forms have been developed by religious orders. What should count in the definition of religion includes the doctrine, ritual processes, the way of living of "followers of the faith", which, in turn, should be influenced by the doctrines and rituals. Furthermore, the political stance and mandate advocated by religious orders should not be overlooked. Whether an order is actually encompassed in the category of "Hinduism" should be determined by all these diverse factors.

It is true that religion has been playing specific functions in various social contexts, thereby surviving in human history. Given this fact, it would be wrong for us to focus solely on the religious sentiments experienced by individuals belonging to certain modalities of worship. I do not suppose that all that matters would be simply the subjective motif and commitment of "individual followers". Furthermore, it would be impossible to identify the nature and qualities of religious sentiments carried by individual people.

Having said so, however, I would like to disclose my concern that the conventional effort to understand religion has placed too much emphasis on doctrine, rituals, distribution among social strata of the followers and so forth. I regret that sufficient attention has not been paid to the understanding of the fundamental and universal structure that should be shared among various orders of religion. I do not intend to say that the "fundamental and universal structure of religion" equals so-called religious sentiment possessed by individual people. The conventional approach to religion, however, has tended to rely on the assumptions that so-called world religion is superior to so-called ethnic religion, and that ethnic religion is superior to "natural religion". Here, against this background, I would like to propose that we all free ourselves from such a stereotyped view that religion can be classified into those three major categories.

Often our attention has been focused on how exquisite the doctrine of religion is, how sophisticated the rituals are, what social status is most predominant among those who follow specific orders of religion, how advanced the arts and crafts are for creating sculpture, paintings and other artistic works symbolizing the core values of the worship. These analytical views are all directed to one specific aim, that is, assigning a particular position to religions based on an assessment of "superiority and inferiority". I am afraid, however, that, while laboring at the prioritization of religion in such a manner, we have overlooked something truly important.

During the Mariai festival, the priests were brandishing snake-shaped leather canes, dancing about frantically with colorful skirts swirling around their bodies. Some of them bit the head off a chicken on a riverbank and threw the head into the center of the river. Spectators were agitated and moved about in chaotic excitement. Women fell to the ground one after another, shrieking and shedding tears, and entering a state of trance. If Brahmins, particularly those in Maharashtra, had witnessed these scenes, they would undoubtedly have been disgusted and would have grimaced in revulsion.

In sheer contrast, the rituals conducted by Brahmins strictly adhere to established protocols, supported by the elaborate doctrines of the order. Therefore, there are distinctive differences between their rituals and doctrines and those of the Mariai cult. How much fundamental difference could there be, however, in terms of the value for human souls that have experienced an evolutionary process for the past tens of thousands of years, I wonder. Although "feuds" might have lasted for thousands of years among different sects, would that antagonism be so fundamental as to be perpetual in people's minds? In addition to internal "feuds" within the boundary of "Hinduism", the Indian Subcontinent is fraught with other conflicts and disputes between Hinduism and Islam or Buddhism. These conflicts will not be resolved as long as people are concerned primarily about doctrine, rituals and the way of life based on these, when pondering on the virtue of religion. What we need is "reform of understanding of religion". Especially in today's context, it would be immensely productive for mutual understanding between different religious sects if effort were made to prove that there is some universal or virtually universal structure of uniformity existing among different religions, despite the apparent discrepancies in the way in which faiths are manifested. The problem is, however, that there are people who do not believe that there is such a universal structure shared by different religions. Actually, it is these people that have driven the sectarian struggles and disputes in the world. While I would like to advise that religion has always been in pursuit of something universal, endeavoring to establish "the sacred", such a concept might be dismissed casually as a theological argument or pedagogical religious philosophy.

The late Wilfred Cantwell Smith, Former Director of the Center for the Study of World Religions, the Divinity School of Harvard University, aspired to advancing the intellectual understanding of religious pluralism and dialogues among faiths across the world, whereby establishing a universal theology or theological perspective. He took an early lead in that undertaking around the mid-twentieth-century. In those days, together with American students, students from various parts of the world such as India, Pakistan, Japan and elsewhere studied at that institute. Through the Center's curriculum design, students were obliged to study religions other than their own. They were encouraged to explore a pathway towards dialogues among different faiths through the comparative studies of religion. Although the late Dr. W.C. Smith's endeavor might have somewhat fallen short of its full achievement, failing to offer a definition of universal theology, I believe that his aspirations brought about great success in the overall initiative.

To be honest, I do not think that the establishment of a universal theology is indispensable, or that it is feasible. On the other hand, I believe that we are urged today to depart from the conventional perception of "superiority and inferiority", which has been used to differentiate one's own religion from others.'

In some faiths, priests or those presiding over the rituals are in the guise of women, and they dance in excitement. Animals are sacrificed as offerings. People enter a state of trance. I presume that these practices have been always in place since the very start of social life in the primitive age. I also speculate that the driving force and desire, which urges us into such actions, still remains in human beings in the modern age, although with some alteration.

One American scientist, who is engaged in research into human cloning technology, says, "Humans and human lifestyles naturally evolve. Therefore, it is only a natural process of evolution for cloning technology to be applied to humans." Could it be really true that humans, especially humans in the religious dimension of life, evolve so dramatically?

It is not yet clear how much time has passed since humans started to use language, thereby initiating social life in a community. At least, however, I do not believe that so much change or evolution has occurred in human souls during the past few thousand years of history. People become conscious of their gender and sex, dancing and singing. They can feel some "sacred" power in blood, water and specific materials. From time to time, they enter an extraordinary phase of consciousness (the sense of metamorphosis). I presume that all these practices have been familiar to us for a long time. I imagine that humans have been engaged in such actions for thousands of years. It must have begun before the launching of so-called world religions such as Buddhism or Christianity.

Certain issues existed on this planet prior to the establishment of the world religions. Indigenous religious faiths were taking care of those problems at that time. It is far from the truth that all those problems have been resolved by the virtues of the world religions. At the same time, it would also be wrong were someone to say that, because those problems already existed before the inception of the world religions, they carry more gravity and importance than issues addressed by the world religions. Here I would like to emphasize that those activities and actions witnessed in the Indian rituals have been with humans for thousands of years, that is, since long before the launching of the so-called world religions. Given this fact, it is essential for people in today's world to reflect upon those actions against the contemporary situation. We should recognize that they must be related to something truly essential for human souls.

WHAT IS HINDUISM?

Hinduism has evolved over centuries, and includes a rich diversity within it. In what is generally called "Hinduism", various races and languages are included, among which conflicts and disputes have emerged from time to time. It would probably be fair to say that the internal feuds within the boundary of "Hinduism" have been much more intense, harsh and on a larger scale than those within Shintoism in Japan.

I have mentioned that it is not clear what modalities of faith the term "Hinduism" stipulates. One of the reasons for this notion is that there have been "internal disputes" taking place within "Hinduism". One element which we need to be aware of is that they are actually "internal" problems for those who take the scope of "Hinduism" broadly. On the other hand, there are other people who support a narrower scope of "Hinduism". For them the conflicts are not internal, but external.

In India, there exist orthodox Hinduism with established *sūtras* and doctrine on the one hand (A), and indigenous religious forms of local origins without them on the other (B). Some people call both A and B "Hinduism", whereas others deny B, accepting only A in the framework of "Hinduism". A and B have not necessarily been on good terms throughout history. While A has continued to enjoy a dominant position and significant advantage over B, there have been feuds persisting between them.

As far as those who support a broader definition of "Hinduism" including both A and B in it are concerned, the strife between the two orders is regarded as an "internal" conflict. Conversely, from the point of view of a narrower definition of "Hinduism" that draws a clear distinction between A and B, the latter should be left out of the legitimate scope of "Hinduism". Should we think that "Hinduism" encompasses both A and B, or that the title "Hinduism" can be awarded only to religious mode A? It seems that Japanese people have been more familiar with the narrower definition when referring to "Hinduism". The problem posed by this approach is that the history of "internal strife", an essential and inherent aspect of this religion, tends to be forgotten or overlooked. I believe that, if this more restricting position allowing the title only to A is taken, we also urgently need to address the question, "what B really is" at the same time.

The strife between A and B actually symbolizes the process of struggle which Hinduism has undergone over thousands of years of history. Today this feud is still a reality in India. Around 1,500 B.C., Aryans migrated to the Punjab in the north-west of the Indian Subcontinent, where they developed the Vedas, originating from their ancient worship of nature. The culture was centered round Vedic rituals, which were presided over by professional priests, namely, Brahmins. These rituals were consolidated, gaining a firm ground in the Aryan population between 1,500 B.C. and 500 B.C. It became a specific religious mode called Brahmanism. It belonged to category A. On the other hand, it is presumed that, by the time the Aryans settled in the new places, there had already existed other religious forms, namely B, among the indigenous people. The Aryan migration provoked religious conflict and strife, which has been persistent through the entire religious history of India. Nevertheless, it would not be correct for someone to interpret the modern conflict between the different orders A and B as a straightforward extension of the ancient feud triggered by Aryan settlement in the new areas, which had already long been inhabited by "aborigines".

In the previous part of this paper, I introduced the worship of a goddess Mariai thriving primarily in Maharashtra, a western part of India, as an example of religious form B.

It is said that people belonging to the Brahmin caste account for about 7 to 8 per cent of the total population of Maharashtra. Obviously, the castes of those who observe the faith in Mariai and other indigenous deities represent a larger portion of the population than those of the Brahmin caste. As I have mentioned earlier, many people of the Brahmin caste are offended by the alternative religious form B including Mariai worship. They trivialize B, declaring that the alternatives are quite alien to their own religion. They reject calling Mariai worship "Hinduism".

It should be noted that what I call the feud between A and B does not necessarily mean antagonism between the so-called "great tradition" and the "little traditions". Roughly speaking, the former represents a pan-Indian cultural tradition, while the latter refers to a local cultural tradition. After the demise of the Gupta dynasty, many aristocrats who had been in the ruling elite, patronizing the "great tradition", escaped from the capital Pataliputra, and migrated to various parts of India. In the new settlements, they encountered the diversity of "little traditions". Such an environment facilitated the fusion between "great" and "little" traditions, promoting the integration of the two. This phenomenon must have been taking place not only during the times shortly after the decline of the Gupta dynasty, but also long before or long after the collapse of the kingdom. Normally, under those circumstances, the two different cultures were either fused together, or, if not integrated completely, they found some way to coexist in an amicable manner. It should be remembered, however, that the "little traditions" usually did not include the aforementioned religious alternative form B, unless under exceptional circumstances.

What is remarkable about the religious modality B is that it has hardly been accommodated in the framework of "little traditions", and that it has been experiencing a persistent conflict with A (which is part of the great tradition). Despite these difficulties and the absence of official recognition from the establishment, the tradition of B has survived many years and still exists in today's India. Oddly enough, not so much attention has been paid to these aspects of Indian religion. It has hardly been raised as an issue so far.

Let us consider the faith in the god Viṭṭhal, a local religion especially well known in Maharashtra. The worship of Viṭṭhal is a religious form unique to Maharashtra and adjacent regions. When Hinduism was disseminated and consolidated in this area, the local deity Viṭṭhal somehow came to be identified with the supreme deity of Hinduism, Viṣṇu. Although the worship of Viṭṭhal has been pervasive among the Marathi community, those who speak Marathi as their mother tongue are not Aryans. In spite of this racial difference between the Marathi and Aryan communities, the Brahmin caste has its place in the former, as it is a social norm for all Hindus. In fact, the Marathi community has played an active and pivotal role in pre-modern and modern India as a major contributor to the enhancement of the Brahmin culture. Interestingly enough, Viṭṭhal worship originating from the local deity in Maharashtra has been well accepted by Brahmins in the traditional Marathi community. On this point, we find completely different approaches taken by today's Indian or Hindu communities to alternative religious modes of an ancient local origin in which indigenous deities are worshiped. Viṭṭhal worship is well tolerated by Brahmins, whereas the faith in the goddess Mariai is categorically denied.

What we face here is a fundamental and inherent problem of

India that began long ago. This problem has hardly been resolved today. It seems that, in Japan, Western nations and also in India or Nepal to some extent, due consideration has not been given to this issue of historic strife between different religious modalities, although it has always been present in society for thousands of years. Indeed the "cultural legacies" created by religious form A, including philosophy, literature, fine arts, performing arts, science and others are of tremendous value. To be honest, they are far superior to those of B in terms of their grace, delicacy and sophistication. For this reason, people engaged in conventional Indian studies have not made special effort to reflect on the other aspect of Indian religion, that is to say, religious mode B. It seems that nobody has ever thought that B could actually be comparable with A.

Contrary to such conventional ideas, however, B might indeed be of significance. It might be so important as to force us to review it seriously alongside the mainstream tradition A. At least it would be fair to suggest that, when pursuing the question "what Hinduism truly is", this element B should be reviewed more carefully than in the past so that the right answer can be revealed to us.

BIBLIOGRAPHY

Bhandarkar, R.G., 1982: *Vaiṣṇavism, Śaivism and Minor Religious Systems* (Reprinted from the Collected Works of R.G. Bhandarkar, vol. IV). Poona: Bhandrakar Oritental Research Institute.

Crooke, William, 1925: *Religion & Folklore of Northern India.* New Delhi: S. Chand.

Danielou, Alain 1964: *Hindu Polytheism.* New York: Bolingen Foundation.

Harman, William P., 1989: *Sacred Marriage of a Hindu Goddess.* Delhi: Motilal Banarsidass.

Stutley, Margaret and James, 1986: *A Dictionary of Hinduism.* New Delhi: Heritage Publications.

Prabhudesai, P.K., 1967-72: *Devīkośa.* Pune: Tilak Maharashtra Vidyapeeth (4 vols.).

Prasad, August 1975, Pune: Prasad Prakashan.

Ranade, R.D., 2003: *Mysticism in Maharashtra, Indian Mysticism.* New Delhi: Munshiram Manoharlal.

Shima, Iwao, 1984: *Hindu Temples at Shaniwar Peth in Poona.* Nagoya: Department of Indian Philosophy, Nagoya University.

Tachikawa, M., S. Hino and L. Deodhar, 2001: *Pūjā and Saṃskāra.* Delhi: Motilal Banarsidass.

APPENDIX

A Short History of the International Conference on Maharashtra: Culture and Society

MEERA KOSAMBI

In the summer of 1983, the late Dr. Günther-Dietz Sontheimer and Dr. N.K. Wagle shared with some of us at the Modern European Conference on South Asia in Tellberg, Sweden, their idea of holding a conference on Maharashtra—not just one, but a whole series. It was to involve scholars from many countries and many disciplines, united by their work on Maharashtra. In those sylvan surroundings, it seemed an exhilarating but slightly unreal idea. What unfolded during the following twenty-odd years has justified the exhilaration, besides proving it to be a very real and even visionary idea.

This was conceived as an experiment in many ways. There was no permanent parent body to monitor the organization and continuity of the conferences, and no steady source of funding. It was chiefly a matter of the commitment of individual scholars devoted to the study of the region, to keep the series going by undertaking by turns the responsibility of holding at least one conference. At the end of each conference, a business session would be held to decide the details of the next. As a full-fledged conference it differed from the session of the Maharashtra Studies scholars that was usually attached to the annual meetings of the Association of Asian Studies in the USA. This conference was to meet about every two years in a different country. As frequently as possible (preferably on alternate occasions), it was to meet somewhere within Maharashtra, so as to enable a large number of Maharashtrian scholars to participate. When it was held abroad, efforts were to be made to bring over as many scholars as possible from Maharashtra, because they generally have few sources of university or government funding. Attendance was to be by invitation only, and scholars could present their papers in either English or Marathi, although the publications would be brought out only in English (containing translations of Marathi papers where necessary). On later occasions, scholars who were not present at a given conference were also invited to contribute papers to the volume of the proceedings. The conference gradually became a longer and richer event with the addition of cultural programs and excursions.

The "First International Conference on Maharashtra: Culture and Society" was duly organized by Dr. N.K. Wagle at the University of Toronto in March 1984, at which were present more than twenty participants from India, Canada, USA, Germany and France. Over the years, Maharashtra scholars were added from countries of Europe (Belgium, Britain, Denmark, Italy, Russia), and from Australia and Japan. The proceedings of this conference were published in two volumes (M. Israel and N.K. Wagle, 1987; and D.W. Attwood, et al., 1988). The second conference in the series was held by Dr. A.R. Kulkarni at the University of Pune in January 1987 (A.R. Kulkarni and N.K. Wagle, 1999). At the third conference at the University of Heidelberg in June 1988, the organizer, the late Dr. Günther-Dietz Sontheimer, introduced the concept of conference themes. For his conference he suggested two themes—"Folk Component in Maharashtrian Culture" and "The Nineteenth Century Social Reform Movement in Maharashtra"—around which was grouped the research of most of the Maharashtra scholars at the time (Sontheimer, 1995 and N.K. Wagle, 1999). It became a test of the successive organizers' innovative ability to identify themes that provided a focus for the research presentations, without restricting them.

The fourth conference was hosted by Dr. Anne Feldhaus at Arizona State University in April 1991. The theme was "Images of Women and the Feminine in Maharashtra" (A. Feldhaus, 1996; and A. Feldhaus, 1998). The fifth conference was organized by Dr. Suma Chitnis and Dr. Meera Kosambi at the SNDT Women's

University in Mumbai in December 1992, on the theme "Continuities and Discontinuities" (M. Kosambi, 2000). The sixth conference was held at Moscow University by Dr. Irina Glushkova in May 1995 on the theme of "Ghar"—house and home (I. Glushkova and A. Feldhaus, 1998; and I. Glushkova and R. Vora, 1999).

The seventh conference was organized by Dr. A.R. Kulkarni at Tilak Maharashtra Vidyapeeth, Pune, in January 1997. The eighth conference was held by Dr. Jim Masselos at the University of Sydney in January 1999 on the theme, the "Body". The tenth conference was hosted by Dr. Jim Laine at Macalester College, St. Paul, Minnesota, USA, in June 2001 on the theme, "Inside and Outside". The eleventh conference was hosted by Dr. Rajendra Vora of the University of Pune in August 2003; the theme was "Paisa" (money). The papers presented at these four conferences have not been published.

The twelfth and latest conference was held by Professors M. Naito and H. Kotani at Senshu University, Tokyo, in August 2005 on the theme of "Marga" (path). The present volume contains the papers presented at the event.

The "International Conference on Maharashtra: Culture and Society" is now an established fact. It has created and sustained a large kinship group of Maharashtra scholars from many countries, to which scholars of the next generation are being added. It is a biennial event we have come to look forward to with excitement, and at times its novel themes have prompted us to branch out into new fields of exploration. As the only participant in all twelve conferences, I look back in wonder and fulfillment on the whole series—on the intellectual challenges it has provided, on the countries and cities it has taken us to, on the new friends we have made within its orbit. The ultimate success of the series of Maharashtra conferences lies as much in the rich scholarship it has produced and the intellectual exchange it has enabled across the divides of space and culture, as in the spirit of bonhomie it has created among the international group through conversations held in various "dialects" of Marathi—Marathi flavored with the accents and grammars of European countries, North America, Australia and Japan.

REFERENCES

Attwood, D.W., Milton Israel and N.K. Wagle, eds., 1988: *City, Countryside and Society in Maharashtra.* Toronto: University of Toronto.

Feldhaus, Anne, ed., 1996: *Images of Women in Maharashtrian Literature and Religion.* Albany: State University of New York Press.

——, ed., 1998: *Images of Women in Maharashtrian Society.* Albany: State University of New York Press.

Glushkova, Irina and Anne Feldhaus, eds., 1998: *The House and Home in Maharashtra.* New Delhi: Oxford University Press.

Glushkova, Irina and Rajendra Vora, eds., 1999: *Home, Family and Kinship in Maharashtra.* New Delhi: Oxford University Press.

Israel, Milton and N.K. Wagle, eds., 1987: *Religion and Society in Maharashtra.* Toronto: University of Toronto.

Kosambi, Meera, ed., 2000: *Intersections: Socio-Cultural Trends in Maharashtra.* New Delhi: Orient Longman.

Kulkarni, A.R. and N.K., Wagle, eds., 1999: *Region, Nationality and Religion,* Mumbai: Popular Prakashan.

Sontheimer, Günther-Dietz., ed., 1995: *Folk Culture, Folk Religion and Oral Tradition as a Component in Maharashtrian Culture.* New Delhi: Manohar.

Wagle, N.K., ed., 1999: *Writers, Editors and Reformers: Social and Political Transformation of Maharashtra, 1830-1930.* New Delhi: Manohar.